M000112306

BRIDGEPORT'S SOCIALIST
NEW DEAL, 1915–36

THE WORKING CLASS IN AMERICAN HISTORY

Editorial Advisors
David Brody
Alice Kessler-Harris
David Montgomery
Sean Wilentz

A list of books in the series appears at the end of this book.

Bridgeport's Socialist New Deal, 1915–36

CECELIA BUCKI

UNIVERSITY OF ILLINOIS PRESS
URBANA AND CHICAGO

Publication of this book was supported by
a grant from Fairfield University.

© 2001 by the Board of Trustees
of the University of Illinois
All rights reserved
Manufactured in the United States of America
C 5 4 3 2 1

∞ This book is printed on acid-free paper.

Library of Congress Cataloging-in-Publication Data
Bucki, Cecelia.
Bridgeport's socialist New Deal, 1915–36 / Cecelia Bucki.
p.   cm. — (The working class in American history)
Includes bibliographical references and index.
ISBN 0-252-02687-X (alk. paper)
1. Bridgeport (Conn.)—Politics and government—20th century.
2. New Deal, 1933–1939—Connecticut—Bridgeport. 3. Bridgeport
(Conn.)—Economic conditions—20th century. 4. Bridgeport
(Conn.)—Social conditions—20th century. 5. Working class—Connecticut—Bridgeport—Political activity—History—20th century.
6. Minorities—Connecticut—Bridgeport—Political activity—History—20th century. 7. Socialism—Connecticut—Bridgeport—History—20th century. I. Title. II. Series.
F104.B7B84   2001
974.6'042—dc21   2001001004

In memory of my father,
Stephen J. Bucki, 1913–2000

CONTENTS

ACKNOWLEDGMENTS

This project has been many years in the making, in the course of which I have worn numerous hats as public historian, community activist, union member, and finally as professor. These experiences have nourished my interest in labor and social history and led me to the people who helped make this project possible. I have accumulated many personal debts. It is a pleasure to be able finally to thank the many people who have helped me along the way.

I gratefully acknowledge the financial support of the University of Pittsburgh history department, the Andrew W. Mellon Foundation, Hamilton College Faculty Research Fund, Fairfield University Faculty Research Fund, and Fairfield University Humanities Institute. The Yale University history department graciously provided me with an appointment as a visiting fellow, allowing me to take advantage of the extensive research sources at Yale.

I thank those scholars who assisted this project, and my career, from dissertation to book, commenting on conference papers and providing timely advice throughout many years: Amy Bridges, John Bukowczyk, Melvyn Dubofsky, William Forbath, Joshua Freeman, Maurine Greenwald, Van Beck Hall, Bruce Laurie, Mark Leff, Nelson Lichtenstein, Mark McColloch, Terrence McDonald, Bruce Nelson, Ronald Schatz, Shelton Stromquist, and Joseph White. Special thanks to my reader at the University of Illinois Press, David Brody, whose astute reading of the early manuscript allowed me to restructure it into its present form, and to my acquisitions editor, Richard L. Wentworth, for seeing it through. For translation of Bridgeport Italian-language newspaper items, thanks to Andrea Graziozi and Maureen C. Miller. Peter Tuckel and Kurt Schlichting shared their expertise in statistical analysis, pooled their data with mine, and provided me with data calculations and graphs.

My greatest debt is to David Montgomery, a master artisan with whom I served my apprenticeship at the University of Pittsburgh. When as a fledgling graduate student I embarked on my first research paper, examining the machinists' struggles on the shop floor in Bridgeport during World War I, I was stumped by the many references to arcane machinist procedures and production practices. Montgomery lent me his well-worn machinist's manual, which explained the methods of twentieth-century machine work. I thought then that this guy is the Real Deal—and so he has proved to be, in matters historical, theoretical, material, and political for these many, many years. Above all, he has been a seemingly endless source of patience and support, for which I am most thankful.

Doing labor history is a collective enterprise, and I am grateful to those who accompanied me on the job, in Pittsburgh and New Haven, through grad school and junior faculty status, and who provided encouragement and knowledge when sorely needed: Eric Arnesen, Jim Barrett, Jackie Dirks, Dana Frank, Julie Greene, Toni Gilpin, Dan Letwin, Chris Lowe, Sylvie Murray, Glenn Wallach, Peter Rachleff, Steve Sapolsky, and Karin Shapiro.

For allowing me to examine records in their possession, I would like to thank Professor Edwin Dahill, West Hartford, Connecticut, for access to the J. Henry Roraback Papers; Myra Oliver, executive director of the International Institute of Connecticut, Inc., Bridgeport; Robert McLevy, business agent of Carpenters Local 99, Bridgeport; and the officers of Painters Local 1719, Bridgeport.

I also wish to thank those who sat for interviews: Jack C. Bergen, Jack K. Donnelly, Frank Fazekas, Ethel M. Freedman, Abraham E. Knepler, L. Herman Lavit, Robert McLevy, Michael Russo, Pearl K. Russo, Josephine Willard, and Peter J. Wojcicki. They graciously opened their homes to me and patiently answered my questions. My father, Stephen J. Bucki, also helped make this historical study real by sharing his memories of growing up in Bridgeport in the 1920s and 1930s. Speaking with them all reminded me of the importance of Bridgeport working people's telling their stories; I hope I got it right.

Ileen DeVault, Grace Palladino, and Sarah DeLone made research trips fun and fruitful with their generous hospitality during my stays in Ithaca, New York, and Washington, D.C. Peter Gilmore, Glenn Davis, and David Pudlin shared with me their personal knowledge of Connecticut labor history and the contemporary labor movement and provided me with sources. Matthew Roth and Bruce Clouette taught me much about Connecticut industrial history and the writing of public history. David Palmquist, formerly archivist at the Bridgeport Public Library, guided me to history sources in Bridgeport and shared his extensive knowledge of Bridgeport history with me. Mary Witkowski, current archivist at the Bridgeport Public Library, helped me snag last-minute local sources and photographs.

Finally, this book was delayed by a grave medical condition. Profound thanks go to my neurosurgeon, Dr. Isaac Goodrich, without whose skill I would not be here to finish this book, and to friends who helped me through the medical crisis and long recovery: Jackie Dirks, Debbie Elkin, Chris Lowe, Mary Ann Mahony, David and Marty Montgomery, Ron Schatz, Glenn Wallach, Cindy Wells. Your kindnesses will never be forgotten.

* * *

Portions of chapter 1 previously appeared as "Dilution and Craft Tradition: Munitions Workers in Bridgeport, Connecticut, 1915–1919," in *The New England Working Class and the New Labor History,* ed. Herbert G. Gutman and Donald M. Bell (Urbana: University of Illinois Press, 1987), 137–56; use by permission of the publisher. Portions of chapters 3 and 4 previously appeared as "Workers and Politics in the Immigrant City in the Early Twentieth Century U.S.," *International Labor and Working-Class History* 48 (Fall 1995): 28–48; used by permission of Cambridge University Press. Portions of chapter 5 and 6 previously appeared as "The Workers' State: Municipal Policy, Class, and Taxes in the Early Depression," in *Labor Histories: Class, Politics, and the Working-Class Experience,* ed. Eric Arnesen, Julie Greene, and Bruce Laurie (Urbana: University of Illinois Press, 1998), 125–49; used by permission of the publisher.

BRIDGEPORT'S SOCIALIST
NEW DEAL, 1915–36

INTRODUCTION

"Not enough democracy was what ailed Bridgeport," proclaimed the labor reporter Mary Heaton Vorse in early 1919 as she assessed the strike waves that had roiled Bridgeport, Connecticut, during World War I.[1] She was referring to industrial democracy, the new proposal, popular with government and labor alike, to give workers a voice on the shop floor. But she also meant political democracy, the participation of all people in their government. This quest for both forms of democracy animated city and national politics then and for the next two decades. Working people, both immigrant and native born, strove to make their voices heard in the halls of political power as well as in the boardrooms and on the shop floors of corporate America.

This book is located at the intersection of twentieth-century American labor, ethnic, political, and urban history. This exploration began with an interest in the dynamics of third-party politics in the New Deal era as a way to understand the range of political thinking in the 1930s working class. But it soon expanded to consider the broader question of how industrial cities functioned in the early twentieth century and how working people affected urban politics. It is built around a case study of Bridgeport from World War I to the mid-1930s. Bridgeport today is an ordinary industrial city, rusted by deindustrialization and tattered by social change, like so many factory towns in the Northeast. Yet early in the twentieth century Bridgeport was a thriving industrial center specializing in the metal trades, a World War I boom town, and the site of some noteworthy events that illustrated a radical tendency in the American labor movement, both economically and politically.

Growing up in Bridgeport in the 1950s, I absorbed the stories and myths of the Socialist mayor who became the best friend of the businessman and the watchdog of the budget, stories told with a mix of cynicism about politics and a sense of disappointment. The only scholarly study of the Bridgeport Socialists, who occupied city hall from 1933 until 1957, was Bruce Stave's analysis, which repeated a "good-government" interpretation of the Socialist administration and emphasized the continuities in Bridgeport city politics during the 1930s and after.[2] Although the conservative end of the story seemed evident enough by the 1950s, something seemed to be missing from the beginning of that story. Had Bridgeport's Socialist campaigns of the early 1930s been *simply* good-government campaigns? If people had voted for just a good-government reform administration, why did many feel something was wanting? Had working people wanted more than good government from their Socialist administration?

This book is not an institutional study of the Bridgeport Socialist Party (SP), nor is it a search for a lost labor party. Rather, it is a study of popular consciousness and the political structures that conveyed that consciousness into government, a "social history of politics."[3] Although Tip O'Neill was not entirely correct when he asserted that "all politics is local," local politics does provide a window on power arrangements that working people could both effect and affect. Urban politics was an area of decisive importance for working-class political identity and mobilization, especially during much of the nineteenth century, when direct confrontation between workers and the state occurred most often at the local level. And even though political power was becoming centralized at the national level from 1900 on, the local level was still decisive for class concerns until the New Deal was well under way. Moreover, looking at urban politics reveals the ways in which American working people saw their political role in the midtwentieth century, particularly during the Great Depression.

Any look at working-class politics in the 1920s and 1930s must grapple with the theory of American exceptionalism, which posits a nonclass-based model of political engagement, and must assess the ways that class and ethnicity were interconnected. In the city this means analyzing how urban machine politics operated (or did not) and how the process of adaptation and Americanization of immigrants affected local, state, and national politics and policy choices. If, as the American exceptionalist explanation goes, the notorious city machine had successfully shaped the consciousness of workers through appeals to ethnicity and community and thus turned workers away from strictly class-based politics, the arrangement was precarious and vulnerable.[4] But while "machine politics" is an appealing shorthand for the complex task of ideological development and voter mobilization in the nineteenth and twentieth centuries, the concept assumes what needs to be proved. The model of machine politics neither predicts nor reveals the dynamics of decision making and patterns of power in the city, nor does it reveal—indeed it denies—the ideological motivations for voting.[5] Where patronage-based politics became a hegemonic model for urban politics, radical and socialist organizations saw their political task as one of weaning workers away from this model. Class-based politics repeatedly challenged this commodification of politics in the late nineteenth century as the Knights of Labor, Greenback-Labor Party, and finally the Socialist Party attempted to gain a foothold in the electoral arena. The SP was sometimes successful in the short term and had its greatest strength in areas of working-class home ownership and union power.[6]

The ethnocultural theory of politics, popular in historiography during the 1970s and 1980s, privileged "ethnic" over "class" affiliations in late nineteenth- and early twentieth-century politics and gave credence to the American exceptionalist model. However, as Richard Oestreicher points out, the seeming dominance of ethnocultural, rather than class-based, political preferences in the nineteenth and early twentieth centuries had more to do with the structure of U.S. politics than any measure of political consciousness among working people, or, as Ira Katznelson has argued, separate spheres of consciousness at home and at work. Three structural facts defined the U.S. political system—an entrenched two-party system, winner-take-all elections, and relative fragmentation of power in the layers of local, state, and national government—and all contributed to the limited ability of class-based issues and organizations to influence the polity.[7] The New Deal era of politics remains an enigma, though historians have attempted with some limited success to identify class and ethnic consciousness in voting patterns.[8]

Complicating this historiography of class politics is the problem of treating class and ethnicity as essentialist, exclusive categories. They are not at all helpful in analyzing popular political consciousness in the 1920s and 1930s. As I will show, in Bridgeport class and ethnicity were tightly intertwined. The process of political mobilization in this era was more difficult because of the re-formation of the working class. From 1880 to 1920 the working class itself was remade by waves of new immigrants, mostly from eastern and southern Europe, who were sojourning to the United States in search of work. While this free-flowing immigration kept the class in flux until new legislation restricted immigration after World War I, immigrant workers began to make their presence known in unionization attempts in coal mining, meatpacking, textiles, and garments, in radical unions like the Industrial Workers of the World, and in the nationality federations of the SP. The contact between native-born workers from "old-stock" groups (the British, Irish, Germans, and Scandinavians) and the new immigrants added to the complexity. To create a successful movement, the working-class culture of old-stock ethnics, who had already established their unions and built links to politics, had to accommodate the emerging class culture of new immigrants, who had their own labor and political traditions. The migration of Mexicans and southern African Americans into industrial regions during and after World War I added further complexity. Although this process could lead to "Americanization from the bottom up," to use James Barrett's phrase, it also bred nativism and racism among native-born workers. This turmoil was reflected in union debates about inclusion of new workers, whether by race, gender, or skill categories, in political debates about the role of unions in politics, and in the stance that the American Federation of Labor (AFL) should take on immigration restriction. These themes played out in the politics of the 1920s and 1930s.[9]

Moreover, *ethnicity* has undergone considerable reinterpretation in recent years, as our understanding of the process of Americanization and "ethnicization" has become more complex. Thus we need to historicize the social construction of ethnicity, to grasp the malleable nature of ethnic categories in the United States in the early twentieth century. The internal class dynamics of immigrant communities, and both internal and external Americanization and assimilation efforts, affected the way that immigrant-turned-ethnic workers perceived themselves in American society.[10] A look at urban politics in the interwar years helps to broaden our understanding of the flexible interrelationship of class and ethnicity in U.S. politics.

In addition, class concerns were often hidden within broader "populist" and "reform" demands—not only work and trade union issues but unemployment relief, social services, honest government, free speech, and free assembly. The first wave of the "new political history" of Progressive Era politics, expressively captured in Robert Weibe's phrase "the search for order," stressed that experts, technology, and managers were the driving force for reforms, often with undemocratic results. But some early analysts of the reform movement of the Progressive Era paid attention to the influence of the working class in "urban liberalism" but did not come to grips with the nature of the labor movement at that time. Some recent studies by labor historians of politics at the turn of the twentieth century link working-class political mobilization to the institutional developments within the labor movement—both "pure-and-simple" and populist-socialist—but the 1930s remain a dilemma.[11]

The New Deal, as understood by observing debates and decisions at the national level, was a pragmatic attempt by Franklin D. Roosevelt and his advisers to save American democracy and the free-market system. Its programs balanced the needs of the American people, who were suffering intense deprivation and threatening disorder, with the business community's acceptance of economic policy changes. The New Deal political coalition, the emerging social welfare state, industrial relations laws, the dynamics of city and state government before World War II—all rested upon political initiatives of groups of workers acting as citizens. But the plans as finally implemented were not shaped by these same working people, which ultimately contributed to the "crisis of liberalism" as it is commonly labeled today.

What can Bridgeport's experience tell us about these national developments in the 1920s and 1930s? Bridgeport, a midsize diversified industrial city, invites a case study designed to explore labor developments, political consciousness, and political change in the period between the wars because the unique Bridgeport evolution from wartime boom town to third-party city provides a fresh perspective on the more general national experience. At the same time its social and economic contours were typical of many industrial cities from World War I to the 1930s. Thus Bridgeport was different but not exceptional. Moreover, Bridgeport's "socialist New Deal" lays bare the limitations of workers' political power at the local level. No program can truly be described as socialist when it is hemmed in by crucial compromises required by the New Deal at the federal and state levels. But Bridgeport's experiment reveals more about the nature of the New Deal, a topic still being debated.[12]

Not many third-party formations were successful in this decade, no matter how much labor radicals wanted such a development to occur. Some recent studies of alternative politics in the 1930s reveal the possibilities for third-partyism. But as traditional institutional political studies, they are unable to reveal the contours of working-class consciousness at the grassroots—the neighborhoods and workplaces.[13] This study of Bridgeport, by contrast, looks at this grassroots level. Moreover, this search for working-class consciousness in Bridgeport in the 1920s and 1930s goes beyond the realm of the workplace to find pro–working class and antibusiness political stances developing around taxes, budgets, and social services. Ultimately, these debates addressed broad political issues such as citizenship, democratic inclusion, and fairness. The debate about these questions was reached and resolved in favor of the Bridgeport Socialist Party in the early years of the depression, as the SP tapped both popular antibusiness anger and the enthusiasms generated by the new Roosevelt administration.

An analytic focus on one city allows us to take an in-depth look at the social and economic changes that gave rise to the new urban politics so influential in national politics in the interwar era. A study of a midsize city also allows us to attend to the multiple political voices of its working-class citizens, voices that might be drowned out in a study of a larger, more complex metropolis. And Bridgeport had independent worker voices in abundance. The city figured in the "new labor history"—David Montgomery's important 1974 article on workers' control struggles during the early twentieth century used the World War I strike waves in Bridgeport to explore aspects of this watershed development in the U.S. labor movement. As I delved deeper into the Bridgeport strikes myself, it became clear to me that fundamental changes in the political ethos of Bridgeport had resulted from this popular upheaval.[14] These strikes, which are missing from the historical memory of today's Bridgeport residents, created a postwar legacy that affected the politics of the 1920s and events in the 1930s.

But the voices of ordinary working people were often hard to hear, and in many cases the historical record has not preserved them. Luckily, in the 1930s the Federal Writers' Project of the Works Progress Administration interviewed scores of ordinary citizens in many states. In Connecticut the project focused on immigrant cultures and experiences. Moldering away on ordinary typing paper and in semisorted form in the Connecticut State Archives, these interviews conducted in Bridgeport from 1938 to 1940 range from topics of immigration and adaptation to family and culture to work, unions, and politics. Though flawed in that they were not usually verbatim reports (though close to it), and their contents often depended on the astuteness of the interviewers and their trustworthiness in their informants' eyes, they provide an unusual opportunity to gauge working-class thought and experience in the 1930s. As such they are superior to present-day recollections, which are often memories told through the filter of more recent experience.[15] Having said that, however, this study has also used present-day interviews, where the chance to ask for explanations of memories has added to the paper historical record. How and why men and women made the decisions to build unions and ethnic clubs, or to join political party clubs, as well as how (and whether) they cast their private ballots are important to the larger question of the 1930s. How did working people view their political options? How did they affect what soon would become the New Deal?

The local newspapers in the 1920s and 1930s, of which there were four in Bridgeport, were overtly partisan and presented various points of view for the same events. Local newspapers sometimes recorded the voices of local, not national, ethnic working-class leaders. These papers sometimes recorded personal opinions, began printing letters to the editor in the late 1920s, and, as in the case of the *Bridgeport (Sunday) Herald* and the *Bridgeport Times-Star,* paid attention to ethnic and labor issues. Moreover, business documents, when available, were more revealing in the 1920s and early 1930s than they are today, giving elitist opinions that business executives often softened in public statements. As such they reveal how local economic and political elites viewed the massive surge of democracy in working-class neighborhoods during World War I and then during the Great Depression.

Why another case study of the 1930s? As I was finishing the first phase of this study, two case studies of the 1930s appeared that touched on labor, ethnicity, and politics. They were Lizabeth Cohen's *Making a New Deal* (1990), on Chicago industrial workers, and Gary Gerstle's *Working-Class Americanism* (1989), on textile workers in Woonsocket, Rhode Island. Cohen succeeded admirably in documenting the creation of a "culture of unity" within the Congress of Industrial Organizations from disparate ethnic groups in Chicago by the mid-1930s. Gerstle revealed the ways in which two groups of immigrant textile workers used the political language of "Americanism" to define their labor agenda. However, neither study made concrete the ways in which working people participated in and interacted with the political system in the 1930s. Moreover, the Chicago ethnic world that Cohen describes is surprisingly monolithic, revealing none of the internal splits that wracked immigrant communities and complicated the process of Americanization and politics. Nor did Cohen integrate this new labor generation with the older one. Before 1936 another group—the "old ethnic" and native-born skilled working class—defined the labor movement through the AFL. The relationship between these two groups of workers in the political sphere is still unexplored. Gerstle's study of Woonsocket uses contested meanings of Americanism to explore in a nuanced way the dynamics of intraethnic dissension as well as interethnic jockeying for power. But his study is limited in that it examines a small one-industry town of fifty thousand, and the relationship between only two dominant ethnic groups. Many cities were more complex.

In Bridgeport the skilled AFL craftsmen who made up the bulk of the Bridgeport SP stepped in to fill a political void created by the crumbling of mainstream parties, the disintegration of traditional modes of ethnic politics, and a fiscal crisis of the city itself. AFL skilled craftsmen, especially building trades workers, were powerful influences within local politics, but they have been curiously neglected in the historical literature of the 1930s.[16]

* * *

This book on Bridgeport workers and politics attempts to fill gaps in earlier studies, the historiography of which I will review in my conclusion. This study situates the workers' world in a changing economic environment and a challenging industrial relations climate, traces the successes and failures of unionism from World War I to the mid-1930s, and links these successes and failures to working-class political organization. Because this is the first modern investigation of Bridgeport, I spent significant time documenting the basic structure of work and the working class and of ethnic communities and their institutions. But in the interest of focusing the story on the political transformations, I have left out many details of work, labor struggles, and ethnic institutions.[17]

The resulting book pursues three avenues of investigation—labor, ethnic, and political—within a chronological framework. Chapter 1 focuses on the effects of World War I in Bridgeport, analyzing the economic transformation of the city into a wartime boom town from 1915 to 1918, with consequent changes in working-class composition and union organization. The powerful swing to the Left during the strike waves of the war years reverberated through ethnic working-class neighborhoods and redefined local political sensibilities and the boundaries of public expression. Chapter 2 traces those wartime changes in politics through the postwar decline and reconversion. Most surprisingly, it reveals the attempt by local business elites to manipulate local parties and the political process in order to control taxes and the city budget. The resulting contest and new political alignments integrated labor's voice in a Republican Party organization that retained hold of city hall in the 1920s.

Chapter 3 analyzes ethnic community life, concentrating on the changing role of ethnic elites in organizational and political life in the 1920s. In particular, it looks closely at the structure and composition of the local political parties, paying attention to the creation of cross-class and interethnic alliances in the Democratic and Republican Parties and the succession of a new generation of ethnic elites. Although the electoral realignment identified by political scientists as the Al Smith revolution did begin in Bridgeport in 1928, ethnic working-class voters remained volatile on the eve of the depression and had not cemented their loyalty to the local Democratic Party.

Chapter 4 examines the economic life of working-class communities in the 1920s, particularly the surviving pockets of union organization, which often had an ethnic dimension. It situates the Bridgeport SP squarely in these union and ethnic associations. The chapter continues into the early years of the Great Depression, tracing its economic effects on working-class communities.

Chapter 5 examines the political consequences of the Great Depression. Bridgeport's citizens, informed by the turbulent economic conditions around them, measured the efficacy of ethnic networks and noted the unraveling of the local Democratic and Republican Parties. Faced with renewed attempts by the business community to control the city budget and relief efforts, the city's voters responded with their own demands for public control and public relief, resulting in the electoral victory of the Bridgeport Socialist Party. The prominence of traditional AFL craftsmen in the SP opens a view onto this sector of the labor movement in the 1930s, revealing both its strengths and weaknesses.

Finally, chapter 6 weighs both the accomplishments of the Socialist reign and its accommodation with liberal business leaders by 1936. The compromise politics of Bridgeport mirrored the dynamics of cross-class bargaining that characterized New Deal politics at the national level. Nevertheless, the choice made by Bridgeport voters in the 1930s suffused the public life of the city with a working-class consciousness that permanently altered its structures of power.

This study reveals new dimensions of working-class experience in the interwar years and provides a counternarrative to the usual tale of the 1920s and 1930s. First, the 1915–19 strike waves had greater consequences than historians have previously acknowledged. The struggle for workers' control, combined with reform rhetoric about industrial democracy, profoundly shaped working people's ideas about their place in an American economy and polity. This legacy, though silenced for much of the 1920s, was reinterpreted by Bridgeporters in the context of the Great Depression to provide the city with an alternative vision of what democracy and the government's role were.

Second, individual ethnic communities were ideologically divided to a larger extent than previously recognized; this had a significant influence on the making of New Deal politics. In the 1920s, the "golden age of ethnicity" as many have called it, immigrant communities settled into U.S. society and produced a profusion of ethnic social and political organizations. Tied to old country politics as they made their way in the American public sphere, ethnic leaders allied themselves with U.S. political parties both ideologically and pragmatically. In the 1920s this often meant allying with U.S. business interests and conservative European governments. But community members were often linked to unions and more radical European politics, just as they had been before World War I. Their loyalty to mainstream American parties was weak, and the Al Smith campaign of 1928 only partially tied them to the Democratic Party. Much depended on how local political leaders treated these new voters. When the depression struck soon after, the ethnic working-class communities in Bridgeport rejected the local traditional parties in favor of a third party that echoed their own class concerns.

Third, the cataclysm of the Great Depression brought out a broad debate about the definition of the public good, pitting previously unengaged working-class citizens against local businessmen and traditional party elites in regard to such issues as taxes, budgets, and city services. Surprisingly, this last point has received little attention from scholars. This study thus establishes the importance of these local and state political issues in shaping the specifics of New Deal liberalism. This early groundswell for a welfare state goaded national political leaders to respond with their own initiatives, which were a compromise between popular sentiment and business sanction.

A New Deal that aimed to incorporate more radical social legislation, restructure political power, and redistribute wealth was halted at the federal level in 1938, just as it had been in Bridgeport two years earlier when Socialists and business interests reached an accommodation. Yet working people had an active influence on these welfare-state decisions, though they did not ultimately have a decisive role in making them. Working people were not merely the passive recipients of federal largesse, as the historical literature has depicted them, but helped to define the public good. This is their story.

CHAPTER 1

Connecticut's
Industrial Fortress

In the opening pages of Mark Twain's 1889 novel, *A Connecticut Yankee in King Arthur's Court,* Hank Morgan, a Hartford mechanic, has been knocked unconscious in a fight and mysteriously awakens in a strange land. He is confronted by an armored stranger on a horse. Thinking the man is from the circus or, worse, an escapee from an asylum, Morgan decides to humor him and follow his orders, "We marched comfortably along, . . . At the end of an hour we saw a far-away town sleeping in a valley by a winding river; and beyond it on a hill, a vast grey fortress, with towers and turrets, the first I had ever seen out of a picture. 'Bridgeport?' said I, pointing. 'Camelot,' said he."[1]

That Morgan the mechanic might conceive of Bridgeport as a fortress was not completely fanciful. In the late nineteenth century Bridgeport was well on its way to becoming an industrial fortress, filled with stone and brick factories and touched by the architectural fantasies of its one-time mayor, the circus impresario P. T. Barnum. Barnum, who had constructed his mansion, Iranistan, in an exotic style, was also responsible for developing East Bridgeport into a factory and residential district, complete with turrets and towers on many of its buildings. Moreover, the inventiveness of Bridgeport mechanics, indeed of many Connecticut mechanics, was becoming legendary.[2]

Bridgeport had experienced slow yet steady growth since its establishment in 1836 from parts of the colonial towns of Stratford and Fairfield. In 1900 its population was slightly greater than seventy thousand, making it the third-largest city in the state after Hartford and New Haven, with new immigrants from eastern and southern Europe diluting its Yankee and Irish heritage. By 1920 its population had doubled and become heavily foreign stock. The port city's location on Long Island Sound—about sixty miles from New York City, near the brass mills of the Naugatuck Valley, and with good rail connections to New York and beyond—made it an ideal setting for industry. In the latter half of the nineteenth century Bridgeport became a metalworking and machine-tool manufacturing center, producing such diverse commodities as ammunition, automobiles, hardware, phonographs, sewing machines, submarines, and turret lathes. It also housed an extensive garment industry. Thus it was an ideal choice for the concentration of war-related production from 1915 to 1918. By 1920 the importance of its industrial production outweighed its size; though it placed forty-fourth in city size in the U.S. census, it ranked twenty-first in number of wage earners and thirty-sixth in value of products produced.[3]

Some of the city's important companies were founded by old Yankee landed and mercantile elites, and many mechanics and entrepreneurs arrived in Bridgeport in the 1870s and 1880s to settle and set up shop. For example, two brothers, Doctors I. DeVer and Lucien C. Warner, moved their small corset business to Bridgeport in 1874, where I. DeVer presided over the company's expansion along with the growth of Bridgeport itself. By the turn of the twentieth century the Warner family owned the city's largest garment factory, and Warners were major investors in two of the city's utility companies and one of the large department stores. Some large employers, like the Bridgeport Brass Company and Bullard Machine Tool Company, remained locally owned. Others merged with similar companies from elsewhere and expanded their Bridgeport plants; for example, Bridgeport's Union Metallic Cartridge Company merged with Remington Arms Company of Ilion, New York. Other financial and industrial interests from New York also founded companies in the city by the 1890s but ran them as absentee owners. Finally, after 1900 a number of Bridgeport's important firms were acquired by large, national corporations. For example, the Singer Manufacturing Company acquired Bridgeport's Wheeler and Wilson Company in 1907, and the Crane Company of Chicago absorbed Eaton, Cole and Burnham in 1904. Bridgeport's Bryant Electric Company became a subsidiary of Westinghouse in 1901, though the Bryant family retained management authority until Waldo C. Bryant's death in 1930. Thus Bridgeport's manufacturers were a mix of locally owned and managed firms and subsidiaries of national corporations.[4]

The board of directors of the Manufacturers' Association of Bridgeport (MAB) overwhelmingly represented the metal trades, whereas the leadership of the Bridgeport Chamber of Commerce (BCC) in 1915 included large retailers, real estate interests, and financiers. In Bridgeport leaders of the real estate and financial sectors tended to be heavily interlocked with the metal trades sector. The largest companies were in the metal trades, the sector that provided the loudest corporate voices in industrial relations and in civic affairs. (See table 1 for a list of major industrial companies and their assets, as well as names of local elites.)

Table 1. Major Bridgeport Firms with More Than $1 Million in Assets in 1920

Firm Name	Product	Assets (millions)	Ownership	Local Elite
Machinery/metal fabricating				
American Chain Co.	Wire and chain	$ 19.6	Bridgeport	Walter Lashar
American Tube and Stamping	Rolled steel	5.1	Bridgeport	Guy Miller
				William R. Webster
Bassick Co.	Iron castings, hardware	6.3	Bridgeport/ Meriden	W. T. Hincks . Bassick family
Bridgeport Brass	Sheet brass, brass products	6.4	Bridgeport/ New Haven	W. R. Webster Guy Miller
Bridgeport Malleable Iron	Forgings	n.a.	Bridgeport/ Naugatuck	Henry Atwater
Bullard Co.	Machine tools	6.2	Bridgeport	Bullard family
Crane Co.	Valves	72.7	Chicago	C. V. Barrington
Handy and Harmon	Precious metals	n.a.	New York	
Holmes and Edwards	Plated ware	20.1	Meriden	
Manning-Maxwell-Moore	Gauges, tools	11.0		
Remington Arms	Ammunition, guns	n.a.	Delaware and New York	
Singer Manufacturing Co.	Sewing machines	n.a.	New Jersey	George Eames
Stanley Works	Rolled steel	15.3	New Britain	
Electrical machinery and supplies				
Bryant Electric (subsidiary of Westinghouse)		n.a.	Pittsburgh	Bryant family
General Electric		374.8	New York	W. S. Clark
Miscellaneous manufactures				
Columbia Graphophone	Phonographs	26.5[a]	New York	
Locomobile Co.	Automobiles	13.8	Delaware	
Warner Corset Co.	Corsets, lingerie	n.a.	Bridgeport	Warner family
American Fabrics	Textiles	4.4	Bridgeport	W. Lashar
Utilities				
Bridgeport Gas Light Co.		4.9	Bridgeport	D. H. Warner
Bridgeport Hydraulic Co.		14.0	Bridgeport	D. H. Warner
Merchants				
D. M. Read	Department store	n.a.	Bridgeport	E. S. Wolfe, D. H. Warner, Sumner Simpson
Howland	Department store	n.a.	Bridgeport	A. M. Cooper

Sources: List compiled from R. G. Dun, *Reference Book, March 1920* (New York: R. G. Dun, 1920); assets and corporate officers from Moody's Investment Service, *Moody's Manual—Industrials* (New York: Moody's, 1921).
a. Assets shown are for 1919.

Businessmen and Politicians in the Industrial City

Local politics was a web of interactions between business elites and the local parties with the goal of a good urban business climate in the years before World War I. Local politics in the thriving city seemed simple enough. The acknowledged political leader in this era was a Republican, John T. King, who had won de facto control of the city in 1911 with the election of his mayoral candidate, Clifford B. Wilson, and their common council slate. King, a Brooklyn-born Irish Catholic who had come to Bridgeport in 1896, had been a bookkeeper, bond salesman, and business lobbyist in the state capital of Hartford before entering Bridgeport Republican politics. After he won the city's lucrative garbage disposal contract, he expanded his influence in the local GOP. Using a saloon-based ward organization, he and his allies overwhelmed the centralized long-time GOP organization before the 1911 election. King's machine, alleged by one local Democrat to "equal that of Tammany," rested on a firm base of Irish Catholic support, along with voters of old Yankee, English, and Scandinavian stock.[5] At the same time King's astute attention to new immigrant groups such as the Italians and Poles enlarged his organization. King was active in Catholic circles and influential in the Knights of Columbus; he had received the papal honor of being named a Knight of St. Gregory. The King machine prospered by paying attention to ethnic community leaders, distributing patronage, and expanding city services in working-class wards.

Wilson, the new mayor, was a Bridgeport-born descendant of a Connecticut colonial family, a member of the Baptist church, and active in the Masons and other fraternal circles. An attorney like his father, he had become successful in local politics and had served as county coroner and as a member of the Bridgeport Common Council before entering the mayor's race. He was mayor from 1911 until 1921. When King's influence rose in the state GOP and he was elected as Connecticut national committeeman to the national Republican Party organization, his ally, Mayor Wilson, followed him to the state level, serving concurrently as Connecticut's lieutenant governor from 1914 to 1921. Wilson's reign as mayor of Bridgeport continued the local political tradition of electing officials who came from old Yankee stock, even as the Irish and other ethnics gained ascendancy.[6]

King's successful ward organization was one half of a powerful city coalition. The other half was the alliance with key local industrialists. The *Bridgeport Herald,* the city's large weekly, disparagingly detailed the workings of the King machine. On the one hand, the "lower five" percent of the city was a King constituency that ran political clubs in the wards, gambling operations, illegal liquor, carnivals, and other amusements, while the "upper ten" percent of wealthy business families received concessions of their own.[7] The most important of King's "upper ten" allies was the industrialist DeVer H. Warner. Warner, heir to the Warner Corset Company established by his father and his uncle, was arguably the wealthiest man in Bridgeport. He was also president of two of the city's utility companies, the Bridgeport Hydraulic Company and the Bridgeport Gas Light Company, as well as president of D. M. Read Company, one of the two large department stores in the city.[8]

The Warners were heavily involved in civic affairs, with a reputation for local philanthropy dating from the Gilded Age. By the second decade of the twentieth century, DeVer H. was carrying on the patrician legacy of his father. A contemporary historical account lauded his attention to parks and recreation, affordable housing, and city health services in Bridgeport, "carrying out in accordance with modern methods and demands ideas which his father attempted to embody in the early development of industrial Bridgeport."[9]

"I am part Socialist, and part aristocrat," he declared to the *Herald* in a feature story on his role as a leading citizen.[10] In private correspondence he was more explicit about his social philosophy. As he explained to Maude Hincks, president of the Bridgeport Equal Franchise League and a member of another prominent financial family, he opposed universal suffrage: "I have come in contact more with the masses than the [upper] classes. I have tried all my life to be fair and just toward them . . . but I am prepared to state that to a certain extent it is not to their advantage to take them out of their natural class. . . . As the world develops it will be more and more a case of the few taking care of the many; the people of brains and energy, unconsciously, if possible, so as not to create opposition, silently caring for the masses. On this basis, the less who vote, the better."[11]

The Warner family's high profile in the city's early industrial growth, as well as a substantial investment in the city, made DeVer H. Warner's leadership role a natural, if not uncontested, one. Even while other leading Bridgeport families were selling out to major national firms or were content to live off their real estate and financial holdings, Warner reaffirmed his loyalty to the city. As late as 1927 Warner, in stanching the flow of rumors that he was selling the Bridgeport Gas Light Company to a national conglomerate, insisted that his utilities would remain locally owned. "The Bridgeport Gas Light Company is a Bridgeport institution, run by Bridgeport people, for Bridgeport people, and will continue to be just that as long as I live, or as long as the Warner group retains control of the situation. Neither price nor profit would influence us."[12] Warner pursued the interests of the city with an astute eye. He reorganized the city's Charities Department, scrutinized tax valuations of out-of-state corporations' Bridgeport plants, and arranged for the MAB to accept a raise in its members' tax assessments in order to boost the city's Grand List (as it called its property tax rolls) and thus allow greater borrowing by the city for improvements.[13]

King's political acumen, coupled with elite support gathered by Warner, proved a potent combination from 1911 on.[14] The alliance of industrialist and political boss had been a traditional configuration of urban politics since the midnineteenth century. Its strong appearance in early twentieth-century Bridgeport corresponded to the city's great growth during the second industrial revolution. By the turn of the new century the city had burst its nineteenth-century economic boundaries and was straining to accommodate its new status as an important producer of machine tools, metal products, and other producer and consumer goods. Landholder, industrialist, financier, and politician alike sensed opportunity in the business of refurbishing the city, providing its residents with basic services, and touting its virtues to lure outside firms. Civic pride aside, a prosperous city meant higher land values, increased construction, more jobs, and more business for public utilities and retail establishments. Businessmen controlled city boards, even as they relied on neighborhood leaders to deliver the votes and to support policy initiatives.

Other prominent industrialists, though often taking independent positions within the Republican Party, participated in city planning and served on financial advisory boards. They were self-made entrepreneurs who had established major local companies (i.e., those with assets of more than $1 million) just before the war and would become more active in city politics in the postwar period. In such a midsize industrial city interlocking directorates tied many of these men together on various company and bank boards. One example was Sumner Simpson, lauded in his obituary in the early 1950s as the city's "Number One philanthropist." Born "a poor boy" in Pittsburgh in 1874, Simpson had come to Bridgeport in 1907 as an assistant to a local factory manager, took over another local company, and through a propitious marriage turned it into the Raybestos Company, foremost maker of brake linings. In the 1920s he became active in manufacturing and civic affairs, serving as an officer in both the Chamber of Commerce and the Manufacturers' Association as well as president of the Bridgeport Community Chest; he sat on the boards of six other local manufacturing firms.[15]

George Eames, who served with DeVer H. Warner on the park board in the early 1910s, typified a lower stratum of business leader active in civic life and the GOP. He followed in the path of his father, Albert, a Yankee machine maker for the Wheeler and Wilson Manufacturing Company. The elder Eames had been active in the city's GOP and had dabbled in entrepreneurial activities, founding the Bridgeport Horse Railroad Company. The younger Eames rose through the ranks of the Wheeler and Wilson Company, eventually becoming company vice president and general superintendent. When the Singer Manufacturing Company acquired Wheeler and Wilson, he became manager of the Bridgeport works. With his family's solid political and business connections, George Eames was influential in the early Bridgeport Board of Trade and the Manufacturers' Association. He did not, however, sit on the board of any major company or bank.[16]

The King-Warner political coalition did not go unchallenged. But the local Democratic Party was dominated by a business elite that matched the GOP's elite in many particulars, including banking and real estate interests. Fewer manufacturers were to be found in Democratic ranks, however, and the lead-

ing activists tended to be midsize wholesalers and retailers. The body of the
Democratic Party was almost exclusively Irish and showed little inclination to
attract newer immigrant groups. Local critics often alleged that King, through
the judicious use of patronage, controlled the faction of the Democratic Party
led by Hugh Lavery, a lawyer, which meant that King was, in effect, running a
double machine. In fact, Democrats also accommodated the Republicans at the
state level, where the GOP was guaranteed a majority because of the rural bias
of General Assembly apportionment. In return for patronage posts Connecticut Democrats often neglected to mount an effective challenge to GOP rule.[17]

Partisanship was still high in this era, as local newspapers remained openly
committed to the party organizations of their choice. After the 1911 election of
Clifford Wilson, the *Evening Farmer*, the local Democratic paper, denounced the
"Warner-Lavery-King public service corporation combination" that now dominated the GOP.[18] Dissident Democratic businessmen continued to rail at King's
control of the city throughout the early war years, but their voices soon became
a whisper. As in many other cities in the Progressive Era, Bridgeport business
"reformers" proposed a commission or city manager form of city government
in the name of efficient, "business-like" (i.e., non–King machine) municipal
administrations. Bridgeport citizens pondered a commission government plan
in 1915 and a commission-manager plan in 1917. When placed on the ballot, the
latter proposal went down in overwhelming defeat, with less than a quarter of
the electorate participating. In the end neither party had worked for passage.[19]
These efforts were primarily weapons in the hands of dissident businessmen to
oppose a business-ward-machine alliance and to move government decision
making to a level far removed from voters. Neither group operated as representative of "the people."[20] By 1915 little enthusiasm was forthcoming for a method of defeating King because of the wartime economic boom. Most factions
within the business community—industrial, financial, and mercantile alike—
decided to unite around the good opportunities.

Immigrants and the City

The industrial city needed the large numbers of skilled and unskilled workers,
many of them immigrants, who were arriving in Bridgeport after 1900. The city,
whose harbor is formed by the mouth of the Pequonnock River and Yellow Mill
Pond, was vertically striated by other smaller creeks and rivers, with many
bridges linking its various neighborhoods. The New York, New Haven & Hartford Railroad line, which ran roughly parallel to the coast, split the city at its
downtown into north and south segments. Factories clustered around the railroad line. Around the factories and south of the railroad line to the shore were
the immigrant neighborhoods—the West End, mostly Scandinavian with increasing numbers of Hungarians; the South End, a mixed neighborhood of recent immigrants; the East Side, the largest voting district of the city and popu-

lated by southern and eastern European immigrants; and the tiny East End, an enclave of Irish and English. These areas were densely settled, a mix of three-story wooden tenements and storefronts, plus small workingmen's cottages and detached double- and triple-decker multifamily houses for the better-off working-class families. The North End continued to be a less congested middle-class area of Yankee and Irish families who were long-time residents, along with certain elite areas like the Stratfield section on the western border with neighboring Fairfield. (See figure 1.)

In 1920, 32.4 percent of Bridgeport's population was foreign born, and 40.4 percent were the American-born children of the foreign born, thus giving the city a population that was 72.8 percent foreign stock. Moreover, 73 percent of the workforce of Bridgeport was foreign stock. These figures reflect large numbers of recent immigrants from the so-called old immigrant groups of English, Irish, German, and Scandinavian origins, as well as the new immigrants from eastern and southern Europe. In 1920 the foreign-born population was 55 percent "new" immigrant, with Italians, Hungarians, and Russians foremost. The "old" immigrants, however, still provided many newcomers to the city in this era, with large numbers of Irish and English. (See table 2.) In this period the African-American presence in the city was small and the Asian community almost nonexistent.[21]

The dynamics of these two immigrant groups, old and new, differed in cultural terms, even as they may have converged in class terms. New arrivals of the old immigrant groups entered American society through settled and highly differentiated communities. They joined existing connections to political parties and trade unions, and they shared relative acceptance in an increasingly nativist age. Thus the immigrant problems of transition and adaptation to the United States in the Progressive Era and World War I were primarily the preoccupation of the new eastern and southern European immigrant communities.

Most of these communities were in flux during the prewar period, with many immigrant workers seeking work and then returning home in a circular migration pattern. But immigrant pioneers who had settled and become ethnic leaders—merchants, saloon keepers, immigrant bankers, undertakers, leaders of large fraternal organizations, some clergy—anchored their immigrant conationals to Bridgeport's economic and political system. These middle-class "brokers" walked a fine line between doing their job of integration so well that the particularistic needs of their community disappeared or so poorly that they were unable to function as bridges. By keeping their communities separately organized and representing their group needs to local authorities, ethnic brokers could keep their communities in line, mediate labor disputes with employers, thwart radical impulses within their communities, and carefully integrate their conationals into local politics.

Occasionally, immigrant elites' support for bettering the working conditions of their people allowed them to upstage radical immigrant leadership. For

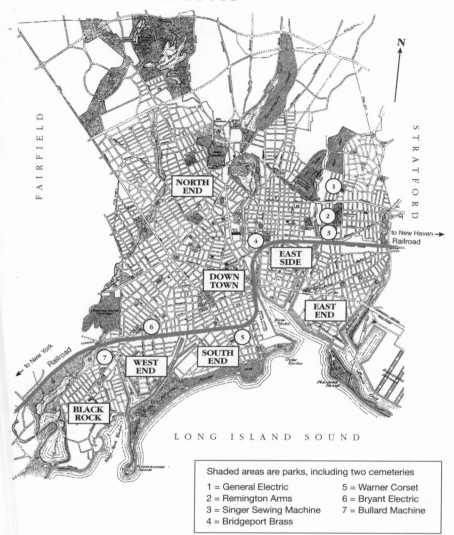

TRUMBULL

FAIRFIELD

STRATFORD

N

NORTH
END

① 1

② 2

③ 3

to New Haven →
Railroad

④ 4

EAST
SIDE

DOWN
TOWN

EAST
END

⑥ 6

⑤ 5

to New York
Railroad ←

⑦ 7

WEST
END

SOUTH
END

BLACK
ROCK

LONG ISLAND SOUND

Shaded areas are parks, including two cemeteries

1 = General Electric
2 = Remington Arms
3 = Singer Sewing Machine
4 = Bridgeport Brass

5 = Warner Corset
6 = Bryant Electric
7 = Bullard Machine

Figure 1. City map, with neighborhoods and major factories, 1920–40. Adapted by Virginia Blaisdell from John Nolen, *Better City Planning for Bridgeport* (Bridgeport, Conn.: City Plan Commission, 1916), 6.

Table 2. Bridgeport Population by Ethnicity

	1910		1920		1930	
Native white/native parents	27,156	(26.6%)	36,816	(25.7%)	37,587	(25.6%)
Native white/foreign parents	37,314	(36.6%)	57,990	(40.4%)	64,979	(44.3%)
Foreign-born white	36,180	(35.5%)	46,414	(32.4%)	40,759	(27.8%)
Black	1,332	(1.3%)	2,228	(1.6%)	3,314	(2.3%)
Other	72[a]		107[a]		77[a]	
Total population	102,054		143,555		146,716	
Selected countries of origin for foreign-born whites						
Austria[b]	3,858		2,697		599	
Czechoslovakia	n.a.		2,227		4,371	
England	3,264		3,491		2,937	
Germany[b]	2,811		1,979		2,100	
Hungary[b]	6,975		6,230		3,983	
Ireland	5,085		4,300		3,184	
Italy	5,021		8,789		8,663	
Poland	n.a.		3,061		3,604	
Russia[c]	4,116		5,395		2,648	
Sweden	1,677		1,783		1,637	

Sources: U.S. Census Bureau, *Abstract for Connecticut,* 1910 (Washington, D.C.: U.S. Government Printing Office, 1911), table 2; U.S. Census Bureau, *Population,* 1920 (Washington, D.C.: U.S. Government Printing Office, 1920), vol. 3, table 13; U.S. Census Bureau, *Population,* 1930, vol. 3, pt. 1: *Population by States* (Washington, D.C.: U.S. Government Printing Office, 1930), table 15, p. 357.
a. Percentage of the total population is less than one-tenth of 1 percent.
b. Includes Poles and Slovaks in 1910.
c. Includes some Poles in 1910.

example, in 1907 one thousand Hungarian workers, led by the radical Industrial Workers of the World (IWW), struck the American Tube and Stamping Company's West End plant and were joined briefly by native-born craft union members. The strike soon became a community cause, with Hungarian merchants donating food and beer, barbers offering free haircuts, and other shopkeepers contributing numerous services. After a prolonged stalemate—AT&S management refused to meet with IWW organizers—three members of the Hungarian elite, Andrew Duka, Joseph Ciglar, and J. Lomnitzer, stepped forward to meet with management. They gained only the reinstatement of the strikers and a promise to arbitrate wages in the future. After intense debate and a slim majority vote the Hungarian strikers decided to return to work. The three notables, however, had demonstrated their mediating ability and their moderating influence, even though they had not eradicated radical sentiments in their community.[22]

Nationally, immigrant spokesmen—Poles, Czechs, Slovaks, Lithuanians—remained tied to the politics of the old country, pursuing the goal of national independence for their native lands by lobbying Congress and the White House on foreign policy. World War I made this task easier for some, more difficult for others. Those immigrants from the Central Powers—Germans, Austrians, Hungarians, and some Poles, Czechs, and Slovaks—found themselves labeled "enemy aliens," and their loyalty was questioned. Their spokesmen assured the U.S. government that they would fight for the Allied cause if the postwar settlement included the breaking-up of empires and the establishment of independent nations. Others denied their loyalty to nondemocratic European leaders. Nonetheless, after August 1914 the mainstream press in Bridgeport speculated about which immigrant groups hated which other groups the most among Bridgeport's Poles, Russians, Austrians, Hungarians, Slovaks, and Lithuanians, and which would return to fight for their emperor or czar and which would join national armies of independence.[23]

Businessmen and the Wartime Boom Town

The year 1915 began auspiciously for Bridgeport, as the city's firms received war orders from the European belligerents. The most significant addition to the city in 1915 was the immense rifle factory of the Remington Arms Company, built on the city's East Side next to the company's older Union Metallic Cartridge Company (UMC) plant. By midyear Bridgeport was producing two-thirds of all small arms and ammunition being shipped to the Allies from the United States, leading some to dub the city the Essen of America. Remington-UMC alone received $168 million worth of war orders. New manufacturing facilities, costing $30 million, or 60 percent of the total industrial construction in the state, were built in Bridgeport from 1915 to 1919.[24]

Remington Arms plant on Boston Avenue, under construction in 1915, occupying 77.6 acres. (Photograph by Lew Corbit, Sr., Historical Collections, Bridgeport Public Library.)

About seventy thousand people flocked to town throughout the war period, augmenting the city's 1914 population of 120,000. An expanded population worked around the clock in war production, while the greater number of single men and the rising number of working women led to the growth of commercial services, laundries, restaurants, and such. Working-class families responded to the housing shortage by doubling up and taking extra boarders on a shift system. Rents soared.

The city's business leaders saw their opportunities and took them. DeVer H. Warner was the first to remind local elites of their responsibilities and to notify newcomers of the tasks ahead: "I believe that the monied interests[,] in justice to the people that have lived here for years, as well as those who have just come, should form new companies, or support existing ones, and loan money to banks in liberal quantity. The worst thing you can say about Bridgeport is that it does not appear to know the great opportunities which have been thrown here. Other cities make great concessions to get half of what Bridgeport has had almost without the asking."[25]

The war boom became the impetus for the modernization of business organization in the city. In the spring of 1915 the newly formed BCC moved to assert its leadership in the public sphere. Spearheaded by a diverse group of retail and service-sector businessmen and a few local manufacturers, the chamber absorbed the memberships of two older organizations, the Bridgeport Board of Trade and the Bridgeport Businessmen's Association, which had often been at loggerheads. "We've never had any real cooperation among the business men before," explained one BCC member.[26] The unified chamber became the vehicle for business boosterism and development plans for the city.

The chamber took the Clifford Wilson administration's modest city development ideas and expanded them into a comprehensive plan. It supported a housing study and recommended new sewers and parks. It appointed its own private-sector Recreation Commission, Health Commission, and Vice Commission to monitor improvements and the city's own commissions in these areas. The city administration supported the chamber's initiatives, and in April 1916 the city's voters approved the largest bond issue in the city's history, $2,275,000. This bonded largesse served the interests of the public, the business community, and politicians alike. Thus the city saw major improvements—a new high school, modernized fire and police facilities and vehicles, paved streets, new bridges on main streets over the city's many rivers, sewage treatment facilities, a new welfare building, a health clinic and almshouse, and improved operations for the health and charities boards.[27] Local businessmen intended to do well by the war. What no one foresaw was the independent action by Bridgeport's working people.

Unionism, from Defense to Offense

"During the war, Bridgeport was a strong union town. Oh boy, you couldn't even smoke cigarettes that weren't union," recalled R. Schmidt, a former union activist who relished the memory.[28] Nationally, the war years saw a massive upsurge in labor activity and union membership, a "new unionism" of workers' control impulses and industrial unionism. The union wave included AFL craftsmen in the metal trades who were opposing management innovations that would subdivide and reorganize their trade. It also included unskilled and semi-skilled immigrant workers who used the new economic boom to enhance their economic position. They, in particular, were energized by the industrial union–social reform unionism promoted by such unions as the International Ladies' Garment Workers' Union (ILGWU) and the Amalgamated Clothing Workers of America (ACWA), as well as the more radical industrial union, the IWW. Nationally, more than four million workers struck from 1915 through 1918, followed by the greatest strike wave yet, strikes by more than four million workers (20 percent of the labor force) in 1919 alone.[29]

Bridgeport epitomized this national trend. The World War I years transformed the city and brought it national attention. What had started as a welcome war boom for local businessmen and city politicians quickly became precarious as skilled and unskilled workers in unprecedented numbers challenged management's power. Strikes—both by unorganized, unskilled immigrants who sought better wages and working conditions and demanded union representation, and by skilled metalworkers who fought to halt the de-skilling of their jobs by scientific management—engaged the attention of the Manufacturers' Association of Bridgeport from 1915 through 1919. The specter of labor radicalism haunted city officials and police as well as the federal government. While the mayor expressed concern for public order, the MAB adamantly resisted labor's demands. The city ultimately became enmeshed in the federal government's planning, as the National War Labor Board (NWLB) sought to build "responsible" unionism and gave Bridgeport manufacturers a model for the handling of industrial conflict.[30]

In the prewar years the labor movement in Bridgeport had been weak, curtailed by the strong open-shop stance of the MAB and further debilitated by the depressed economic conditions of 1914. Effective unions existed mostly in the building and printing trades. A ten-hour day was standard in the city's shops. Lodge 30 of the International Association of Machinists (IAM), led by reform-oriented members of the Bridgeport Socialist Party, was small and ineffective; many of its members were unemployed because of the economic slump. But in the early years of the war the confrontation between workers and managers in the metal trades reached fever pitch, and the IAM bore the brunt of management's reorganization. Nationally, employers in the metal trades began a systematic attempt to control production and rationalize shop-floor processes through technological innovation, subdivision of tasks, and the application of the principles of Taylorism or scientific management.

The expanded Remington-UMC quickly came to dominate the city's economy. It was the largest employer in Bridgeport, had the most European (and later U.S.) contracts, subcontracted to smaller machine shops the work of building specialized production machinery, and gave orders to larger Bridgeport firms for ammunition components. At the same time Remington-UMC competed with all these shops for workers and set the pace for Bridgeport's handling of labor unrest.

AFL members embarked on organizing drives in the city's workplaces once the war boom got under way in the spring of 1915. Unionists from the building trades began the action by pressing their demand for the union shop at the city's construction sites, while IAM Lodge 30 announced a drive for the eight-hour day (that is, a forty-eight-hour week, because the workweek included Saturdays). Within days machinists at Remington-UMC and other machine shops struck. Remington-UMC's management, in order to avoid delays in production, broke ranks with the MAB and agreed to the shorter hours. Other Bridgeport machine shops had little choice but to follow suit, and by August 1 most machinists were back as work.

All was quiet for two weeks. But on Monday, August 16, one thousand women corset workers struck the Warner Corset Company, demanding the eight-hour day, elimination of fines and other work rules, and recognition of their union shop committee. "Chaos reigned in manufacturing circles," declared the *Herald* as unskilled and semiskilled workers struck the city's factories, garment shops, foundries, rubber works, and laundries, all demanding the eight-hour day, pay raises, and elimination of irksome work rules. "It seemed to be in the air that any workman or workwoman who wanted shorter hours, without loss of pay, need only let it be known and walk out of the factory," observed the *Herald*. "Others, on learning the cause of the walkout, followed suit, until in the course of a day the entire factory was depleted of help."[31]

"Personally, I think Bridgeport has gone bughouse," declared a spokesman for the Crane Company.[32] Many strikers were foreign-born workers who conducted strike meetings in Italian, Hungarian, Slovak, and Polish. Sympathy strikes spread the movement, as other factory operators refused to work on goods transferred from the struck shops, and jitney drivers declined to carry nonstrikers to their jobs. All told, about fourteen thousand workers struck that summer. Finally, most companies agreed to the eight-hour day (with modifications) and some wage concessions. However, employers remained adamantly opposed to the recognition of union shop committees. The AFL organizers dispatched from Washington, D.C., attempted to enroll unskilled workers in various federal (directly affiliated) locals, while the craft unions that had started the eight-hour drive moved to consolidate their position.[33]

The eight-hour movement of the summer of 1915 was two tiered. Though the

IAM had first raised the eight-hour demand, most of the twenty-five hundred striking machinists were back at work when strikes swept the rest of the city. The separate walkouts of more than eleven thousand unskilled laborers and semiskilled operators ultimately carried the movement and the drive to unionize the city. The contrast between the craft unionists' aloofness and the mass strike movement among the less skilled reflected the considerable distance separating these two groups of workers during the first year of war mobilization.

Immigrant workers in Bridgeport had seized the opportunity of the new war economy to improve their lot. Their spontaneous uprisings constituted virtually a general strike around the major demand for the eight-hour day. Yet these actions revealed definite ethnic cleavages. "Each nationality congregated among its own" at the general strike headquarters, the Fraternal Order of Eagles Hall, noted the *Herald.* When sudden strike violence occurred, it invariably involved members of just one ethnic group. At the Crane Company gates, for example, Polish strikers "rioted" when Polish scabs attempted to cross picket lines; police arrested two Polish picketers.[34]

All members of one ethnic group, regardless of their workplaces, met together to hear union leaders in their native language. While obviously necessary because of the language difficulty, the separateness of this strike activity revealed the lack of a central labor leadership that could bring all workers together in this early phase of the war boom. This was less a problem in workplaces that tended to employ many conationals, as seemed true of smaller manufacturers, but it was a major obstacle in larger plants that employed many different nationalities. The AFL organizers hastily ordered to Bridgeport by the national tried to overcome ethnic difficulties by enrolling everyone in catchall locals—which also solved the immediate problem of craft jurisdiction—and willingly acceded to worker preferences for language locals.[35] Strikers mixed symbols of ethnic nationalism with American patriotism. For example, fifty Italian strikers from the Siemens Rubber Company marched down Main Street carrying both Italian and American flags.[36]

In the maelstrom of events the traditional ethnic leaders who had so carefully tied themselves to the American mainstream seemed to have played no role in this unrest and rarely made an appearance. Though there were many reports of neighborhood solidarity and sympathy actions, ethnic workers on the East Side did not meet in their own halls. Five hundred Slavic metalworkers crowded into the St. Joseph T.B.& L. Hall, an old Irish temperance organization, to hear a Polish orator urge them to join the union. Slavic workers in general were eager to hear union messages, but traditional church and fraternal leaders stayed away. Only Father Andrew Komara of the Slovak parish, St. John Nepomucene Church, supported the strike the following year. Two weeks after a molders' union fund-raiser at Eagles Hall, the general strike headquarters, Komara opened his church hall to a fund-raiser run by the Slovak members of that union. He was also the only community leader to address the MAB, warning it to expect that radical appeals would attract Slovak workers unless the manufacturers treated their workers better.[37]

In contrast, Hungarian workers in the West End were able to use their community hall for their strike meetings—actually a tradition since the AT&S strike in 1907. Five hundred Hungarian strikers attended a meeting at Rakoczi Hall where an IAM organizer joined Zador Szabados, editor of the New York–based *Elöre*, a Hungarian socialist paper, a good example of the openness of ethnic community leaders and the IAM to leftist speakers. In the Hungarian community left-wing community leaders clearly commanded the greatest respect. Many immigrants found that the pull of the Left was strong. Joseph Ettor, a national IWW organizer, claimed that his union had five hundred new members in Bridgeport by summer's end, mostly Italian, Russian, and Jewish immigrants. Indeed, so strong was the IWW's pull on Italians that the Italian officers of the masons' helpers' local almost succeeded in turning over their local to the IWW before officers of the national masons' union intervened.[38] Thus radical ethnic spokesmen guided the strike movement of 1915. But ethnic separateness remained a weakness in the effort to build a long-lasting strike coalition.

When the unskilled made fewer demands for formal organization during the war, Bridgeport managers dismissed the strike wave as merely a straightforward demand for a wage increase, noting that workers seemed willing to work the old ten-hour day as long as the last two hours were at premium pay.[39] Metal trades employers, however, were more concerned about the organizing efforts of AFL craft unions, such as the IAM and the Metal Polishers, which threatened management's plans to institute high-volume war production on the shop floor by using specialized machinery and scientific management practices.

The Bridgeport IAM planned an organizing campaign in the burgeoning war production plants. Though the union's power was greatest in the small specialty machine shops with highly skilled workers, the key to union strength in the city lay in organizing the Remington-UMC complex, which was expected to employ about sixteen thousand workers at full operation. Though the leadership of IAM Lodge 30 remained in the hands of craft-oriented machinists, many of whom were active in the Socialist Party, the 1916 organizing committee in Bridgeport quickly became dominated by more radical newcomers who espoused mass action and industrial unionism.[40] Leading the campaign was Sam Lavit, a machinist with six years' residence in the city. A Russian Jewish immigrant, he was described by one IAM member as "a fine agitator . . . who would get up and speak at a meeting and put the stuff across. He understood Industrial Unionism and he wanted the Bridgeport workers to understand it."[41]

The organizing committee broke with traditional craft structure (for example, IAM Lodge 30 accepted as members all qualified, apprenticed machinists within the geographic area) by setting up a plant-based lodge, Remington Lodge 584, and two ethnic lodges, Scandinavian Lodge 826 and Polish Lodge 782. The four lodges together formed the new District Lodge 55. The machinists also recruited a committee of active women from the Corset Workers' Union to begin organizing the women at Remington-UMC.[42] Lavit and other members of the main organizing committee pursued novel tactics, in addition to shop-floor contacts, to garner publicity and heighten enthusiasm for union membership. For example, that spring organizers tossed reams of cards out of an office window to the downtown streets below; printed on the card was simply the phrase "25,000!" leaving people to speculate about what it meant. The next week they tossed out more cards, this time reading "25,000 by May 1st!" In the third week the cards read "25,000 by May 1st—Join the Machinists Union!"[43]

The great gap between skilled craftsmen and semiskilled and unskilled workers, though narrowed by management's steady destruction of the machinists' craft, proved difficult to close as the organizing campaign got underway. Splits within the ranks of munitions workers quickly became apparent, as many skilled machinists refused to support the grievances of the less-skilled workers, especially women. Ethnic frictions also lurked beneath the surface. For example, it was common knowledge among Bridgeporters that Swedes preferred to work in small shops where, according to Mr. Pederson, a Swedish-American tool

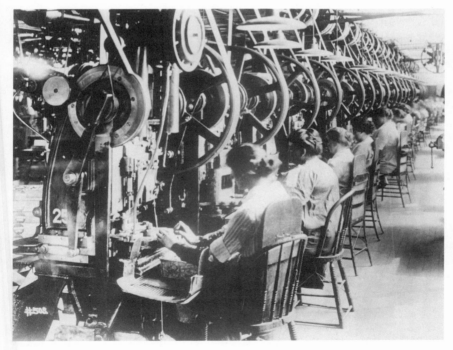

Women cartridge makers at Remington Arms–Union Metallic Cartridge Company, 1915 (Historical Collections, Bridgeport Public Library.)

grinder, "they are better recognized for their work."[44] By the war many Swedish machinists were clustered in these machine shops, citing ethnic solidarity and the employer's preference for all-around skill there. Moreover, as Sidney Johnson explained, they disliked the new situation in newly expanded factories like Bullard Machine Tool Company, a well-known maker of turret lathes and automatic machinery, where "Poles, Slovaks . . . would always try to chisel into a better job without regard to their ability."[45]

Pederson explained his view of the situation in the big shops during the war: "The employer's main interest is the rate of production rather than first quality work."[46] The Bullard Machine Tool Company eliminated craft classifications altogether from the production workforce during the war, when the company switched to making cannons and other ordnance. The massive war boom in Bridgeport allowed the company to reorganize its production; the U.S. War Department funded Bullard's expansion to a large new plant in the city's West End where the company implemented this new production scheme. The company made up for the reorganization by providing "liberal advantages" in the form of fringe benefits and other welfare measures.[47]

The failure of the old union leadership to combat the deteriorating shop-floor conditions or to deal effectively with the new munitions workforce caused an upheaval within the ranks of the Bridgeport IAM. In April 1917 Lavit was elected as District 55's business agent, and other organizing committee members were elected as local officers.[48] Interpreting this stunning victory as a repudiation of exclusivist craft unionism and an endorsement of industrial unionism, the new officers embarked on a bold course. They made special efforts to appeal to semi-skilled immigrant workers.[49] In addition, IAM District 55 attempted to bring order to management reform. In August 1917 Lavit sent letters to all Bridgeport employers of machinists, stipulating new union rules under which IAM members would work. By including a minimum wage rate for *seven* machine-shop classifications—from the highest through the lowest levels of machine workers, instead of the old craft standard of one or two union classifications and wage levels—District 55 signaled its intention to include most metalworkers under the IAM banner. Most important, the union intended to replace the myriad individual rates created by scientific management with a union-sanctioned plan. Lavit attempted to negotiate these demands with Bridgeport employers through the fall of 1917 with no success.

The situation suddenly changed, however, in the spring of 1918 when seven hundred toolroom machinists at Remington Arms walked off the job on Good Friday in a dispute about holiday pay. But in limiting their demands to only their own classifications, toolmakers and toolroom machinists returned IAM District 55 to protecting the status and wages of skilled machinists while ignoring the less skilled. But when the War Department announced that it had decided in favor of the machinists, Bridgeport employers refused to comply. Enraged by their employers' intransigence, more than seven thousand machinists ignored appeals to patriotism and put down their tools. By the end of June the stoppage included craftsmen from twenty-two machine shops, seven hundred men from Remington's toolroom, and one thousand each at two other munitions plants, Liberty Ordnance and the American-British Company.

The machinists returned to work as the newly created National War Labor Board assumed jurisdiction over the dispute. At NWLB hearings Bridgeport manufacturers revealed the purposefulness of their actions in reorganizing production and undercutting skilled craftsmen. Militant Bridgeport machinists were equally adamant in their opposition to this reorganization, which they referred to as "evil working conditions." But national IAM leaders had become more worried by the radical trend within their rank-and-file, compounded by the AFL's wartime no-strike pledge. The national office asserted its control over NWLB hearings. A subdued Lavit, now flanked by national IAM officers, limited his remarks to the grievances of the skilled machinists, retreating from his efforts to represent the less skilled.[50]

Americanization

The tension caused by the incessant labor agitation during the war years heightened the atmosphere of coercive patriotism that was suffusing the wartime boom city. Local political leaders had early declared for the British cause and combined an antipathy for labor with general alarm about possible German saboteurs in the city. Bridgeport took on the appearance of a military camp. Pacifist demonstrations were suppressed, and speakers from the Connecticut Council of Defense staged war rallies on factory grounds. The council was appointed by the governor to coordinate material aid to the war and to boost patriotism in both home and factory. The state deployed militia units, and agents of the Army and Navy Military Intelligence Bureaus were engaged in plant surveillance in the city. A navy submarine guarded the harbor, ostensibly against German attack.

Even before U.S. entry into the European war, local fears of radicalism found an obvious target in the "hyphenates," the foreign-born residents supposedly loyal to their countries of birth.[51] In the wartime environment of Bridgeport the serious business of war production took place alongside frequent newspaper exposés of alleged spy activities and bomb threats. An opinion column in the *Herald* conveyed a common point of view on "Americanism" and war patriotism. "If you are in America now, whether born here or not, stand by the American flag, the American people, or get out. You can't serve two gods. You can't serve two countries. You must be either American or not American."[52] Though meant to encourage citizenship, measures were often harsh, and as the war progressed, Americanization became more coercive. In April 1918 Gov. Marcus C. Holcomb issued a proclamation that forbade the use of any language other than English in any public or private elementary school in the state (exempting only language classes and private schools' devotional services) and also forbade aliens from teaching in any public or private school.

Connecticut provided a model for the rest of the country in setting up the Connecticut Council of Defense. The National Council of Defense (NCD) soon advocated similar agencies elsewhere in the nation, and George Creel's Committee on Public Information of the NCD coordinated efforts to reach unions and immigrant groups. The Connecticut Council of Defense recruited volunteer "Four Minute Men" and "Minute Women" to canvass neighborhoods and exhort captive audiences at factory gates and movie theaters on the evils of hoarding, slacking, and the like; men who ignored draft notices caused great concern. In Bridgeport these volunteers were local Democratic and Republican Party activists as well as industrialists' wives. Factories sponsored Liberty Bond drives; the Union Metallic Cartridge Company led the city's factory campaign for employee subscriptions, with more than $320,000 pledged in October 1917 added to a $150,000 pledge from the workforce of its affiliated plant, the Remington Arms. Once the United States entered the war, the state Council of Defense carried out a military census of all alien males aged twenty-one and older who were living in Bridgeport. The council found about nine thousand Austro-Hungarian aliens and five hundred German aliens, all of whom were required to register with the police as "enemy aliens." Immigrants rushed to the courts for citizenship papers as major employers like Remington Arms announced they would hire only citizens or those with first papers, that is, those who had applied for citizenship. More onerous was the proclamation that enemy aliens would no longer be allowed to live within a cordon sanitaire around each war plant. This was a special hardship for immigrant workers because most plants were in the heart of immigrant neighborhoods; the simple solution was to apply for citizenship.[53]

Antiwar sentiment had been silenced early on. The Bridgeport Socialist Party, which had established eight language branches during 1915–16, steadfastly held to the national SP's antiwar declaration. Bridgeport police, however, had already barred the Slovak branch of the SP from holding an antiwar meeting in March 1917, even before the U.S. government's declaration of war.[54] After the 1917 Russian Revolution, Russian organizations in Bridgeport became suspect as well. Nicholas Hourwich, son of the New York left–socialist leader Isaac Hourwich, was arrested in Bridgeport on charges of sedition as he addressed the Bridgeport branch of the Union of Russian Mechanics. The SP members in the Central Labor Union, an umbrella group of all AFL locals, tried to curb prowar sentiment among unions, while, in contrast, the radical (but non-SP) leaders of IAM District 55 led strikes while they vigorously sold Liberty Bonds.[55]

Immigrants and their leaders voiced their worry for their homelands while assuring Americans of their devotion to the United States. The task was considerably easier among groups whose homelands were allied with the U.S. war effort. The first task was raising money for victims in the old country. After hostilities began in Europe, immigrant groups in Bridgeport sponsored benefits, such as those for the "Armenian-Syrian Relief Fund" and "Polish War victims." Ads for the latter event, a classical concert featuring Polish performers, stressed the special tragedy of Poles forced to fight each other as conscripts in the Austrian or Russian imperial armies and appealed to Americans to "assist these persevering Poles" by buying tickets to the concert. Later, the Polish Citizens Committee, made up of Polish fraternal orders in the city, hosted a concert that featured the pianist Jan Paderewski and raised $50,000 for Polish aid. These Polish efforts were tied to Roman Dmowski's Polish National Council and thus to the United States and its allies. A Czecho-Slovak Relief Fund opened at National Slovak Sokol Hall to collect money for war relief. Immigrants who had not taken out first American citizenship papers could join the independent army in their homeland. About two hundred Polish immigrants in Bridgeport signed up for the independent Polish Army fighting in France. Similarly, Slovak men from the city went to France as part of a Slovak Army unit. The Slovak fraternals of the city pulled together a Slovak League, whose women's auxiliary knitted and sewed garments and made surgical dressings for this army unit. Polish and Slovak aspirations for an autonomous homeland contributed to their allegiance to the U.S. war effort, even though those born within German or Austro-Hungarian territories were listed as enemy aliens. The Slovak Minute Women performed Red Cross work and sold Liberty Bonds in their community.[56] Similar sentiments engulfed the Irish-American community, whose animus toward Britain had initially made Irish Americans reluctant to support the Allied war effort. But now Col. J. H. Murray of Bridgeport offered Governor Holcomb the services of the Hibernian Rifles, the drill team of the Ancient Order of Hibernians, for the war emergency.[57]

Things were more difficult for groups whose wartime loyalties were divided. The Polish community was split by the establishment of KON (Komitet Obrony Narodowej, or Committee of National Defense) by Polish left-wingers in the United States. KON endorsed Gen. Jozef Pilsudski's effort to achieve Polish national independence by allying with Austria against Russia. Mainstream Poles, and their Catholic allies, supported the Dmowski's Polish National Committee and its alliance with Russia to achieve independence. After the United States entered the war in 1917 on the Allied side, KON members were suspect while members of Dmowski's group were welcomed in Washington. The Polish Socialist Alliance sold its building on East Main Street in Bridgeport to contribute money to Pilsudski's war effort, thus putting it at odds with U.S. war goals. The large Magyar community was at once tied to Germany and its culture and stung by the early appearance of anti-German feeling in Bridgeport. The Bridgeport Hungarian newspaper, the Magyar-language *Bridgeport*, published statements of outrage against Hungarians' alleged mistreatment in the United States. Many Hungarians in America supported the independence aims of Mihály Károlyi, the Hungarian statesman who favored breaking with Germany; the

Hungarian community's loyalty was nonetheless suspect. And indeed the relationship was complicated. For example, Bridgeport's Rakoczi Aid Association
lost heavily by investing in Hungarian war bonds.[58]

Americanism, ethnic nationalism, and interethnic antagonism were echoed
in the banners carried by groups in the massive July Fourth parade held in
Bridgeport in 1918, in the midst of machinist strikes. By 1918 all groups had declared their loyalty to the United States, but tensions among the nationality
groups increased. Magyars denounced pan-Slavism, Poles opposed German and
Russian aggression, and Slovaks clamored for self-determination. The Bridgeport Fourth of July Parade, inspired by the National Committee on Public Information's plans for a ceremony at Mt. Vernon, became the state's major celebration. Governor Holcomb himself stood on the reviewing stand. The parade
consisted of two parts, the first a contingent of twenty-five hundred state guardsmen, the second the "Loyalty Division" marshalled by Bradford Pierce, the president of the Bridgeport Chamber of Commerce. The Loyalty Division was made
up of assemblies of men from the city's Russian, Lithuanian, Slovak, Italian,
Polish, Irish, German, Swedish, Hungarian, "Czecho-Uhro-Russian," Rumanian,
Greek, and Armenian communities. Also marching in it were the Sons of the
American Revolution, numerous other Yankee fraternal organizations, eleven

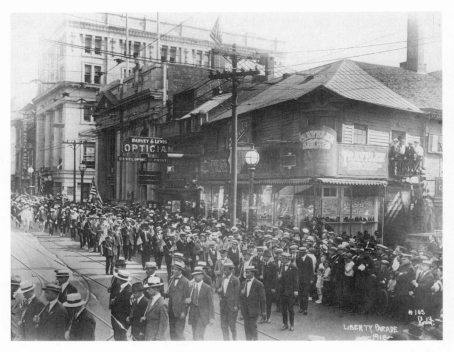

Loyalty Division, Fourth of July Parade on Main Street, 1918. (Corbit's Studio, Bridgeport.)

bands, and three drum corps. Each man in every contingent carried a small American flag, and groups vied for the record of carrying the most big American flags—won by the group of five hundred Germans accompanied by a large boys' choir. There was hostility within the ranks of the Loyalty Division, however. The Magyars, marshalled by the fraternal leader John Dezso, carried a pennant declaring, "We are all Americans in the Fight." Marching directly behind the Magyars, the Czechs carried their own banner: "Things we hate, Kaiserism, Prussianism, Militarism, despotism, and Magyarism."[59]

* * *

Unions walked a fine line between legitimacy and subversion. Considerable patriotic pressure came not just from management and government but from other workers. The workforces at the Lake Torpedo Boat Company and the Locomobile Company, who in 1917 had struck against nonunion wages, in June 1918 threw "unpatriotic," or prostrike, workers into Long Island Sound. Indeed, in the fervor whipped up on the Fourth of July in 1918, the workforce at Lake Torpedo Boat voted to work on the Fourth and to contribute three hours' pay to the government as an extra contribution to the war effort. In the spring and summer of 1918 local newspapers pressured striking machinists to return to work, and Lavit appealed to his members to await the NWLB decision on labor relations in the city. The *Bridgeport Times* warned the public that the fomenters of strikes were "socialists and frequently socialists of the I.W.W. stripe [who were] German in sympathy."[60] In addition to the federal government's stepping in to solve Bridgeport's labor troubles, the mayor (now also a colonel in the Home Guard, an early version of civil defense) and the common council passed a "work or fight" ordinance that authorized the police to sweep through the city during the strikes and arrest any adult male without a draft card who was not at work. More than five thousand "slackers" without draft cards, mostly the foreign born, were arrested during the summer strike days and turned over to the draft board for induction.[61] While the IAM's newspaper, the *Bridgeport Labor Leader,* carefully avoided political or antiwar statements, IAM members showed their patriotism by selling war bonds all during the troubled summer. Many machinists were confident that the NWLB, in light of the previous War Department decision and the classification schemes already set up in U.S. shipyards and arsenals, would accede to the Bridgeport machinists' demands.[62]

On the contrary, in August 1918 the NWLB rescinded the War Department decision and ordered a basic eight-hour day with pay raises for *all* war workers, with the smallest raise (5 cents) going to the skilled craftsmen. It allowed no adjustment in job classifications but did order the installation of employee shop committees in sixty-three large and small metalworking companies in the city. The decision was consistent with the NWLB's philosophy of attempting to bring "industrial democracy" to the workplace while upholding "existing conditions," whether union or nonunion.[63]

The skilled workers were incensed at the decision and dubbed their 5-cent increase a "jitney feast"; they voted another walkout. Five thousand machinists struck, calling on President Woodrow Wilson to take over the Bridgeport factories, as had been done in nearby Springfield, Massachusetts, when those employers had refused to abide by an NWLB ruling. William Johnston, the national IAM president and a member of the NWLB, initially supported the strikers but within the week bowed to government pressure and ordered the lodges back to work. The strikers voted to forfeit their lodge charters rather than obey the Grand Lodge. The stalemate lasted until September 13, when President Wilson issued a back-to-work order and threatened to rescind the men's military exemptions. The strikers quickly returned to work.

The strike in the summer of 1918 was essentially the initiative of skilled machinists. Few production workers or women workers from Remington-UMC took part in strike activities. Ironically, the government's decision spurred significant union efforts among Remington-UMC women for the first time. The women, incensed that Remington-UMC was not abiding by the government decision, which stipulated a minimum rate of 32 cents an hour for women workers, signed IAM membership cards. Women workers noted the inadequacy of the decision's provision for equal pay for women in men's jobs and petitioned the local NWLB board for an extension of the decision to women younger than eighteen years, who had been excluded. The women's organization was growing rapidly. By the end of October IAM Women's Lodge 1196 had one hundred members and was granted a charter.[64]

Industrial strife was by no means abated by the NWLB decision, which had required that the city establish a labor representation board. The three labor representatives chosen at a citywide conference of shop committee delegates (themselves elected at government-supervised voting by all employees at each workplace) were Sam Lavit and two other IAM leaders. Employers, however, refused to deal with them, and the NWLB declined to force employers' participation on the local board. The declaration of the armistice in November 1918 cut short developments in the city's industrial relations.

After war ended, both business and the IAM concentrated on the consequences of demilitarization, especially unemployment. The petitions of manufacturers and unions alike succeeded in putting off the cancellation of government contracts for a few months. But by March 1919 all government war contracts were canceled, the wartime government apparatus was dismantled, and the Bridgeport office of the NWLB was closed. The government-sponsored system of shop committees, foundering as it was, ceased to operate.

Even with the end of the war, manufacturers and politicians continued to fear labor agitation. Indeed, at the back-to-work vote taken in September 1918 radical machinists had shed their neutral political stance to form the American Labor Party to run candidates in the November 1918 city election.[65] Large-scale unemployment demonstrations organized by the IAM District 55, IAM wom-

en's activism on behalf of women's suffrage, reports of "Bolshevik" displays in
ethnic neighborhoods (such as a funeral at which everyone wore red carnations),
and the outbreak of strikes in nonmunitions industries concerned Mayor Clifford Wilson and his police superintendent.[66]

Their fears were not unfounded. In July 1919 the Corset Workers' Union, dormant since 1916, struck the Warner Corset Company and four other corset shops
in town, demanding a forty-four-hour week and a 20 percent wage increase (demands first formulated by the IAM at its unemployment demonstrations in January). Sam Lavit then announced an IAM drive for the forty-four-hour week, a
wage increase, and a minimum wage rate for all workers in the city's machine
shops. This call to represent *all* machine-shop workers, regardless of craft status, was answered by the ten thousand skilled and unskilled workers at shops like
Bryant Electric, Remington–Yost Typewriter, Hawthorne Manufacturing, and
American Graphophone, who joined the three thousand corset workers on strike.
The machine-shop workers asked for IAM sponsorship, and Lavit enrolled them
as IAM members and wired the national office for strike benefits.[67]

Labor activity in 1919 contrasted sharply with the exclusivist machinist strikes
in the summer of 1918. Disunity was overcome during the postwar strike wave
that engulfed immigrant communities throughout Connecticut. In Bridgeport,
as well as other cities in Connecticut and around the country, factory-wide
walkouts united skilled and unskilled workers of all ethnic groups in 1919.[68]

It also led to an open split among IAM members. At a rump session of IAM
Lodge 30 in June machinists who were displeased with Lavit's rule narrowly
passed a resolution to abolish District 55 and reaffiliate the Bridgeport lodges
with the New Haven district. This move would have deprived Lavit of his position as district business agent. The *Herald* characterized the dispute as a rebellion of the "old guard" of IAM Lodge 30 against Lavit's rule, noting that Lavit's
support came from "the temporary, the new members," many of whom were
leaving town with the closing of the war industries. The other three IAM lodges
had not had time to vote on the resolution when the national IAM acted. The
Grand Lodge secretary refused to sanction the ongoing strikes, appeared at a
meeting of IAM Lodge 30, and announced Lavit's removal from office by order
of the Grand Lodge. The charges against Lavit included his having called unauthorized strikes, his being a "Bolshevik" and "IWW," and (worst of all) his
allowing nonmachinists, such as the clerks in the accounting department at
American Graphophone, to become members of the IAM. When a full meeting of Lodge 30, including the strikers, responded with an overwhelming vote
of confidence in Lavit, the lodge's charter was revoked. The Grand Lodge chartered a new Lodge 116 with "loyal" IAM members and appointed John J. Egan
as its president. This union split was a conservative AFL response to the radical
industrial unionists in its midst. While the garment industry strikes were settled favorably for the union, most of the strikes by metalworkers were lost as a
result of the IAM's disarray.[69]

The 1915 and 1919 mass strike waves had convulsed the city for months at a time, as workers from many factories and workplaces struck to demand recognition of their shop committees and the improvement of wages and working conditions. The strike waves of 1915, with the unanimous demand for the eight-hour day, had consisted of parallel but separate movements of skilled craftsmen and unskilled immigrant workers. The strikes during 1916–18 were the results of a complex interplay of forces—the introduction of mostly immigrant men and women workers to the new semiskilled jobs created by management reorganization, combined with craftsmen's fears of de-skilling and their hostility toward these new workers. Faced with the choice of either building a broad new union movement with these new immigrant workers or retreating into an ever-narrowing world of craft privilege, craft unionists seesawed between these alternatives during the war. Immigrant workers, who were earning unprecedented piecework wages in the flurry of war production but were harassed by anti-alien legislation and "100% Americanism," chose to participate only sporadically in the strikes from 1916 to 1918. The result in 1918 was a stalemate between the IAM and Bridgeport manufacturers that was mediated by agents of the National War Labor Board.

The war and the NWLB provided radical unionists like Lavit with an opportunity to confront both employers and the conservative AFL craft unions alike with the power of unskilled and semiskilled workers. It also gave the radical unionists the opportunity to harness the "workers' control" impulse of craftsmen to the aspirations of most industrial workers for some form of "industrial democracy" in the workplace. Lavit and other radicals elsewhere used the reformist wing of the NWLB, personified by the NWLB chairman Frank Walsh, to press this agenda in the face of the strong antiunion stance of U.S. corporations and the resistance of conservative unionists.[70]

1919: Red Scare

The wartime push for industrial democracy had radicalized Bridgeport workers' notions about their own organizations. But the 1919 strikes in metalworking were lost or compromised by four factors. First was the intransigence of manufacturers unwilling to endure the government-imposed labor solution. Second was the federal government's campaign against the feared "Bolshevism" among Bridgeport's workers. The third was the intolerance of conservative craft unionists who would brook no deviation from traditional union practice or membership. The final blow came from the economic downturn that affected the boomtown from 1919 through 1923.

In 1919 both managers and conservative trade unionists could agree that the greatest danger lay in workers' moving even further to the left. The IAM Grand Lodge had dealt a crucial blow to the organizational integrity of the strikers by revoking Lodge 30's charter. The expulsion of Lavit from the IAM by national

IAM officers did little to strengthen unionism in the city. Many ousted IAM Lodge 30 radicals, whom Lavit called "the conscious minority that have made American history," did march further to the left, ultimately joining the Amalgamated Metal Workers of America (AMWA). The AMWA was an independent industrial union formed in 1920 by the merger of various IWW metalworker organizations, revolutionary shop committees, and expelled IAM lodges such as the famed Micrometer Lodge of Brooklyn. The AMWA claimed a national membership of twelve thousand in late 1920, with Bridgeport as one of its seven district headquarters. AMWA Lodge 30 in Bridgeport continued to publish its weekly newspaper, the *Progressive Labor News* (the successor to the *Bridgeport Labor Leader*), which now included a Spanish-language column. Lavit briefly left the city to organize for the AMWA in New York and Chicago, then resumed his role as "stormy petrel" [sic] of the city's workers in 1920.[71]

AMWA Lodge 30 served as a general union for all radical workers, not just metalworkers, throughout the city (one local newspaper characterized its members as "gaunt, gray-haired workers with fanatical eyes and drooping mustaches").[72] For example, the Bridgeport Rubber Workers Union, organized as an AFL federal local during the war, left the AFL following Lavit's ouster from the IAM and joined the AMWA. Its last publicized strike was a bitter conflict about the firing of two of the union's committeemen at the Siemons Hard Rubber Company in late 1920. Described by police as a "particularly violent" strike, the Italian workers, 210 men and 40 women, were led by John Vernon, born Theodore Giumelli, who had been their leader during the wartime strikes as well. A company lockout destroyed the union, and Vernon found himself blacklisted for the rest of the decade.[73]

The blacklist and unemployment soon took their toll. "A lot of the workers here came from other cities, and they drifted back to their hometowns or other places looking for work. . . . Besides that, a lot of the active men were blacklisted, and couldn't have bought a job for any amount of money," Mr. P, a former IWW member and AMWA activist told an interviewer from the Federal Writers' Project of the Works Progress Administration. "I used to grab my grip and go out selling on the road."[74]

The Palmer raids further disrupted the radical infrastructure within immigrant communities. The IWW, the Communist Party, and the Communist Labor Party were the national targets of U.S. Attorney General A. Mitchell Palmer on November 7–8, 1919, and January 2, 1920. In Bridgeport the sole targets of the November raids were Russian radicals. Eighty-seven men were arrested in Bridgeport on those nights, dragged from their homes and Russian social clubs. A good number from Bridgeport were eventually deported. "There were I.W.W.'s, anarchists, socialists, and embryo bolsheviks—in six months they scattered the whole organization," recalled Mr. P. Though only "Russians" (and probably Ukrainians as well) were the targets in this city, this police action sobered all immigrant communities.[75]

Nonetheless, AMWA Lodge 30 survived and rallied radicalized workers after 1919 to a variety of causes. The events organized and supported by the AMWA in these years illustrated the broad multiethnic labor coalition that was the legacy of the war years. For example, the AMWA in early 1921 sponsored a mass fund-raiser "to purchase supplies for the relief of the women and children in Russia." Lodge members also sponsored and supported a fledgling chapter of the World War Veterans in Bridgeport, a prounion veterans group opposed to the antiunion activities of the American Legion. The AMWA provided the organizational basis for a Consumers' League challenge to new meter charges imposed by the Bridgeport Gas Light Company on home use. On May Day 1921 the AMWA and the Amalgamated Clothing Workers of America cosponsored a mass meeting at which Paul Blanchard of the ACWA shared the podium with the national secretary of the Irish-American Labor League and a representative of the Welsh Miners Federation. And the AMWA sponsored the first Bridgeport meeting in defense of Sacco and Vanzetti, complete with a speech by the "Rebel Girl" Elizabeth Gurley Flynn.[76]

The remaking of the postwar world; the concern about the future of Russia; the political grievances of Italian, Irish, and Welsh labor; the impassioned cause of industrial unionism—these were the issues that linked the diverse radicals of 1919–21. At Bridgeport's founding meeting of the "Workers Educational League" in the spring of 1921, the radical Swedish workers who had organized the meeting sold Communist Party and IWW literature and made ambitious plans to gather the IWW, Socialist Labor Party, AMWA Lodge 30, and the "radical bakers, . . . Swedes, Hungarians, Spaniards and all other radicals" into one citywide coalition.[77] But soon gatherings such as these retreated into friendly ethnic enclaves, the activities of some small circles of unionists, and the memories of now-silent workers. The postwar radical union coalition was broken, and the AMWA made unemployment its main issue in 1921.

While munitions workers in Bridgeport had felt the effects of the cut in war orders by mid-1919, the rest of the city felt the lag only in the winter of 1920–21, as the entire nation fell into the postwar slump. Bridgeport saw its population decline by about thirty thousand from the wartime peak of 175,000, as immigrant workers left after the war, many returning to Europe. National unemployment rates were 21 percent in 1921 and 15.4 percent in 1922. Because Bridgeport depended so heavily on war orders, its unemployment rate was no doubt higher. Factory reports illustrate the local economic dislocation. By the summer of 1921 the Remington Rifle factory, which had employed more than 9,000 people at the height of the war, was closed and the plant sold to General Electric Company. Its sister plant, Union Metallic Cartridge Company, which had employed 6,000, now reported 2,800 on its payroll. The Bullard Machine Tool Company, which had expanded to 2,600 employees during the war, closed during the summer of 1921. Locomobile, which with 1,700 workers had shifted from touring cars to Riker trucks for the duration, now reported 100 on the payroll. Bryant Electric, another major employer with 1,500 wartime employees, now registered 500. Bridgeport Brass (3,000 during the war), Singer Sewing Machine Co. (2,400), and American Tube & Stamping (1,600) all reported significantly fewer employees. It is little wonder that employers encountered few objections to the implementation of their employee representation plans, which were their answer to union unrest.[78]

Bridgeport's unionists responded to the postwar depression in a variety of ways. The Metal Trades Council of the Bridgeport Central Labor Union (CLU), led by the long-time Socialist Karl Lang, presented its own activist program in an attempt to smooth over the IAM's ouster of Lavit and to continue the strike agitation of 1919. Borrowing the rhetoric and strategy of the radical AMWA Lodge 30, the Metal Trades Council urged workers to ignore the "boss's" shop committees and join with the city's existing unions to form "one big local" to carry out collective bargaining in the city.[79] Outside the metal trades, members of the building trades', barbers', bakers', and milk-truck drivers unions all succumbed to wage cuts in 1920–22, but only the drivers lost their union. The city was treated to the new spectacle of strikebreakers, mostly African-American men in their army uniforms, as they marched through Bridgeport streets to defeat a dockworkers' strike. The Metal Trades Council in late 1920 set up a soup kitchen to serve the growing number of unemployed in the city. By early July 1921, when it closed the kitchen due to lack of funds, the Metal Trades Council had distributed 37,500 meals and 816 family food baskets, had received donations from 22 bakeries, and had raised about $1,300 in cash.[80] Trying a different tack, the Amalgamated Metal Workers organized mass rallies for unemployment relief from the city, proposing to raise the money by taxing every working citizen, and held a "slave auction" on Main Street that put unemployed men on the auction block to sell their services for the week.[81]

In these demonstrations about city relief, metalworkers once again faced the manufacturers of the city. The city's Board of Charities had attempted to meet relief demands out of the regular 1920–21 budget, but its funds were inadequate for the coming year. A plan by GOP mayor Wilson to ask the Connecticut legislature for permission to issue $500,000 in city bonds to finance a work-relief fund met with stern opposition from the MAB, itself in the midst of an assault on the city's finances and tax structure. Wilson successfully played on manufacturers' fears of radicalism to induce their support.[82] The MAB agreed to support a reduced amount ($300,000) in bonds, with the proviso that the governor appoint a special relief commission, rather than the city Board of Charities, to administer the fund. Such a commission, dominated by prominent local industrialists, was set up. This Special Relief Commission eventually handed over the money to the GOP-dominated Board of Charities but laid its own rules regarding eligibility, the rate of pay for work relief, and the hours of work.[83]

The *Herald* reasoned at that time that manufacturers feared labor radicalism and looked to John T. King, "with his national financial power and his friendship with labor organizations . . . to turn the balance to such an extent as to prevent radical socialistic ideas from becoming the aim of the unemployed." But the Special Relief Commission was an industrialist, not an elected, entity. It was at this point that Lavit accused the manufacturers of trying to take over city government, a charge that the GOP repeated against the Manufacturers' Association and its Democratic candidate in the fall 1921 election.[84] It was the beginning of a useful friendship between Lavit and the Republicans in city hall.

* * *

Wartime agitation brought a number of social changes to Bridgeport that lingered into the 1920s and beyond. The first was a decision by major industrialists to replace their stark antiunionism with sophisticated labor management. Second, organized labor briefly raised its profile, creating the potential for an active, independent working-class constituency in the city for the first time. The last legacy was in the political sphere. Local politicians had an opportunity to create a new political coalition that incorporated these working-class elements. This was a development that would take unusual twists in the 1920s.

CHAPTER 2

Manufacturers, Politics, and Postwar Problems

The war had profoundly changed the city of Bridgeport. Working people's actions during the turbulent war era had bolstered their capacity to mobilize economically and politically. Labor's ability to preserve a measure of power in the postwar era now depended on the few labor organizations that survived the managerial and government repression of 1919. Here agitation by radical unionists forced the city to face the reality of widespread unemployment. In offering a generous relief plan to the unemployed and angry metalworkers, city officials hoped to reclaim the loyalties of these newly active working people. What they accomplished was exactly that but at the cost of alienating their business allies, who themselves were struggling to survive in the postwar economic downturn. Thus began the unraveling of traditional politics in Bridgeport.

The economic pressures of the reconversion phase of the postwar period strained the cozy relationship between local Republican politicians and business leaders. While employers tried to stabilize the shop floor, they were also mindful of their bottom lines, which were undergoing severe strain in the 1920s economy. The city was reeling under several pressures. Mayor Wilson's Republican administration faced a rising unemployment rate, an enlarged population in need of city services, and a newly active ethnic working class with disruptive potential. To assuage the working population the city needed more revenue. On the other hand, manufacturers faced the end of a lucrative war market, a newly competitive peacetime economy, and a potentially uncontrollable labor force. Each chose a different path to stability. The GOP's easiest solution was to maintain the city's development trend and the increased spending for social services. Manufacturers' easiest solution was to control costs, both labor costs and taxes. The ensuing power struggle over these conflicting goals reordered the political coalitions of the city and cost Bridgeport manufacturers their public image as civic leaders. Elected officials, by contrast, lost the legal authority to control the finances of their city to a business-dominated Board of Apportionment. But the local GOP emerged as the champion of democracy, home rule, and working-class interests. A new class alliance appeared. By the mid-1920s Bridgeport's politics were a different state of affairs than that of Calvin Coolidge's New Era.

"It has become almost universally recognized in our country," proclaimed John E. Edgerton, president of the National Association of Manufacturers (NAM), in 1929, "that the interests of labor and capital[,] also of management and public[,] are inseparable and practically indistinguishable."[1] Moreover, he implied, mutual interest would lead to society's recognition of business's leadership qualities in the separate spheres of business and politics. During the 1920s business leaders moved boldly to claim this role.

Battles about federal legislation in the early 1920s forced business at both the national and state levels to inject itself into the political arena to remove government from industrial relations, to lobby for an end to "class legislation," and to promote public spending on business needs such as highways while prudently budgeting other government spending. Businessmen's fear of losing their vaunted position in Washington compelled their lobbying efforts against the AFL.[2] As Charles R. Gow, president of the Associated Industries of Massachusetts, explained to the annual meeting of the Manufacturers' Association of Connecticut (MAC) in 1923, the Associated Industries had succeeded in getting its legislative agenda enacted in Massachusetts the previous year not by "the old method of secret lobbying, underhanded solicitation, and private conferences in executive chambers, but . . . in the open by organizing and compiling the facts and the figures and by presenting the opinions of people whose opinions were bound to be respected, and by laying those facts and figures before the authorities, for their consideration, in such a manner that there was but one action possible under the combination of circumstances."[3]

Connecticut manufacturers similarly sought to rally their forces and make their needs known at their state capital. "How many manufacturers of the management and sub-management class take a really constructive interest in government? How many lend their energies to the selection of sound-thinking men for public office?" cried a 1924 editorial in *Connecticut Industry*.[4] Connecticut businessmen had little need for concern at the state level, however. By mid-decade prominent members of the MAC or Chamber of Commerce occupied the governor and lieutenant governor's seats and General Assembly leadership positions. Similarly, Connecticut's congressional representatives, all Republicans, mirrored the business makeup of state government. They included Rep. Schuyler Merritt, chairman of the board of Yale and Towne Company of Norwalk, and Rep. Edward Goss of Waterbury's Scovill Company. U.S. Sen. Hiram Bingham, a former history professor at Yale University, consistently worked on behalf of Connecticut industrial interests. Indeed, in 1929 the Senate censured him for employing the executive secretary of MAC as a staff member of his subcommittee on the Smoot-Hawley Tariff Bill. Finally, the leader of the state's Republican Party, J. Henry Roraback, was head of the state's largest utility company, Connecticut Light & Power, and had enriched his company through favorable utility legislation.[5]

Connecticut's constitution, which had not been fundamentally changed since its ratification in 1818, gave virtually all power to the strongest of the branches of government, the General Assembly. All town and city governments were open to legislative control by special acts of the General Assembly; county government had little presence or importance. The state constitution preserved the rural dominance of the lower house, though state senate seating had been amended in 1901 to represent the urban population somewhat more fairly. So, for example, in the 1920s the small town of Union, population 257, had two state house representatives, the same number as Bridgeport, which had population of 150,000. This malapportioned government—dubbed a "rotten-borough" system by one local analyst—plus GOP control of state patronage, ensured that the state Republican Party's probusiness attitudes would dominate and that urban, immigrant constituencies would rarely be heard. Reform impulses within the GOP, originating in the state's largest cities, were easily stifled.[6] The state was known for its lax labor regulation, low level of social services, and a rigid "pay-as-you-go" fiscal policy.[7]

The General Assembly routinely used "special legislation" to carry out corporation enhancements (such as utility legislation), to the benefit of state businesses. Also through state special legislation the assembly could intervene in the workings of any town or city. While home rule was usually respected in many towns, the cities often came under legislative scrutiny.

Political Crisis, Taxing Times

Though the Manufacturers' Association of Bridgeport (MAB) proved itself capable of smoothly handling industrial relations in the 1920s, developments described in chapter 4, it found itself constrained in the messy political realm of municipal party politics. Even though state government was in solidly probusiness hands by mid-decade, political leadership at the municipal level was being contested.

Bridgeport's population had grown enormously during the war, and so had the city's budget. While the number of properties on the Grand List had doubled, the budget had tripled, going from $3.2 million in 1915 to $9.8 million in 1919. The tax rate increased from 18.0 mills to 29.3 mills in the same period. Moreover, in 1920 the city labored under a bonded debt of nearly $11 million, up from the modest $2.6 million it had incurred for city modernization in the prewar period.[8] (See table 3 for the city's Grand List and tax rates, 1915–40.)

Different local business sectors, however, had not agreed on a strategy to check

Table 3. Bridgeport City Finances

Fiscal Year	Grand List	Tax Rate (mills)	Expenditures (millions)
1915–16	$115,154,912	18.0	$3.200
1920–21	239,201,117	29.3	9.800
1921–22	244,925,794	28.9	9.599
1922–23	240,149,209	33.3[a]	7.959
1923–24	236,637,534	29.2	9.252
1924–25	260,089,867	28.2	8.847
1925–26	257,173,589	27.4	9.026
1926–27	252,701,570	27.4	9.781
1927–28	256,794,919	26.9	11.047
1928–29	264,217,255	29.7	8.759
1929–30	264,289,069	28.8	8.647
1930–31	267,809,479	29.5	10.039
1931–32	269,253,146	29.5	10.590
1932–33	266,073,576	29.4	10.297
1933–34	242,180,641	34.7[b]	11.453
1934–35	234,354,338	29.3	10.647
1935–36	233,201,400	31.8	10.887
1936–37	232,613,300	30.0	10.479
1937–38	236,245,385	28.6	10.818
1938–39	243,971,415	28.4	10.782
1939–40	248,234,875	28.3	10.534

Sources: City of Bridgeport, "Grand List," *Municipal Register* (Bridgeport, Conn.: City of Bridgeport, 1940), p. 240; "Board of Apportionment Report (Combined Tax Districts)," *Municipal Register* (Bridgeport, Conn.: City of Bridgeport, 1916–40); "City Auditor Report," *Municipal Register* (Bridgeport, Conn.: City of Bridgeport, 1916–26); "City Comptroller Report," *Municipal Register* (Bridgeport, Conn.: City of Bridgeport, 1927–40).
 a. The city levied an additional "special tax" of 6 mills to relieve deficits caused by extensive relief spending.
 b. The city levied an additional "special tax" of 4.9 mills to relieve deficits caused by extensive relief spending.

city spending. Three basic approaches emerged from the plethora of individual grievances and political rivalries. The first was the search by the Bridgeport Chamber of Commerce for a way to bring public pressure on Mayor Wilson's GOP administration in 1920, which the organization initiated by hiring an independent urban expert to investigate the city's finances. When the investigation revealed nothing damaging, the BCC leaders were momentarily stymied, though they continued to talk about the idea of commission government and charter revision.

Small merchants and real estate agents aggrieved about tax assessments favored another approach. Dissident small merchants petitioned the state legislature in 1921 to change the legislation that governed the city tax commissioner's office. They brought forward the first accusations of tax manipulation to control votes and party loyalty, along with the charge that city officials had artificially inflated the valuations of properties on the Grand List in order to increase bonding levels (state law limited cities to a borrowing capacity of 5 percent of the value of their Grand List). The dissident merchants wanted the legislature to abolish the appointive office of city tax commissioner—occupied by an ally of John T. King's—and to restore an old system of elected tax assessors. The BCC's executive secretary appeared before the legislature in support of this bill, as did a number of real estate agents, attorneys, and merchants.

The bill, widely interpreted in Bridgeport as a move against the King machine rather than a step forward in fiscal responsibility, received little backing. In fact, the officers of some of Bridgeport's largest firms, Bullard Machine and Bryant Electric, to name two, as well as numerous small companies, real estate interests, and the Bridgeport Taxpayers League, urged the governor to veto the bill. As the corporation secretary of Atlas Shear Company told the governor, "It will be more advantageous to the City and to the Manufacturers to allow the single Tax Commissioner as at present, rather than go back to the old form of Assessors."[9] Manufacturers were clearly opposed to a political move that would take finances back to an open electoral arena rather than toward regulation. However, Gov. Everett Lake, a Republican, signed the bill, stating his preference for an elective rather than an appointive office.[10]

The BCC then bore the brunt of popular dissatisfaction with the recent political moves against King. Its large membership included many small businessmen who were tied to King and unhappy with the BCC's support of anti-King maneuvers. With many members threatening to resign, the chamber finally resolved that "the Chamber as an organization cannot be active politically. Its members with citizenship obligations ought to be active politically."[11] The chamber as an organization thus bowed out of partisan debate.

A third path to municipal control emerged in the aftermath of these legislative moves. Responsible businessmen should replace machine politicians in city hall, it was argued. Here manufacturers and Chamber of Commerce leaders could agree. Consequently, by the fall of 1921 individual managers and businessmen had directly intervened in party affairs to win leadership and promote their candidates. Their initial efforts centered about the local Republican Party. The Republican Voters League (RVL), with George Eames, Walter Lashar, C. E. Bilton, Guy Miller, and A. M. Cooper as leaders—all officers in either the Manufacturers' Association or the chamber and based in the silk-stocking Fifth ward—moved to capture the GOP city convention. This effort failed. Clifford Wilson won renomination for mayor amid a fragmented convention.

The Democratic Party, through its new youthful leader, the attorney John Cornell, then solicited business leaders' participation in its party, and the RVL bolted from the Republicans. The Democrats, with RVL support, then nominated Fred Atwater for mayor. Atwater was a long-time Democrat, president of Columbia Nut and Bolt Company, a director of People's Savings Bank (the city's largest savings bank), and on the boards of both the Manufacturers' Association and the Chamber of Commerce.[12]

The 1921 election resounded with the basic issues that would recur in 1923 and

1925—the city budget and taxes. As John T. King put it, "The only big issue for ten years has been the control of the tax list," and he accused manufacturers of hiding their true property values. The King GOP organization defended Clifford Wilson's ten-year record of questionable dealings. In spite of its opposition to Wilson in the previous election, the *Bridgeport Herald* became Wilson's sole supporter; it condemned the Manufacturers' Association as a "tax-dodging organization." While DeVer H. Warner was still reported to be backing the King organization, he was noticeably quiet.[13]

The Democratic Party and the RVL took the offensive, with Atwater calling for a city hall housecleaning and citing financial irresponsibility, lack of planning, and neglect of schools. Adding to Atwater's "broom-sweeping" rhetoric, the RVL accused the King machine of using the tax office to reward "good" manufacturers and punish "bad" ones. Atwater received strong backing from the *Bridgeport Times*, the Democratic daily. The *Bridgeport Sunday Post* and its two dailies, the *Morning Telegram* and the *Evening Post*, were officially nonpartisan but leaned heavily toward Atwater, calling for an end to city debt and financial recklessness. Reform rhetoric, combined with the GOP's internal disarray and dissatisfaction with Wilson's leadership, swung voters away from the Republicans and into support for the manufacturers' candidate. With a large crossover vote from the Republican column, Atwater won with 53.7 percent of the vote, and Democrats swept all but two of twelve wards.[14]

The new Atwater administration began 1922 determined to adjust the city's budget. The newly installed president of the city's Board of Apportionment and Taxation, William E. Burnham, himself a midsize manufacturer, declared, "There will be no extravagance" and inaugurated a campaign to cut expenditures and collect back taxes through liens and foreclosures.[15] Schools, easily the most burdened city budget item with the greatly increased population, bore the brunt of the Atwater ax. Schools were forced to hold half-day sessions to accommodate the overflow of students in a second afternoon session, and schools were even closed for one week in March 1923 when teacher salary appropriations fell short. The board also forced the closing of Bridgeport's popular Normal School, which was a training school for teachers.[16]

Manufacturers cooperated fully with Mayor Atwater, even though the tax rates could not be reduced immediately. Manufacturers' apprehension about labor radicalism seemed so great that the first move by the newly elected Democratic mayor in November 1921 was to levy a special 6 mill tax to augment the Relief Fund for the coming winter. Indeed, Atwater's expenditure for relief exceeded that of Clifford Wilson's administration.[17] At an executive board meeting of the Manufacturers' Association in early 1922, one after another expressed dismay at Atwater's decision to use the 1920 Grand List to set taxes, rather than compile a new list (the 1920 list having already been proved, in their eyes, to reflect the machinations of the old Wilson-King regime). Nonetheless, members of the MAB told their president, George Eames, manager of the Singer Company, that they would "pay as assessed to support the [Atwater] administration." Soon after, Atwater and his tax assessor personally addressed the assembled manufacturers, explaining the city's valuation methods and asking their cooperation.[18] This cooperation paid off for the industrialists. As a satisfied Manufacturers' Association Tax Committee concluded in 1923, the city had reduced the valuations on its Grand List by about $4 million, practically all in reductions to manufacturers' assessed inventories, and Bridgeport manufacturers had saved about $120,000 in local taxes through this arrangement. Nonetheless, as Guy Miller, head of the Tax Committee, warned his fellow businessmen, "The reductions secured were not necessarily permanent and . . . the chances were that a hostile administration would mean an increase in industrial taxation."[19] The third path to municipal reform, electing business candidates, seemed to have worked well during these two years.

Atwater and his backers then moved to the next step, the permanent alteration of city government. Atwater himself explained his perspective: "While my experience in politics has been very limited, nevertheless I have always believed in the city manager or commission form of government, taking it from a business man's standpoint. Taking a plan whereby the city control can be in the hands of permanent and qualified business managers would seem to be the most advantageous for the interests of the people and the taxpayers at large."[20] The issue of commission government or some newer variant like the city manager system, lingering in Bridgeport since the war period, had been batted about within the Chamber of Commerce since 1920, where the ideas played to mixed reviews. While a number of chamber leaders pressed for it, other major players, like the Hydraulic Company's Albert Lavery, expressed skepticism that any new government structure could be kept out of the hands of the Republican machine.[21]

By the early 1920s national reformers had noted the flaws in commission government, and city manager–council plans or strong mayor plans were in vogue. In Bridgeport, Atwater appointed a charter revision committee; after a year of deliberation it proposed a strong mayor charter. The proposed charter would replace the ward-based common council and weak mayor structure with a four-year mayoral term (as opposed to two), with large appointive powers, and eight at-large council members with staggered two-year terms. The probusiness *Bridgeport Post* urged support for the charter as a way out of partisan corruption. Other observers accused Bridgeport's industrial leaders of feeling secure in their hold on the mayor's office and wishing to consolidate their power. As the *Herald* put it, "The manufacturers and other financial interests . . . would not be annoyed 'protecting their interests' every two years, for once a 'strong' mayor is placed in power he would stick until the crack of doom." The charter revision proposal was placed on the November ballot.[22]

However, manufacturers soon found that traditional political parties were not so easily controlled. The Democratic central committee was angered that Atwater, a Democrat, had ignored its directions on patronage distribution; after the 1921 election Atwater had declared that because he had been elected with the help of Republicans, he would distribute patronage to both parties. Moreover, the influence of businessmen was disputed within the party itself. Cornell, the local Democratic chairman who had initially welcomed the RVL, now protested manufacturers' intrusion into party politics, declaring, "It is now a question of the Democratic Party against the Doughboys." The RVL-manufacturers' bloc, the moneyed men with the "dough," was the problem. However, Cornell's "organization" Democrats were not able to control their convention in October 1923 and Atwater won renomination.[23]

The Republican Party, having reorganized after the defection of the RVL, nominated a solid pro-King ticket with the long-time GOP activist F. William Behrens at its head. Behrens, a German-born meat merchant, had built a solid reputation in his ten years as charity commissioner and was credited with upgrading the almshouse and Hillside Home, the city's old-age facility. Moreover, because Behrens was an immigrant and a small merchant, his nomination signaled the emergence of a new direction in the Republican Party—away from candidates who were members of the Yankee elite.[24]

The partisan lines were again drawn, with the GOP claiming that business interests dominated the Democrats and Atwater repeating the charges of GOP corruption. The political squabbling and internal divisiveness resulted in a low voter turnout for both parties, and Behrens won with a narrow margin of 84 votes out of 26,280 cast. Voters, however, made their preferences clear on a number of issues. They soundly defeated the proposed strong mayor charter and voted decisively to reopen the city's Normal School.[25]

Though this election victory was a less-than-spectacular affirmation of support for King's organization, it was a clear repudiation of Democrat Atwater and the budget economies of the Manufacturers' Association. A triumphant King warned the business community on election night, "I have no quarrel with industry. I am a conservative in politics but I think the time has arrived that the business people of this city look to the propriety, sincerity and ability of busybodies who have created themselves the leaders of every civic movement. . . . I want to say to the Chamber of Commerce and the Manufacturers' Association that the people of this town are not arrayed against them in their proper capacities." Eames defended the local political activities of the MAB, protesting that manufacturers were "deeply interested in the welfare of Bridgeport." The definition of business's "proper capacities" now became the test for votes.[26]

Behrens's inaugural message in 1923 focused solely on the tax question, and he announced his intention to "readjust taxes."[27] He started by asking manufacturers for data from their federal tax returns. The Manufacturers' Association, in an uproar, quickly assembled a delegation to meet with the mayor to demand an explanation. The mayor planned to reduce the tax rate but intended to simultaneously raise assessments by about 20 percent for manufacturers and merchants and 10 percent for home owners, in effect increasing the business proportion of the local tax burden. The dismayed manufacturers decided to delay their public protest, but they reminded Behrens of the "depressed conditions of industry" and called upon the city "to live within its present income."[28] As a result of reassessment, however, 2,415 appeals were filed with the Bridgeport Board of Tax Relief. Similarly, the following year $10 million in tax appeals were filed against valuations on the 1924 Grand List, $4.7 million of which were corporate claims.[29] The actions of the electorate and politicians had thwarted the businessman's route to local power through business candidates and charter reform.

Forsaking City Hall

Manufacturers then abandoned the local electoral arena entirely. Bridgeport's activist manufacturers had already spearheaded a move by the Manufacturers' Association of Connecticut to reorganize and regularize the entire state tax system. Both the state Chamber of Commerce and MAC had undertaken an analysis of state revenue and spending patterns. The 1921 General Assembly embraced their suggestions for limiting state indebtedness, raising money from user fees, and using a small corporate income tax to reduce dependence on the property tax. The state's property tax, the main source of state and local revenue, was levied on three broad classes of property: real estate, buildings, and fixed machinery; tangible personal property, such as domestic animals, autos, furniture, merchandise, and inventory on hand; and intangible property such as stocks and bonds. Towns and municipalities assessed property and collected the tax, relying on it for most of their revenues and paying a small percentage into state coffers. But state and local government reliance on the general property tax had hit manufacturers, especially the metal trades, hard during the postwar slump, since property and large inventories of unsold goods were taxed regardless of loss of income.[30] Connecticut manufacturers felt that they were bearing an undue portion of the state's tax bill (54 to 75 percent of tax revenue, according to various estimates). "The manufacturer is taxed but is deprived of representation. His needs are for the most part disregarded," lamented an editorial in *Connecticut Industry.*[31]

Nationally, business groups were alarmed about the steep rise in taxes nationally, the state and local portions of which had doubled from 1913 to 1922. Business groups pushed for a shift in taxes to all classes of citizens. As James A. Emery of the National Association of Manufacturers explained, "Taxation is a badge of citizenship," and he proposed such devices as a general sales tax, which would make taxes real to the average citizen. Similarly, Charles Fay, a business spokesman, argued that on the municipal level the poor should be made to pay taxes so that they would be motivated to repudiate fast-spending urban machine politicians.[32] Industrialists, then, sought a dual goal of reducing taxes in gener-

al and of shifting the burden from the manufacturing sector to other taxpay-
ing sectors. Their aims were thus in opposition to the interests of home owners
and to the mercantile business sector, whose share of the tax burden would be
raised, and to the working-class community in general, whose services would
be curtailed if revenue decreased.

Not surprisingly, Bridgeport manufacturers placed themselves at the forefront
of the state manufacturers' efforts to redress this perceived grievance, even
though Connecticut had kept its budget and indebtedness well in hand.[33] Guy
P. Miller of Bridgeport headed the investigation by the MAC's Taxation Committee of local taxing methods. Miller pointed an accusing finger at manipula-
tive local politicians who were milking manufacturers for the benefit of other
groups of taxpayers. "There is a tendency on the part of assessing officials to
increase the burden of manufacturers disproportionately . . . notwithstanding
the fact that the prosperity of the three groups [manufacturers, merchants and
home owners] in many circumstances depends upon the success of the manufacturer who is obliged to compete in the markets of the world whereas the
competition of the other group is largely local."[34]

In so openly claiming a privileged position for manufacturers, MAC hoped
to compel agreement from the other business sectors as well as the general public. Miller went on to delineate the methods of calculating assessments. "Prior
to the war the local taxpayer made the best bargain possible with the assessor,"
and local manufacturing groups did this by accepting a certain percentage of
the total tax burden and distributing it among their groups' members. In this
way manufacturers avoided furnishing actual valuations to the assessors, but this
left them open to manipulation by local officials, who could easily raise the
group assessment. Miller explained, "It has been found easier to raise assessments than rates and a popular political trick is to reduce the rate a mill or so
and increase assessments more than enough to make up the difference."[35] Apparently, this was the crux of the Bridgeport difficulties.

At this same time William Blodgett, the Republican appointed to serve as state
tax commissioner, announced that his office would undertake an investigation
of the state's property tax system, citing uneven assessments across the state, the
failure of local tax officials to record real estate transactions in order to obtain
"fair market value" of property, and the continued difficulty of assessing personal property. His goal was a uniform, modern system of taxation free from
"the present corrupting and demoralizing influences" that the "tax structure
now encouraged." Through the state tax commission's Board of Equalization,
Blodgett targeted Bridgeport for a thorough investigation.[36]

At this point the state's desire to regularize the tax system in municipalities
merged with the desires of Bridgeport manufacturers to free themselves from
the grasp of local politicians. Commissioner Blodgett's hearings into the Bridgeport tax system revealed, he said, a "capricious and arbitrary" system that had
raised industrial assessments in the Wilson administration, decreased them

during Atwater's reign, and increased them again under Behrens. More important, the Behrens administration had shown favoritism in compromising on assessments for certain unnamed manufacturers. For these reasons the tax commissioner recommended special legislation to allow the state to oversee tax matters in the city.[37]

The result was a bill, dubbed the "Ripper Bill" by the Bridgeport press, to strip taxing powers from elected officials in Bridgeport and place them with a new board of apportionment and taxation to be appointed by the governor. The current system had a board of three elected assessors, an elected tax collector, and a bipartisan board of apportionment and a board of relief appointed by the mayor; the Ripper Bill would have a governor-appointed board of apportionment, which, with greatly enhanced budgetary powers, would then appoint the assessor, collector, and board of relief.

This piece of legislation, introduced during the 1925 spring session of the General Assembly, caused the polarization of politics and altered the configuration of power in Bridgeport. While the measure was ostensibly the product of the state tax commissioner's office, its local backers included members of the now-disbanded RVL and the major manufacturers who had instituted tax appeal lawsuits against the Behrens administration. These included locally based companies, such as Bridgeport Brass, American Chain, Bridgeport Hydraulic, and Bridgeport Gas Light Company. The Warner interests had been publicly involved from the start of the tax investigations in 1923, when Guy Miller, late of Bridgeport Brass and now an officer of the Warner-controlled Hydraulic Company, took on the task of investigating taxes for MAC. State representative Al Lavery of neighboring Fairfield, now vice president and treasurer of the Hydraulic Company, sponsored the Ripper Bill in the General Assembly. Finally, DeVer C. Warner, son of DeVer H., chairman of Mayor Behrens's Tax Revision Committee, resigned from that committee, stating that Behrens had no intention of changing the makeup of the current system.[38]

It was now generally understood in Bridgeport that the Warner-King alliance had crumbled. The Warner Corset Company, through the postwar slump, continued labor troubles, and the extreme change in fashions, had posted a deficit in 1921 (and would again in 1926). The Bridgeport Hydraulic Company had also been engaged in litigation with the city over taxes and the rate the city paid to the water company for water and hydrant service. Bridgeport Hydraulic had won its case in Superior Court, where the city was ordered to refund about $38,000 in tax overpayments.[39] At the same time the Connecticut Supreme Court had ruled that past certificates of error granted for tax abatements, many from the Atwater years, had been illegally issued and that back taxes had to be paid on those accounts. This decision hit friends and foes of the Behrens administration alike. The city tax collector and the state tax commissioner had pressed this case, which Tax Commissioner Blodgett saw as vindication for his bill to regulate tax matters in the city.[40]

Supporters of Blodgett's Ripper Bill confronted those rallying around Mayor Behrens's bill, which was designed to revamp the tax structure of the city while keeping financial authority in the hands of elected officials. Behrens rushed to the state capital to defend his administration's efforts to rectify the excesses of the past and promised to take the politics out of taxation. Cheered by the more than two hundred Bridgeport citizens who packed the Hartford hearing room in favor of Behrens, city officials remonstrated that the abatements they had granted included cases of impoverished widows or families with ill breadwinners who would lose their homes if forced to pay.[41]

Officers of the Bridgeport Chamber of Commerce appeared at the hearing to support Mayor Behrens, revealing the falling-out between business groups in Bridgeport. The chamber had originally welcomed the investigation of the city's taxes, beginning a series of public forums soon after Blodgett announced his investigation but also cooperating with the mayor's tax committee. But as a result of membership pressure, the BCC's policy became one of "cooperat[ing] in every way possible with the City administration."[42] The BCC's board of directors was violently split over the Ripper Bill, with former RVL leaders like A. M. Cooper, a large merchant, and other opponents, such as former mayor Atwater, arguing against helping the Behrens administration. But a majority of BCC board members—including the heads of savings banks and mercantile establishments who were themselves hostile to manufacturers and dismayed at Blodgett's attack on home rule—decided to aid Behrens. The BCC board assembled en masse in the mayor's office to present him with technical amendments to his bill in return for their support. The next day, George Crawford, the BCC president; William Hincks, a Democrat; and A. M. Cooper, former leader of the RVL, testified before the General Assembly on behalf of Behrens's bill and in opposition to the Ripper Bill.[43]

Strongly in favor of Blodgett's bill were the leaders of the Manufacturers' Association of Bridgeport. The MAB had decided not to take an official position but instructed its manager, Alpheus Winter, to poll individual members and present those findings at the public hearing. Winter testified that he had surveyed the heads of forty-eight large firms, all of whom wished to remain anonymous, representing assessed valuations of more than $51 million on the Grand List. Thirty-four of these firms, representing 69 percent of that list, favored the Ripper Bill, according to Winter. Moreover, as George Eames had stated early on, manufacturers were most incensed about the assessments of "goods in process" (i.e., inventories)—set at about $41 million in Bridgeport, compared to $16 million in Hartford, $21 million in New Haven, and $28 million in Waterbury.[44]

Blodgett himself took the high ground, saying that both parties were to blame for the state of affairs in Bridgeport: "Those who have controlled administrations have seemed more than willing to seize the State's delegated power to tax and use it as an instrument for political advantage to outdo the opposing faction for control of the city." The Ripper Bill passed the General Assembly overwhelmingly. The ease with which the bill passed was ascribed to the much-discussed King rivalry with the state GOP boss, Roraback, but the clear victors were the manufacturers of Bridgeport.[45]

Gov. John H. Trumbull's appointees to the Bridgeport Board of Apportionment and Taxation confirmed that sober-minded, anti-King businessmen would now be in charge of the city's finances. Indeed, relieved from seeking electoral approval, they would now carry out the program begun during the Atwater administration. The new chairman was William E. Burnham, a wealthy retired industrialist who owned a number of metalworking shops and was director of a number of Bridgeport trust banks. A member of the RVL, he had been on the old board of apportionment and taxation since the Atwater administration and was responsible for inviting the state investigation. The six others were either members of the RVL or Democrats from midsize businesses, though partisanship seemed to matter little. With two exceptions, all were members of the city's elite, listed in the *Blue Book* and the membership rolls of the prestigious downtown Algonquin Club.[46] Mayor Behrens protested to Trumbull that some of the governor's appointees were officers of companies that owed back taxes. Trumbull rejected Behrens's appeals to reconsider his appointments, noting that his appointees were "men of the highest standing and integrity."[47]

Sharply escalated rhetoric set the tone for the 1925 city election as the implications of the Ripper Bill became clear to the general public. Mayor Behrens had championed the cause of the average taxpayer the year before. "The City of Bridgeport is made up largely of homeowners who work for a daily wage," he declared. "Whether they are rent-payers or tax-payers their interests must be safeguarded."[48] King now added to that appeal, calling on "rank and file taxpayers whether you own a cottage, a two-family house or a four-family house, whether you have an investment of real estate in the business section or whether you be merchants," to support the Behrens administration in the election. King noted that only manufacturers were able to conceal assets under the new tax system. The Behrens reelection campaign emphasized home rule and the meddling of industrialists in city affairs as major issues. "Shall a group of intriguing manufacturers be permitted to control the assessors board?" asked Behrens.[49] The Republican Party, calling itself the "Party of Progress," emphasized the physical improvements to the city, "the best paved streets in the state; model institutions for the care of the sick and needy; adequate sewage and sewage disposal systems; modern grade and high schools; exceptional parks and recreational facilities including two free golf courses; public safety of unequalled efficiency; modernized health clinics."[50] Behrens was not exaggerating. Compared to other Connecticut cities, Bridgeport at this time was outstanding in the range of its public facilities.

The GOP, moreover, moved to champion working-class issues. Mayor Wilson had begun the overture to labor unions in the winter of 1920–21, when he agreed to the radical metalworkers' union demand for unemployment relief. By

1925, when the Republican Party was back in power, it was actively involved in settling labor disputes, an unprecedented occurrence in the history of the city's labor relations. After a garment strike turned violent, the city prosecutor declined to press charges against the strikers who had been arrested, and a GOP police superintendent overruled a police captain's order that limited picketing. More surprisingly, former mayor Wilson and other prominent Republicans mediated a textile strike later that fall.[51]

The Bridgeport Socialist Party (SP) was a persistent participant in local politics through the 1920s. With Jasper McLevy, a slate roofer, trade unionist, and later a small contractor, as its mayoral candidate, the SP received 6.3 percent of the vote in 1921 and 6.2 percent in 1923. The SP was given coverage only in the *Herald,* a paper that prided itself on its progressivism and independence. Because the weekly *Sunday Herald's* circulation compared favorably with that of the largest daily in town (the *Post*), the SP received wide attention, if not votes.[52] The SP's election appeals combined calls for municipal reform that evoked the Progressive Era with Socialist positions on public ownership. Calling attention to the "double machine" politics of the King organization and the need for "unbossed" government, the SP also condemned the Ripper Bill as the work of "a group whose only interest is to exploit the wage-earner to the last ounce." McLevy reminded voters of Atwater's opposition to the eight-hour day during the strike wave of 1915 when Atwater, a manufacturer, had stated that shorter hours would just mean more dissipation in local saloons. Finally, the SP embarked on a campaign of rallies on street corners and at factory gates, forcing both the Republicans and Democrats out of their club rooms to do the same. Prominent leaders of the major parties attended SP rallies. McLevy noted that the rallies taught the politicos "what the issues of a campaign are and [they] get a line on what argument to use. While we do not get the benefit, we have the satisfaction of educating them."[53] The SP undoubtedly moved the GOP further along its path of laborist appeals by 1925; in this context the SP chose not to outdo the GOP in worker rhetoric but to expose the political machine at work. Though the SP seems to have lost the majority of its votes to the GOP in 1925, its campaign presence reinforced the GOP's antimanufacturer appeal.

By contrast, pitched battles within the Democratic Party in 1925 once again produced the businessmen's candidate, this time an attorney, Thomas Cullinan, which confirmed the silk-stocking label attached to the Democratic Party. Cullinan defended the investigation of the tax office, repeated the charges of past corruption and manipulation, and decried the GOP's attempt to stir popular hostility toward industrial interests. "Shall class be arrayed against class?" he asked. Answered King, "The issue in this campaign is that . . . the large taxpayer be forced to pay their just proportion of taxes. If this is arraying class against class then we accept the guilt of the charges."[54]

Finally, an "Independent Republican Committee" ad reminded Bridgeporters that the election choice was between John T. King and jobs: "Thriving industries in other cities won't do YOU any good. . . . LET'S ALL DO OUR DUTY AS CITIZENS AND PROTECT THEM FOR IF THE WHISTLES DON'T BLOW WE DON'T WORK."[55] To make sure that citizens did their duty the Manufacturers' Association helped its members plan a get-out-the-vote campaign; most allowed workers to vote on company time.[56]

The tactic seems to have backfired. With the largest number of Bridgeport citizens voting in any recent city election, Behrens was returned to office, with a vote of 16,032 to Cullinan's 14,386. Only two of the twelve contested common council seats went to Democrats, one of whom was William Crawford, the son of the BCC president, in the silk-stocking Fifth District. It appeared that even King's recent involvement in the Harding administration's national scandals, prominent in the news during the campaign season, did not hurt the local GOP slate.[57] A triumphant John T. King capped the election celebrations by publicly calling on the GOP treasurer to return the $250 campaign check from DeVer H. Warner. "I despise double-dealing," he explained.[58] The split between manufacturers and the GOP was complete.

The major manufacturers of Bridgeport had openly organized a political faction within the Bridgeport Republican Party, the RVL, to capture that party for their own ends. When that failed, they successfully overran the Democratic Party to put their man in city hall. When their candidate and their program of financial cuts was repudiated at the polls in 1923, manufacturers abandoned the electoral arena and achieved their goal of controlling the finances and taxes of Bridgeport through state legislative action. In so doing, manufacturers lost any claim to civic leadership. Bridgeport manufacturers' version of industrial democracy in the workplace, an employer-controlled and -directed program, paralleled their idea of political democracy in Bridgeport, an employer-controlled and -directed administrative body mindful of business interests.

However, in the political sphere their GOP adversaries did not retire to a brooding defeat but rallied new supporters around them to keep a firm grasp on what political powers were left to them. The Bridgeport Republican Party, locked in a financial struggle with its erstwhile industrialist supporters, relied increasingly on social services to its ethnic working-class constituents to rally support for its candidates. Gradually, the GOP turned from reliance on the patronage allure of these expenditures to emphasize its support for trade unions, as the unemployment crisis of the winter of 1920–21 gave Mayor Wilson a chance to redeem himself in the eyes of the radical IAM, which he had attempted to suppress during the war years. Sam Lavit, whom Wilson had tried to run out of town in 1919, was counted as a GOP supporter in 1921. While this belated overture to labor did not forestall Wilson's defeat in 1921, it had long-range effects. When Democrat Atwater became mayor, his Board of Apportionment even increased relief expenditures while cutting other areas of the budget. When the GOP returned to power in 1923, no longer concerned with courting industrialists, it continued its friendship with labor unions and by 1925 had mediated labor disputes and intervened with the police department to allow unfettered union picketing.

Bridgeport resumed a lively street agitation by 1921, with all parties making use of rallies on street corners and at factory gates and with radicals of all stripes holding forth on soapboxes at the downtown plaza—dubbed the "Hyde Park of Bridgeport" by one local paper. Bridgeport police had stopped requiring permits for public rallies or meetings. By contrast, in other strike-prone cities like Waterbury, police prohibited gatherings well into the mid-1920s. And unlike a much-publicized incident in nearby New Haven, union organizers in Bridgeport were never run out of town by the police in the 1920s.[59]

To be sure, the Bridgeport Republican Party had not transformed itself into a working-class party. GOP rhetoric merged the anti-industrialist sentiments of the city's working class with a general anti–big business theme that had been a staple of populist appeals to middle-class constituents. The GOP's willingness to acknowledge the class organizations of the working-class community did not make Bridgeport a union paradise, nor did it revive the organizing fever of the war years. But anti-industrialist feeling remained high in Bridgeport long after the World War I strikes precisely because of its salience in the political sphere. Public opinion in Bridgeport in the 1920s thus did not fit the national profile of that decade as an antiunion and probusiness era.

Local Parties

The 1921–25 municipal electoral arena provided an opportunity for union issues to be heard. But what did it accomplish for political inclusion of diverse peoples, from different racial, ethnic, gender, and class backgrounds, in the 1920s? Nationally, this decade has been interpreted politically as the decay of the "System of 1896," a national politics characterized by Republican hegemony in the Northeast, steadily declining voter participation, and an expanding administrative state. The ethnic and cultural antagonisms previously kept in check by this party system were revived in the 1920s, even as class conflicts seemed to subside. At the same time the Progressive Era arguments about private interest versus public good remained. In their rush to modernize, consolidate, and streamline the political system to save it from the greedy grasp of "The Interests," Progressive elite reformers contributed to the bureaucratization and centralization of national politics. The "search for order" in the early years of the twentieth century had replaced the messiness of democratic politics with the administrative state. Bridgeport elites copied what the previous decade's "progressive reforms" had enacted nationwide in the name of efficiency but now in service to business interests. Bridgeport city politics, then, comfortably fits this national model.

Moreover, changes in the rules governing access to the ballot had a deliberate antidemocratic influence on the composition of the "political universe."

Personal registration laws, extended residency requirements, and literacy tests, along with poll taxes in the South, were intended to make voting more difficult for immigrants, African Americans, and working-class citizens generally. The result by 1920 was a new pattern of age and class stratification in voter turnout, with upper-class and older voters the more active participants. Turnout also had a gender bias after the granting of women's suffrage in 1920, though women's lesser participation was not enough to explain away the lowered overall turnout. By the 1920s an entire generation, as well as waves of new immigrants, had grown up under a system of lessening involvement in electoral politics.[60]

The municipal politics of Bridgeport, while not a simple reflection of national politics, contained most of the same elements and illustrated many of the underlying tensions of politics in the 1920s. Here, though, it led to the unraveling of local political arrangements, not voter apathy. One important, though not quite decisive, fact was that Bridgeport remained a competitive newspaper town in the interwar period, allowing for a diversity of political voices. The four locally owned newspapers in the city, none of which was swallowed up by national newspaper chains during this period, lent their own influence to the political atmosphere. The co-owned *Morning Telegram* and *Evening Post* were Yankee in cultural stance, probusiness and antiunion, but did not have a monopoly in Bridgeport. The *Times* and *Star*, which merged in mid-decade, were Democratic leaning (though officially nonpartisan) and reported on ethnic and labor issues. The eclectic *Bridgeport Sunday Herald*, whose masthead proclaimed "No Fear—No Favor—The People's Paper," consistently brought controversial political issues to the fore, heightened the consideration of ethnic issues, and opened its pages to coverage of independent and Socialist Party politics. In addition, both the *Times-Star* and the *Herald* began printing letters to the editor in the late 1920s.[61]

The twin principles of home rule and democracy resonated strongly where urban and immigrant constituents were underrepresented in the political system. Such was the case in Bridgeport. Not only was Connecticut's state legislature malapportioned, giving rural legislators undeserved power, but the U.S. Congress refused to reapportion congressional districts after the 1920 census, leaving the burgeoning urban areas underrepresented at the national level for the entire decade. Added to this environment was the pressure from nativists that led to immigration restriction, the pressure from reformers that produced strict voter registration requirements, and the demands from industrialists that resulted in the suppression of labor and radical organizations. All these developments gave the appearance in the 1920s that the political system was insensitive to the needs of the lower classes and unresponsive to pluralist ideals. Under such circumstances a local party willing to listen to working-class needs, to support (or at least not to oppose) labor action, and to court new ethnics could count on more votes than the "better element" could muster. Of course, such a cross-class and multiethnic coalition based on expediency rather than principle could be vulnerable in changing times.[62] What happened to this alliance is instructive.

A local Republican Party with a prolabor policy would seem to be at odds with the national party, given its conservative, business-oriented stance. And more than once John T. King wished that local politics could be divorced from national party concerns.[63] He also faced opposition from the state party. Like other urban GOP insurgents against the corporate free-enterprise leadership of the upstate organization of J. Henry Roraback, King supported proposals for extended social welfare legislation and the stricter regulation of utility companies. However, King's stance seemed motivated solely by political rivalry. When compared to the activities of Frank Healey of Windsor Locks, Connecticut's attorney general, and Isaac Ullman of New Haven, both outspoken activists of the "progressive" wing of the GOP until the mid-1920s, King was not actively engaged. Despite his progressive leanings, King fell into lockstep in national GOP campaigns. King stumped for Coolidge in Bridgeport during the 1924 campaign; his message was the standard Republican litany of the protectionist tariff and the full dinner pail.[64]

The GOP had dominated Connecticut since the 1890s and continued to do so into the 1920s through Roraback's assiduous attention to the needs of both industrialists and rural Yankee farmers. The Democratic Party, by contrast, had controlled the executive branch of state government for only six years between 1892 and 1930 and had never once controlled the state's powerful lower house. Democrats, whose state leadership was almost entirely Irish, had carried over few of the Yankee supporters from the era before William Jennings Bryan and in the 1920s governed only a few small urban areas of the state. The state Republican Party, while still decidedly Yankee in its ethnocultural leanings, courted Irish constituents and after 1920 began to pay closer attention to new ethnics as well. In this inclusiveness it mirrored the successful coalitions, if not the policy preferences, of the GOP urban machines of King and Ullman.[65]

International events after the war helped the Connecticut GOP immensely. In the first instance, Irish opposition to Woodrow Wilson's alliance with Britain, as well as controversy about the League of Nations, alienated many Irish in Connecticut from the Democratic Party and briefly enlarged the Republican Party. "The best among the Knights of Columbus are turning from the Democratic Party and they do not want to turn directly to the Republican Party but will turn toward a personality," a GOP stalwart reported to Roraback in 1919. "King is clever enough to see this and is working it for all it is worth."[66] King, of Irish Catholic stock himself, already had good credentials with Irish groups and the Irish-dominated Roman Catholic diocese. So did Mayor Clifford Wilson, King's protégé, who, though himself from an old Yankee family, was known for his pro-Irish statements.

Other state GOP leaders aided this circumstance. The vociferous campaign in Congress by U.S. Sen. Frank Brandegee, R-Conn., against the League of Nations drew the Irish vote to the Republican Party, even as Brandegee was losing votes from others because of his opposition to women's suffrage. As Roraback put it in the 1920 campaign, "One loyal Irishman is worth a carload of pacifists, ministers and college professors." Indeed, in the GOP sweep of Connecticut in 1920 reform Republicans and Independents who waged a determined battle against Brandegee conceded Irish, German, and Italian voters, like their counterparts nationwide, to the regular GOP ticket.[67]

The Irish predominance in both parties in Connecticut was still evident in the late 1930s, even after the realignment of new ethnics in the political system was already under way. "The Irish, taken as a group, take a more active part in government problems," noted a reporter from the Federal Writers' Project in 1939, speaking of Bridgeport. "Unlike many of the other nationalities, the Irish play an important role in politics. Although the Irish still have a large percentage of municipal workers, they take part in politics not only because they want jobs, but because they look upon it as giving them prestige in the community. On many occasions they taunt the other nationalities for not taking as active a part as they do."[68] Indeed, one well-wisher labeled a 1925 gathering at the German-born Behrens's market as the "Irish Parliament." The Irish members of

"The Irish Parliament," dinner at Behrens's Meat Market, ca. 1925. (Photograph by Corbit's Studio, Historical Collections, Bridgeport Public Library.)

the Bridgeport GOP styled themselves the "decent" element in their community, and derided the Irish Democrats as the "saloon element."[69] Neither party, of course, was immune to this charge. In 1924 King turned most of his local power over to Arthur Conner, a Twelfth District saloon-keeper-turned-bank-official and U.S. postmaster.[70]

King's appeal "to organize and fight" the American Protective Association and "the KLU [sic] KLUX KLAN" attracted his Irish supporters, though his Republican organization was repeatedly undermined by upstate Republicans' refusal to condemn the Klan; luckily, the same dilemma in the national Democratic Party canceled this issue out.[71] The local Democrats were also vocal in their opposition to the Klan. The Klan carried out a flurry of activity in Bridgeport in 1923, holding meetings at Summerfield Methodist Episcopal Church and at the British St. George's Hall on the East Side, which also accommodated most ethnic groups of the area. The mostly Irish Bridgeport Police Department kept a close eye on Klan activities, given its anti-Catholic bias. Of all nativist voices, the Klan briefly had the largest following in Connecticut. But the Klan enjoyed little political clout in Bridgeport, unlike in Danbury and more rural towns where it was stronger. In one particular exchange that received widespread notice, John Cornell, the Irish Catholic leader of the local Democratic Party, was surprised to find that his offhand remarks in St. George's Hall to a meeting of the Aheppa Society, a Greek fraternal organization, had offended six Klan members in the back of the hall. The six walked out amid "booing and jeering" from the Aheppa members, who denied having invited them.[72]

While the GOP remained the more successful party in Bridgeport during the decade, the Democrats held on to a core of loyal Irish community leaders. Democratic leaders early put themselves at the forefront of the Irish nationalist cause, organizing the Bridgeport branch of the American Committee for Relief in Ireland in 1921. Francis J. Brennan and Thomas M. Cullinan, prominent Democrats, organized the kickoff event, at which Cornell, the rising city leader, was elected permanent chair. In attendance were dignitaries from the Diocese of Hartford, as well as the Democratic Party leader David E. Fitzgerald of New Haven. The committee raised money for Irish relief through the city's Catholic parishes.[73]

At the same time Yankee sentiment was still strong. The mayoral position in Bridgeport remained a Yankee preserve for some time. Both parties put up men of illustrious family standing in the city, and they were either attorneys or owners of midsize businesses. Behrens, the Republican mayoral candidate in 1923, became the first non-Yankee mayor since the brief reign of the Irish "stoker mayor" in 1903.[74] As late as 1929, when the Democrats were in striking distance of city hall, they chose as their mayoral candidate Edward Buckingham, a Yankee professional whose forebears had arrived in Connecticut in the 1600s.

Throughout the 1920s the Bridgeport parties, like most municipal parties everywhere, relied on leaders at the ward or district level to carry on the public life of the party and to dispatch voters to the polls. Party power depended on multiple linkages to voters and to money and influence at various levels of the city and state. Who were these local party leaders? The twenty-four elected representatives who comprised the Bridgeport Common Council—two from each of twelve voting districts—were key to this mobilization of partisan support. The common council approved mayoral nominations to city boards, enacted ordinances, granted special waivers and variances of those ordinances to constituents, and oversaw the purchases, contracts, and physical improvements of the city. Running the city meant forging a coalition of disparate and often contending interests, smoothed over by down-to-earth arrangements between party leaders and private entrepreneurs who brought supplies and services to the city. Much of the successful tax agitation of the Manufacturers' Association was aimed at extracting the financial decision-making power from these men. But the members of the common council, regardless of their diminished role in financial planning as a result of the Ripper Bill, remained the emissaries of their neighborhoods. They were the "ex-plebes," as Robert Dahl called their counterparts in his study of New Haven politics, ethnics who had moved to a higher socioeconomic status but were nowhere near the standing of elite business and financial leaders. Common council positions were not terribly prestigious, because they were part time and poorly paid. Nonetheless, they were the building blocks of Democratic and Republican partisanship as well as a foot in the political door for these individuals and their followers.[75]

Party regulars in Bridgeport did not constitute a diverse circle. In the years 1920–28 sixty-seven candidates—all men—ran for council seats on the GOP ticket. More than 80 percent had British or Scottish surnames (we'll call them Yankees) or Irish surnames. Almost half were businessmen, retailers, professionals, or managers; the largest subgroup was independent businessmen of modest means. Another 40 percent were employees of various skill levels, while 12 percent either listed no occupation or cannot be identified. The handful of eastern and southern Europeans on this list were contractors, businessmen, or retailers.

On the Democratic side the situation was much the same. Eighty-two council candidates (all men, of course) were presented to the voters of the city from 1920 to 1928. Again, ethnic representation was limited; more than three-quarters had Yankee or Irish surnames. The Democrats were equally middle class—44 percent came from business or professional ranks—while 30 percent were employees (either blue collar or white collar). The eastern and southern Europeans on this list were, however, from the employee ranks, not from the ranks of businessmen, as were those in the Republican Party.[76]

Commonalities abounded. Membership in the Knights of Columbus, Elks, Foresters, or Odd Fellows was a common tie for many candidates of both parties. Indeed, few factors separated the Democrats from the Republicans at the local level. While the business and professional ranks dominated, a few candidates, mostly Democrats, identified themselves as union members. For example, one was a legislative representative for the Brotherhood of Railroad Trainmen, one a former officer of the bricklayers'-union-turned-independent-contractor. The new leader of the Central Labor Union, Milton McDonald, ran on both the Democrat and the Socialist lines in 1924, an unusual year. The most well-known labor Democrat, John J. O'Neil, Sr., had been a founder of the Bridgeport CLU. A staunch Fenian, he was an AFL state organizer and founder and owner of the labor newspaper, the *Bridgeport Advocate;* he was succeeded in the 1920s by his son John J. O'Neil, Jr. The lists of GOP council candidates also included union members, though they often weren't identified as such.[77]

An equal number of council candidates were foremen at the larger industrial works of the city, leading to speculation about pressure on workers to belong to the "correct" party. It was perhaps not a coincidence that one Republican city council member was a foreman at H. O. Canfield Company, a well-known industrial employer of Italians, the most overtly Republican of the city's ethnic groups. Only one member of the elite, William Crawford, sat on the council during this period, as a Democrat representing the Fifth District. His father, George Crawford, had been president of the Chamber of Commerce. The others, while clearly not members of an elite, represented a middling economic stratum and only a segment of the ethnic mixture of the city. The common council represented a group that might oppose manufacturer intrusion on the city's prerogatives and could be induced to support union endeavors at times. Its class inclinations were by no means set, however, and could be swayed by the atmosphere of the times.

A look at the next higher level of local elective offices—General Assembly seats and the state central committee posts—shows that the holders of these positions were members of a higher social group. The personal and professional rewards were higher here. The state central committee, consisting of representatives from each state senatorial district, directed party affairs and elected the committee members to represent the state at the national party. In the Republican Party, which controlled both the state and the city for most of this period, Bridgeport delegates to the state central committee in 1920–28 held lucrative connections. For example, in the early 1920s John T. King did not hold a position in the local Republican Party but served on the GOP state central committee from the twenty-first state senatorial district. The thirteen men and women on the central committee were from predictably Yankee or Irish backgrounds and from professional or business occupations. The GOP members of the General Assembly were also an economic cut above the common council members, mostly lawyers and businessmen. From 1920 to 1928 the Democrats were out of power at the state level, but serving on the Democratic State Central Committee, with its links to national party affairs, was potentially rewarding. All thirteen Democratic committee members from Bridgeport were Yankee or Irish and, like their GOP counterparts, were professionals or businessmen. But the Democratic Party candidates for General Assembly seats had a slightly more plebeian cast and included some craftsmen.[78]

By 1924 both parties had moved to create women's slots on the state central committees, including a national committeewoman. But the two parties differed locally in their attention to the new female voters in their midst. The question of women's suffrage had animated Connecticut politics and parties during the war period. A number of mainstream Republican women were prominent in the Connecticut Women's Suffrage Association, while more radical women activists worked through the National Women's Party, with its prolabor stance and more militant tactics. In Bridgeport, GOP women leaders represented the "respectable" suffrage voice and, after the suffrage amendment was ratified nationally, moved quickly to enroll and mobilize women in Bridgeport politics. By 1921 Bridgeport's GOP women had set up district women's clubs in every voting district. Ella Fleck, a staunch suffragist, doctor's wife, and King supporter, led the GOP women, appointing one woman in each district to run women's affairs. Republican women kept their clubs separate from the men's clubs and met on different nights than the men. They justified this structure by arguing that the women often needed to ask simple questions about politics and did not wish to be ridiculed by the men. These clubs held such affairs as card parties, and a fall hayride and husking bee, and one club sponsored a women's dance orchestra. The Fifth District women's club even had its own club rooms. All women's leaders were either Yankee or Irish, and they appear to have made no special effort to reach new ethnic women, perhaps leaving that task to ethnic clubs.[79]

The Democratic Party, by contrast, was less successful, both at organizing its affairs and at opening its organization to newly enfranchised women. Faced with the task of organizing the new women voters, Bridgeport Democrats chose to establish a citywide women's group rather than copy the more ambitious district structure of the GOP. Prominent Democratic women such as Mrs. William T. Hincks, Mrs. Lynn W. Wilson, and Mrs. Fred Atwater—all wives of wealthy and prominent Yankee leaders—tried to organize women into the party, hosting the statewide meeting of Democratic women in 1920. They were less successful at their district level. Unreconstructed district organizations took some time to integrate women into their social events. For example, women were not allowed until 1925 to attend the annual Twelfth District Democratic Social Club sheep roast on the Sunday of Labor Day weekend. Described as a "big family gathering," the event represented a major change in party get-togethers.[80]

The structure of party politicking changed in the 1920s throughout the nation and in Bridgeport. The neighborhood tavern, a site of male sociability and often the locus for neighborhood and work solidarities, had also served as a place for local politics before Prohibition. The neighborhood bar was a contact point for electioneering politicians meeting their public. "In the days of the saloon, many political questions were settled for the district over the bar," recalled Mrs. O, a County Limerick native who was the widow of a successful Twelfth District tavern keeper. "Just before Election Day both parties came around treating the house. . . . Tonight it might be the Republicans, tomorrow might be the Democrats. . . . It wasn't just your district, it was leaders from every district in the city."[81]

In the 1920s, with the loss of the saloon as a political space, local party leaders had to remake their method of meeting residents and gathering their followers. At the same time political activity became removed from the streets and other public spaces. In the early 1920s the Republicans and Democrats followed the Socialist practice of rallies at shop gates and on street corners in order to appeal to workers but abandoned this after 1925. Only the SP continued to meet workers at their factories or the public on street corners. The major parties, on the other hand, began extensive use of the radio and returned their campaign gatherings to the fraternal and ethnic halls and the new political club rooms.

In many cities, large and small, the 1920s was the heyday of the political club, a group of like-minded individuals who located their organization in a room or building in the district and carried out social functions and party fund-raising. They became the mainstay of partisan activity, providing office space for local politicians and, increasingly, the primary sites for election speeches and rallies. The Republicans in Bridgeport responded to these new structural demands by incorporating their district organizations as district clubs, buying buildings as district headquarters, and eventually charging membership dues. In 1920s Bridgeport the expenditure for club property was often large. The Eighth District Republican Club went so far as to place the club in the hands of a holding company, with the district leaders as majority investors, to protect the thousands of dollars they had invested in their new clubhouse from "the whim of politics." Some Democratic clubs followed the Republican trend of arranging formal district incorporation of their clubs, though they did so less enthusiastically than the GOP.[82]

These clubs were the province of grassroots leaders and supplemented, rather than took over, official party tasks such as election day duties. In Bridgeport the town chairman appointed the district chairs, who were responsible for election day duties. The tasks of the district chairs were separate from the district club affairs, and they did not sit on the town central committee but reported to it. The most influential role the district club members played was in electing the district leader, who did sit on the town central committee and had a say in party policy, strategy, and patronage. John T. King's success in elections, it was said, was the result of his building an efficient district club system that delivered the important get-out-the-vote effort.[83]

Both the alertness of King's political organization to potential leadership qualities in district citizens and attention to women's participation in the party are illustrated by one woman's story of her introduction to the Bridgeport

GOP. Mrs. X, a fourth-generation German American, had recently moved to the city's East Side after her husband took a job at the Remington offices during the war. She recalled that her husband, who had been a Democrat in New York, immediately joined the Republican Party in Bridgeport. "You wouldn't know that there was any other Party in Bridgeport at that time," she noted. In 1920 she and her husband had organized a carnival day for Remington City, the housing complex sponsored by Remington Arms Company for better-paid war employees (most were foremen or white-collar employees, though some skilled manual workers lived there too). The voluntary neighborhood association, made up of owners of the area's semidetached units, raised money for ornamental shrubs, landscaping, and other neighborhood niceties. King himself walked up to her during the carnival and said, "We'd like to have you in our group." Only days later a woman from the Twelfth District GOP club invited her to attend the primary convention and meet other women activists from her district. Soon thereafter she accepted the captaincy of her precinct. Mrs. X then sponsored information meetings, gathering neighbors to her house during the 1921 election to meet the candidates. Accompanied by King and the district leader Arthur Connor, Mayor Clifford Wilson spoke at her house "packed with [fifty to sixty] women . . . Outside the street was crowded with cars, and the men stood outside on the porch listening." Party activists like her were crucial to the mobilization of votes during primaries and general elections. "I had a system," she explained. "I went to the women and asked what time they would be ready. I told them to have their hats on and to be ready when I sent the cars to call for them. . . . I saw that all my people got in before the polls closed and that they had the right tickets [for the primary]."[84]

The primaries were important arenas for party activists to implement policy or end unpopular leadership. Both of Bridgeport's major parties were plagued by splits in numerous districts, the GOP over King's leadership and the Democrats over the intrusions of the manufacturer-inspired Republican Voters League into their midst. The clubs often contained the factionalism, and most commonly factions within each club put up rival primary slates. In a few badly factionalized districts there existed separate clubs that vied for the district's primary vote. Particularly strife-ridden were the Democrats in the Sixth District, where two rival clubs battled for control, and the Fifth, which produced both of the Democratic businessmen who ran for mayor and was the home of the Republican Voters League.[85] (See figure 2 for the location of city voting districts.)

In the Twelfth District two entrenched factions of the Democratic Party, one said to be tied to King's double machine, warred over the club. Indeed, Twelfth District Democrats went to court to settle the question of club membership, resolve insinuations that members held dual memberships in the Democratic and Republican clubs in the district, and decide rightful leadership of the club. By 1927 Cornell was barely holding onto control of the Democratic Party, and William Flanagan, who chaired the city's Democratic central committee, was considering abolishing all district clubs.[86] By contrast, the Twelfth District Republican club, run by Connor, was remarkably stable. The only intrusion on the affairs of the GOP club in this district was the creation in 1924 of the Twelfth District Hebrew Republican Club, the first separate Jewish organization within the city GOP. This club and its ladies' auxiliary were made up of lawyers and shopkeepers (and their wives) from the main business blocks of the neighborhood. The club's rooms were separate from the regular GOP, and it carried on socials, pinochle and whist nights, and sponsored talks on citizenship and nat-

Figure 2. City map, with voting districts, 1920–40. Adapted by Virginia Blaisdell from John Nolen, *Better City Planning for Bridgeport* (Bridgeport, Conn.: City Plan Commission, 1916), 6.

uralization. On citywide party issues the Jewish Republicans backed the King-Connor leadership and supplemented rather than rivaled the activities of the regular district club.[87]

So where were the new ethnics? And where was the working-class rhetorical emphasis on taxes and labor support coming from in the middle years of the decade?

CHAPTER 3

Ethnics in the 1920s

After the dislocations of the 1920–22 postwar depression eased, American workers faced a stabilized and ascendant corporate power determined to control the workplace. They confronted a work environment shaped by the wartime experiments in technological innovation and rationalization. They, as well as their employers, grappled with a newly competitive national and international economy. Finally, they faced a corporate America that challenged union power everywhere it appeared and offered in return the glimmer of a new prosperity. This was a perilous decade for workers' power and identity, both on and off the job.

In addition, World War I and the subsequent immigration restrictions changed immigrant communities. These immigrants-turned-ethnics faced the threatening disintegration of their communities under the pressures of Americanization, cultural change, and the rise of the younger, U.S.-born generation. Within all this internal change ethnics faced the challenge of joining the American electoral system in a meaningful way. All this meant profound changes in the social and cultural life of the American working class.

What did these changes mean for Bridgeport's ethnic workers and their families? In the first two chapters I showed what the effects of the war and postwar economy had done to employers' local political relationships. These chapters also hinted that local power resided in working-class votes, though voters did not yet have a labor-defined agenda. Working people took advantage of the possibilities in this decade of change and reorganized themselves along ethnic and electoral lines.

In the Neighborhoods

Bridgeport's Slovak minister, Igor Bella, put the issue very simply in 1938. His community's goal was "Americanization, not assimilation . . . absorbing the American way-of-life, and at the same time preserving the culture of one's own nationality."[1] His curious distinction between Americanization and assimilation—a distinction not made by sociological writers of the time—signals the complexity of the task facing all new immigrant groups, that is, eastern and southern Europeans, in the 1920s and 1930s. This process involved not only fitting in with American society but redefining their relationship to the old country.

Drawing on Old World organizational traditions, immigrant pioneers had built on the kinship- and village-based chain migration from eastern and southern Europe to create the myriad fraternal benefit organizations—landsmanschaften, *societàs di mutuo soccorso,* religious communities, parish councils, ladies' sodalities, and athletic and singing societies—that dotted U.S. immigrant colonies by 1900. These provided health and accident insurance and death benefits, conducted recreational and social activities, embodied the moral ideals of the community, and often monitored the conduct of the community. No ethnic community was homogeneous; all were stratified by class, region, and religion.[2]

By the turn of the twentieth century these local groups had often merged to create national organizations designed to represent ethnic concerns to the U.S. government. In addition, immigrants' nationalist visions of the old country had given a particular dynamic to each community in the United States before World War I. The three main types of old country nationalism manifested in immigrant Bridgeport between the 1880s and World War I were an *integral* nationalism that demanded language or religious unity; a *pluralist* nationalism that appealed to common geographic origins and history, irrespective of religion or even native language; and a *socialist* nationalism, which explicitly tied nationalistic aspirations to class goals. The alternative was Americanization.

For example, the Polish Roman Catholic Union, founded in 1873 and dominated by priests who tied being Polish to being Catholic, represented an integral nationalism. In opposition, other Polish community leaders gathered in Chicago in 1880 to found the Polish National Alliance (PNA), which saw the American Polish immigrant communities ("Polonia") as the "Fourth Province of Poland." The Fourth Province's mission was to combine with the three partitioned parts of historic Poland to fight for a free and unified homeland. In this pluralist-nationalist model the PNA was secular and nondiscriminatory, even allowing Jews to join—though, doubtless, few did. The PNA was more popular in Polonia; after 1896 the PNA always had a significantly higher membership than the Polish Roman Catholic Union. Further complications in the Polish case stemmed from religious differences. An independent Catholic movement, the Polish National Catholic Church, had split from Rome in 1900 and contended that Polish Roman Catholics were not nationalist enough.[3] Along with the Polish Socialist Alliance all these groups had halls on Bridgeport's East Side.

Similarly, religious differences divided the Slovak community, whose nationalist fervor was slower to coalesce than that of the Polish community. The National Slovak Society, founded in 1890, was a pluralist-nationalist organization that attempted to transcend the confessional divisions among Slovak Roman Catholics, Greek Catholics, Lutherans, and Calvinists. Its chief rival for allegiance was the Catholic Slovak Union, which admitted only Catholics. The Slovak Wreath of the Free Eagle, founded in Bridgeport in 1890 and growing to moderate size and influence, was another smaller federation open to all Slovak Christians.[4]

The next wave of ethnic national federations in the United States consisted of the gymnastic societies ("Sokols," or Falcons) founded in the 1890s, following the central European custom of nationalistic physical culture. The Polish Falcons' Alliance, started in 1887 with the help of the PNA as a youth-oriented gymnastic group, had a militant nationalist orientation; by 1907 the Falcons were sponsoring military training of its members and helped form the Polish Army in France during World War I. The Bridgeport Polish Falcons retained their hall in the South End in the 1920s. The Slovak Gymnastic Union Falcon, known as the National Sokol, organized in 1896 by nationalist community leaders to champion the cause of the Slovak minority in Hungary, was also strongly secular. Slovak Catholic dissidents broke away from this group in 1905 and formed their own Slovak Catholic Sokol with the slogan "For God and the Nation." In Bridgeport this meant organizational rivalry and quite clear separation. For example, the National Sokol had a hall on Hallett Street on the East Side that it shared with the National Slovak Society, while the Catholic Sokols had their own hall across the street.[5]

Socialist groups within each ethnic group tied nationalist aspirations to goals of progress and social transformation rather than political independence per se. Moreover, because so few of their countrymen could vote in the United States, they stressed the fate of the homeland and decried the simplistic electoral orientation of the Socialist Party of America.[6]

The eastern European Jewish community divided itself between religious and secular orientations, focusing on social and political improvements in the United States, often with the financial help of wealthier German Jews of an earlier migration. The more localistic associations soon merged into national groupings, concerned with cultural preservation (yiddishkeit) in a new land or, increasingly in the period just before and during World War I, Zionist aspirations for a homeland. Standing outside the conservative localistic organizations were the socialist groups, most prominently the Workmen's Circle (*Arbeiter Ring*). The Workmen's Circle envisioned its fraternal body to be part of a three-part organic community, joining with the trade union and the political party to transform society. More important, this fraternal organization successfully kept many Jewish businessmen and professionals in a socialist orbit.[7]

Representative life histories of early ethnic notables in Bridgeport illustrate both the functions of ethnic leaders in this era and the upward paths of these immigrant self-made men. Consider the Magyar community, the only ethnic group in Bridgeport to be closely settled in one neighborhood. In 1898 Joseph Ciglar, designated "patriarch of the Hungarian colony," built the first hall in the West End enclave that became the main site of Hungarian settlement in Bridgeport through the 1940s. A mecca for social activities, Ciglar's Hall contained a roller skating rink and one of the first motion picture houses in the city. It also served as the first home of two Bridgeport fraternal benefit organizations—the Rakoczi Aid Association (established 1887) and the Hungarian Aid Association (established 1892). Three years after emigrating from Hungary to the United States, John Renchy settled in the West End of Bridgeport in the mid-1880s and opened a tavern. He and Ciglar founded the St. Stephen Roman Catholic Church, and Renchy became a national officer in both the Rakoczi Aid Association and the Hungarian Aid Association. Both Renchy and Ciglar became active in local politics. Stephen Varga came to the United States in 1890, first to the coal mines of Pennsylvania and then a few years later to Bridgeport. After working for some time in the Cornwall and Patterson machine shop, Varga went into business for himself by opening a cafe. John Dezso, who would serve sixteen years as national president of the Hungarian Aid Association, was a real estate developer who opened up the Villa Park area of neighboring Fairfield to immigrants before and during the war period. It was he who laid out new lots in neighboring Fairfield with Hungarian street names. All these men became prominent leaders in Hungarian fraternal circles. The Hungarian notables owed their prosperity, which was unusual for Bridgeport's immigrant elite, to the two Bridgeport-based Hungarian fraternals, the Rakoczi and the Hungarian Aid. They became, respectively, the third-and fourth-largest Hungarian fraternals in the United States, projected the Bridgeport officers into leadership beyond the local community, and brought significant national insurance business to Bridgeport. The role of fraternals in shaping the Hungarian community both socially and geographically was decisive. Indeed, the fast-growing Rakoczi Aid Association, which prided itself on its pluralist nationalism, played a determining role in the location of the Hungarian enclave. The Rakoczi bought an entire block in the West End adjoining its new hall; it then subdivided the block, bounded by Bostwick, Hancock, Cherry, and Pine Streets, and sold house lots to arriving conationals.[8]

Before the 1920s Bridgeport's Italian community showed little interest in larger nationalist concerns and remained more strongly attached to regional identities. Italians had dozens of associations in Bridgeport by 1919, all locally oriented and often anticlerical. The unification of Italy in the midnineteenth century had not drawn many southern Italians into the unification process, and the immigrants from those regions felt more connected to their local origins than to the nation of Italy. In fact, Italian ethnic leaders in Bridgeport were aggressive Americanizers. Two community pioneers, Louis Richards and Frank D'Elia, founded the first Italian fraternal group in Bridgeport in 1898 and named it the George Dewey Sick Benefit Society, after the U.S. naval commander who defeated the Spanish fleet at Manila Bay. Clearly, American nationalism and enthusiasm for the Spanish-American War was more appealing to them.[9]

The prominence of Italians in Bridgeport society and politics was related to their numbers and to the astute leadership of the pioneers. The proclaimed "pappa" of the Italian community, Richards, an undertaker, exemplifies the ethnic leader who combined entrepreneurial skill, economic defense of the community, and contact with Americans to reach an esteemed position among his own. Richards, or Luigi Ricciardo, as he advertised in the Italian newspaper *Sentinella*, was born to a middle-class family in Benevento and had come to the United States when he was twelve. He then worked at a variety of construction jobs and, after arriving in Bridgeport in 1890, became foreman at Canfield Rubber Company, one of the few factories in the city that would employ Italians in those early years. He moved on to open his own barber shop and then became a labor contractor in construction.

"All the Italians that came here would look up to Louis Richards for help, either in getting a job or for other reasons," recalled an early resident.[10] Richards's earliest and most celebrated political victory, however, came as a byproduct of his role as labor padrone in 1900. Richards had furnished men to Bridgeport contractors for the extensive improvements to the New York, New Haven & Hartford Railroad line throughout the city, as had another Italian padrone, Dominic Marino of Boston. Richards's men, all from Bridgeport, were forced to live in Marino's barracks and buy provisions from him. Richards saw this as a challenge to his own padrone business and as a hardship on the local Italian laborers and prompted state intervention in the labor contracting business. He was instrumental in sponsoring a state investigation of labor conditions for contract laborers in Bridgeport and for passage of a state "anti-padrone" law.[11]

All immigrant groups were deeply affected by World War I. In 1920 immigrant communities faced the difficult realities of a new Europe, a nativist America, and a triumphant corporate economy. Most important, now that many immigrants' nationalist dreams had been realized by the creation of new nations from the ruins of the Austro-Hungarian Empire, Bridgeport's immigrants had to choose. They could return home (a decision that, given the new American immigration restriction laws, could be a permanent one) or could choose to settle down in the United States. Their immigrant-to-ethnic journey was just beginning.

However, the decision to stay in the United States did not mean abandoning immigrant customs and institutions. Indeed, the chroniclers of fraternal organizations and foreign-language newspapers refer to the 1920s as the "golden age" of ethnicity, when membership and readership reached all-time highs. What, then, were the structural changes that Bridgeport's immigrant-turned-ethnic communities underwent?

Churches, fraternal and mutual benefit organizations, and athletic and cultural clubs remained the main socializing institutions in ethnic communities in the 1920s. (See table 2, p. 20.)

While the nationalist strands of the prewar period—integral, pluralist, or socialist—had less meaning in 1920s ethnic communities, their legacies were apparent nonetheless. Nationality issues often combined with labor and political issues. Secularists, non-Catholics, and socialists from each eastern European ethnic community supported socialist or prolabor governments in Europe. But middle-class ethnic leaders opposed these governments, as did American businessmen and foreign policy makers. In the mid-1920s this conservative stance helped cement ethnic relationships with mainstream American political parties. In both the Slovak and Hungarian cases these conservative nationalistic views eventually led to their approval of fascism. Finally, the retreat from European affairs, as in the Polish case, aided the more rapid accommodation to an American society without the wholesale assimilation of these ethnics. Thus the larger group in the Polish community, which opposed the Pilsudski government in Poland, turned inward and focused on making their way in American society. *Wychodztwo dla wychodztwa,* "the emigrants for themselves," became the dominant Polish-American slogan, wielded by Polish grocers and businessmen in their desire to keep their community close about them. It might usefully have served as well as a slogan for most eastern European ethnic elites in the 1920s.[12]

But not all communities were so successfully dominated. In the Hungarian-American community dissension between defenders of the defunct Bela Kun revolutionary government and supporters of its right-wing successor, the Horthy regime, kept this community split. Hungarian monarchist supporters in Bridgeport received sympathy from the local Bridgeport press. But revolutionary activity in Hungary in 1919 had excited the Hungarians of Bridgeport and had a lasting influence on them. The left-wing Hungarian branch of the Socialist Party, which had joined the Workers (Communist) Party, continued a vibrant existence in the West End, now augmented by pro-Kun refugees from Hungary. According to the Bridgeport Police Department, the Hungarian Workingmen's Federation, the "communist club," had seventy-five to eighty active, dues-paying members in 1921 and distributed about five hundred copies of each issue of its paper, *Elöre.* Federation members established a singing society, the Liberty Workingmen's Singing Society, and maintained a hall on Spruce Street in the center of the West End in the 1920s and 1930s. The benefit organization linked to the Workingmen's Federation had enough broad-based support to receive funds from Hungarian churches and fraternal organizations to build a Workers' Home, or "Self-Educating Place," in nearby Fairfield. In most large Hungarian communities in the United States, a "grand committee" deliberated for the community and functioned as a coordinating body representing all groups. The Hungarian Workingmen's Federation in Bridgeport was influential enough to force the reorganization of the Bridgeport Grand Committee in 1929, limiting the influence of pro-Horthy supporters. The Socialist Labor Party, though small, remained active in the Hungarian community, as did a band of Wobblies.[13]

Similarly, the Russian Revolution made political adjustments in many communities more complicated. The small Armenian community, settled in an enclave of the Twelfth District along Yellow Mill River, split between those favoring Soviet rule and those opposing it. The Russian community was hopelessly divided. Miss Pospelova, a social worker for the YWCA's International Institute, reported in 1923 on her failure to make progress in the Russian community. "Half of them suspect me of being a Bolshevist as I came recently from Russia; the other half is equally sure I have been sent to spread propaganda against the Russian workers." While the Palmer raids of 1919 and 1920 had scattered much of the Russian Left, pockets of Ukrainian anarchists and a United Russian Trade and Educational Union were still distributing newspapers in 1921. Support for the Soviet Union and for radical unionism survived through the decade. The political tensions in this community had grown by the late 1920s when Igor Sikorsky, the aviation manufacturer whose company was absorbed by Connecticut's United Aircraft Corporation, moved his plant from Long Island to Stratford and sponsored right-wing Russian immigration to Stratford and the East Side of Bridgeport.[14]

Though ethnic women's activities were rarely given space in the Bridgeport mainstream press comparable to that given the men's fraternal groups, myriad women's groups flourished. Most were societies attached to the various religious institutions, concerned with parish affairs, the keeping of the altar (the Catholic altar societies) or attending to the ritual needs of the home (Jewish women's Talmud Torah auxiliaries). They reached married women who were often uneducated. Other ethnic women's groups were geared more to public action and attention. The Polish Women's Alliance had been set up just before the war because Polish women activists felt that the dominant groups were not addressing their concerns. Ukrainians and Lithuanians set up women's alliances, in 1915 and 1917, respectively, to provide insurance and education for women. The Polish National Alliance established a new PNA Women's Department in the 1920s. By the 1930s the Bridgeport Sokols had women contestants in national and international gymnastics competitions. The Polish Falcons also began admitting women in the 1920s. Only Italian organizations seemed generally unresponsive to women's needs. This may explain why Italian women were the heaviest users of the Bridgeport International Institute, sponsored by the YWCA.[15]

The inclusion of women was not only a response to the growing demands of women in the 1920s but part of an answer to the general issue of attracting the second generation. This was a problem larger than any other facing the new ethnics in the 1920s. The communities tried to address this question while they attended to the Americanization of their first generation, a stance that encouraged the preservation of ethnic culture in the process of adapting to American society. First, this included the use of English. In the early 1920s the Foreign-

Language Information Service reported that U.S.-born children of immigrants preferred to read American newspapers and that even the first generation, after acquiring some English, turned to the American papers for general news. Many fraternal newspapers began including English pages by 1930 after bitter internal debate about whether they would be abandoning their native language. The Magyar-language *Bridgeport* by 1931 had on its masthead *Szellemben Amerikai, Nyelvben Magyar,* "American in Spirit, Hungarian in Language." Many second-generation Jewish men joined Jewish lodges of American fraternals like the Elks and Odd Fellows, a halfway station between ethnic loyalty and Americanization. Proving its Americanism and recovering from World War I antipathy, the Connecticut German sängerfest opened a new category of songs, English language. The prize was an American flag.[16]

Tensions between the generations persisted, however. The Rakoczi Aid Association, through its journal *Rakoczi Szemle,* promoted the cause of its "powerful and safe" association in preference to American insurance companies that were making inroads into the Hungarian community. In the 1920s both the Bridgeport Hungarian Aid Association and the Rakoczi Aid Association worried about the preponderance of elderly among their members because fewer young people were joining; before the war many immigrants had returned to Hungary in their old age, which relieved the fraternals of the financial burden. Nonetheless, in the early 1930s, when John Dezso, president of the Hungarian Aid Association, proposed changing its name to American Aid Association to attract the second generation and a more general clientele, he was met with a resounding no. As one Bridgeport Hungarian explained, "Most of the young people hardly attend church and have their own clubs along the American style . . . they don't care about nothing."[17]

Organizations attempted to attract the interest of the second generation through sports programs—the Sokols and Falcons were most successful. Bridgeport Swedes turned an informal soccer group into a formal club in 1920, but for most ethnic groups baseball held the key. By mid-decade the fraternals had a well-organized system of local and regional baseball competition. The debate was not just one of which sport to play—basketball seemed a particular bone of contention—but how to approach sports. As one observer noted, "the old program of nationalistic physical culture" was under assault. The Polish Falcons had devoted most of their organizational energy before 1920 to the military fight for Poland's independence; most of their energy in the 1920s was taken up with the issue of whether their sports programs would continue to be nationalistic or assimilationist. In the short term the generational problem was solved by the Sokols' holding many dances for their youth in addition to the sports programs.[18]

In the postwar period as immigrants settled in, ethnic communities spread to the less crowded neighborhoods of second settlement. This was not the suburbanized embourgeoisement of workers; rather, it was the search for better housing. More economically stable immigrant families moved from the crowded inner-city neighborhoods of first settlement to better housing away from the center of town. But in many cases the move was only a half-dozen blocks or so from the six-family wooden tenements to better single- and double-decker houses previously occupied by skilled workers who had immigrated earlier and now were moving farther out. (See figure 2, p. 66, and table 4.) These areas included voting districts 6B, 8, 9A, and 9B to the east and north, where home building accelerated; the Twelfth District, which was expanding east into neighboring Stratford; and the Swedish neighborhoods of the Fourth District, which were growing west into Fairfield. Many recalled that savings put aside during the war allowed them to buy houses or at least to reclaim from boarders the front parlor of their rented apartment.[19]

This movement of immigrants to better neighborhoods caused some flight on the part of middle-class Americans. "Americans have resented what they consider an invasion of their better living sections," stated a social worker at the YWCA's International Institute in 1919, as American families moved to the outer districts.[20] One middle-aged black woman, who had lived in Bridgeport since 1898 and worked as a domestic for families in the Seventh and Eighth Districts, told an interviewer that by the war "most of the people she worked for moved to Westport, Fairfield and Stratford."[21] Starting in the early 1920s, many of the most prominent industrialist families of Bridgeport, as well as some middle-class Americans, began their steady flight to the suburbs. The pastor of the Park Street Congregational Church, located on Washington Park on the East Side, noted the same trend. Park Street Church, organized in 1868 as part of the settlement of the East Bridgeport–Washington Park area by skilled American workmen and middle-class elements in the heyday of P. T. Barnum, had long

Table 4. Color and Nativity of the Population by Voting District, 1930

District	Native White/ Native Parents	Native White/ Foreign-born Parents[a]	Foreign-born White	Black	Other	Totals
1	1,756	1,187	917	60	19	3,939
2	2,247	3,959	2,776	495	11	9,488
3	2,579	6,248	4,869	55	0	13,751
4	2,184	3,016	1,975	60	6	7,241
5 (a and b)	5,438	5,365	3,187	114	0	14,104
6 (a and b)	4,744	9,601	5,596	491	7	20,439
7	2,220	2,633	1,609	348	13	6,823
8	3,177	5,245	2,868	570	1	11,861
9 (a and b)	4,312	8,521	4,880	18	6	17,737
10	1,171	5,195	3,501	301	7	10,175
11	965	3,388	2,185	145	2	6,685
12 (a and b)	6,794	10,621	6,396	657	5	24,473
Totals	37,587	64,979	40,759	3,314	77	146,716

Sources: U.S. Census Bureau, *Population,* 1930, vol. 3, pt. 1: *Reports by States* (Washington, D.C.: U.S. Government Printing Office, 1930), table 23, p. 365.
a. Also includes mixed parentage.

served a native-born community. But by 1921 "the trend of movement has been
steadily away from our neighborhood to the West Side, North End and the suburbs, and we have lost many members to churches in those sections," Rev. Gerald H. Beard wrote. He hoped, however, to keep the church going as a community service.[22] Bridgeport's "Hell's Kitchen" was only about four blocks away,
but so too were the nicer artisan houses of more skilled Slovak workers. To the
south of Washington Park in the Tenth and Eleventh Districts, vacant storefronts
in the mid-1920s testified to the spreading-out of better-off ethnics.

Moving to the outskirts of town was often a quality-of-life decision for working-class people from rural origins. Statement after statement attested to the
yearnings of those families financially stable enough to achieve ownership of a
yard and vegetable garden. For years many Hungarians traveled on weekends
from their Bridgeport apartments to tend their vegetable gardens on lots they
owned in the Villa Park and Tunxis Hill sections of Fairfield before they could
afford to put up a small house and move there.[23]

Most working people, however, stayed in the city. Ethnic neighborhoods became increasingly differentiated by economic status. For example, the Slovak
community now had three distinct colonies on the East Side: the blocks of first
settlement south of the railroad tracks in the Tenth and Eleventh Districts still
inhabited by factory laborers; the better-off mechanics and artisans along Arc-
tic Street north of the railroad tracks of the Tenth District and into the Ninth
District; and the businessmen and professionals (a small group) who by the early
1930s were scattered on the better residential streets.[24] Bridgeport's factory districts were strung out in a roughly east-west line that followed the railroad tracks
through the lower third of the city near the coastline. Though ethnic clustering
existed at some factories, workers had also become used to crisscrossing the city
to work, especially in the wartime boom days. A 1923 transportation survey revealed that of the more than thirteen thousand factory workers contacted, 41
percent still walked to work, another 22 percent traveled only within the central trolley zone, and 37 percent now made longer trips that required a transfer
from outer zones. But the trolleys could also be a meeting space for working
people living nearby or working in the same area. "Everybody knew each other
from the trolley rides," remembered Robert McLevy, who lived in the Oak Street
section of the Sixth District.[25]

An assertive ethnicity in the 1920s was achieved through the increased appropriation of public space, as Bridgeport ethnic organizations staged ethnic festivals that increasingly dominated the streets of Bridgeport. Though similar displays had been reported in larger metropolises before this time, their appearance
in Bridgeport, as in so many other medium-sized cities, reflects the maturation
of an ethnic sensibility.[26] The Italian community made the most ostentatious display of its presence. The persistent fragmentation of the Italian community into
provincial organizations, despite its elite's strongest efforts, surely encouraged
this active style. In particular, the celebrations of patron saint days by mutual

benefit organizations, sporadically organized in the prewar period, became elaborately staged and frequent events during the 1920s. The St. Anthony festival, begun in 1925, was a two-day affair on the East Side. It centered around the light-bulb-strung blocks of Pembroke and Willard Streets in the East Side's Hell's Kitchen area that were bedecked with both Italian and American flags. The festival began with a street parade featuring the statue of St. Anthony on Saturday, included an evening band concert by the Bridgeport Marine Band on the lot of the Bridgeport Brass Company, Sunday mass at Holy Rosary Church, and neighborhood fireworks on Sunday night. Similarly, the Mount Carmel Society held its two-day festival in honor of Our Lady of Mount Carmel with two street parades, one in the North End and one on the East Side, a band concert and fireworks on Saturday night in two city parks, a Sunday mass, and a picnic at Pleasure Beach. The Faetana Society also celebrated for an entire weekend with a march through the streets, a picnic, and fireworks. Attendance at these events was always reported to be in the thousands.[27] The use of streets and city parks, the donation of a private company's lot, and the presence of a military band all suggest acceptance of this group by the city's political and economic leaders.[28]

Including Ethnics in Politics

The issue of ethnic incorporation into the political parties was resolved both within the regular party clubs and through outside organization. As already noted, only some small ethnic diversity was reflected in the slates for common council and district chairs. Yet the ties established between key party leaders and ethnic networks in the city were crucial to partisan success. While the old ethnics were well integrated into the political parties, some also supplemented their participation through the activities of citywide, partisan, ethnic interest groups like the Erickson Swedish Republican Association. However, the new ethnics had larger challenges facing them, both from nativist public opinion and from the Americanization needs of their recently settled communities.

The local Republican Party courted new immigrants in the prewar period, while the mostly Irish Democratic Party rarely did. In return for rounding up votes in this period, ethnic notables and their allies traditionally received minor appointive positions within the party or the city administration. Before the 1920s the ballot positions that new ethnics received from the party organization were in lesser, though potentially lucrative, posts such as city sheriff or justice of the peace. This, combined with the appointive positions like notaries public, created a politics of and by ethnic notables, set into a dependent framework of ties to local American politicians.

The large Italian community in Bridgeport was ripe for political attention in the early twentieth century. Richards was particularly astute at courting the attention of the Yankee elite. "One time he wanted to show the American people that he was the leader of the Italian people," recalled a sixty-year-old woman who had come to Bridgeport in the 1890s, "so he made a parade on Main St. with all the Italians. He got all these Italians from some of the contractors in the city and when they marched on Main St. all the American people were surprised and they said 'That man is a big man with his race.' So after this all the Americans used to have respect with Mr. Richards, and when he said something to the American people they used to listen with two ears open."[29]

The Italian community remained riddled with provincial differences, a proliferation of organizations, and personality clashes. That Richards was able to dominate political leadership was largely the result of his championing all Italians, rather than any particular regional group, and the mutually beneficial alliance he had established with the Republicans. By then he had acted as a court interpreter for Italians, a popular way to get noticed by political leaders, and had caught the eye of local Republicans. In 1894 he gained a place on the Republican ticket as a city sheriff. As an immigrant banker and labor contractor himself, Richards protected Italian business community interests through his position in the Republican Party. As Richards himself told it, "Well, when I became sheriff . . . when the other [Irish] officers tried to raid the Italian establishments, . . . I would prevent them from doing so by telling them that if they raided the Italians I would raid the Irish two to their one." In a similar vein Richards explained his citizenship methods. "When I started to take hold of matters of the Italians in this city I was able to push many of them through. There were times that I knew how hard it was for some of these to go through the strict [citizenship] test, but I also knew that these people would make darned good citizens even if they could not read and write well."[30]

The local Republican Party cultivated ethnic pride and self-assertion in important ways. In 1904 Richards and D'Elia received political acknowledgment when they were invited to the inaugural reception of President Theodore Roosevelt.[31] A more striking example of ethnic recognition by local politicians was the manner in which Columbus Day became a state holiday in Connecticut. The Columbus Day holiday campaign began with a 1908 extravaganza arranged in Bridgeport by the community leaders Luke Petruschell, a barber, court interpreter, and chairman of the United Italian Societies; James Massey, editor of *Il Sole;* and Louis Richards. With Richards as grand marshal the four-mile parade was supported by Italian societies from the entire state. Led by a float constructed by Bridgeport immigrants from Genoa, the parade included a delegation from every society, including the Italian Socialist Federation. Bridgeport's Republican mayor reviewed the parade and delivered a speech praising the Italian contribution to the city and the nation. Here was a fundamental recognition—by the dominant city and state party—of the largest immigrant group in Bridgeport and the state. Richards then carried the cause of Columbus Day with him as he campaigned for upstate Republicans during the 1908 campaign season. The impressed and grateful state politicians enacted the Columbus Day measure in the next legislative session.[32]

During the 1920s subtle but definite changes in ethnic participation in partisan politics took place in Bridgeport. The majority Republican Party under King strengthened its organization after the defection of industrialists in 1921 by paying greater attention to its ethnic constituents, particularly Germans and Italians, to supplement its Irish stalwarts. German Americans slowly reentered American public life after the intense hostility of the war years and through Mayor Behrens became key players in local Republican politics. Some reporters suggested that King's courting of German Americans was calculated to hold down the Socialist vote in the city. And indeed, after a brief fling by the Bridgeport Steuben Society in canvassing for Robert La Follette, the Progressive Party's presidential candidate in 1924, the German community remained staunchly Republican. In 1925 German-American voters set up a permanent German Town Committee, modeled after the Republican Town Committee (the local central committee), to coordinate electoral efforts. Behrens's active membership in the German singing group Schwaebischer Maennorchor was a pivot around which much GOP activity turned. At the 1928 annual outing of Schwaebischer Maennorchor at Behrens's Stepney Farm, reporters noted almost as many Irish, mostly police and city hall workers, as Germans. Similarly, the Republicans renewed their links to traditional Italian notables in the community.[33]

Increasingly, in the 1920s ethnic communities became markedly more aggressive, both in their internal political organizing and in their demands upon the parties for places on the ballot. In Bridgeport and other Connecticut cities eastern and southern European political activists spearheaded the organization of political clubs in order to direct party affairs in their neighborhoods. Their Americanized leaders began demanding more patronage and more prominent positions on the party slates. Because these communities now represented a large potential electorate, party officials had to take their bids for some power seriously.[34]

At the state level the Connecticut GOP began taking great pains to curry favor with the state's growing ethnic voters. In the mid-1920s the secretary of state nomination became an "Italian position" on both the Democratic and Republican slates, as the state parties recognized the increasing part played by new ethnics. Attention to the "foreign vote" in the state GOP meant that during campaigns, "'old liners' dropped into the Allyn House headquarters [state GOP headquarters in Hartford] only to wait one or two hours to penetrate the inner sanctum because the chairman was occupied with a group of Italians, a colored group, a committee of French from eastern Connecticut or a committee of Poles from New Britain."[35]

Such attention at the state level meant more attention locally. In the early 1920s the GOP in Bridgeport honored ethnic leaders by appointing some to various city boards such as the Health, Charities, and Recreation Commissions, where their communities' interests presumably lay. These ethnic leaders, generally businessmen or professionals, included the Polish doctor Bronislaus Smykowski, the Italian undertaker Richards, the German-Jewish lawyer Jacob B. Klein, and the Hungarian Catholic priest Stephen Chernitsky. None commanded a dominant position on these boards. Throughout the decade, moreover, new ethnics were conspicuously absent from the most important appointive boards and commissions, such as police, fire, public purchasing, and zoning, which remained in the hands of influential Yankee and Irish-American citizens.[36]

Some ethnic group representatives chose to gain recognition through activity within the regular GOP clubs. Hungarians, a sizable minority of the Third District in the city's West End, sought representation in both the Democratic and Republican clubs and were given the common council nomination by both parties at various times during the 1920s. A fairly solid record of GOP wins in the area allowed John Renchy, the real estate developer, and Stephen J. Mak, a storekeeper, to occupy one of the seats for a good part of the decade. But the Third District GOP dealt with Hungarian voters separately. Although other more assimilated groups, such as the considerable number of Swedes in the area, usually rallied at the regular district GOP headquarters, the GOP held campaign rallies for Hungarians at Rakoczi Hall. The notables of the important Hungarian Catholic parish were solidly Republican, and only Republican officials and district leaders spoke at the parish party in honor of Father Chernitsky.[37] Ambitious Jewish notables, mostly lawyers, were active in the GOP, but with the exception of the Twelfth District they refrained from setting up separate clubs before 1928. They did not often appear as common council nominees but were most frequently found as notaries or as appointees to the city court bench.[38]

Other ethnics, however, felt the need to press their representation in politics as a separate group. From 1920 to 1928 twelve ethnic political clubs, all tied to the Republican Party, incorporated and registered with the office of the town clerk, a sure sign of sufficient financial backing and long-term interest. For example, the Bridgeport Polish Republican Club, a citywide club that had been in existence for twelve years and had a declared membership of 125 men, incorporated in 1924. Most of the new clubs were not tied to specific boundaries. For example, the St. John's Slovak Political Club, which was started in 1921 by two Slovaks who eventually ran for common council on the Republican ticket, appealed to all Slovaks across the city.[39] Several more ethnic clubs, which did not register with the town clerk but were mentioned in local newspapers, popped into view for particular campaigns.

Many of these clubs grew out of the ethnic networks already in existence. As one recent Italian immigrant remembered about his initiation into American politics in the 1920s, "I used to go [to the Italian clubs on the East Side] and I played cards with all the people. . . . In these clubs, I remember the people they would all talk about politics. I didn't know what these politics was all about at that time, and I was always asking the people everything. Some of these Italians started to make like a political club after this. . . . I asked some of the men in the club what you had to do to be a voter, and they said that I had to learn to read and write. I told them that I was learning and some day I would be a voter."[40]

The ethnic political clubs' ability to bring out their community of voters on election day made them useful to the political parties, though the parties had rarely tolerated such formalized structures before. As observers noted, ethnic political clubs were valuable in integrating groups into the mainstream political bodies, but at the same time they could reinforce separateness.[41] Another self-limiting tendency of these organizations in Bridgeport was the devaluation of the concerns of women in their communities and the ignoring of the female vote.

Italians in Bridgeport were among the most favored of the new ethnic groups in the Republican Party by the mid-1920s, as measured by terms of appointment to city commissions, justices of the peace, and common council nominations. These slots went to notables like Louis Richards, Louis Abriola, and the D'Elia family, who had early been important in recruiting Italians to the GOP. In return, Michele Altieri, who served as secretary of the Italian-American Republican Town Committee, proclaimed in *La Sentinella* that Italians should support the local Republicans, "the ticket that represents the true liberty and protection of our community . . . and gives us recognition at every occasion." At the same time he appealed for the support of three Italian Republican nominees, Donato D'Elia, Joseph Petriello, and Luigi Abriola: "We must affirm ourselves in politics . . . it is necessary to support our own countrymen."[42]

The Italian community, as the largest ethnic group in the city, constructed an extensive organizational presence in GOP city politics in the 1920s. The Italian GOP maintained a network of district clubs separate from the regular party clubs and financed its own activities. These clubs were coordinated by the Italian General Committee (later the Italian-American Republican Town Committee), whose incorporation petition in 1921 announced its goal to be the "social and moral development and Americanization of the Italian element." The key leaders in these 1920s clubs, of course, were the new office seekers; Michele Altieri, Joseph Cubelli, and Michael Iassogna all made their way onto the local Republican ballot during the decade.[43]

A clear victory for Bridgeport Italian Republicans was the nomination and subsequent election of Cubelli, a businessman born in Calitri, Italy, as state representative in 1924 and then state senator in 1926. This prize—an Italian added to the Bridgeport slate for a state office—was the result of the flexing of Italian political muscle. The importance of such a position, besides its relatively greater prestige, was that it gave local Italians *direct* access to state Republican leaders, rather than indirect access through the regular Bridgeport GOP organization. Expressing a long memory of American political duplicity, one Bridgeport Italian remembered, "Before when the Italians were not strong and when they did not have the citizen papers these [Irish and American] politicians wanted to step on the Italian, now that they are citizens, most of them these people they want to promise to the Italian a lot of things so that they will get the Italian vote. . . . the Italian they used to believe these politicians" in the early 1920s.[44]

Thus, though they remained within the circles of the Republican Party, Italians found the need for more aggressive tactics. For example, Italians in the Ninth and Tenth Districts incorporated their clubs in 1927. The goals of the clubs reflected the desire to push the GOP further: "[we] as a whole have been ignored in the matter of political preferment and . . . [our] nationality has never been recognized in police and fire appointments."[45] Clearly, the motivation of this club was not to break with existing political alliances but to push beyond their imposed limits.

At the same time these Italian Republican clubs took charge of the city civic festival that "belonged" to Italians—the Columbus Day celebrations. Now the Italian GOP clubs arranged the parade and fireworks that had once included all Italian organizations in the city. Italian GOP leaders appeared to have accomplished a near hegemony in culture and politics in their community.[46]

Had ethnic politics come far from the "villainous ward-heeler" stereotype of Progressive Era days? The *Bridgeport Sunday Herald,* carrying the banner of intelligent voting and progressive reform into the 1920s, thought not. In the same issue in which the paper reported the opening of the new Ninth-Tenth District Italian-American Republican Club, a *Herald* editorial declared that Bridgeport had no room for the "hyphenated American" organized for "selfish purposes."[47] Similarly, the *Herald* warned black leaders to aspire to "true citizenship" rather than to equate votes with patronage: "More than half the rottenness in politics today comes from this exchange of the ballot for patronage." (Black leaders from Hartford and elsewhere had warned Republicans not to take black votes for granted.)[48] For the *Herald* these critiques were part of its systematic assault on machine politics rather than on ethnic representation as such. While attacking what it perceived as the "boss"-like use of new ethnics' votes by the local Republicans, the paper also reproached the Democratic Party for its minimal attention to all groups in Bridgeport. For example, in the 1922 election the *Herald* pointed critically to the overwhelmingly "green" (i.e., Irish) complexion of the Democratic slate. The *Herald* also reported in 1921 that the Republican Voters League was being called the "Klu [*sic*] Klux Klan of Bridgeport" for failing to make nominations from the various religious and ethnic groups.[49]

Ethnic activists themselves often reinforced this image of the ethnic politician as manipulator of the uneducated. Zygmunt Czubak, a lawyer, carefully distinguished between his Polish Republican Club, "a very good element, an aggressive and sincere type" loyal to the upstate Roraback GOP machine, and the "so-called 'King' faction, under the guidance of a certain Dr. Smykowski . . . [and] the Reverend Dr. Ratajczak." Claiming that the days when one needed the clergy to reach the Polish community were past, he noted that "even though the clergy wield some influence, yet, you will notice after due observation that, this influence is held only over the un-citizen or non-voter, and very, very few voters will tell you anything different." His club met at the secular-oriented White Eagles' Society Hall. Here the deferential politics of the immigrant past, attached to the city's King machine, was being challenged by an Americanized leadership loyal to the upstate GOP organization.[50]

Other ethnic organizations in the 1920s rejected such ethnic appeals for political purposes. Sven Murberg, an officer of the Swedish-American Association, rejected leaflets from the Republican Voters League addressed to Swedish voters in the Third District during the hard-fought 1921 election. "A plea to national pride or prejudice is un-American," he explained. Similarly, Abraham Lodge No. 89 of B'nai B'rith objected to the letters sent out by the Twelfth District Hebrew Republican Club that appealed for GOP support by noting the large number of GOP appointments of Jews. "The Jews vote as American citizens only—and not as a class or religious body," protested the lodge. Clearly, the issue of ethnic appeals created controversy within ethnic groups themselves, as well as within nativist or "Americanization" ranks.[51]

Ethnic politics remained difficult throughout the 1920s simply because new ethnics still lagged behind in citizenship. In 1930, for example, even after the increased activity of ethnic leaders in Bridgeport and the upswing in electoral interest caused by the 1928 election, 21 percent of Bridgeport's adults, male and female, were still not citizens. The rates of naturalization varied widely by ethnic group. While old ethnic groups like the Irish, English, and Scandinavians had citizenship rates of 70 or 80 percent for both male and female immigrants, the rate of naturalization for new immigrant men ranged from a high of 46.3 percent for Hungarians and 45.9 percent for Italians to a low of 36.2 percent for Lithuanians. Only 26.0 percent of Lithuanian immigrant women were citizens, and even for Hungarians the women's rate was only 37.3 percent. The rates for eastern European nationalities were even lower when we consider that Jews, considerably more Americanized than other eastern European immigrant groups, were also subsumed under these various national categories.[52] (See table 5.)

For new ethnics the problem was twofold: overcoming the negative consequences of fairly recent arrival and penetrating the political life of the city or country. First, this generation of immigrants took an average of ten to twelve years between arrival and application for citizenship. Moreover, fewer new ethnics registered to vote once they had become citizens. The director of immigrant adult education in Bridgeport noted that in 1930 Italians led in attendance at Americanization classes. But he estimated that of the twenty-five thousand Italians in the city, both native and foreign born, only about four thousand were registered voters.[53]

Given the proliferation of Italian political clubs, this information is startling. Italian GOP leaders seemed either unwilling or unable to enroll a majority of their community in the electoral process. Undoubtedly, they took the time to get citizenship papers and voter registrations only for those they knew and those who were pledged to follow their lead on election day. For example, in the Tenth

Table 5. Naturalization Rates for Foreign-born White Residents Twenty-one Years of Age and Older by Sex and Country of Birth, 1930

	Males			Females		
	Population	Naturalized		Population	Naturalized	
City totals[a]	19,999	10,530	(52.7%)	18,607	8,687	(46.7%)
England	1,339	1,003	(74.9%)	1,450	1,013	(69.9%)
Irish Free State	1,144	920	(80.4%)	1,511	1,128	(74.7%)
Sweden	827	499	(60.3%)	737	499	(67.7%)
Germany	1,029	683	(66.4%)	959	647	(67.5%)
Poland	1,826	692	(37.9%)	1,678	507	(30.2%)
Czechoslovakia	2,081	1,071	(51.5%)	2,100	826	(39.3%)
Hungary	1,835	850	(46.3%)	2,000	746	(37.3%)
Russia	1,424	819	(57.5%)	1,137	579	(50.9%)
Italy	4,527	2,076	(45.9%)	3,605	1,156	(32.1%)
Canada-French	437	175	(40.0%)	355	157	(44.2%)
Lithuania	448	162	(36.2%)	358	93	(26.0%)

Source: U.S. Census Bureau, *Population,* 1930, vol. 2: *Statistics by Subjects* (Washington, D.C.: U.S. Government Printing Office, 1930), table 25, p. 478.

a. Includes foreign-born whites from countries other than those listed.

District, which was 69 percent foreign born in 1920 (predominantly Italian and Slovak), only one-fourth of the foreign born were naturalized citizens. Moreover, of the 6,382 adults (all those aged twenty-one or older, native and foreign born), only 1,315, or 20.6 percent, were registered to vote. Even in 1927, after the Italian political leaders had begun to exert their will in GOP political affairs, the number of registered voters in this district had reached only 1,588 (1,129 men and only 459 women), still a minority of those eligible to vote. This meant that mobilization of the full electorate remained to be accomplished.[54]

Connecticut state law made the voter registration process unwieldy. The potential voter was required to submit a written "to be made" application to the town selectmen in advance of the swearing-in date (this was one of the few tasks that town selectmen in cities were elected to perform). The applicant did not need to be present in person—filing was often the task of ward heelers and other party activists. The resident himself or herself then had to appear before the town selectmen on one specified date before the election to complete the registration process. The resident then had to pass a literacy test, defined as the ability to read three selected lines from the Connecticut Statutes or state constitution. The process was complete when the resident was sworn in by the town selectmen and added to the voter list. The elected Board of Registrars, made up of representatives of the two major parties, was assigned the duty of maintaining the voting list, the caucus list (with party identification, to be used in primaries), and the roll of personal tax. This office also supervised the annual door-to-door canvass of the town to confirm the voting lists and make up the personal tax assessment. Ethnic party leaders considered their representation in these offices to be crucially important to their community's political participation, both in enrolling immigrant voters and in keeping them on the rolls.[55]

A final peculiarity of Connecticut tax law stopped many citizens, new and old, from exercising their voting rights. Connecticut law levied an annual "personal tax" on every man and woman aged twenty-one to sixty (women were added to the personal tax list when they gained the vote in 1920) who lived in the city. The Bridgeport Board of Registrars collected the tax each January; the penalty for failure to pay was a fine or imprisonment to work off the tax. Originating from the early nineteenth-century principle that only property holders or taxpayers had citizenship rights that extended to decision making, the personal tax had been a true poll tax in nineteenth-century Connecticut and was still often referred to as a poll tax in the 1920s and 1930s before its repeal in 1935. Given the role of the Board of Registrars in assessing the annual personal tax, many working-class Bridgeporters (as well as others throughout the state) thought that the annual $2 personal tax was a prerequisite for voting. One foreign-born housewife explained why she did not register to vote: "I vote, I pay tax. My man pay tax. One tax enough in the family."[56]

One suspects that the alleged dependence of machine politicians on immigrant voters actually rested with relatively few voters indeed. A problem for all immigrant cities, then, was one of political mobilization in the era of declining voter turnouts.[57] Even if many in their community remained outside the circle of citizenship, Italians became the most visible, and the most vigorous, of the GOP constituencies in Bridgeport. As Yankees and Irish Americans in general began to shrink from active partisanship, new ethnics in Bridgeport stepped in to take their place. While "popular politics," distinguished by nineteenth-century-style electoral hoopla and crowd activity, had declined in much of the country by the 1920s—even in Bridgeport, lamented the *Times-Star*—the Italian politicians reinvigorated city elections.[58] Borrowing from the style of their ever-growing street festivals in the 1920s, Italian GOP leaders orchestrated political marches, complete with brass bands, during the campaign season to continue a visible electoral ritual in an era when politics had moved behind club room doors. For example, on the night before the 1924 presidential election the Italian Republican clubs staged the only campaign parade of the season. It assembled in the Italian districts and then marched to a meeting hall in the center of town, to be addressed by Louis Richards, Paul D'Elia, and John T. King. For the first time Italians made an effort to gain their women's participation; they rode in cars in the march. The Italians, and the Socialist Party's persistence in its street corner campaigns, were all that was left of a nineteenth-century political style.[59]

The expansion of ethnic politics in Bridgeport before 1928 did not come about solely from assertive behavior on the part of the ethnic communities. The structure of local politics and the relationships among constituencies was undergoing change as well. The GOP, for example, needed the participation of new ethnics in order to counter the business challenge by the Republican Voters League.

Mayor Behrens and the Republican Party stayed in power until 1929 by cementing relations with ethnic leaders and by riding the wave of popular indignation about the revaluation of the city's Grand List under the direction of the governor-appointed "Ripper Board" of Appropriation and Taxation, which had raised valuations on residential property. Similarly, GOP accusations that the 1927 Democratic nominee, former mayor Atwater, was antilabor, because he opposed the eight-hour day, had strong resonance in the city in 1927.[60]

Populist themes were still important in Bridgeport politics in the late 1920s, but clearly the key ingredient in the GOP's successful city campaigns was the party's outstanding organizational apparatus. Giving ethnic leaders more access and control in the party assured them of votes, however imperfectly mobilized those communities were. The chief weakness in the structure, however, was precisely this incomplete mobilization of the potential electorate, a weakness that would become apparent in subsequent years.

The 1928 Presidential Election

By the late 1920s the local electoral sphere showed signs of strain. The incumbent local Republicans, having fended off the businessmen's challenge, still faced internal problems. The previously cooperative leaders of immigrant communities chafed under the clientelist relationships that had made the system work. The local GOP's populist appeal for partisan loyalty staved off charges of machine corruption for some time, and through 1927 the party maintained a solid core of about sixteen thousand voters. Its success, however, depended on a weak and divided local and national Democratic Party. Even more troubling, less than half of the potential electorate participated in Bridgeport's elections, a turnout similar to the national one. This left a large group of unattached citizens as potential loose cannons on the electoral deck. The Bridgeport GOP might have survived, however, had not extraordinary changes in the electorate in 1928 upset the political balance in Bridgeport and other cities of the Northeast.

The 1928 contest between Herbert Hoover and Al Smith coincided with the historical development of immigrant working-class communities, shaking loose older partisan alignments and drawing new voters into the electoral sphere. In Bridgeport, as elsewhere, Catholic ethnic communities rallied to the candidacy of Al Smith, whose religion provoked the greatest national controversy in this presidential campaign.

The 1928 election is a central event in the literature on U.S. politics in the interwar years. Here debates about critical election theory, ethnocultural politics, and models of partisan mobilization all intersect. Beginning with Samuel Lubell's identification of an "Al Smith revolution," the 1928 election became a key element of critical election theory. It has been analyzed as a watershed in the transformation of national politics and the transition to a Democratic majority and the New Deal system. Moreover, the 1928 election has been interpreted as a clash of two cultures—a stark duality that set urban, Catholic, new ethnic, and "wet" against rural, Protestant, old ethnic, and "dry." Recent studies have unraveled this neat and all-encompassing duality, but intolerance still looms large in any analysis of the political climate of the late 1920s. Finally, although ethnic participation was high in the 1928 election, the *permanent* incorporation of new groups into the polity was not easily accomplished in this era. Thus the 1928 election was not a shaper of 1930s voting patterns. And, while new ethnics proved themselves interested in the Democratic Party, organization Democrats were little interested in acknowledging their presence.[61]

The analytically useful focus is on the qualitative effects of the 1928 election on Bridgeport politics. The 1928 election mobilized new voters, affected party loyalties in Bridgeport, and undermined the ethnic politics of traditional notables of the 1920s. First, the 1928 election mobilized more new voters in Bridgeport than any other single election of the twenty years before 1940, thus greatly expanding the electoral participation of the city's people. Second, the leadership of the local Democratic Party was challenged from within, and a new set of Irish leaders took over. Third, new ethnics who were already involved in electoral politics increasingly abandoned their traditional leaders and their attachment to the Republican Party. However, new ethnics were only imperfectly incorporated into the Democratic Party by the rising ethnic leaders who scrambled to organize the new voters in the 1929 municipal election. The 1929 city election, which brought a Democrat back to the mayor's seat and Democrats to the common council, turned on the dilemmas of a local Republican Party caught in financial improprieties and had little to do with the lingering effect of Al Smith. The 1928 election in Bridgeport did not prefigure the politics of the 1930s, but it did hasten the crumbling of the existing political order.

The Connecticut Republicans responded to the difficult 1928 campaign with an eye to their very mixed constituency, as they attempted to downplay the ethnic and religious issues raised nationally in order to keep the many Irish and other Catholic ethnics in their party. Connecticut Republicans thus focused all their attention on economic policy. Manufacturing leaders throughout the state were the most prominent boosters of the Republican effort. As Edward O. Goss, president of Waterbury's Scovill Manufacturing Company, GOP presidential elector from Connecticut, and father of state senator Edward W. Goss, reminded readers of the *Bridgeport Sunday Herald*, "The wage earners of the state must not be misled by non-vital issues." Early attempts by GOP manufacturers to influence workers by placing campaign cards inside pay envelopes had fizzled, and the Republicans quickly turned to a barrage of newspaper advertisements. The *Hartford Times*, a Democratic paper, characterized the GOP campaign as "the quadrennial beating of the tom-toms to scare Connecticut factory workers into line."[62]

In the Bridgeport area papers GOP ads relied exclusively on the tariff issue. A typical full-page ad from the Connecticut GOP featured photographs of the state's largest manufacturing plants—Scovill, General Electric, Pratt & Whitney, Winchester—and drove home the message that Connecticut's jobs and consumer prosperity depended on the Republican tariff: "Let's keep what we've got. . . . Keep workingmen's cars parked at these factories! Don't go back to Democratic depression! Protect yourself!"[63] These slogans would, of course, come back to haunt the GOP a year later.

Bridgeport industrialists spoke up in a full-page ad just days before the election. Sixteen local business executives, including A. H. Bullard, DeVer H. Warner, Sumner Simpson, and Carl F. Siemons, signed an ad for Hoover, declaring, "Let's keep what we've got—Prosperity didn't 'just happen.' Let's elect as President America's best business administrator—Herbert Hoover—and keep our jobs and our prosperity." Other local industrialists signed smaller ads under the aegis of the Bridgeport Hoover Engineers Committee, while the Engineers Hoover Committee at the Bullard Machine Tool Company was allowed to hang a Hoover-Curtis banner across Fairfield Avenue in Black Rock near the plant. Most local GOP businessmen signed a final ad on the Sunday before the election simply proclaiming "Prosperity." Richard Howell, editor of the *Bridgeport Sunday Herald*, ridiculed the GOP state ticket, calling it a "well balanced ticket of three bankers, one manufacturer, one merchant and one physician." Howell hinted that whose interests the Republican Party represented in Hartford was no great mystery.[64]

Hoover's running mate, Charles Curtis, toured the state in October and declared loudly to a Bridgeport Republican rally that "bigotry was not the issue."[65] But many rank-and-file Republicans were acutely aware of the religious tension surrounding the campaign. Intolerance hurt the Connecticut GOP, because many Irish and other Catholic groups had become stalwarts in the state GOP machine. As the GOP leader Roraback later ruefully noted, the intemperate remarks of diehard anti-Catholics did affect the GOP vote in the state: "Great indiscretion was manifested among Republicans, particularly the women, in expressing the same views [about Catholics]. . . . The issue was very bitter and the bitterness has not yet gone." He insisted, nonetheless, that many Catholics had "stood loyally by the ticket . . . being subjected to many humiliating remarks of so-called Republicans." Luckily, he noted, the issue had not cost Republicans a statewide victory.[66]

The religious issue became hotter as the campaign wore on. The *Catholic Transcript,* newspaper of the Diocese of Hartford (which encompassed all of Connecticut), declared that while it would not get involved in politics, it would monitor and report on instances of religious bigotry. Late in the campaign the *Bridgeport Sunday Herald* editorialized against bigotry in an editorial headlined "The Viper of Intolerance" and placed blame squarely on the Protestant churches. The circumspect *Bridgeport Post,* the businessman's paper that generally supported Republican national policy, held to a carefully worded neutrality during the campaign but felt compelled to denounce the shrill atmosphere at the end of the campaign that kept "hate fires burning."[67]

The Connecticut Democrats spent relatively little on newspaper ads but relied on news stories, feature articles, daily contact with voters, and the general furor about Smith's candidacy to publicize the campaign. While the state Democratic Party's delegation had earlier agreed to go to the national convention united for Al Smith, the party had split over the state leadership of Thomas Spellacy, who was accused of doing Republican bidding in the state. Reform Democrats nominated Charles Morris and Augustine Lonergan for, respectively, governor and senator in 1928. This rise of a new faction within the Democratic Party, though it did not topple the GOP's statewide hegemony in 1928, would become formidable in the 1930s.[68]

Smith received much coverage from the local media. The *Herald,* for example, ran a full-page feature story on a prominent Connecticut citizen and muckraking journalist, "Ida M. Tarbell Explains Why She Votes Democratic Ticket," while the paper reminded readers that Democrats and Republicans agreed on tariff and economic issues. Bridgeport's local radio station, WICC, broadcast a dramatic reading of the life of Al Smith, based on the Norman Hapgood biography, *Up from the Streets.* For the first time in a long time Bridgeport Democrats rallied large crowds for their campaign events. Franklin Roosevelt, well known and well liked in Bridgeport for his judicious handling of navy industrial issues during the world war, spoke on behalf of the Democratic ticket in Bridgeport to twelve hundred Democrats under the auspices of the Fifth District Democratic Club, while Eleanor Roosevelt held forth at a major women's rally in Bridgeport hosted by the Smith-Robinson League of New Voters of Fairfield County. A last bash by the Democratic Women's Club drew twenty-five hundred to the ballroom at the Pyramid Mosque. Finally, an estimated thirty thousand Bridgeporters turned out to greet Al Smith on his whistle-stop through the state.[69]

As the AFL returned to its nonpartisan stance after the La Follette experiment of 1924, it faced the reality that neither party had seriously courted the labor vote. On the other hand, neither Hoover nor Smith was perceived as antilabor, and the AFL and the railroad brotherhoods had won some favorable legislation under Republican rule. The AFL made no endorsement. Similarly, the Connecticut Federation of Labor made no endorsement, but Connecticut labor leaders were strongly in favor of the Democratic candidate. John J. Egan of Bridgeport, secretary of the Connecticut Federation of Labor, headed the Al Smith labor campaign statewide, while other federation officials and local officers served as subchairmen in each congressional district. Noting that about 60 percent of labor men in the state had been Republican in the past, Egan proclaimed himself fully confident that those who had not been completely won over to the Democratic camp by election time would at least split their ticket for Smith. John J. O'Neil, Jr., loyal Bridgeport Democrat and labor leader, became head of the Smith campaign in Bridgeport and named a committee that included nearly every Central Labor Union delegate except the Socialists, even winning over the former Socialists Minor Treat and Karl Lang. Labor in the state and in Bridge-port carried out its campaigning apart from the regular Democratic Party.[70]

The Socialist Party in Bridgeport cranked up its election apparatus in con-junction with the national candidacy of Norman Thomas and James Maurer and fielded its own state and city slate headed by Jasper McLevy for governor. The SP "offer[ed] itself as the political party of the producing classes, the workers in farm, factory, mine, or office," and called for the panoply of labor legislation it had championed for some time, as well as for civil liberties reforms, higher income taxes for upper brackets, and public ownership of natural resources and the banking system. The national literature highlighted the problem of techno-logical unemployment and the call for an unemployment relief plan, and the Socialists condemned both major parties as "two wings of the same bird of prey."[71] McLevy, as the party's standard-bearer in Connecticut, picked up this theme. "We are living in an age of concentration of industry and capital, and in the natural course of this development the political institutions represent-ing the two big groups have drifted into the same course," he exclaimed at the first big campaign rally of the season. "Grocery stores, drug stores and cigar stores are being organized on a chain-store basis, and the political parties are in the same position." The SP's rhetorical target was corrupt government, which it contrasted with European socialist municipalities that provided "clean and honest administrations," with support for strikes, the workers' housing projects in Vienna, inexpensive transportation, and low utility rates.[72]

McLevy rehearsed points that he would put to great use in a few years. Point-ing to the "usury" of the Connecticut system of levying high interest rates on delinquent property taxes, McLevy pointed to Socialist Milwaukee's system of charging only 6 percent additional interest on unpaid taxes. He stated, "Almost every thrifty person desires to own a home to properly house his family and have some economic security in his declining years. It is the solemn duty of a just government not only to aid him in the accomplishment of this lofty purpose but to protect and guard him against financial shylocks."[73]

The SP was aided in its campaign by the unprecedented attention of the *Herald,* which printed the SP platform, covered SP rallies, and in the last weeks of the campaign even carried political cartoons from the Socialist paper *New Leader,* under a caption "As the Socialists See the Campaign." The *Herald* pro-claimed two weeks before the election that the SP was the only party to actual-ly debate issues and asserted its disgust with the changing nature of politics. In "Socialists Retain Their Sanity," the paper editorialized, "If American politics is a joke, any vote at all is a waste of time and energy. If it is a serious matter, a vote for the socialist party is not a vote wasted, because such a vote at least reg-isters a protest against organizing hypocrisy and buncombe into a national in-stitution." A respectable turnout of about eight hundred citizens heard Norman Thomas speak at Bridgeport Central High School at the end of October.[74]

The Smith campaign caused a shake-up in grassroots politics in Bridgeport.

Al Smith's mass appeal to Catholic ethnics brought over many who had been enmeshed in the local Republican organization or who had forsaken their allegiance to the Democratic Party after World War I. GOP state leaders rightly feared an Irish bolt to the Democrats. The Republicans acknowledged that the Irish were "not naturally Republicans" but had come over on the League of Nations issue in 1920 and then the KKK imbroglio in 1924.[75] Nationally, the Foreign-Language Information Service reported that no monolithic "foreign vote" existed and cited the contrasting endorsements within each ethnic circle.[76]

The "traditional" Republican non-Catholic ethnic groups in Bridgeport— the Swedes, the Germans, and the Jews—were very active. The John Erickson Republican Club, part of a national organization of Swedes, held rallies for Swedish voters in the Third and Fourth Districts. Many Jewish middle-class activists in Bridgeport were committed to Hoover but used this campaign as an opportunity to establish their own political clubs independent of the GOP club structure. Thirteen Jewish businessmen incorporated the Hoover Republican Club in September 1928, and Jewish Republicans from the city's Fourth District set up the Fourth District Independent Hebrew Republican Club to "enlist the support of all the Jewish business and professional men in the district for Hoover." Roraback reported to GOP national headquarters that the Republicans had received about 80 percent of the "Hebrew vote," though he also admitted that "we lost a number of the younger and more irresponsible members of that race."[77]

But key defections from Italian and Polish ranks were what worried Bridgeport GOP leaders. The Polish Republican Club, headed by Americanized professional men, rallied Poles at the St. Joseph National Catholic Church. But the Roman Catholic pastor, normally strongly Republican, sat out the campaign.[78]

The pressures on traditional political arrangements were most obvious in the Italian community, nearly monolithic in its Republican affiliations before this time. Ominously, the first disturbance came from within the party, as rivalry exploded between Italians and others over the state ticket and then over the Italian state senator from the city's Twenty-third Senatorial District. The *Herald* ominously noted, however, that "the Italian vote is said to be leaning toward the candidacy of Governor Al Smith for the presidency, and Republican leaders are doing everything in their power to keep this vote in the Republican column."[79] The tempo of the defection picked up, as Angelo Paonessa, the Democratic mayor of New Britain, presided over the organization of the statewide Italian Committee for Al Smith in mid-September. Two delegates from the Bridgeport Italian Democratic Al Smith Club, including the long-time Democratic loyalist Antonio Abriola, helped coordinate the Bridgeport participation. Emil A. Napolitano, a "faithful worker" for the GOP for twenty years and a justice of the peace, publicly renounced his Republican affiliation, claiming that Italian candidates and Italian voters were given only promises by the GOP; he now declared himself a "full-fledged Democrat."[80]

The Bridgeport GOP depended on its black common council page, Charles Ross (who, it seems, held the only African-American patronage slot), to be "the Moses to tote Negro votes to the polls." Many black leaders in Bridgeport remained loyal to the Republican Party rather than join a defection to the Democrats, and the state GOP reported that blacks in Bridgeport voted for Hoover. However, John E. Robinson, a local black leader, insisted that his community was now divided in two, the "standpat group" loyal to the GOP and a new "progressive group" looking for new political leadership. Frank W. Campbell, an officer of the new Bridgeport Non-Partisan Association, declared in a letter to the editor of the *Herald* that "the Afro-American group has been republicanized for years, but they are waking up in Bridgeport as well as other cities and towns." Citing recent Democratic recognition of black candidates elsewhere, he declared that "the democrats are giving the race man something and not by say-so but by action."[81]

The tide was changing. The *Herald* reported that foreign-speaking Catholics, "heretofore . . . solidly Republican," were now displaying only Smith-Robinson signs in their windows. The Bridgeport Democratic leader John Cornell wore a satisfied smile as he proclaimed to the *Times-Star*, "There has never been such a campaign as this wherein voters have worn their allegiance on their sleeves and glorified in letting everyone know where they stood."[82]

Al Smith Clubs popped up in all districts, even rivaling the regular Democratic district clubs as vehicles for newly mobilizing ethnics. Concentrating for the first time on registering women voters, the Democrats also set up separate Women's Al Smith Clubs in many districts. Lacking many officeholders in their ranks, the Democratic get-out-the-vote effort relied on volunteers, a decided disadvantage. A new city leadership appeared in the person of Archibald McNeil, Jr., a coal wholesaler. The McNeil family, of illustrious standing in the city, traced its ancestry to the 1780s in Bridgeport, and Arch Senior had been the first president of the prestigious Algonquin Club. The elder Archibald McNeil had been an important influence in the Bridgeport and national Democratic Parties and a close friend of William Jennings Bryan. The son had been the first in Bridgeport on the Al Smith bandwagon in 1926, beginning in his local power base of the Fifth District, and played the most prominent role in Bridgeport's 1928 campaign. It was he who brought new Irish community leaders to the fore in the Democratic Party.[83]

Both numerically and proportionally, more Bridgeport voters entered the electoral system in 1928 than in any other election year from 1921 to 1940. In all, 10,375 "newly made" voters were enrolled in 1928, a 26 percent increase over the previous year's voter list (the usual increment each year averaged two to three thousand). The women's column gained 5,672 newly enrolled voters, while the men's rolls increased 3,395. Both Republicans and Democrats saw "women 70 and 80 years of age, barely able to hobble, becoming voters for the first time."[84] The Bridgeport GOP conceded that new voters were about 60 percent Democratic and 40 percent Republican. But in the hotly contested Third District, in the largely Hungarian West End, which had voted Republican in the last municipal election, "an unusually large number of applications, by both men and women . . . has been filed entirely independent of the party organization," noted the neighborhood *Black Rock News*. The paper speculated that this "indicat[ed] an exceptional enthusiasm in the forthcoming election."[85]

The transfer of party loyalty occurred at the grassroots level. Once again, neighborhood clubs and family relationships were often the ties that now brought newly awakened ethnics into the Democratic camp. Liberat Dattolo, who had come to the United States in 1915, explained how he wound up voting Democratic in the late 1920s: "That time . . . all the people were on the Democratic side, and these men in the [political] clubs used to tell me that the Republicans had all the money and the Democrats were for the poor working people. . . . These people said that all the Irish people had the clubs, and they were mostly Republicans, and they were no good. Sometimes we used to get some men like [Antonio] Abriola in the club, and he used to tell all the people to be Democrats."[86] Thus the Al Smith campaign benefited from both newly mobilized voters and voters who switched party loyalty.

Moreover, the 1928 election established the high level of voter participation in Bridgeport that continued into the 1930s. Registered voters as a percentage of the voting age population (citizens twenty-one and older) jumped from roughly 60 percent before 1928 to nearly 71 percent in 1928 and leveled off at about 70–75 percent for the 1930s. Similarly, the turnout for the 1928 election (the percentage of voters who cast ballots) rose to 93.8 percent. The turnouts in the 1932, 1936, and 1940 presidential elections were not far behind. Women's participation lagged somewhat behind men's. By all measures, Bridgeport citizens reached a new level of participation in the political process, as was the case nationally. (See table 6.)

Al Smith won in Bridgeport, with 24,448 votes, or 53 percent of the votes cast. It was the first win for the Democrats since the manufacturer-dominated municipal election of 1921 when Fred Atwater had received 53 percent, or 16,226 votes. In 1928 the Democrats lost at the state level as usual, but a key portent for the future was that the cities of Bridgeport, New Haven, Hartford, and Waterbury went Democratic. Bridgeport also sent Democrats to the state capital. More important for the structure of Bridgeport politics, all but three districts elected Democratic candidates to the common council, which broke the Republican monopoly. Only the First District, which was the sparsely populated downtown area; the Third, where GOP Swedes carried the district despite the newly organized Democratic Hungarians; and the Fifth, the silk-stocking ward, retained Republican majorities.

Various ethnic constituencies were represented on both slates but now with a subtle shift, because party sometimes overshadowed ethnicity in the voters' choices. The most prominent new ethnic on the local Republican slate, Joseph

Table 6. Bridgeport Election Results, 1920–40

Year (Campaign)	Potential Electorate	Registered Voters	Total Votes	Turnout	Democrat	Republican	Socialist	Other
1920 (president)	61,274	37,105	33,869	91.3%	31.3%	63.6%	3.8%	1.3%
1921 (mayor)		37,827	30,280	80.0	53.7	39.8	6.5	—
1922 (governor)		36,417	24,714	67.9	47.1	49.7	3.1	—
1923 (mayor)		36,209	26,280	72.6	46.7	47.1	6.2	—
1924 (president)		38,527	32,347	84.4	19.3	62.1	17.9	0.7
1925 (mayor)		39,573	31,163	78.8	46.2	51.5	2.4	—
1926 (governor)		38,820	24,778	63.6	29.7	67.7	2.6	—
1927 (mayor)		39,958	29,780	74.5	40.7	54.3	5.0	—
1928 (president)		49,025	46,008	93.8	53.1	45.7	0.8	0.4
1929 (mayor)		48,117	37,770	78.5	55.6	38.8	5.2	0.3
1930 (governor)	69,922	48,829	37,446	76.7	57.9	38.2	3.3	0.4
1931 (mayor)		51,546	42,698	82.8	41.9	21.9	35.3	0.8
1932 (president)		54,642	49,713	91.0	50.5	40.1	8.7	0.8
1933 (mayor)		55,497	46,345	83.5	35.3	15.8	48.4	0.4
1934 (governor)		55,475	41,418	74.7	29.9	26.4	40.0	3.8
1935 (mayor)		55,803	43,823	78.5	20.3	23.7	55.4	0.7
1936 (president)		59,696	53,409	89.5	64.2	27.1	3.7	5.0
1937 (mayor)		57,994	41,554	71.7	21.6	9.7	68.7	—
1938 (governor)		58,961	46,174	78.3	30.5	18.8	47.8	2.9
1939 (mayor)		58,653	40,211	68.6	26.7	14.6	57.5	1.2
1940 (president)	86,132	62,408	54,632	87.5	65.3	34.6	—	0.1

Source: U.S. Census Bureau, *Population, 1920, vol. 3: By States* (Washington, D.C.: U.S. Government Printing Office, 1920), table 13, p. 162; U.S. Census Bureau, *Population, Vol. 2: Characteristics of Population, 1940* (Washington, D.C.: U.S. Government Printing Office, 1920), table A-37, p. 854; Registrar of Voters, *Book of Elections,* 1920–40; City of Bridgeport, "Official Returns of Election," *Municipal Register,* 1921–40.

Cubelli, who was running for reelection as state senator from the Twenty-third District, lost to the Democrat, an Irish-American machinist. The young Jewish-American lawyer, David Goldstein, captured the state senate seat in the Twenty-second District (called the "Irish" district) for the Democratic Party; he had been opposed by an Irish-Catholic Republican. Two first-generation ethnics were elected as Democrats to the common council, an Italian in the Eleventh District, and a Slovak in the Twelfth (both districts were on the ethnic East Side)—a new practice for both areas and a surprise to many, given the supposed GOP lock on these districts. Though a mostly Irish sea of candidates overwhelmed the new ethnics in the Democratic Party, the Irish and Italian Democrats had already forged some social ties. The Italian Eleventh District candidate, Joseph Massicotte, an accountant in a local manufacturing firm, was active in the Knights of Columbus, as were most of the Irish candidates. On the other hand, the successful Slovak candidate, Andrew Nagy, a meat cutter, had his own independent constituency. Nagy was from the Kassa region of the old Hungarian empire, an area that had furnished some of the earliest Magyar and Slovak settlers to Bridgeport, and he was supreme secretary of the First Slovak Union.[87]

Tension existed between new ethnics and others within the Republican Party at this time, the beginning of an internal rejection of the Behrens organization and its dependence on traditional ethnic elites. On the other hand, although the Irish leaders in the Democratic Party welcomed voters from eastern and southern European backgrounds, they made little room for the newcomers in the party structure. Indeed, throughout the state, Democrats had an opportunity to woo disgruntled Italian GOP leaders "but the stupidity—or the treachery—of the local Democratic leaders dashed these plans," according to the *Herald*.[88]

The 1929 Municipal Campaign

Ethnic party allegiances had undergone serious change during 1928. The Al Smith revolution had touched the rank-and-file voter, but had it influenced the leadership? The municipal election of 1929 revealed the shape of the future. In early 1929 the Democrats on the new common council began the financial probe they had been threatening from the sidelines for several years. The Yellow Mill Bridge project, a major construction effort funded with city bond money, had run seriously over budget, and allegations of favoritism in the letting of contracts seemed to doom William Behrens, the incumbent GOP mayor.

Once again, the main campaign cry of the local Democrats was GOP corruption. In late 1928 some Democrats, led by John J. O'Neil, Jr., the local labor leader, formed a "Buckingham for Mayor" committee within the Democratic Party. Edward T. Buckingham, a Yale Law School graduate with Yankee forebears who had settled in in Connecticut in the 1600s, had been the Democratic mayor of

Bridgeport from 1909 to 1911, had served as state workers' compensation commissioner from 1913 to 1928, and had actually gained the most votes of all local Democratic candidates in 1928, even though he was running for a relatively obscure position on the board of education. A Congregationalist, he made much of his support for the cause of Irish freedom and was well regarded by workers and manufacturers alike for his fair decisions on labor compensation cases.[89]

Pledging a "clean, honest, decent government" for Bridgeport, Buckingham was supported by leading local manufacturers and the "Ripper Board" of Apportionment. Thanks to a working relationship forged by Al Smith activists and the manufacturers' organization, the erstwhile Republican Voters League (RVL), the Democratic Party now represented a formidable challenge in the municipal arena. Even the businessmen who led the Young Men's and Young Women's Republican organization followed the RVL and stumped for the Democrat Buckingham, not the Republican, Behrens.[90]

Thus, despite the new ethnics in its membership, the Democratic Party was presenting the same face as it had in 1921: a Yankee mayoral candidate and industrialist supporters. Nor did Democrats offer many other slots to new ethnics in the 1929 contest; their municipal slate was overwhelmingly Irish. In an interesting change Germans, usually strong GOP supporters, now made up the second-largest group on the Democratic slate, although they were a distant second. Only one new ethnic, Luciano Veronese, ran as a Democrat, for the relatively unimportant position of town selectman. Nonetheless, Buckingham and his campaign workers doggedly pursued the new ethnic vote, with speeches at Greek, Lithuanian, and Hungarian halls and rallies sponsored by the Twelfth District Slovak Club and the Colored Political and Civic Association. Hotly disputed claims for the allegiance of African Americans and Italians spilled across the letters to the editor pages of the *Herald*.

The local Republicans, staggering from the defections of the previous year and bickering within, allowed Behrens to run for reelection in an effort to vindicate his administration. It seemed to many observers that one GOP faction, which was grouped around John Schwartz, a building-supply contractor who served as building commissioner, wanted to see Behrens and his supporters defeated in order to clear the way for their group. The *Herald* illustrated the turnabout in local Republican fortunes. The newspaper, which had supported King until his death in 1926 and his Republicans through all the difficult years, now turned away, editorializing: "When John T. King was running the republican party a conscientious paper could support it. King's policies were expensive, but they built up the city of Bridgeport. . . . During all the years John T. King ran the government of this city there was less corruption than there has been in the four short years now closing under the gang which occupies his shoes, but does not fill them."[91] In other words, the paper no longer viewed local Republicans as "defenders of the people," as they had been in 1925.

Curiously, given the rupture of grassroots ethnic support for the GOP, more new ethnic candidates appeared on the Republican ballot than had ever been allowed before. Clearly, despite the growing friction between traditional ethnic leaders and the party, the party could not do without their participation. Donato Delia ran for sheriff, while the Hungarian Albert Bodnar in the Third District and Michele Altieri in the Tenth tried to win back these ethnic districts for the Republicans. Indeed, Italian GOP leaders were desperate to keep their constituency in line. Rousing Italians to "the great contest," *La Sentinella* urged voters to compare the number of Italian names on the GOP line to the slate offered by the "other party." The paper called upon its readers to vote "Italianly" (*Italianamente*) and "with all your Italian feelings" for Behrens and the Republicans, "true friends of our people."[92]

The GOP was swept from office with a greater margin of victory for the Democrats than in the 1928 Bridgeport totals, though with a lower voter turnout. Buckingham captured nearly 21,000 votes (56 percent of the vote) to Behrens's 14,660, with the SP gaining 1,968 votes. The only Republican candidate to win was Robert Cherry, a member of the typographers union who won a seat on the common council from the First District, thanks to ticket splitting. In the Italian Tenth District, the GOP candidate, Michele Altieri, lost his common council race by only 38 votes (of 1,530 cast). The spoiler in this district turned out to be Peter Wojcicki, a popular Socialist who garnered 102 votes. Indeed, the Socialist slate, which claimed 5 percent of the vote, ensured Democratic victory in many races. In the heat of the last days of the campaign, the local newspapers took little notice of the New York stock market crash.

The newly enfranchised ethnic voters, however, were not yet firmly wedded to the Democratic Party. What was certain was that the traditional ethnic political leaders were no longer in control of their communities. For example, the Polish leaders in the GOP, Dr. Smykowski and Reverend Ratajczak, had not raised their heads at all during the 1928 or 1929 election seasons. Italian community notables felt the situation had gotten out of hand. Although they had rebelled against the politics of deference that had frustrated their ambitions within the local GOP, they still expected deference from their constituents. The Italian-American Republican Central Association, operating from its faltering center at the Sons of Italy hall, represented the old politics of Richards, the D'Elias, Cubelli, the Altieris, and their followers. As they ruefully noted, the local landslide for the Democrats in 1929 had meant a great loss for their leadership.[93]

Ethnic politics was now a competitive arena, and many activists now bid for constituents. "There has been too much of this business of a man opening a store and putting ["Political Club"] on the window, gathering 20 or 30 voters and engaging in the sale of beverages," noted Joseph Adiletta, the Republican president of Enrico Caruso Sons of Italy Lodge. Challenging these "speakeasy politicians," Adiletta called for them to "meet in a large place and bring the politics of the city out in the open."[94] In the late 1920s traditional Italian and Polish notables still had prestige, but American politics was passing them by. They had been aided in the 1920s by members of the second generation who aspired to elite status but were ultimately overshadowed by the popular mobilization of the Al Smith campaign.

Although the Al Smith campaign had opened the door to the participation of new ethnics in the electoral process, it had left the question of political leadership unresolved. The Democratic leaders had to consolidate the new voters into their organization. Would appeals to ethnic solidarity work? And how much power would they have to hand over to ethnic members of the party? On the other side, the fading traditional ethnic leaders as well as ambitious newcomers had to find the appeal—ethnic, religious, economic, or ethical—that would rally voters behind them. Clearly, ballot slots and patronage were insufficient.

CHAPTER 4

Working People, 1922–32

"The long arm of the job" affected every aspect of the lives of Bridgeport working people, as was noted in the famous contemporary study of another 1920s city, *Middletown*.[1] But work was different than it had been before and during the war. The forces of technological and managerial change, the rightward turn in U.S. politics, the ascendance of business thinking—all combined to make work a locus for new perceptions of modern life and identity. Ethnic working-class institutions survived in the 1920s by adapting to the Americanizing ethos of the time and following their middle-class leaders into the American game of electoral politics. Just as ethnic institutions hung onto their separate organizations, so did the remnants of leftist parties and labor unions. Unions either adapted to the new tone, for example, in the AFL's 1923 proclamation, *Industry's Manifest Duty*, or resisted managerial innovations until the unions were defeated. Both adaptations contributed to the patterns of organization in Bridgeport.[2]

While it is often convenient to speak of decades—1910s, 1920s, 1930s—this chronological division too often simplifies the story. Labor historians have called the 1920s the "lean years" because of the dire effects of the era on the labor movement, whereas others have heralded it as the "age of prosperity" because of the tremendous vigor of the economy. But this prosperity lasted in Bridgeport (and much of the country) only from 1922 to 1929—never mind that for most working people, the prosperity did not reach deep enough into their economic level to alter their lives. For most working people the period between the end of the postwar recession and the beginning of what was to become the Great Depression in 1929 was nothing more than seven years of steady work. As an unskilled immigrant worker recalled the year 1929, "We were not surprised by hard times. . . . It was normal, it happened to us before in 1922 and 1923."[3] This chapter surveys the legacy of unionism and radicalism as it was manifested in Bridgeport workplaces and neighborhoods in the 1920s, the social effects of the early Great Depression, and the consequent organization in the workplace.

Bridgeport's conversion to a peacetime economy was long and wrenching. The productive capacity of the city, which expanded during the war years to its 1919 peak of 42,862 wage earners producing $208 million worth of products, was not reached again during the 1920s and 1930s, although its population remained steady. Only another world war would again bring significant economic expansion.[4] The munitions and machine tool industries were doomed to excess capacity after the First World War. Companies like Remington Arms–UMC Company successfully switched from producing munitions to making sporting guns, cutlery, and business machines. Others, like the Lake Torpedo Boat Company, found their markets suddenly nonexistent. This firm was a casualty of the postwar era. Similarly, some Bridgeport products, such as the deluxe touring cars produced by the Locomobile Company, lost their competitive edge to auto companies in the Midwest.

Some Bridgeport firms made the successful switch to the new growth industries of the 1920s, producing parts for the automobile and electrical industries. The expansion of the electrical machinery and parts industries saved the 1920s economy of Bridgeport. The General Electric Company (GE) was a concrete expression of this new trend; in 1921 it purchased the giant Remington Arms rifle plant to establish its own operations in the city. By the end of the decade GE ranked among Bridgeport's largest employers. Bridgeport even captured an early lead in the new aviation field with the location of Sikorsky Aircraft Company on its border in Stratford in 1929.[5]

Bridgeport remained the "Industrial Capitol of Connecticut," its moniker reflected in the call letters of its first radio station, WICC, which was established in 1924. Yet no single firm dominated the economy in the 1920s, and the city's industrial base remained a mix of locally owned corporations and subsidiaries of national corporations. During the decade the Bridgeport Chamber of Commerce made extensive efforts to bring more industrial firms to the city.[6] The city was also a mercantile center for the surrounding region. Thus, while 60.3 percent of Bridgeport's labor force in 1920 was engaged in manufacturing, a significant minority of people worked in commerce and in white-collar jobs. From 1920 to 1930 the number of people gainfully employed in the manufacturing and mechanical sector decreased, while the number working in trades, services, and the professions grew. This included a growing number of women in professional jobs as teachers and nurses. (See tables 7–9 for labor force numbers.)

The decade brought prosperity and opportunity to some and stability for many. The high points of industrial activity in Bridgeport came in 1923 and 1929, though the city never approached the level of 1920. For the stabilized working class of the 1920s, jobs in Bridgeport's factories were steady, but the job market

Table 7. Occupations of All Gainfully Employed Persons Ten Years of Age and Older, 1920 and 1930

	1920		1930	
Manufacturing	38,506	(60.3%)	32,448	(50.6%)
Transportation	3,234	(5.1%)	4,070	(6.4%)
Trade	6,185	(9.7%)	8,903	(13.9%)
Public service	1,202	(1.9%)	1,454	(2.3%)
Professional	2,960	(4.6%)	4,093	(6.4%)
Domestic/service	3,928	(6.1%)	5,054	(7.9%)
Clerical	7,644	(12.0%)	7,539	(11.8%)
Agriculture/extractive	237	(0.4%)	504	(0.8%)
Totals	63,896	(100.1%)	64,065	(100.1%)

Sources: U.S. Census Bureau, *Population,* 1920, vol. 4: *Occupations* (Washington, D.C.: U.S. Government Printing Office, 1920); U.S. Census Bureau, *Population,* 1930, vol. 4: *Occupations* (Washington, D.C.: U.S. Government Printing Office, 1930).

Table 8. Bridgeport Labor Force by Sex, 1920 and 1930

	Males				Females			
	1920		1930		1920		1930	
Manufacturing	31,203	(64.5%)	25,925	(55.5%)	7,303	(47.0%)	6,523	(37.5%)
Transportation	3,037	(6.3%)	3,704	(7.9%)	197	(1.3%)	366	(2.1%)
Trade	5,180	(10.7%)	7,474	(16.0%)	1,005	(6.5%)	1,429	(8.2%)
Public service	1,199	(2.5%)	1,442	(3.1%)	3	(0.0%)	12	(0.1%)
Professional	1,759	(3.6%)	1,994	(4.3%)	1,201	(7.7%)	2,099	(12.1%)
Service	1,923	(4.0%)	2,193	(4.7%)	2,005	(12.9%)	2,861	(16.5%)
Clerical	3,835	(7.9%)	3,471	(7.4%)	3,809	(24.5%)	4,068	(23.4%)
Agriculture/ extractive	233	(0.5%)	499	(1.1%)	4	(0.0%)	5	(0.0%)
Total	48,369	(100.0%)	46,702	(100.0%)	15,527	(99.9%)	17,363	(99.9%)

Sources: U.S. Census Bureau, *Population,* 1920, vol. 4: *Occupations* (Washington, D.C.: U.S. Government Printing Office, 1920); U.S. Census Bureau, *Population,* 1930, vol. 4: *Occupations* (Washington, D.C.: U.S. Government Printing Office, 1930).

Table 9. Bridgeport Population (Ten Years and Older) in the Labor Force and the Manufacturing Labor Force by Sex and Ethnicity, 1920 and 1930

	1920		1930	
	Labor Force	Manufacturing Labor Force	Labor Force	Manufacturing Labor Force
Males				
Native-born/native-born parents	24.8%	20.7%		
Native-born/foreign-born parents[a]	25.3	22.5	55.9%[b]	47.8%[b]
Foreign-born	47.7	54.9	41.1	49.7
Black	2.0	1.8	2.5	2.4
Females				
Native-born/native-born parents	27.8	19.3		
Native-born/foreign-born parents[a]	41.1	40.1	75.7[b]	68.5[b]
Foreign-born	28.7	39.4	21.7	30.6
Black	2.3	1.1	2.6	0.9

Sources: U.S. Census Bureau, *Population,* 1920, vol. 4: *Occupations* (Washington, D.C.: U.S. Government Printing Office, 1920), table 2, pp. 1065–68; U.S. Census Bureau, *Population,* 1930, vol. 4: *Occupations* (Washington, D.C.: U.S. Government Printing Office, 1930), table 12, pp. 275–77. Data on other races not available.

a. Includes one foreign-born parent.

b. The 1930 census no longer separated native-born children of foreign-born parents from the general category of native-born persons for midsized cities like Bridgeport.

expanded little during the decade. The increased productivity in industry and new forms of management control had reshaped the workplace fundamentally, destroying jobs for some while creating new jobs for others.

A majority of industrial workers in Bridgeport worked in large factories. According to the 1919 *Census of Manufacturers,* thirteen, mostly metalworking, plants in Bridgeport—each of which employed more than one thousand employees—employed 64 percent of all Bridgeport wage earners.[7] The world of paid work in Bridgeport was, like elsewhere, a predominantly male world, though the city had a female participation in the waged labor force that was higher than the national average. Moreover, the world of work was overwhelmingly a world of the foreign born and their native-born children, a characteristic that diminished only slightly in the 1930s. Foreign-born workers held the majority of unskilled laborer and semiskilled operative positions, mostly in metalworking, and this was the largest category in the male manufacturing workforce in the 1920s and 1930s. But foreign-born men were also represented in skilled positions. In 1920 half of the city's machinists and carpenters, along with 83 percent of the brass and iron molders and casters, were foreign born.

Bridgeport's great industrial expansion in the metal trades had attracted those with apprentice training in these skills, while the city's physical expansion created a ready market for those with construction skills. Since the 1880s immigrants from northern and central Europe had joined native-born Americans in dominating many skilled metal trades and building crafts in the city. Newly arriving British, German, and Swedish immigrants found a niche in Bridgeport's foundries and machine shops. Many were already prepared with European apprenticeship training or were able to gain entrance because of community solidarity with a foreman or craftsman from their ethnic group, church, or lodge.

Less commonly, eastern European immigrants entered the skilled trades by virtue of an apprenticeship in the old country or an unusual opportunity to learn in the United States. Peter P. Wojcicki, a long-time leader of the Polish Socialist Alliance in Bridgeport, had learned the machinist trade in Warsaw before emigrating to the United States. Though he knew no English, he found a job as a machinist by "pointing to a machine and *showing* the boss the skills he had."[8] Contact with the German community, especially the Lutheran Church, often facilitated entry into skilled trades for some Slovaks, Hungarians, and others who spoke German. Stephen Havanich, a Slovak who had trained in Hungary as a cabinetmaker, credited "the German influence" for the Slovak impetus to learn trades. "Even now [1940]," he noted, "most of the tools used by the Slovak tradesmen are referred to by their German names."[9]

Ethnic antagonism continued in the workplace during the 1920s and 1930s. One Polish machinist recalled that even in the 1930s, when he was working as a toolmaker at Singer Sewing Machine Company with mostly English or German workmates, "we [were] always having arguments about what nationalities make the best machinists." He had come to Bridgeport as a child and had learned the machinist trade at the local trade school, a new avenue for advancement in the early part of the century. By the beginning of the war, he had worked his way up from machinist helper to toolmaker at the Union Metallic Cartridge Company and was one of the privileged workers who retained his skill in the face of managerial reorganization.[10]

Immigrants worked in many independent crafts as well. In 1920 three-quarters of the city's bakers were foreign born, as were almost all the tailors and shoemakers; most came from southern and eastern Europe. Even the hierarchy of trades was similar to that in the Old World. "In Italy," explained an Italian-born mason, "the good mason is like the sculptor, the engineer—he is higher class. The barber and the tailor is low class." This was so because the latter trades "anybody could learn, easy." An Italian tailor explained that when he had arrived in the United States in 1921, he found that he could not set up shop as he had in Italy, so he got a job in a coat and suit factory while studying design. He then started his own tailor shop in Bridgeport in the late 1920s, which he held on to throughout the depression.[11]

But by the 1920s the independent crafts, just like independent retailers of all sorts, were under assault by the new methods of manufacturing and marketing. Although the mason's trade continued in some construction in the 1920s, the Italian mason complained that the use of concrete "had ruin[ed] the mason trade." Havanich, the Slovak cabinetmaker, set up a steamship ticket and foreign-exchange business in the 1920s; he explained why he was no longer in his trade: "Machinery. . . . those working at the trade are no longer considered to be craftsmen, instead they are assemblers, just as in any other type of work." An immigrant trained in Italy as a tailor and barber complained that his barber shop was no longer making enough money. By the midtwenties a price war in the barber shops had "spoiled everything." This trend only accelerated in the 1930s. A Polish barber agreed that "the business is good for nothing." In the 1930s his three sons were training to be mechanics.[12]

Despite industrialists' attention to new styles of management in the 1920s, finding work, especially for operators and laborers, still depended on personal, familial, or community contact with employers. Mr. A.T., who came from Italy to Bridgeport in 1923 to join his older brother, recalled that his brother arranged a laborer's job for him in the old-fashioned way, by talking to his foreman, also an Italian, at the Crane Company. One Slovak worker related that he had worked in foundries "since I was 18 years old in the old country." After some years in Ohio and Pennsylvania, when he finally arrived in Bridgeport after the war, his relatives told him to "see Jankura, the man in the employment office in Bridgeport Brass Company. They told me he was a Slovak, and might give me a job because I was the same nationality." Jankura gave him a job. The company had hired Stephen Jankura as employment manager in the early 1920s. In the 1930s he was honored as a leader in the Slovak community solely by virtue of his management position at the brass mill.[13] Centralized managerial procedures did not replace the prewar pattern of job recruitment. Thus the Bridgeport Brass Company combined company unionism, welfare policies, and personnel management with old-fashioned ethnic ties in order to cement relationships between management and its workers. Similarly, the recommendation of the immigrant pastor who remained on good terms with the Manufacturers' Association, or membership in the fraternal lodge that refrained from political arguments, might help members to get a job.[14]

Immigrant women were clustered in industrial jobs. U.S.-born daughters of foreign-born parents were found equally in manufacturing and in clerical jobs in the 1920s. Those in clerical positions were generally from northern European backgrounds. Even in the late 1930s employment agencies found it hard to place Italian-American or Jewish-American women in white-collar positions. The clerical sector, though growing in this period, provided opportunities for only some Bridgeport women.[15] As many women were running machines at corset factories as were working as stenographers and typists in 1920. In 1930 more Bridgeport women were working as domestic servants than as stenographers and typists. Married women searching for work encountered discrimination in some factories—GE, for one, rarely hired married women, except under special circumstances—and experienced difficulty in finding day care.[16]

African-American men and women, who accounted for just 2 percent of Bridgeport's population, occupied only a few categories of work during the decade. A few black men held more skilled manufacturing positions, but most were laborers in brass mills and cartridge factories. Black women had even fewer options; in 1920 and 1930 the vast majority were domestic servants. Women did not break the color line in industry until World War II.[17]

On the Job

With the battles about unionization and de-skilling won by management, manufacturing in the city settled into stable patterns until 1929. Major Bridgeport manufacturers, which now took the sophisticated industrial relations approach exemplified by Rockefeller-influenced management specialists, moved to create harmony on the shop floor, with shop committees, new welfare capitalist employee benefits, and a "new spirit in industry."[18] The steady technological advances and the stabilization of the Bridgeport economy meant that workers no longer could easily change jobs. Manufacturers in Bridgeport carefully managed the size of the local workforce during the 1920s to ensure this stability. The Manufacturers' Association recruited workers to the city through extensive advertising in regional and foreign-language newspapers in order to avoid labor shortages. They paid careful attention to the equalization of wage rates in many companies throughout the city and adopted a GE-devised wage scheme regarding starting rates. All this effort was in the interest of forestalling labor unrest and preventing competition among factories for workers.[19]

Bridgeport employers waged the Open Shop Drive and instituted the American Plan in the early 1920s, just as their counterparts did in industrial centers elsewhere in the country. While the open shop clothed itself in the rhetoric of free choice and an end to union "monopoly," it was clearly aimed at ferreting out union organization.[20] On the other hand, the American Plan entailed establishment of the employee representation plan (ERP), designed as a substitute for outside unionization and to promote workers' trust in their bosses.[21]

In the 1920s Bridgeport employers enthusiastically instituted employee representation committees, bonus and stock ownership plans, such amenities as lunch rooms, cooperative grocery stores, life insurance and sick benefit organizations, and baseball teams to wed their employees to the firm and to discourage participation in similar ethnic or union institutions. Twenty Bridgeport manufacturers, employing an estimated thirty thousand workers, had functioning ERPs in place in the spring of 1920. The "Bridgeport Plan" adapted the federal government's wartime shop committee system to the postwar period but now with no outside government regulation and no outside union representation. These employee representation plans for each firm usually had a structure of three worker representatives from each department, an executive committee made up of chairmen of the department committees, and an equal number of management representatives to administer a grievance procedure. All workers were allowed to vote in department elections, though eligibility for committee positions was restricted by certain criteria. At a minimum committee nominees had to be U.S. citizens and have three months' tenure at their jobs—some shops required a year's service. In the absence of strong union pressure the selection process resulted in committee delegates who were older, had longer service records, and were proportionally more native born than the workforce as a whole. The plan did not include a citywide committee of employee representatives (as was part of the National War Labor Board [NWLB] structure), because each company preferred to focus on its individual labor force. Indeed, managers were determined to leave behind this citywide aspect of the NWLB plan.[22]

The largest Bridgeport manufacturers supported the concept of employee representation plans. Alpheus Winter, the former local NWLB examiner and now general manager of the MAB, pronounced the ERPs to be "reasonably successful . . . in large plants presenting complicated problems." In a review of the plans eight firms—Remington Arms, Bridgeport Brass, Bullard Machine, Singer, Holmes and Edwards, Max Ams Machine, Automatic Machine, and Nilson Machine—affirmed that the plans had improved employee morale. Stanley H. Bullard, whose shop had inaugurated a plan two months before the August 1918 NWLB decision mandating shop committees for the duration of the war, insisted that the plan had preserved the "close-small-shop-relationship despite our very great increases in plant and workmen." Others, like the managements at Locomobile Company and Columbia Graphophone, weren't so sure.[23]

As labor conflict seemed to subside, managers grew bolder in promoting the "business man's view" of the economy. George S. Hawley, MAB president during most of the 1920s, noted that employers "use the committee [the ERP] as a means of education of both management and men . . . [for] the creation of good will and better understanding as well as the peaceful settlement of disputes." For example, in 1923 Bridgeport Brass inaugurated classes for members of its shop committees, 200 to 250 people, to explain the financial workings of the company. Using such visual aids as three-dimensional colored blocks, the lessons illustrated the dollar value of sales, the costs of factors of production, the way wage rates were determined, and finally the "real" level of profits (about 5 percent, management claimed). In addition, other lectures featured more general topics, such as "What Economics Is about and Why It Should Interest Us," "What Determines Prices," and "What Banks Are for and How Things Are Paid for." The company was pleased to report that the classes were widely attended. C. F. Dietz, president of Bridgeport Brass and chairman of the Industrial Relations Committee of the Manufacturers' Association of Connecticut, noted that his company's goal was to combat "the seeds of discontent" spread by propagandists. Bridgeport Brass also used petitions gathered at its ERP meetings to lobby on behalf of favorable tariff bills before Congress.[24]

However, the National Civic Federation polled major employers and found that by 1929, company interest in forms of welfare capitalism had diminished and many fringe benefits and most ERPs had disappeared. Bridgeport Brass and the New York, New Haven and Hartford Railroad, two of the strongest advocates of company unions in the state, had both abandoned their ERPs by 1929. Clearly, many companies thought that they no longer needed such weapons against labor unrest.[25]

The exemplar of the new industrial relations nationally was the newest employer in Bridgeport, General Electric. GE had leased the giant Remington Rifle factory in 1920 (and bought the whole facility in 1921), and a management team moved from Schenectady to set up operations in Bridgeport. Throughout the decade GE steadily transferred production assembly divisions from other plants to the Bridgeport site. By 1929 it employed more than thirty-three hundred men and women making appliances, electrical parts, and industrial components for other GE assembly facilities. Nationally, GE's innovative management had pioneered in using works councils (ERPs) as a substitute for unionism; introduced a wide variety of benefits for long-term employees, such as pensions, paid vacations, stock options, and life insurance; and sponsored a mutual benefit association for employees' own contributions toward sick pay. It also rationalized production and introduced the Bedeaux system of premium pay to the city. Its company newsletter, the *Bridgeport Works News,* filled its pages with information about plant production, benefits granted to employees that month, a column on new consumer products and their availability to employees at a discount, citizenship news, a women's section with wedding announcements, a sports column, and a safety column done in black dialect with a blackface cartoon.[26]

The Bridgeport GE employee clubs active in the 1920s included the Athletic Association, which ran the gym on company premises; baseball and basketball teams for the city's Industrial League; and a Women's Athletic Association, as well as the Firemen's Association, Foremen's Association, Sunshine Club, French Point Club, and the Quarter Century Club. Yet this profusion of club activity was not evidence that the entire workforce was involved. The few figures published by the company indicate that workers were selective in the company benefits they used. For example, while 94 percent of Bridgeport GE's employees took out additional life insurance through the company plan, only 44 percent (the next-to-lowest participation rate of any GE plant) were members of the GE Mutual Benefit Association (GEMBA), a situation that management deplored. Moreover, an examination of the lists of officers and the department representatives of GEMBA reveals a preponderance of English, Irish, and German surnames among both men and women members; this would seem an indication that new ethnic workers had declined to participate.[27]

Those workers may have been attracted to other options. The 1920s were the years of the greatest participation in immigrant fraternal benefit societies, which may have provided more congenial group surroundings and more in the way of community support than the company association, perhaps at a lower cost.

The sports pages of the Bridgeport newspapers show that the ethnic leagues, the Building Trades Council league, and other community groups were just as active as company sports leagues. In addition, two blocks from the GE plant on Bridgeport's East Side were three Sokol gymnasiums maintained by Czech and Slovak fraternal groups. Finally, even as national industrial relations experts discussed and critiqued GE's company unionism and velvet-gloved approach in the 1920s, the pall of company retribution for union sentiment hung over the Bridgeport plant. Mr. R., an Italian-born worker who had transferred from the Schenectady plant to Bridgeport in 1929, recalled his anger at receiving only a 12 percent bonus when he had been promised 25 percent the first month. But when he talked to his workmates about protesting, they advised him "to keep [his] mouth shut."[28] Clearly, unionization of this workplace would be difficult.

Unions

The political power of working people, whether exercised independently through the Bridgeport Socialist Party or through the mainstream Democratic or Republican Parties, depended on how well they were organized at the workplace. If they were organized, local politicians would be forced to address economic matters and other working-class issues, instead of relying on their usual ethnic group appeals around cultural issues. Where did unionism survive in the 1920s?

Bridgeport workers faced very different kinds of employers, depending on their industry. Bridgeport industry had three different work worlds that retained worker organizations, each with its own legacy of union organization and each with its own pattern of relations among coworkers. They were the machine tool and metal trades, the building trades, and the clothing and textile trades. In the most important manufacturing group and the largest companies—the machine tool and metal trades—industrial unionism raised its head only sporadically until 1925 and not at all thereafter. The postwar economic dislocation and the Open Shop Drive left few workers with union experience in these plants. The unskilled and semiskilled workers among the new immigrants benefited little from the few pockets of metal trades craft unionism that survived. These employers effectively replaced an independent labor voice with company unionism and seemingly reigned supreme. The building trades remained the most important and secure arena of union power in the 1920s, involving a large male workforce that was mostly native born or old immigrant. Finally, the secondary clothing and textile sectors of Bridgeport industry were part of a fiercely competitive national market. Here new immigrant workers clung to their unions wherever they could for as long as they could.

First, the world of the clothing and textile workers drew workers from the city's South End, the Hungarian West End, and the Slavic and Italian Tenth and Eleventh Districts on the East Side; this world was markedly different from that inhabited by most U.S.-born workers. In relating their job experiences, many workers expressed ethnic antagonism, so it is clear that ethnic separateness remained a continuing problem for union efforts in the 1920s. The employees of Warner Corset Company, the Wolf and Abraham Company, and the Salts Textile mill resembled the workforces that had struck in 1915 and 1919 and secured union representation into the 1920s. Workers here faced the speed-up and stretch-out experienced by other workers in these northeastern industries during the 1920s (stretch-out referred to making one worker responsible for running more machines).

Labor relations in the Bridgeport needle trades depended on activity in nearby New York City. Both the International Ladies' Garment Workers' Union (ILGWU) and the Amalgamated Clothing Workers of America (ACWA) kept a watchful eye on affairs in Bridgeport. The city had one of the largest concentrations of production in the corset industry. The Warner Corset Company was one of the larger employers in the city, with two to three thousand workers for in-house manufacturing, along with a varying number of home workers. The strikes in the summer of 1919 at Warner and other corset shops, which involved a total of three thousand strikers, were called by the ILGWU as part of its New York campaign to consolidate wartime gains. The union briefly gained a wage increase, an end to fines and charges for thread, and a forty-four-hour week (that is, a half day on Saturday). But by 1921 the local had slumped into somnolence, the forty-eight-hour week again became the norm, and wages slipped to less than $15 a week. The ILGWU local there blamed its weakness on the company's new personnel department, Warner's profit losses on the new anticorset fashions of the 1920s, and ethnic rivalries within its workforce. The workforce was split—the U.S.-born workers intolerant of immigrants, and Italian and Hungarian immigrants often dominating entire departments and distrustful of each other. After a series of unsuccessful strikes, Warner succeeded in crushing the union by 1926, and the company remained nonunion until the early 1930s.[29]

The pattern was different in the case of two other active shops in the 1920s, the Wolf and Abraham boys' and children's clothing manufacturer, and the Salts Textile Company. Both industries faced highly competitive markets for their products and consequently put pressure on their workforces to increase production, generally through speed-up and stretch-out. The mostly immigrant workers in these two shops successfully united to resist their employers' efforts to squeeze the last ounce of profit in order to survive the competition. Because the ACWA and its allied organization, the Amalgamated Textile Workers, were not members of the AFL, events in these two unions went on largely outside the purview of the official labor movement in Bridgeport. But because they involved large numbers of immigrant workers, and because they also involved the direct intervention of politicians in the city, these strikes illustrated the evolving links among local Republicans, labor unions, and ethnic workers during this period.

The Wolf and Abraham shop, which contracted work from New York City manufacturers and employed about six hundred inside workers and two hundred home workers, was located in the heart of the Hungarian West End. After winning its strike in the summer of 1919, ACWA Local 223 faced continuing management pressures to increase production rates and decrease wages. Similarly, Salts Textile Company faced the new 1920s economy with difficulty. The British stockholders sold out to their New York counterparts in the early 1920s, reduced the workforce to about six hundred in 1925, and introduced complex piece-rate plans for its mostly immigrant workforce.

Here Sam Lavit's organizing ability was called into play for the last time. Barred from the AFL after the war for his militant role in the IAM, he found refuge in the independent ACWA after the Amalgamated Metal Workers had faded. Here his fluency in Yiddish, as well as his knowledge of the immigrant workers he organized in the garment and textile shops during the 1920s, helped sustain those groups. However, he slowly moved further from the radicalism of the war years. As Mr. P, a member of the Workers (Communist) Party by then, remembered it, "He [Lavit] sold out . . . right after the funds ran out. . . . He came out openly for Republican candidates." Lavit's union career became a mixed bag of devotion to industrial unionism and pragmatic actions to cement his relationship with local Republican politicians whose intervention was crucial to the success of any strikes in this era. He became an exemplar of the "new unionism" of the 1920s, working with cooperative employers to manage the production problems of the plant and forging a middle way between ACWA accommodation to friendly managers and the more militant attitudes expressed by those of his rank-and-file affiliated with the Workers Party. By 1928 his health and personal devotion had flagged, and he retired from the labor movement, reappearing as a labor relations mediator later in the 1940s.[30]

The Jewish and Italian workforce at Wolf and Abraham carried out plantwide strikes in the fall of 1921 and spring of 1923, causing Lavit to bring labor difficulties to the attention of local elites. The settlement of the weeklong strike in 1923 came about with the help of a board of arbitrators, composed of Stewart Brice of the Bridgeport Chamber of Commerce; Lynn Wilson, editor of the *Bridgeport Times;* and William Lavery, the GOP president of the Bridgeport Common Council. But by the spring of 1925 the deal had unraveled, and a six-week strike in April and May 1925 pitted the union against a determined employer threatening to move out of town and now supported in his antiunion stance by the Chamber of Commerce. Only an arbitration session presided over by GOP mayor Behrens and federal mediators brought about a partial settlement, but the factory closed six months later and moved its operations to New Jersey.[31]

What was special about this strike was worker unity in support of the union, unlike the situation at Warner Corset Company, and the overt support given the union by GOP political leaders. Local political support was often important leverage for workers, both morally and in the crucial battle ground of police and city courts.[32] In the 1925 strike a sympathetic GOP police commissioner over-

ruled the police department and allowed mass picketing, and GOP city prose-
cutors either declined to prosecute or city court judges handed out slight sen-
tences to arrested strikers. The Twelfth District Hebrew Republican Club protested Lavit's treatment at the hands of a special police officer, and prominent
GOP lawyers agreed to be incorporators of a new prounion garment shop in
town to keep a unionized presence in the industry.[33] None of this, of course,
saved the union jobs at Wolf and Abraham, because the plant was one that could
easily transfer its operations elsewhere. The ACWA only regained its strength
in Bridgeport and the rest of the state in the early depression years.

The Salts Textile Company, with its plant on the East Side, made cotton and
silk plushes and velvets as well as upholstery fabrics. It had once recruited English immigrant weavers to its plant but by the war period had a mixed workforce of twelve hundred English, Slavic, and Italian men and women; the workforce was about one-quarter female. Skill levels and working conditions varied
among the weavers, many of whom operated more complicated plush looms
with two warps and two shuttles or complex Jacquard looms. During the war
immigrants had eagerly sought the well-paying jobs at Salts. But when the company faced continuing competitive pressures, management bore down on the
workforce. Weavers struck in summer of 1925 over the introduction of the Dyer
system of premium pay, which the plush weavers complained was simply a
speed-up. The strike committee, made up of representative ethnics and an equal
number of men and women, appealed to Sam Lavit, then in the midst of the
Wolf and Abraham strike, to take over their strike as well. While some workers
were supporters of the Amalgamated Textile Workers Union, an independent
union supported by the Amalgamated Clothing Workers, others were interested in the AFL's United Textile Workers.[34] They affiliated with neither but chose
Lavit as their organizer. Labor disputes punctuated the period from 1925 until
1929 when the Sidney Blumenthal Company, which owned the large Shelton
Looms in the nearby town of Shelton, bought the Salts mill. The four hundred
Salts workers refused to accept Blumenthal's offer in 1929, insisting instead on
wage parity with the twenty-two hundred workers at Shelton Looms. Solidarity between the Shelton Weavers Club and the new Saltex Weavers Club, with a
strong contingent of Workers (Communist) Party members, kept the union alive
in Bridgeport.

Some patterns repeated themselves here: as in the earlier disputes at Wolf and
Abraham, Lavit was quick to call in federal mediators as important tools in creating a settlement (a tactic he had used to its full extent during the war), and
again Lavit was able to assemble an arbitration committee of local political
notables to avoid a second strike in 1925. But at Salts, Workers Party activists
supplanted Lavit's organizing efforts as management became more intransigent.
The independent union local remained tied to the Workers Party for the rest of
the decade.[35] These examples provide a window on the many strands of activist and radical tendencies within workplaces and neighborhoods. But as vola-

tile as these union activities were, they remained separate from the traditional centers of organized labor in the city.

The perspectives and actions of skilled workers in mainstream AFL unions, like the building trades and some metal trades, were key to the labor politics of Bridgeport in the 1920s and 1930s. Nationally, the AFL lost 30 percent of its membership between 1920 and 1924, with even larger losses in those unions that had gained the most members during the war years. The machinists' union, for example, lost a quarter of a million members and fell below its 1914 membership total. The building trades, which had lost fewer members, became a much more potent force in the AFL for most of the 1920s. Along with this change in composition came a change in strategy. As the depression of 1920–22, the Open Shop Drive, and hostile courts drove unions nationally into retreat, the AFL embraced new attitudes toward employers who tolerated a union presence. The AFL's manifesto, *Industry's Manifest Duty,* issued at its 1923 convention in Portland, Oregon, exemplified this "strategy of defense." Here the AFL offered labor's cooperation with management to achieve greater efficiency, discipline, and productivity in exchange for a recognition of labor's vital role in industry. AFL unions clamped down on radicals and stunted internal democracy through the ruthless suppression of dissent.[36]

Similarly, the Connecticut labor movement, like the national AFL, survived the depression of 1920–22 and a fierce open-shop drive but with little real power. The Connecticut Federation of Labor (CFL) was proud that it had been able to prevent the passage of antilabor legislation by the General Assembly, a group that Ira Ornburn, secretary of the CFL, called "the most reactionary men in all walks of life." But union activists were not able to gain passage of any prolabor legislation during the decade. Given to political nonpartisanship, the CFL was conservative and often timid in an openly antiunion state and prone to accept the moderating influence of its attorney, Cornelius J. Danaher, a Republican who volunteered his services but had little innovative will. By mid-decade Patrick F. O'Meara, a New Haven plumber who was president of the CFL, had announced that the employer onslaught of the early 1920s had abated and urged the 1926 CFL convention to cooperate with friendly employers: "I implore everyone connected with the movement not to do anything that will interrupt this great progress."[37]

Ornburn, an official of the New Haven Cigarmakers' local, held the powerful position of CLF secretary until 1924. A fervent Democrat, he went on to become president of the Cigarmakers International Union in the late 1920s. As a strong conservative, Ornburn diligently policed the labor movement to thwart leftists (especially from his home labor council in New Haven) through his newspaper, the *Connecticut Labor News,* opposed a labor party and the endorsement of La Follette in 1924, and ferreted out former Wobblies and supporters of industrial unionism. On many of these issues he was usually opposed by most Bridgeport delegates to the CFL. When he left his post in 1924 to become a part of the national Democratic Party's labor bureau for the presidential campaign, John J. Egan of Bridgeport became CFL secretary, a position he retained until the late 1930s.[38]

AFL unionism survived in Bridgeport, successfully in the building trades and hardly at all in the metal trades. The major spokesmen—among them, Egan, Milton McDonald, and Jasper McLevy—came out of these sectors. All three were prominent craft unionists in the 1920s. All three became consequential in Connecticut politics, each through a different route—Egan of the IAM became the Republican-appointed state commissioner of labor in the 1940s; McDonald, the youngest of the three, received a Democratic appointment as a mediator for the National Recovery Administration and as an official of the state labor department in the early 1930s; and McLevy became the Socialist mayor of Bridgeport in the 1930s.

Egan became the voice of conservative AFL unionism in Bridgeport and the state in the 1920s and 1930s. A confirmed craft unionist, he headed the "conservative" IAM faction that had allied with Lavit during the war in order to defeat the Socialist leadership of IAM Lodge 30 but then turned on Lavit's radical industrial unionists.[39] Egan was installed as president of the new Lodge 116 in 1919, when the Grand Lodge removed Lavit and revoked Lodge 30's charter. Strongly convinced that craft unionism was the tried-and-true approach, Egan had castigated the national IAM for too many "new propositions. . . . Old-age pensions, machinists' homes, insurance features or any other policy that means an indirect benefit to the members will not create interest in our organization; what the members want is the money in their pay envelope and an organization that will protect them, and when they need a job will get them one."[40] His solution, though, was to imitate the building trades' organizational structure and walking delegate system, completely unmindful of the vastly different working environment of most machinists. Clearly, he had only craftsmen in small shops in mind. Egan was active in the 1928 Al Smith campaign for the Democratic Party and then became a loyal Republican and used his position in the CFL to influence state politics.

Milton J. McDonald, leader of the plumbers' union in Bridgeport, was one of the young labor leaders to emerge after the war. No radical, he was nevertheless interested in ending factionalism, promoting labor legislation, and maintaining a high profile for unionism. In 1923 he was elected president of the Bridgeport Central Labor Union in coalition with Socialist forces, ousting the "Greybeards" from their "self-satisfied" leadership, as the Herald put it.[41] Elected president of the Connecticut Building Trades Council by the end of the decade, he became heavily involved in the Democratic Party statewide.

Jasper McLevy was the quintessential skilled craftsman of the Second International Socialist movement. Born in 1878, he was the oldest of the nine children of the Scottish immigrants Hugh and Mary McLevy. After a grammar school education he began an apprenticeship in the roofing trade, the trade of his father. Although he was raised as a Presbyterian, he soon eschewed religion and began attending socialist discussions at Charles Porzenheim's tobacco shop on Main Street. In 1900 he joined the newly united Branch 10, Local Bridgeport, of the Socialist Party of America (SP) and quickly became active in the AFL. An organizer for and later president of the Bridgeport Central Labor Union, he became well known in Connecticut labor circles and was credited with passage of the state workers' compensation law in 1913. He also served as national president of the International Slate and Tile Roofers' Union of America during the war years. As for his political career, he "learned to 'Stump' in the School of Hard Knocks" and felt most comfortable on a soapbox. In 1911, during the best of the Socialist Party's prewar electoral campaigns, he had garnered 25 percent of the mayoral vote. A "constructive socialist" along the lines of Milwaukee's Victor Berger, McLevy stood squarely on the right during the SP's factional battles of the prewar era. But he remained loyal to the antiwar stand of the SP during World War I, and he and others slowly began to rebuild their organization in Bridgeport in 1921. While working at his trade through the 1920s, he devoted his time to electoral work for the Socialist Party and labor lobbying at the local and state levels.[42]

With strong representation from the Socialist Party, Bridgeport labor leaders put themselves in the forefront of an activist labor solidarity agenda that mirrored the activity of "labor progressives" nationally. Never revolutionary, they were activists in an era given to retreat. The Bridgeport Central Labor Union (CLU), through the leadership of Milton J. McDonald and Minor Treat—a printing pressman, Socialist, and veteran of World War I—mounted organizing drives in the city, carried on the state La Follette campaign, and pressed social legislation on a reluctant CFL.

The Bridgeport CLU found itself with a dwindling membership and worsened conditions as a result of the 1922 depression. The workweek had gone from 44 hours a week to an average 48 to 50—and 55 hours in some industries—while skilled workers' wages in the metal trades had plummeted. The CLU planned an all-out organizing drive in the trades and in the factories in 1923, a plan that was met with skepticism by craft unionists like Egan. Another attempted organizing drive in 1925 also met with little apparent success.[43] The CLU, to judge by the names of the local secretaries listed in the *Bridgeport City Directory,* was overwhelmingly Irish and old immigrant. There were, of course, new ethnic enclaves within the CLU—the barbers were largely Italian, a Jewish bakers' local met at the Labor Lyceum sponsored by the Workmen's Circle, the molders included a Slovak contingent, and the building trades had a mix of ethnic groups. Most unions held their meetings at Metal Trades Hall on Main Street, while the carpenters and painters met at Carpenters Hall, also in the downtown area. The CLU no longer sponsored Labor Day parades; the parade was replaced by an afternoon picnic, with baseball games that pit the building trades against the metal trades. By the end of the decade even picnics were few and far between.

However, it would have been impossible for either the Socialists or the AFL activists to create a union drive without approaching the structure and ideology of the radical industrial unionism of the war years, and it was unclear who wanted to return to those days. McDonald, who was too young to have been part of the factionalism of the war years, attempted to heal the rifts in the IAM. But when he invited Sam Lavit to join him at the 1925 Connecticut Federation of Labor convention, Egan, the CFL secretary, refused to allow Lavit to enter.[44]

In the 1920s the building trades accounted for one-sixth of the city's wage earners who held nonsupervisory manufacturing positions, numbered about forty-eight hundred workers in 1930, continued to provide the most persistent voice of labor, and represented the greatest number of organized workers in the city. Because the building trades relied on a local economy, they were insulated from the open-shop industrial relations policies in other industries and could take advantage of prosperous conditions in local construction and highway expansion. This local perspective also meant that they were more in touch with local political decisions about infrastructure spending for city roads, buildings, parks, and such. In addition, because of Bridgeport's proximity to New York City, Bridgeport craftsmen could threaten to leave Bridgeport contractors for the strongly unionized and high-wage New York construction work. Indeed, unlike the labor forces of the other big cities of Hartford and New Haven, Bridgeport's construction labor force was 95 percent unionized, whereas both Hartford's and New Haven's were 50 percent open shop.[45]

Building trades leaders became the activist cadre of Bridgeport unionism throughout the 1920s. Socialists had a presence, though not a decisive hold on power, in the building trades unions before the war, but they made a strong mark in the 1920s. One whose prominence predated the war was Jasper McLevy. Other key Socialists who attained positions of leadership during the 1920s included Jasper's brother Charles, who had moved up from local president to district president to business agent for the Carpenters' District Council in 1926 and for the next fourteen years. Another was Peter Brewster of the painters' union, who became business agent for his local in 1929. Both unions had many active Socialists among their lesser officers. The membership of the carpenters' union was largely Yankee, English, and Irish, with an increasing number of Slavic, Italian, French-Canadian, and German carpenters and cabinetmakers. One local was entirely Swedish.[46] The painters' union too was a mixed group, with many Jewish and eastern European members. The Bridgeport painters' union included Irish and Jewish Socialists, and even a Hungarian Communist, among its leadership in the 1920s. Thus building trades unions reached further into ethnic communities than the labor movement as a whole in the 1920s.[47]

The Socialists and many nonsocialists who attained positions of power in the Bridgeport labor movement during the 1920s were attuned to a social unionism that went beyond guaranteeing the economic well-being of building trades workers. Many were interested in promoting the labor movement as a whole and pushing for political reforms that were of interest to the entire working class. They were, however, craft unionists and did not question the structure of the labor movement itself in this era. Thus, while their activities kept unionism in the public eye during the lean years, they did not appreciably change the fortunes of most workers in the city's industries.

The Socialist Party

The Bridgeport Socialist Party (SP) had been founded from a merger of the locals of the Social Democratic Party and the Socialist Labor Party in October 1900, fully nine months before the unity conference that created the Socialist Party of America nationally. Connecticut was one of sixteen states where the parties had united in advance of the squabbling national factions. Both Jasper McLevy and Fred Cederholm were initiated as members of the new Branch 10 of Local Bridgeport in that October meeting. Max Schwab, a German immigrant butcher and local organizer for the SLP, became the city secretary of the new Bridgeport SP. A body of workers and small tradesmen, the Bridgeport SP left little in the way of memoirs or reminiscences of the early days. The party reached its height of prewar influence in the 1911 city elections, when McLevy garnered 25 percent of the vote (more than 3,600 ballots) and Fred Cederholm, a machinist, won the common council seat from the city's large Twelfth District.[48] They began printing a local paper, the *Examiner,* in 1913 and published through 1918 under increasingly straitened conditions. Their influence could best be observed in the growth of the trade union movement in Bridgeport. McLevy's influence at the state level grew during 1914 and 1915 as he led a lobbying force of Bridgeport Socialists and unionists to convince the Connecticut Federation of Labor to sponsor a workers' compensation bill in the Connecticut General Assembly.[49]

The Connecticut SP represented an important stratum of the Connecticut working class. Composed primarily of native-born Americans and old immigrants of modest means, with a few intellectuals such as the sociologist Robert Hunter, the Connecticut party was never known as radical. Ella Reeve Bloor, the state organizer for the party from 1908 to 1910, recalled her initial difficulty in being accepted by the state committee's Catholic members because she was a divorced woman. J. E. Beardsley, the state secretary, explained the party's success in winning support from Catholics. "A speaker knows when he comes to Connecticut for the Socialist Party that he is to speak for political Socialism and not for the I.W.W. or any other economic body. . . . Nor is our speaker allowed to air his personal grudges against the church from our platform." In other words, complained the leftist *International Socialist Review* in 1914, the majority of the Connecticut party was "in the habit of confessing their sins to a priest," a habit that would incline members toward docility. Connecticut Socialists, then, were disposed toward "vote-catching and office-seeking," not "break[ing] the fetters of wage slavery."[50]

Well, yes and no. The task of a political party, ran the reformist thinking, was to capture the machinery of state to make it work for the benefit of the working-class majority. The might of capital, however, could be met only in the economic arena, where workers were armed with their other weapon, the trade union. This careful separation of economic and political struggles, so common to the Second International, informed McLevy's view of Socialist goals as well. When he ran on the Socialist ticket for mayor in 1911, he was also president of the city's Central Labor Union, and the majority of delegates were also SP members. He refused, however, to allow the CLU or individual locals to endorse the SP or vote to contribute money to the campaign. Similarly, McLevy had urged the unions not to endorse candidates from the mainstream parties either, arguing that the practice led to "corrupt efforts" by "old political machines" to "swing and pledge the labor vote." The Socialist intellectual Robert Hunter warmly praised this stance, noting that it was "in accord with the policy of many European Socialists, who have urged the unions not to endorse Socialism so long as there was the slightest danger of disrupting the trade union movement."[51]

Although they were a minority, a number of foreign-language federations were loosely affiliated with the Bridgeport Socialist Party. The Bridgeport Polish Socialists had organized a Polish Socialist Alliance (PSA) in 1900. There was apparently an Italian Socialist group before 1910, though it is unclear whether it was affiliated with the Socialist Party. Just before the war Jewish and Slovak branches were growing. The flurry of labor activity in the summer of 1915, as well as concern over the war in Europe, nurtured the growth of the Bridgeport SP, for nine language branches, as well as a chapter of the Young People's Socialist League, existed by the end of the year.[52] As war fever hit Bridgeport, the Socialists faced a repression that grew stronger once war was formally declared.

The Bridgeport SP, reviving after the disasters of the World War I period, continued the McLevy orthodoxy. In particular, this allowed Socialists in their most important unions, the building trades, to stick to their union international's ban on "politics" in the locals and thus keep peace between Socialists and those affiliated with other parties. "We weren't allowed to discuss politics [in the union], you know," remarked Robert McLevy, Jasper's nephew and a carpenters' union member since the 1930s. Carpenters' and painters' locals sometimes did vote to support specific members if they were running for political office (as Democrats, Republicans, or Socialists) in the early 1920s, but this became less common by 1930.[53]

The Socialist Party's transition to the 1920s was a painful experience. The war crisis, the leftward swing of the foreign-language branches and others in the wake of the Russian Revolution, and government repression spelled the end of the SP as a national political force by 1919, when the party formally split. The Bridgeport SP was only a shell of its former self, reduced in 1921 to occupying a desk at the back of another group's hall, while the Russian and Hungarian branches moved to join the Workers (Communist) Party. Trade unionism, antiwar sentiment, and a lack of enthusiasm for the new Bolshevik experiment bound the SP survivors together.[54]

But it can be argued that the Socialist members kept the Bridgeport labor movement alive, and sometimes lively, in the 1920s, despite the SP's weakened state. While Socialists in Bridgeport only occasionally brought forward social and political issues that were not already approved by the AFL or the various international unions, they effectively rallied non-Socialists around them in pursuit of these goals long after the CFL had abandoned them. For example, at the state level the Bridgeport Socialist unionists presented and successfully carried resolutions for the release of Eugene V. Debs, imprisoned for criticizing government prosecutions under the 1917 Espionage Act, and Tom Mooney and Warren Knox Billings, held since 1916 in the fatal bombing of a San Francisco parade. But the Bridgeport Socialists were unsuccessful when they submitted a resolution for recognition of the Soviet government and the opening of trade and in their protest of the CFL's enthusiasm for a labor bank. The Connecticut SP threw its weight behind a lobbying effort in Hartford for an old-age pension bill, an idea initiated by the Fraternal Order of Eagles and supported by the CFL. But beyond this, the SP began pushing a bill for employer-funded unemployment insurance in 1925. By 1928 McLevy reported that the Bridgeport CLU had endorsed this cause and was starting a campaign to gain publicity for the measure. Similarly, the Bridgeport SP began to work publicly in support of the coal miners' strike in 1926, working with the CLU and various individual unions. The CLU went beyond strike support to announce that it was "committed wholeheartedly to the cause of government ownership and operation of America's coal mines." Calling for a public hearing on the issues of the strike and the serious hardship it was causing in the city, the CLU began an attack on "profiteering" in soft coal. The Bridgeport Common Council was forced to set up such a hearing.[55]

The party began a major effort to rebuild its base in the late 1920s, as Fred Schwarzkopf, then the secretary, told national headquarters. "We here in Bridgeport have decided that we are no longer going to look for excuses why we should not do some real constructive work. The methods of yesterday seem very adaptable for our present needs. And so we are going out as often as possible, personally visiting our former members and new possibilities. The result of our efforts so far has been that we now have more paid-up members than we have had during the past twelve years," reported Schwarzkopf.[56]

Who, then, were the Socialists of Bridgeport? A collective biography of the Socialists can be constructed from the list of candidates who appeared on the Socialist Party ticket in Bridgeport in the 1920s. An analysis of the 70 names (66 men and 4 women) reveals that 53 percent (37) were skilled workers, with machinists and toolmakers heading the list, followed by building tradesmen. The next largest categories were owners of retail businesses (8) and salesmen (3). Only one "professional," a newspaper reporter, appeared on the list. The four women were wives of other candidates; none listed an occupation. The largest ethnic group was American/British/Irish by surname (32), with Jewish (16) and German (16) the next largest. Three Scandinavians, two Slavs, and one Italian rounded out the list.[57]

A look at representative individuals reveals a pattern of ethnic affiliation that overlapped the occupational categories. Most had been in the party for a long time. In addition to Jasper McLevy, they included such founders as Max Schwab and Fred Cederholm. Schwab, born in Germany in 1860, had come to the United States in his midtwenties and in 1892 established a butcher shop in Bridgeport. He was active in the Socialist-leaning Workmen's Sick and Death Benefit Society.[58] Cederholm, the former member of the common council, had been born in Denmark. Blacklisted from his occupation as a machinist for his activities on behalf of the union in 1915, he had been an IAM staff organizer ever since. He too was a member of the Workmen's Sick and Death Benefit Society.

Jewish members of the group, mostly foreign born, were members of Workmen's Circle. Solomon Snow was born in Austria in 1864 and emigrated to Bridgeport in 1885. The father of eight, he was a painter and active in the Workmen's Circle. Isadore Kravetz was a paperhanger. Both he and Snow were active in Painters Local 190. George Ribak, a used clothes dealer, was also a member of the Workmen's Circle; he came from the Russian territory of Latvia. The youngest of the foreign-born group, Fred Schwarzkopf, was an Austrian Jew who had come to Bridgeport at age three, joined the SP in 1914 when he was nineteen, worked as a carpenter, and served as secretary of Carpenters Local 115 in 1917–18. He had amassed a large socialist library, including the complete series of Haldeman-Julius Little Blue Books. Unlike the others, he was not active in the Workmen's Circle; rather, he listed himself as a member of both a Jewish and a German branch of the Odd Fellows, as well as lodges of the Knights of Pythias and the Masons (AF&AM).[59]

The Slavic members of the group included Peter P. Wojcicki, who had been born in Warsaw in 1887 and who was a machinist who served an apprenticeship in Warsaw before coming to the United States. He was linked to the others by occupation and was a leader of the Bridgeport chapter of the Polish Socialist Alliance and an officer of the Polish Mutual Benefit Society. He was fluent in Polish, German, and Russian. Stephen Havanich, a Slovak, was also tied to the others by trade. A skilled cabinetmaker, he had been a member of the carpenters' union and briefly flirted with the Wobblies during World War I. During the 1920s he set up his own business making musical instruments, and he served his Slovak community by selling steamship tickets and insurance. Like so many from the Austro-Hungarian Empire, he bridged the nationalities—he spoke Slovak, Hungarian, and German—and was a member of the Slovak Union Sokol and the German Workingmen's Singing Society.[60]

The "new immigrant" Socialists belonged to the radical fraternal groups of their communities. The Workmen's Circle claimed to be the largest single Jewish organization in Bridgeport during the 1920s. Although it was radical and secular, it joined with other Jewish groups in common community activities. Its split with middle-class Jewish leaders centered around the growing influence of Zionism in the Jewish community.[61] The Polish Socialist Alliance, while distinctly a minority current in the generally conservative Catholic Polish community, was highly visible nonetheless. The PSA bought a new building on the East Side in 1923 and sponsored many cultural activities, historical plays, Polish songs, and dances. The Bridgeport International Institute, a YWCA-sponsored service agency for immigrant communities, noted the popularity of the PSA in the mid-1930s and reported that its membership was about five hundred. The PSA officers, however, were economically distinguished members of their working-class community. Of the seven officers in 1931, six appeared in the *Bridgeport City Directory*. Four were machinists and one was a carpenter, a contrast to the unskilled and semiskilled majority of Polish workers.[62] Their championing of Polish culture and identity made them welcome and worthwhile community members.[63]

Of the native-born Americans in the Bridgeport SP, most were craftsmen—carpenters, painters, printers, or machinists—and most were union activists. Union membership created ties with non-Socialists. Peter Brewster was a painter who had held most major offices in the Bridgeport and Connecticut painters' union, as well as the Bridgeport Central Labor Union. Everett Perry, the oldest native-born candidate, was from Massachusetts, had been a member of the United Brotherhood of Carpenters all his working life, and had joined the SP in 1914. Other SP members included Jasper McLevy's brother Charles, the business agent of the Carpenters District Council, which had more than twelve hundred members in the 1920s; Karl Lang and Minor S. Treat, both of whom had served as president of the Central Labor Union; and Harry Williamson, president of the local printing pressmen's union. They were privileged members of the working class, mostly from native-born and old immigrant groups, most from the generation born in the 1880s. They had maintained union organization despite the antiunion atmosphere of the 1920s because generally they represented crafts with local labor markets and because the technological attack on their skills was limited.[64] Moreover, because many were full-time union functionaries or were self-employed, they were removed from the influence and pressures of employers, both antiunion employers and those tied to one of the major parties. While this set them apart from the majority of Bridgeport workers, it also gave them the organizational resources and skills to make an independent bid for political power.

Thus the Bridgeport Socialists were a labor aristocracy. For skilled workers class consciousness carried contradictory impulses, both a collectivist labor appeal and an exclusiveness born of the contours of their unionism. Craft unionism, premised on controlling entry to the trade and defining the standards of workmanship, defended its control over work by barring employers' intrusion into these areas. While some trades fell before employers' restructuring of the work process in the early decades of the century, other craftsmen carved out protective niches for themselves rather than redefine their place in a new working class.[65] There were parallels between this craft union thinking and that of the Socialists of the Second International, a class perspective that often refused to rethink its relationship to new workers and new ethnics.

The Bridgeport SP exhibited many of these limitations in its social relations. Ideologically, the Bridgeport SP waffled between a class analysis of politics and a more broad-based "producer" perspective. It sometimes combined its appeal for social justice and a class party with a rhetoric of honesty and efficiency for the benefit of all citizens of all classes. Their leaders' ability to transcend these limitations, and their effectiveness in representing the entire working class, would be tested after 1929, when even the stable crafts were threatened.

Labor and Politics

Many Bridgeport trade unionists, like their counterparts nationwide, embraced the theory and practice of a labor party, especially in the World War I era. In fact, Bridgeport was the first city in that era to field a labor party, in November 1918. The American Labor Party (ALP), formed by the militant machinists of Sam Lavit's IAM, had taken this step to move beyond their defeat at the hands of the NWLB that fall. Echoing the economic demands of the machinists' union, the ALP resolved to "exercise their political rights as an instrument of industrial emancipation thus paving the way for an autonomous industrial Republic (shop control in the factories, mines, mills, and other establishments wherein workers are employed)." The ALP endorsed President Woodrow Wilson's Fourteen Points and also the platform of the British Labour Party. The SP, which dominated the Central Labor Union at that time, refused to allow the CLU to endorse the ALP and even expelled three members who supported the ALP.[66]

The Bridgeport ALP prompted the founding of a labor party at the state level, with a goal of "political, industrial and social democracy." With Hartford as another strong center, the Connecticut Farmer-Labor Party gained the endorsements of the central labor councils of Hartford, Meriden, New Britain, New London, and Stamford, as well as that of individual locals throughout the state. They contributed delegates to the 1919 Chicago convention to set up a national labor party. These organizations unsuccessfully attempted to gain support for the Connecticut Farmer-Labor Party in the Connecticut Federation of Labor. The Connecticut Farmer-Labor Party effort had a longer life in Hartford and, while not successful itself, seemed effective at penalizing the Democratic Party there for its coolness to unionism. The Bridgeport group, however, decided to endorse the Democrats in 1919 as a way of punishing the GOP mayor Clifford Wilson, whom they saw as antilabor. This caused a split between Bridgeport and the rest of the state organization, and the Bridgeport ALP disappeared.[67]

The standard-bearer for a "labor" party in Connecticut had long been the SP.

But in the challenging days of the early 1920s, the Bridgeport SP attempted to build a political coalition with non-Socialist trade unionists. The local SP had run a slate in state and local elections even in the difficult years but did little campaigning. Debs garnered 3.76 percent of Bridgeport's vote when he ran for president in 1920, slightly higher than his national average. Bridgeport SP members began campaigning extensively only in the 1921 municipal election. In 1922, while sharing candidates statewide with the Connecticut Farmer-Labor Party, the Bridgeport SP invited local labor to help fill the Socialist slate for local offices. Labor Democrats, shut out of the local Democratic Party in its new business-men's orientation, reacted favorably. "Many conservative labor leaders in Bridge-port have expressed an eagerness to co-operate with the Socialists this year," reported the *Sunday Herald,* and more than one hundred labor representatives gathered at Metal Trades Hall to endorse a "Socialist-Farmer-Labor" ticket. The ticket received 708 votes on the SP line and 69 on the Farmer-Labor line, for a meager 3 percent of the vote, but this total had deprived some Democratic candidates for common council of a winning margin in a tight race.[68] This formation of a labor political bloc prepared the Bridgeport labor activists for cooperation in coming elections and resulted in reopening the Democratic line to some labor leaders at the district level in 1924.

This trend culminated in the 1924 La Follette campaign, which highlighted both the potential of the moment and the serious rifts in thinking between Socialists, labor progressives, and their middle-class allies. The 1924 campaign has been interpreted as both the peak of labor party sentiment among American unionists and the abrupt end of such sentiment. The labor coalition, the Conference for Progressive Political Action (CPPA)—made up of progressives in the Committee of Forty-Eight, Farmer-Laborites, and the SP—was an uneasy one from the beginning. In particular, accepting La Follette's ultimatum regarding an independent campaign effort built around a trust-busting anti-monopoly platform was difficult for those who wished for a genuine labor party. But many labor progressives outside the SP were unwilling to turn away from the two major parties, whose labor supporters had formed an effective labor bloc in Congress in 1920–24. The AFL, never interested in abandoning the two-party system, only reluctantly endorsed La Follette after being spurned by the Democrats and even then nearly abandoned that endorsement as the election drew near. Because La Follette insisted that no state or local tickets be run on a Progressive Party line, unionists at the state and local levels found themselves tied to one of the two major parties.[69]

Connecticut exhibited all these contradictions. But the campaign in Bridgeport, rather than being a swan song for the Socialists, became a vehicle for the SP's resurrection as a vital part of Bridgeport politics.[70] When the La Follette–Wheeler ticket was announced in 1924, Connecticut progressives, labor, and the SP set up a state committee.[71] Both the Bridgeport and New Haven central labor bodies endorsed the ticket. In a tumultuous convention the CFL voted to endorse La Follette, despite strenuous opposition from Ira Ornburn and his New Haven paper, the *Connecticut Labor News*. Ornburn had already resigned his post as secretary of the CFL to take up his appointment as head of the labor bureau for the eastern region of the National Democratic Committee.[72]

In Bridgeport the SP eagerly threw itself into the campaign. On the state campaign committee for La Follette were the Bridgeport locals of the painters, Metal Polishers, ACWA, Corset Workers, and the CLU. Jasper McLevy was on the executive committee and spoke throughout the state during September and October. All the Bridgeport delegates at the CFL convention in September, Socialists and non-Socialists alike, voted to endorse La Follette.[73] Similarly, labor Democrats in Waterbury and New Haven, like state senator Joseph Tone and two ward chairmen (both union members) in New Haven, endorsed La Follette. They had little to lose at the state and local levels, given the general conservatism of the Connecticut Democratic Party.[74]

The *Sunday Herald* gave much coverage to the campaign and endorsed La Follette, and the unionists were joined by other groups, notably the German Steuben Society and some African-American groups that stumped for the Progressive candidate. In Bridgeport the SP opened its ballot line to select progressive candidates from other parties because La Follette's national headquarters refused to allow state tickets. The Bridgeport SP endorsed Milton McDonald, a plumber running on the Democratic line in the Twenty-third State Senatorial District, and John J. O'Neil, Jr., the Democratic labor leader, for the common council seat for the Sixth District.[75]

Bridgeport Socialists, however, soon added to the confusion surrounding labor's political intentions and nearly destroyed the coalition they had so carefully built. The Fourth Congressional District, Fairfield County, had been dominated for many years by U.S. Rep. Schuyler Merritt, a conservative Republican who chaired the board of Yale and Towne Company. Democrats in that district nominated William English Walling of Greenwich as their candidate. Walling, a former left-wing Socialist intellectual who became an adviser to Samuel Gompers, had split with the Socialist Party in 1917 by launching vociferous attacks on the party's antiwar stance, accusing it of being pro-German. Walling explained his hopes to force a political realignment to make the Democratic Party a labor and progressive coalition, but he opposed formation of a third party. The Bridgeport La Follette supporters refused to allow the Fourth Congressional District's La Follette committee to endorse Walling, which would have meant giving him the SP line. By late October Walling and the Bridgeport La Follette forces had reached a compromise, and Walling appeared at La Follette rallies with endorsed Democratic candidates and Socialist spokesmen.[76]

Manufacturers fretted publicly about a large La Follette turnout, fearing that it might throw the presidential election into Congress. Both locally and nationally, the National Association of Manufacturers (NAM) engineered a get-out-the-vote campaign to encourage voting by "the better element" among its members' workers. The Manufacturers' Association of Bridgeport, lately deep into local politics, geared up for the campaign. Bridgeport factory owners made arrangements to allow their employees to vote. Coercion was not unknown in Connecticut. La Follette rallies were broken up in Darien and Meriden, and Connecticut workers reported that they were forced to contribute to Coolidge and threatened with the loss of their jobs.[77]

Republicans need not have worried, as Bridgeport gave Coolidge 62.5 percent of the vote. As Bridgeport's La Follette chairman, Minor Treat, ruefully noted, his committee did not have enough workers at the polls to prevent Republican poll workers from giving false advice to voters—for example, one voter looking for the Progressive line was shown the Prohibition lever instead. While La Follette got 18 percent (4,552 votes on the Progressive line, 1,243 on the SP line), slightly higher than his national average, labor candidates in Bridgeport did not pick up most of the La Follette votes but only votes on the SP line; they did no better than the other Democratic candidates. Statewide the Democratic campaign was a shambles.[78]

Socialists had crisscrossed the state and had gotten immense coverage in some areas. Their obstinacy on the Walling issue had nearly cost them the labor coalition they had built, but they had reasserted their place, if not their preeminence, in Bridgeport politics and the Bridgeport trade union movement. Backing La Follette had not been a wasted effort for them. When state labor progressives met to decide the future, enthusiasm for a labor party had decisively waned. The national decision of the CPPA, the labor coalition, to return to its nonpartisan stance, as well as La Follette's death the following spring, meant that no new party was launched. As the delegates to the 1925 CFL convention voted a resounding no on a resolution for a labor party, John J. O'Neil, Jr., the Bridgeport typographer who had returned to the Democratic camp, exclaimed, "We had learned our lesson."[79]

It is true that local labor activists aligned with one of the two major parties did not campaign with the Socialist Party again in the 1920s. But the SP continued to mount state and municipal campaigns for the rest of the decade. The Bridgeport SP received 5 to 6 percent of the municipal vote for most of the 1920s, a modest and unimpressive showing. The electoral action was in the Al Smith revolution in 1928. Nonetheless, the SP soon looked like a reasonable voice in the municipal arena, given the acrimony in the local Democratic and Republican organizations. The *Bridgeport Sunday Herald*, which had established itself as a progressive voice during the La Follette campaign, began giving wide coverage to SP municipal issues. In 1928 Jasper McLevy began writing a guest column on city politics for the paper, and the *Herald* was enthusing about other elements of a progressive agenda for American politics.[80] While none of this exposure resulted in victories for the Socialists, it established them, and McLevy especially, as legitimate actors in Bridgeport's public sphere.

The 1920s have been dubbed the lean years for a reason: American workers had few choices and little power. While skilled workers in the city's metal shops—such as tool-and-die makers whose jobs had been strengthened by management reorganization—could assert some power vis-à-vis management by virtue of their skills, Bridgeporters did it in a nonunion context. The skilled workers who retained effective unions during the 1920s, such as the building trades or select occupations like motion-picture operators, did so because of the particularities of their labor markets. Theirs was the experience of a significant minority but a minority nonetheless. In the dominant metalworking industry the postwar move toward industrial unionism had been stopped cold. But in the few volatile areas of labor relations in the garment and textile industries, workers whose ethnic makeup and work background mirrored those in the metalworking shops were not docile. Subjected to the speed-up and stretch-out suffered by these declining industries elsewhere, they worked for employers who could not buy labor peace with steady wages. Finally, the continued viability of the Socialist Party in Bridgeport was significant. Socialists preserved union organization in the lean years and would have plausible answers to the economic disaster that confronted all in 1929.

Economic Survival after the Crash, 1930–33

For the most part, 1929 had been an auspicious year. Bridgeport's payrolls were 17 percent higher than in 1928, and retail sales were up 16 percent. The city led the state in the number of building permits issued. The city's industries were continuing to expand into new sectors. The Remington Arms plant had begun production of new business machinery, while Sikorsky Aviation continued its new building program, expanding its workforce from a handful that spring to nearly three hundred by fall.[81] Nonetheless, overall industrial activity showed signs of slippage in Bridgeport in the few months before the October 1929 stock market crash. Led by declines in the construction industry, machine tools, and other nonferrous metals production, Bridgeport joined the state and nation in the downward spiral.

Bridgeport's unemployment rate in late 1932, according to the Connecticut Unemployment Commission, was 27 percent, similar to the rate for the state's other industrial cities and towns. This rate was well above the 20 percent unemployment in the two larger cities, Hartford and New Haven, which had a much larger white-collar base. The Unemployment Commission estimated that 15,000 to 16,500 were jobless in Bridgeport, part of the statewide total of 140,000 to 150,000 without jobs.[82] The industrial sector in Bridgeport hit its low point in January 1933, when the number of workers in the major factories sank to only 55 percent of its 1929 average, and the number of man-hours worked was only 35 percent of the 1929 level. The average person still working in the city's largest plants put in only 30 hours a week that spring. According to data supplied by Bridgeport manufacturers, the average common laborer, who earned 48 cents an hour in 1929, had collected a pay packet of $23.52 for an average workweek of 49 hours. In 1932, however, he was making 44 cents an hour and working only 35.7 hours, thus taking home a weekly pay of $15.70. Similarly, an all-round machinist in the city in 1932 earned only 68 percent of what he had in 1929. Thus by 1933 even workers who had jobs found themselves in worse condition. The Manufacturers' Association of Connecticut brightly pointed out that deflation had lowered the cost of living by 25 percent, thus making up for the decline in wages.[83]

Among Bridgeport's largest locally owned industries, both the Bridgeport Brass Company and the Bullard Machine Tool Company posted operating deficits in the early 1930s. The Warner Corset Company was rumored to be in difficulty as well, though as a closely held family firm it did not report to the public. Large local retailers, such as the D. M. Read Company, also posted deficits in these years. A flurry of plant closures and company acquisitions and mergers, mostly involving small and medium-sized firms, further weakened the economic base of the city. One large workplace, the Underwood-Elliott-Fisher Company, the office machine company that had moved its portable typewriter division from Hartford to Bridgeport in 1919, transferred the division back to Hartford in 1932. This company was the only one to offer to take Bridgeport workers when it moved.[84]

Since the period of 1910–25, when some large Bridgeport companies had become subsidiaries of national corporations, the fear had always hung over the city that work would leave, because local loyalty no longer existed. Most large national corporations with plants in Bridgeport, such as General Electric, Westinghouse and its local subsidiary, Bryant Electric, and DuPont, with its subsidiary Remington Arms, weathered the early depression. General Electric had, in fact, increased its production facilities in the city in 1930, transferring the radio division from Schenectady to Bridgeport. Making parts for this new product was responsible for keeping the Bridgeport works active, as was the transfer in mid-decade of the refrigerator division, which supplied an expanding consumer market. GE workers could buy these new products from the company at a 25 percent discount, with company installment plans available for financing—an ironic condition, given the economic woes.[85] In January 1933 the *Bridgeport Sunday Herald* started a reader survey, "When Will I Get My Job Back?" The answer seemed to be not anytime soon.[86]

As companies struggled to survive the collapse or to take advantage of weakened rivals in the marketplace, managers paused to consider the volatility of their workers. State industrial leaders credited their own astute managerial techniques for the "lack of violence and disorder." Citing the effects of education programs and social work among their workforces, managers "explain[ed] problems of management and the effects of economic laws to their workers," thereby raising workers' awareness of "business costs and business methods." Connecticut employers were more concerned with the plight of the "higher classes of workers," who they thought were enduring "the greatest suffering, certainly mentally and probably physically" because they had taken advantage of prosperity "to adopt what they accepted as higher standards of living." One Bridgeport manager, for example, pleaded with the MAB for a way to help some of his skilled workers, who were in danger of losing their homes.[87]

On the other hand, Connecticut managers reassured themselves that unskilled workers, though badly hit, were "habitually thrifty and their manner of living makes them hardy. They are accustomed to hardships and are resourceful in meeting them."[88] Social workers at the Bridgeport International Institute repeated this notion in a more romantic tone: "We feel closer to the real heart of the foreign communities because of their great need. . . . The closer one gets the more one can appreciate the beauty of their simplicity, their faith, and their ability to endure."[89]

Bridgeport companies, like their counterparts nationwide, used the depression to reorganize production, retool, and introduce new technologies to their plants. They also began substituting women workers on a number of jobs, because women's pay rates were lower. In addition, the segmented nature of women's employment, with many jobs in the less depressed sales and service sectors, meant that women kept jobs, even as their male relatives were being laid off from hard-hit industries. Nonetheless, the large number of women industrial workers in a mixed-industry city like Bridgeport meant that women too were affected.[90]

The economic despair brought on by joblessness and wage cuts had contradictory effects on neighborhood ethnic businesses in the city. In the 1920s ethnics had begun to desert the neighborhood grocer and butcher for the lower prices in the American chain stores that proliferated in the neighborhoods of second settlement. But many returned to their ethnic compatriots in the early 1930s. Ethnic workers now needed their neighborhood grocer, not because they were unfamiliar with American ways or stirred by ethnic solidarity, but because they needed credit. This the chain store did not provide. The return to that immigrant era strategy of survival carried with it its own tensions. "If I had money we would buy the food in the market uptown and save plenty of money, but I can't do that because I owe too much money in this grocery store," explained one shopper at a corner grocery on the Slovak East Side. Others grouped around her testified that even though they now had jobs, they were afraid to take their business elsewhere because their neighborhood grocer might withhold credit from them the next time they lost their jobs. Some lost their fear of this possibility, however. The attitude of a second-generation Polish couple in the West End points out the tensions between this fear and the pressing need to stretch the family budget. The previous year they had shopped at Nick's, the neighborhood grocer, who had "carried" them for three months. "He's awfully nice. . . . Nick gave us credit—but his prices are higher. He carries good meat, but it used to cost us about twelve dollars a week and sometimes that was without our meat bill." Now that they had an income, Mr. and Mrs. C shopped at the Giant and the Liberty, two American chain stores in the neighborhood.[91]

Ethnic merchants lived on the margin themselves, and some storekeepers were forced into bankruptcy. At the same time some families took up new entrepreneurial ventures to substitute for wage work. As Mrs. Kurmery, a second-generation Hungarian, explained to an interviewer from the Federal Writers' Project, in 1930 her unemployed husband "thought he'd see what he could do with a bread route. He began selling bread and cake. Then we bought the store from the woman, too. . . . When we opened up business was very slow. Well, finally we got in such depth [*sic*] because people were getting the bread, but they didn't pay us." While she continued to run the store, her husband finally found a factory job that allowed them to pay off the bills they had accumulated at the store. Individual proprietorship was not a marker of economic upward mobility in this era but often its opposite.[92]

Others took a decidedly less legitimate route. Mrs. S, a Portuguese immigrant, was arrested for selling homemade liquor in her kitchen. "I lost my job eleven months ago. My husband left me with four children and I had to find some way to make money. I couldn't get a job and selling hooch seemed to be the best way," she told reporters. The local newspapers reflected the dismal scene. While ads announced store sales and "drastic new price reductions" at the Poli Palace movie house, reports of arrests for stealing food or coal began to fill newspaper pages. Home foreclosures became more commonplace, and the "unemployed, evicted tenants and out-and-out derelicts" set up a "Hoover City" in a wooded lot behind St. Vincent's Hospital in the North End.[93]

Beyond family strategies, communities persevered by turning to traditional ethnic and religious institutions or by trying to unionize. But fraternal organizations, which traditionally extended sick and death benefits to their members, were geared for only the most minor of relief activities. None could cope effectively with the massive unemployment of its members. Most ethnic fraternals, although revamped in the 1920s with modern insurance and actuary planning and consolidated into large national organizations, were hard-pressed to sustain their national memberships.[94]

But local groups did what they could to hold on to members and were helped along by emergency funds from their national headquarters. Indeed, local organizations provided valuable, honest, and extensive help to their members. No significant scandal or financial misdeeds seemed to have tainted the ethnic organizations of Bridgeport during this time, though a few ethnic bank failures reflected badly on those individual entrepreneurs. The vitality of these organizations in the late 1930s and the 1940s, as indicated by membership numbers, attested to continued allegiance. The energy of ethnic institutions by mid-decade was closely related to their roles as organizing bases for politics and unions in these communities. In addition, new ethnic organizations, like the International Workers Order, which combined ethnic culture, inexpensive insurance, and radical causes, grew tremendously during the latter half of the decade. Bridgeport shows little evidence that ethnics turned away from their institutions, as Lizabeth Cohen says happened in Chicago.[95]

Bridgeport fraternals lowered their dues or held fund-raising events to pay the dues of unemployed members in arrears. In 1932 three fraternal groups in Bridgeport—the Slovak National Sokol, Slovak Catholic Sokol, and Polish White Eagle Society—announced new, more lenient rules for unemployed members, and the Catholic Sokol inaugurated a small loan program for its members. The Rakoczi Aid Association held a fund-raising banquet in the Hungarian community, the proceeds of which were turned over to the society's treasurer to pay the dues of unemployed members.[96]

Some ethnic communities with a more diverse economic base had for some time carried out specifically philanthropic activities. The Jewish community was the best organized in this area. The Jewish Welfare Bureau, established by better-off German-Jewish businessmen in the early years and now run by the prominent professionals and businessmen of both German and eastern European groups, continued its general social work, handling marital disputes, family difficulties, and all juvenile delinquency cases among Jews. In 1936 the organization set up the Hebrew Free Loan Association "to aid those people who needed rehabilitation through loans, not relief." The Hebrew Sick Benefit Association of Bridgeport, a more traditional self-help organization set up by new immigrants in 1902, also offered free loans and saved its members from being placed on relief rolls. The Jewish community wished to keep its members from becoming wards of other private or public agencies. Both the Jewish Welfare Bureau and the Catholic Charitable Bureau received funds to care for "their own" from the Bridgeport Community Chest drives set up in the mid-1920s.[97]

The Swedish Welfare Association, established in the mid-1920s to aid unfortunate members of the community, was made up of two delegates from each of the city's Swedish churches, fraternal organizations, and singing societies, as well as the Swedish local of the carpenters' union. During the 1930s the group held a series of benefit concerts and other events to raise money for needy members. A measure of their relative prosperity was the ability of a group of Swedish citizens in 1931 to purchase the Burns Mansion in the West End for a new Swedish community center. It was to be shared by sixteen Swedish organizations and the estimated eight thousand Swedes in the city. The Swedish Welfare Association funded the purchase by selling two hundred shares at $100 per share, available on an individual basis or to organizations at a maximum of twenty shares each.[98]

Other groups also moved toward charity drives. The Hungarian Ladies Aid Society held a charity ball in December 1931, a "big success" with prominent Hungarian leaders and city politicians on hand, to raise money to "make Christmas pleasant for the unemployed." Bridgeport Lithuanians in 1932 moved to form a coalition group, the Bridgeport Lithuanian Council, to coordinate aid to needy families in their community. The twelve Lithuanian societies in the city each sent two delegates to council meetings. Political ward clubs in ethnic districts rounded out the group of institutions providing charity.[99]

* * *

The first stirrings of union organization in Bridgeport began in the 1930s, as they did nationally, in the very industries that had been in the vanguard of the great strike wave of 1919—metalworking and the garment trades. Outside the building trades, little union activity prevailed in the early years of the depression. The exception was the old Salts Textile Looms (now renamed Saltex Looms), where 350 workers walked out of the Bridgeport shop in early March 1931 in sympathy with six hundred weavers at the Shelton plant over wage cuts and the requirement to operate two looms instead of one. Workers at both plants were organized by the National Textile Workers Union, an affiliate of the Trade Union Unity League (TUUL).[100]

The TUUL, an industrial union federation founded in 1929 by the Communist Party (CP) to provide an alternative to the AFL, also made small organizing inroads in the metal trades in Bridgeport. But the CP's most visible accomplishment was the creation of Unemployed Councils in Bridgeport, Hartford, New Britain, and Stamford. Organizing by neighborhoods and using the ethnic links of the Hungarian Workers Home in the West End, and the Russian Mutual Aid Society and Polish International Labor Defense on the East Side, the Bridgeport Unemployed Council staged demonstrations to demand extensions of city relief funds, an end to foreclosures, and an end to the state's deportation of relief recipients who had no established settlement in Connecticut. The city groups rallied the unemployed for coordinated hunger marches in the springs of 1930, 1931, and 1932, appearing in Stamford, Hartford, New Britain, and Bridgeport, among other towns. While in many cities police harassed or arrested CP speakers and Unemployed Council members who visited city hall, Bridgeport's atmosphere was relatively benign. Rallies in Bridgeport attracted about 150 to 300 people between 1931 and 1933, but aside from one arrest of a CP speaker in early 1930 and the harassment of one relief recipient who had allowed the Unemployed Council to meet in her home, Bridgeport saw no harassment comparable to that reported in the rest of the state. The city reinforced its reputation for tolerance of radical activity, and the CP activity contributed in a small way to the crescendo of popular dissatisfaction with "politics as usual" by 1933.[101]

Unions used a variety of survival strategies—self-help, compromise, and finally politics. The building trades, especially the carpenters and the painters, had made considerable gains by 1929, but these slowly ebbed away in 1930. Business agents for both the carpenters and plumbers had their hands full with keeping members in line and patrolling work sites to ensure that members weren't working under scale or forced into kickback arrangement with their employers. They were also on the lookout for employers who exploited apprentices or forced union carpenters to work overtime at straight pay. Locals also worked to provide relief funds to their members, sometimes paying the dues of unemployed members.

Both locals faced the challenge of union contractors' suddenly going "open shop." Legal actions against unions once again loomed large. The increased threat of injunctions against unions caused the building trades to seek greater political influence. The building trades included many with political tendencies in their ranks—a goodly number of Democrats, including the rising star Milton Mc-Donald of the plumbers, as well as veteran Socialist activists such as Charles McLevy, business agent for the carpenters, and Peter Brewster, the painters' business agent. What united them on the political field was the common cause of labor standards. This was true for day-to-day policing of union conditions, where due regard was given by friendly local government, or in federally funded construction projects, where the 1930 Davis-Bacon Act required the payment of "prevailing wages." In addition, having friendly judges, appointed through traditional state party structures, could reduce the threat of injunction.[102]

The first real signal of a new era in labor politics came in the 1930 state elections. The Bridgeport building trades began an unprecedented political campaign that united their diverse political loyalties and created the climate for a labor-oriented politics in Bridgeport. The carpenters started a countywide campaign to defeat the county sheriff, Simeon Pease, in the election because the Republican, as a member of the Fairfield Board of Education, had authorized a "notorious" nonunion Rhode Island contractor to build a new high school in that town, depriving union men in Bridgeport and Fairfield of jobs. Pease was also accused of building a new house for himself using nonunion labor and cement blocks manufactured by inmates of the county jail, located in Bridgeport. This successful electoral campaign, led by Charles McLevy, developed over six months from the local grievances of Bridgeport carpenters to involve the Building Trades Council, the Central Labor Union, and finally the Connecticut Federation of Labor in its cause. The campaign was the first of its kind in recent local memory. The momentum built by this issue was so great that inmates working in the jail's cement block factory went on strike during the election campaign. As John J. Egan, CFL secretary and now a Republican, reported the satisfying result to the convention of the Connecticut Federation of Labor: "It made little difference whether a labor man be a Socialist, Republican or what not: if he was a labor man he was against the election of Simeon Peace [sic]. My only wish is that organized labor would display more of this spirit."[103] This was indeed the point, for the campaign brought together Socialist, Democratic, and Republican labor leaders and raised public interest in fair labor conditions. This increased political activity by Connecticut unions helped create a favorable climate for Socialist campaigns in Bridgeport.

The other union action was in the garment trades. Here the connection between political clout and union activity became even clearer, as the unions got a sudden helping hand from the Democratic governor Wilbur Cross, a moderate elected in 1930. The "sweatshop problem," as Joseph Tone, Cross's new labor commissioner called it, became the target of a sustained state campaign—

actually the first such campaign for the Connecticut Department of Labor—to rectify abusive and exploitative conditions in the state's factories. The launch of the campaign against the "sweatshop scourge" was timed to coincide with the start of the Connecticut state election season in 1932.

In the early 1930s the most readily available work for Bridgeport's women and girls was work in new garment sweatshops, which developed rapidly in the depression until they were routed out by a newly vigilant state government in 1932. Clothing contractors fleeing the higher prices, stricter labor laws, and unionized conditions in New York City set up fly-by-night shops in vacant Bridgeport buildings or parceled out home work in the poorer immigrant neighborhoods of Bridgeport, where shop rents were cheap and where desperate families worked for substandard wages. In August 1932 Commissioner Tone revealed to the press examples of the shocking conditions and low wages under which Connecticut women and girls toiled. Investigations by the Connecticut and U.S. Departments of Labor revealed that women and children were earning as little as 9 cents an hour in their kitchens, assembling garters, cutting and stitching trim, and sewing buttons. By contrast, factory work in these same lines earned Bridgeport women close to $10 (or about 21 cents an hour) when a full week's work (48 hours plus) was available. Egan, the CFL secretary, called attention to the "truckloads [of needlework] being dumped on the East Side of Bridgeport to be distributed among the poor for home work."[104] Tone's "vice squad" dramatically arrested a series of shop owners in New Haven and Bridgeport for violating the state's rather lenient labor laws on maximum hours of work for women and minors (fifty-five hours per week, whereas the surrounding states imposed a maximum of forty-eight hours). It was a successful campaign that rallied the public, labor, social workers, church groups, the Socialist Party, and even employers to condemn "unscrupulous and low-grade employers."

As the Manufacturers' Association of Connecticut (MAC) finally put it, instead of providing welcome employment for the state's unemployed, sweatshops were "a scourge on the backs of legitimate manufacturers, a constant threat to industrial peace in the commonwealth, and a drag on the well-being of Connecticut communities."[105] Connecticut manufacturers had eventually decided to support the state's antisweatshop activity because the sweatshop upset community stability, stirred radical agitation and labor unrest, brought threats of greater state legislation on labor issues, and undercut the established clothing manufacturers in the state. "Legitimate manufacturers" thus agreed with *Connecticut Industry*'s editorial cartoon, "Mac's Philosophy," in which Old Farmer Mac proclaimed, "I never did have any use for these fly-by-nights who allus take the cream and leave the skim milk to us fellows that pay the taxes."[106]

The MAC argued, however, that stricter enforcement of laws already on the books, not new laws, was the remedy needed. Even with public attention riveted on the issue and a U.S. Women's Bureau investigation under way, business groups achieved their goal of minimal new state legislation. The Republican-dominated General Assembly in 1933 passed only a new minimum wage law for minors (enacted in the wake of the National Industrial Recovery Act [NIRA]) and gave authority to the Department of Labor only to require employers to register with the department when they set up shop in the state; employers refused to countenance the lowering of the maximum hours of work to forty-eight.[107]

The political climate had changed with the victory of Franklin D. Roosevelt in November 1932 and his "One Hundred Days" legislative blitz in early 1933. The needle trades unions—ACWA and ILGWU—had held on through the antiunion 1920s in their stronghold of New York City, though they had disappeared from Bridgeport. But they returned to Connecticut in the early 1930s. During its own antisweatshop offensive in Pennsylvania, New Jersey, and Connecticut, the ACWA targeted the largest established shops in Bridgeport in the spring of 1933 as part of its tristate Shirtworkers campaign. Now bolstered by the NIRA Section 7(a)'s implied federal protection for union organization, workers staged a series of two- and three-week strikes that produced more than three thousand ACWA members with union contracts in Connecticut by July, including eight hundred in Bridgeport. Another three hundred at Bridgeport's Commercial Shirt Company joined them in August. Most were Italian, Polish, and Slovak women machine operators and Jewish male cutters. Bridgeport Socialists walked their picket lines, cementing ties that were remembered in November.[108] The ILGWU also began a New York drive to organize cloak and dress shops in early 1933, followed by an "out-of-town drive" to organize the contract shops in Connecticut and elsewhere. Bernard Schub, the new ILGWU organizer assigned to Connecticut, was a member of the SP and quickly established a supportive relationship with Jasper McLevy and the Bridgeport Socialists.[109]

"Rock-a-by baby, in the tree top / When you grow up, you work in a shop / When you get married, your wife'll work too / Just so the rich may have nothing to do. / Hush-a-by baby in the tree-top / When you grow old, your wages will stop / When you have spent the little you save / Hush-a-by baby, off to the grave."[110] The strikers who sang this song in July 1933 on the picket line outside the doors of the Stylecraft Leather Goods Company in Bridgeport's South End expressed deep-seated class grievances born of three long years of depression. They were part of a large national movement of working people roused to action at the workplace by the passage of the NIRA in June 1933. The atmosphere in the city had become electric.

CHAPTER 5

Capturing City Hall:
Depression Politics, 1930–33

On the evening of November 7, 1933, tens of thousands of people converged on Bridgeport's downtown business district in a spontaneous celebration of that day's municipal election. The Bridgeport Socialist Party had won a stunning victory, garnering more than 22,000 votes, or 48 percent of the vote cast, in a three-way race. The SP elected a mayor and twelve of sixteen common council candidates, as well as candidates to a score of lesser offices. The enthusiastic crowd stopped traffic on Main Street, then formed an impromptu victory march from downtown across the Stratford Avenue Bridge and over to cheer the Socialists at their East Side storefront headquarters. Marching bands and contingents from several Italian fraternal societies accompanied them. Many carried brooms on their shoulders, a dual symbol of a clean sweep in the election as well as a cleaning-up of city politics. One witness to this mass display of political sentiment, Michael Russo, an organizer for the Bridgeport Unemployed Council, recalled that the crowd acted "like a revolution had come here."[1]

The issues in the Bridgeport municipal elections in the early 1930s were grouped around three main themes. First was the question of taxes—who within the body politic should pay for the city's services and relief activities. Second was the debate about what to spend money on, or, conversely, which services were expendable in a crisis economy. A final theme was an increasingly general disillusionment with politicians and the political process.

New Public and Private Responses to Unemployment

The employer class had not been idle from 1930 to 1933. Two major questions preoccupied urban elites and residents across the United States in the early 1930s:

first, who should pay the bill for the effects of the economic catastrophe and, second, who should control the social programs that were established. Welfare issues had changed in the late nineteenth and early twentieth centuries. From colonial times town governments had cared for their poor. Since the Gilded Age this aid had often been privatized and handled by "professional" charity agencies and social workers who labeled their charges the "deserving" and the "undeserving" poor. Nonetheless, the boundaries between public and private welfare remained porous. In the heady days of municipal reform in the early twentieth century, cities streamlined their growing relief programs by creating departments of public welfare, partly to fend off accusations of corruption and incompetence by private charity organizations. An uneasy working relationship developed, with a mix of public and private funding and administration. Both sectors continued to believe in local self-sufficiency, however, and neither contemplated the effects of extended unemployment on their limited system of social provision.[2]

As unemployment and deprivation spread in the United States from 1930 to the economic nadir of 1933, debate intensified about the merits of private versus public remedies for unemployment. President Herbert Hoover believed that voluntarism and private relief sufficed for the temporarily displaced, and he urged companies to adopt voluntary "Share-the-Work" programs. Local chambers of commerce launched "Buy Now" campaigns, encouraging increased consumption for the sake of economic recovery. Lawmakers at all levels debated the advisability of using public revenues for relief.[3]

Industrialists by and large looked to the private marketplace and understandably opposed groups that sought to place the burden of recovery squarely on their backs. Business leaders' ideas about their responsibility to society were forceful but limited. The manufacturing sector attempted to solve the social welfare dilemma through a simple schema of *group responsibility* (i.e., businesses' responsibility to their own workforces) and *community responsibility* (i.e., local government's responsibility for the improvident or for the casual workforce). These terms come from the definitive statement and policy recommendation in *Unemployment and Its Remedies,* published by the Manufacturers' Association of Connecticut in 1933.[4]

Group responsibility was the term used by forward-looking employers who in the 1920s had pioneered "welfare capitalist" programs for their long-term employees. As scholars of welfare capitalism have observed, these initiatives were based on rigorous company control of eligibility and benefits. In the early 1930s major industrial employers argued that they were responsible only for their own employees. In-house unemployment funds sprang up in firms that had experimented with welfare plans before and during the 1920s.[5]

General Electric was in the forefront of this initiative, just as it had been in 1920s welfare capitalism. But the example of GE also illustrated the limits of liberal business thinking. GE's Unemployment Insurance Fund derived from a 1 percent deduction from workers' paychecks that was matched by an equal contribution from the company. GE president Gerard Swope was adamant about the "joint and equal" feature of the contribution, steadfastly refusing to consider a plan funded by the company alone. In his famous 1931 speech, "The Stabilization of Industry," he urged employers to follow his lead on unemployment funds and other benefits in order to head off a federal mandate. He also argued for cartelization by industry associations, with government oversight. Based on the "associationalism" of Hoover's Commerce Department in the 1920s, such large-scale economic planning was echoed by other business-sponsored schemes like the U.S. Chamber of Commerce's Harriman Plan, though the others rarely included welfare plans.[6] Similarly, the chairman of the Connecticut State Emergency Committee on Unemployment, the industrialist James W. Hook (who also sat on Hoover's Emergency Committee for Employment) also advised Connecticut companies to set up unemployment reserve funds; the alternative, he warned, was a compulsory public unemployment insurance fund "that will force upon industry a disproportionate amount of the load." The crucial difference between Hook's proposal and a public unemployment fund was that, much like the GE plan, employers would be responsible only for their own workers and would control disbursements from this joint fund.[7]

The Manufacturers' Association of Connecticut opposed state legislation that proposed to interfere with the marketplace or increase taxes on industry. MAC president E. Kent Hubbard editorialized in 1931 against the "flood of inimical social legislation" being proposed at the state and national levels, "legislation which would further increase the burdens of manufacturing industries. Those who are responsible for such legislation do not seem to realize that the prosperity of the individual citizen of the state is dependent, in a great measure, upon the prosperity of industry." As MAC vice president John H. Goss of Waterbury's Scovill Company put it, government palliatives would be "encroachments on our individual obligations . . . more dangerous to our social order than infringement of our individual rights."[8]

Both the final report of the government's Connecticut Unemployment Commission, *Measures to Alleviate Unemployment in Connecticut,* issued in December 1932, and the MAC's *Unemployment and Its Remedies,* issued a few months later in early 1933, strongly urged voluntary company-based unemployment reserve funds and opposed a compulsory unemployment reserve system or state-run unemployment insurance plan.[9] Both recommended that the state encourage the establishment of such unemployment funds by exempting them from taxation.[10] Bridgeport followed the national pattern, guided by industrialists like William R. Webster, chairman of Bridgeport Brass Company, who also served as chairman of the National Association of Manufacturers' Employment Relations Committee; George S. Hawley, president of the Bridgeport Gas Light Company and a member of the MAC Special Committee on Unemployment Relief; and W. Stewart Clark, works manager of Bridgeport GE. In Bridgeport,

GE's representation on the city's voluntary business and community organizations had a tremendous influence. As one Bridgeport YWCA staff member put it, "There is quite an attitude of acceptance [in Bridgeport] that the policies of the General Electric are very perfect and most liberal."[11]

The employer-controlled unemployment fund at GE was not as generous as it seemed. As one Bridgeport GE worker remembered, the unemployment plan became one by which the company could reward favored employees. "They had all kind of gimmick rules and regulations," recalled Frank Fazekas. "In fact they could wiggle that any way they wanted to give to who they wanted—and they could find many reasons not to give it." The unemployment benefits were helpful to those who got them, but the other company strategy, short time, helped the company avoid paying out unemployment contributions to others. Fazekas explained that his brother, who had been laid off even though he had more seniority than Frank, was able to collect $13 a week from the GE unemployment fund and "a basket—two quarts of milk and certain other things . . . from the city." Frank, on the other hand, was still on the job but on short time, and "it was getting so slow and I was working about maybe two days a week and I would say, 'jeez that ain't even half of my pay.' . . . I was making $8 and $6 a week. I said 'lay me off!'"[12]

The second part of the business formula for relief from the economic crisis was *community responsibility,* that is, *local* government's responsibility for the improvident or for the casual workforce. Congress agreed. As Hiram Bingham, the Republican senator from Connecticut, put it, "It is not the business of Washington to look out for the general welfare of the States. It is the business of the States to look out for the general welfare of the people."[13] But Connecticut's state government was not given to innovative responses to the depression crisis. The outgoing Republican governor and the incoming Democrat, Wilbur Cross, had jointly agreed in late 1930 to set up the Connecticut State Emergency Committee on Employment, modeled after Hoover's committee, with a $10,000 appropriation to investigate the situation. This committee was replaced in July 1931 by the Connecticut Unemployment Commission, whose duties were similarly limited. The most relief that Cross proposed to the 1931 legislature was $100,000 for state forest work-relief, with the addition of an accelerated construction calender for previously authorized projects that would use the budget surplus built up in the prosperous 1920s. Governor Cross, the former dean of the Yale Graduate School, had been elected in 1930 as a reformer and as a challenge to the GOP hold on state offices, but Cross staunchly believed in traditional "pay-as-you-go" planning and balanced budgets, as did many state executives and legislatures at the time. As he told the Annual Governors Conference in 1932, "The doctrine of lavish government expenditure as a promoter of economic prosperity is unsound in theory, . . . The best service the government can render the business community in time of depression is . . . to maintain unimpaired its own financial stability and credit, as a rock to which the business world may look and take heart."[14]

Indeed, Cross took that stance to its maximum. Hard-pressed representatives of charity agencies in two Connecticut cities, Hartford and New Haven, told the *Survey* in 1932 that community sentiments were definitely opposed to federal relief, but the secretary of the New Haven Community Chest acknowledged that there was "a widespread feeling that the possibility of state funds has not been sufficiently explored."[15] A conference of Connecticut mayors, meeting in Bridgeport in April 1932, urged the governor to call a special session of the legislature, which was next scheduled to convene in January 1933, to pass measures to deal with the crisis of the cities. The mayors suggested a number of measures, including a gasoline sales tax for relief funds, forcing banks to reduce interest rates and mortgage rates, and a moratorium on second mortgage payments. The governor demurred.[16]

While state officials were unmoved by the plight of cities, the Connecticut Unemployment Commission and MAC made recommendations on how cities could meet their "community responsibility" to take care of the needs of those not cared for by company plans—these included the "chronically unemployed," casual and transient workers, and "unemployables." Both organizations lavished attention on the Waterbury Plan and the special Hartford work-relief project, which were privately run and not subject to control by public officials. Both were instructive examples of the power dynamics surrounding debates about the collection and distribution of relief funds in this era. They relied on private money—in Waterbury, workers' contributions matched by company contributions, and in Hartford, donations to the Community Chest—and were administered by private charity agencies. Money was solicited from both business and the public and then put in the hands of business leaders, bypassing local governments.

So too the Bridgeport Community Chest attempted to control relief expenditures. The Community Chest, an entity administered by major industrialists wearing their philanthropic hats, had been set up in the mid-1920s to consolidate the myriad fund drives by charity groups that besieged local elites in the city throughout the year. A board of directors arranged the annual drive and then parceled out yearly grants to the various private social agencies of the city, such as the Red Cross, the YWCA, the YMCA, and including the Catholic Charitable Bureau and the Jewish Welfare Bureau. Employers pledged a given amount to the annual drive and then collected donations for the Community Chest within their own firms. For example, GE management—W. Stewart Clark of GE was chairman of the Community Chest's board of directors in the early 1930s—urged employees to donate an average day's pay; in 1930, 98 percent of them did, for a total exceeding $23,000.[17]

In early 1931 the Manufacturers' Association of Bridgeport, the Chamber of Commerce, and the Community Chest created a new organization, the Citizens Emergency Committee for Unemployment Relief and Employment. Executives of the city's leading industries, utilities, and retail establishments made up its membership (the mayor was invited as well), and its purpose was to oversee charity, eliminate "duplication and waste," and promote "an intelligent distribution of existing work among our breadwinners in such a manner that each family will receive a relatively equitable share," that is, work sharing.[18]

But this private charity had its limits. As the *Bridgeport Sunday Herald* columnist known as M.J.R. noted, by 1932 the charitable drives of the Community Chest had reached too deeply into humble pockets: "You might canvass the men engaged on public works through the department of public welfare and discover that most of them contributed a year ago to the Community Chest. . . . Of course, the idea of the framers of the Community Chest was to lessen the burden of the wealthy by compelling the city employees and the factory help to contribute." It was time, he argued, for the "men and women of means to . . . subscribe the [needed] amount."[19]

M.J.R. had hit upon the crucial question. Who should pay for relief from the economic disaster? The private company plans extracted money from worker and company alike, reducing workers' take-home pay while giving a tax break to companies that set up reserve funds. The charity drives also extracted money from rich and poor alike. Both company plans and charity drives kept relief funds and work-relief projects in private elite hands, not in public coffers or under democratic community management.

The history of voluntary charity agencies in the United States in the 1920s reveals a trend toward "broadening the base" of donations beyond the usual well-to-do donors. In 1913 Cleveland became the first city to experiment with a single fund drive for local charities. This development got a boost from the federal government's endorsement of War Chests during World War I, which coordinated community fund-raising for war-related services and relief. During the 1920s Community Chests appeared in many cities and towns, led by major corporate donors and heads of private agencies who sought to make charity more efficient and effective by running one annual combined appeal for donations. Community Chests developed workplace-based funding drives in the form of the payroll check-off, reaching into the pockets of ordinary workers. The Community Chest movement was not fully inclusive—religious and ethnic charity organizations outside the mainstream had to apply for funding. But by the late 1920s the national Community Chest movement conceded that public expenditures from taxes and other revenues far exceeded the amount raised by private charity and called for "teamwork" between public and private agencies. Nonetheless, many Community Chests and their corporate leaders insisted on overseeing the relief effort in the early 1930s, fearful of profligacy and corruption on the part of elected city officials.[20] A good example is Bridgeport, where key industrial leaders, such as Sumner Simpson, president of Raybestos Company, and W. Stewart Clark, works manager of GE, were president and chairman of the board of directors, respectively, of the Bridgeport Community Chest, and also leaders of the Citizens Emergency Committee for Unemployment Relief and later the Committee of One Hundred on Municipal Affairs, created to investigate city finances.

The unsympathetic eye with which Connecticut industry viewed the plight of the city during the depression was most vividly illustrated in an editorial cartoon published in the Manufacturers' Association's periodical, *Connecticut Industry*. (See figure 3.) Here an executive scolded a delinquent schoolboy, labeled "Municipalities," and coached him in an after-school tutorial. On the blackboard were the lessons to be learned. Most important was the lesson that "Mayors and others should junk their tin cups and dark glasses—and use their pencils—Taxpayers are interested in savings plans—not elaborate schemes for state retail sales, gasoline, manufacturers and income taxes."[21] In light of the massive unemployment situation and failure of private industry and charity to deal effectively with it, this posture looks both ungenerous and unrealistic.

MAC'S PHILOSOPHY

Figure 3. Reprinted from *Connecticut Industry* 10 (August 1932): 15.

Bridgeport very quickly turned to public funding of unemployment needs, while other cities maintained a greater reliance on private relief. Bridgeport was at the extreme, because city government by 1932 was responsible for more than 92 percent of all relief expenditures, compared to New Haven's 81 percent and Hartford's 65 percent, a trend that had been obvious since 1930.[22] Bridgeport's reliance on public relief was the product of historical experience and the creation of an extensive welfare system in the city during the previous downturn. In the postwar depression of 1920–22 the city had embarked upon an ambitious and expensive work-relief program to forestall public unrest; in essence, this program had been forged in the crucible of World War I's mass strikes and radical activity. When an economic downturn again became apparent in late 1929, the city's Board of Public Welfare—still managed by Angus Thorne, the Republican appointee who had presided over the 1920–22 relief effort—quickly returned to the earlier plan. In addition to the direct relief usually available to poor families, the board instituted an extensive work-relief plan from February 1930 until April 1931, when funds finally ran out. The men were put to work in the Public Works Department, repairing roads and parks, painting and repairing city buildings, and cutting firewood to be distributed by the Department of Public Welfare to families on relief.

Bridgeport's work-relief plan, geared toward male breadwinners, was one of the first implemented in the nation during the 1930s.[23] The wage rates were generous enough at the beginning: 50 cents per hour for a guaranteed forty-eight-hour week for all unemployed, regardless of family size. These rates seemed too generous to manufacturers; in fact, with so many factories working short time, a worker was often economically better off if totally unemployed and thus eligible for city work relief. Because relief jobs included skilled trades work, building trades unions were equally displeased when the Department of Public Welfare cut even these wages. Under fiscal pressure the hourly wage was soon reduced to 40 cents.

But the funds, bolstered by the sale of short-term deficiency bonds and a 0.8 mill tax increase, ran out in the fall of 1930. At this point the city's business community stepped in. The Citizens Emergency Committee on Unemployment and Unemployment Relief announced its intention to coordinate its own review of the city's needs and relief efforts. Eventually, businessmen cooperated with Democratic mayor Buckingham's plan to keep the tax rate constant, cut the budget, and to ask the General Assembly to authorize Bridgeport to issue $1 million in city bonds to fill relief coffers. The Republican- and rural-dominated legislature agreed to a bond bill of only $500,000. But in a bow to local business pressure, the legislature placed that funding in the hands of a committee of prominent Bridgeport businessmen named in the bill rather than in the hands of the city government. This private committee then parceled the money out to the city Welfare Department and oversaw its relief efforts.[24] Attention now turned to the question of taxes and the public purse.

Taxes and Budgets

While pressure mounted during 1931 for federal assistance to states and localities for their relief efforts, the Hoover administration pondered the growing federal deficit brought on by economic decline and increased federal spending, modest though that spending was. The question quickly became one of tax policy. Angered at the lack of federal action on the question of unemployment relief, Gifford Pinchot, the governor of Pennsylvania, stated what a growing number of observers considered the obvious: "Local relief means making the poor man pay. . . . The forces behind the stubborn opposition to federal relief is fear lest taxes to provide that relief be levied on concentrated wealth."[25]

The traditional unpopularity of taxes, combined with the dire economic situation in which individuals and businesses found themselves, sparked a massive tax revolt at the local level during 1930–32 throughout the nation. An estimated three to four thousand taxpayer groups sprang up across the land in the early 1930s, organized to lower taxes at the state and local level. In 145 cities with populations greater than fifty thousand, tax delinquency had risen from 10.8 percent in 1930 to 25.2 percent by 1933. While some of this was the result of home owners' inability to pay, it was aided and abetted by large real estate holders who agitated for tax reassessments, tax freezes, or spending constraints. The most notorious tax strike took place in Chicago in the early 1930s; legal challenges to the city's property assessments had resulted in a delay in levying property taxes from 1928 to 1930 while the county carried out a complete reassessment. When taxes were finally levied, major real estate holders banded together to challenge the assessments. When the tax challenges in Chicago failed in court, the Association of Real Estate Tax Payers (ARET) urged all taxpayers to resist paying the new taxes. By offering free legal representation on threatened foreclosures, ARET gained a considerable following of small home owners, as did other groups like the Polish United Home Owners of Illinois, but small home owners were not the driving force behind the organization. ARET conducted its campaign as an attack on the "tax eaters," the political machines with their padded budgets and patronage games. These attitudes and the widespread problem of tax delinquency alarmed municipal experts, bankers, and civic leaders, who mounted a "Pay Your Taxes" campaign throughout the country.[26]

The Socialist Party, governing a number of towns and cities at this time, challenged the notion that cities were spendthrift and that the best city was the city with the lowest tax rate. Daniel Hoan, the Socialist mayor of Milwaukee, addressed the issue in his 1933 pamphlet, *Taxes and Tax Dodgers,* where he claimed that "civilization may be judged by the amount of service that the people in a community demand, and what they can afford to pay for, and not by how low a tax rate they have." Contending that government service was less expensive than a comparable private service, he stated his solution: "Not lower taxes, but fairer taxes." The SP favored steep income and inheritance taxes and deplored the taxpayers' leagues that used "the bogey of 'high taxes' for no other purpose than to undermine public confidence in the serviceability of organized government, and to keep the tax burden falling on the poor instead of the rich."[27]

In this era the "serviceability of organized government" was the key ideological issue underlying much political debate between business interests, which wanted no state interference, and both the liberal business leaders and the public, who wanted government intervention in the economy to solve an economic collapse. On the state and municipal fronts the former wanted lowered government expenditures, period. The latter two wanted full-service government but battled about who should pay for it and how it should be run. Bridgeport city politics resounded with the noise of this battle about social policy and social spending.

At the root of the contest for control of relief funds was the elite perception that patronage politics dominated city politics. Elite hostility to urban machines had its roots in the Gilded Age and had animated Progressive Era municipal reform movements. Indeed, some analysts have contended that the inability of social and economic elites to eliminate or regulate patronage politics derailed the beginnings of a welfare state in the Progressive Era.[28] Elite reformers were unwilling to place social spending in the hands of the political parties. During the depression, business leaders conceded that private charity could not meet the crisis and tried to both limit their own tax burden and control disbursement of relief funds.

The broadening of the base of taxation was the banner under which Connecticut manufacturers supported a proposed legislative study in 1933 to restructure the state tax system, which relied heavily on real estate and personal property taxes. MAC warned that the state had seen "the removal of a number of industrial concerns from the state of Connecticut because of what they felt were unjust tax burdens." Here was the specter of the runaway shop, used not only as a weapon to thwart labor organization but as a strategy to escape the financial burden imposed upon businesses by cities everywhere in the state.[29] In Bridgeport history the tax revolt in the early 1920s by major industrialists, brought on by the manipulation of tax assessments by politicians, had led to reform that reduced manufacturers' portion of the local tax burden. But even with tax reform Bridgeport firms still routinely appealed their tax assessments in an attempt to lessen their obligations.[30]

The debate about who should pay to alleviate the distress of unemployment influenced the state Unemployment Commission's recommendations in 1932. Though they had praised private business unemployment plans as the best, James Hook and his colleagues on the commission conceded that public relief was imperative; Connecticut cities could not meet the emergency and needed state aid. The commission recommended that legislation be drawn up to arrange state-provided funds for work relief (not charity, the commission noted); this money would be distributed as loans to municipalities according to guidelines laid out by a new state commission for the emergency. Most important, the money "should be administered locally under the supervision of a local committee, approved by the state" commission. Finally, "if funds for relief require the placing of additional taxes, the burden on real property should be eased and more equitably distributed on the general public through a broader base of taxation."[31] The proposal combined both the business goal of a wider tax base and the elite goal of keeping relief money out of the hands of elected officials.

As MAC put it, "The tax base must be broadened. . . . Taxes should be at low rates designed to fall upon a large number of people." This meant shifting taxes, which in Connecticut relied heavily on real estate and personal property, away from manufacturing and toward sales and other consumer taxes. Nationally, Congress hotly debated a national sales tax, which, as Sen. George H. Moses, a New Hampshire Republican, succinctly explained, was "based upon the surest foundation for one's ability to pay—namely one's ability to buy, and he who buys most, pays most—as he should. Under such a tax the rich are soaked, and the poor do not escape." But as the Socialist leader Norman Thomas quipped, "It's a wonder they don't put a tax on tickets to the bread line." A coalition of Democrats and progressive Republicans responded to President Hoover's proposed Revenue Act of 1932 by substituting a more progressive tax plan—a steeply graduated income tax; higher estate, gift, and corporate profits taxes; and a return to various excise taxes. However, the new federal revenue was not intended for relief but to make up for the shortfall in tax receipts stemming from the business decline. State and local governments remained in charge of relief efforts.[32]

Connecticut's Senator Bingham, the former Yale history professor, had argued in early congressional debate about relief that "if we take away from the localities concerned the need of providing for their own suffering, we do away with just that much incentive toward their taking part in local self-government. . . . It is an attack on the very self-respect of local communities. . . . It is upon the development of sturdy, self-reliant citizenry that this Republic must in the long run depend for its long life. If we build up a body of citizens who are always depending on the central Government we will make weak citizens rather than strong citizens."[33]

But this elite definition of respectable citizenry proved unpopular to Bridgeport citizens who accepted their civic responsibilities and agreed to pay their fair share. They saw no contradiction in calling upon government for relief assistance. The burden of relief crystallized the debate about private versus public needs and private versus public responsibility. The crisis in fiscal affairs directly influenced the municipal elections of 1931 and 1933. Ironically, in the battle about municipal priorities that raged in 1931–33, Bridgeport business leaders moved to deprive Bridgeport's "sturdy, self-reliant citizenry" of democratic control of city finances precisely because those same citizens rejected a business-endorsed municipal solution in favor of the local Socialist Party's.

City Politics, 1930–33

The 1933 Bridgeport city election was the culmination of efforts by *two* differ-ent reform movements in the city, with two different constituencies and two different goals. According to Alan H. Olmstead, the astute local columnist for the *Bridgeport Times-Star,* the first was an "official reform" movement, "fostered by big business men who were no longer busy with their factories." This first movement, using ideas from the Progressive Era, aimed to bring about a "com-mission government," with an appointed financial board of businessmen to take charge of the city's taxes and spending. For business groups a plan that com-bined a reduced tax rate, strict budget controls, a "broadening" of the tax base, and a lowered expectation of public services was the precondition for a revival of the economy and their businesses. Olmstead described the second reform movement as "the quiet discontent of the mass of people."[34] The features of that grassroots movement—a desire for budget oversight by elected officials, a fair system of taxes, an adequate level of social services, and a guaranteed standard of living through either full employment or work relief—revealed the popular political culture of the early depression. The two reform movements were dia-metrically opposed.

Like so many other American cities in 1932–33, Bridgeport faced its inability to meet its debt obligations or its payroll. It confronted both mounting costs for unemployment relief and declining tax revenues because of the devaluation of real and personal property and the inability of citizens to pay their tax bills. As already noted, Bridgeport was unusual in that it was one of only a few cities in Connecticut that had pledged to cover unemployment relief out of public cof-fers. Between 1929 and 1934 the budget of the city's Department of Public Wel-fare went from a modest 4.2 percent of the city budget to 23.1 percent. Because the city budget paid so much of the relief expenditures early on, when other com-munities were relying on private relief drives, the city would soon be more vul-nerable to fiscal crisis. The combination of relief expenditures and interest and debt service would bring Bridgeport close to insolvency by 1933. (See table 10.)

Table 10. City Budget

Fiscal Year	Total City Expenditures	Relief	% of Budget	Interest and Debt Payments	% of Budget	Tax Rate (mills)
1915–16						18.0
1929–30	$ 8,647,049	$ 359,627	4.2	$1,654,719	19.1	28.8
1930–31	10,038,866	916,440	9.1	1,494,820	14.9	29.5
1931–32	10,589,769	1,298,934	12.3	1,506,570	14.2	29.5
1932–33	10,296,530	1,580,479	15.3	1,953,522	19.0	29.4
1933–34	11,452,597	2,641,399	23.0	2,112,951	18.4	29.8

Sources: Data derived from City of Bridgeport, "Office of Comptroller, Annual Report," *Municipal Register* (Bridgeport, Conn.: City of Bridgeport, 1929–34), Schedules A–E.

In the fall of 1931 money had again grown tight in the city's budget. The city gave relief or jobs to an average of 3,145 people a month in 1931, double the 1930 average of 1,636. The city sold $300,000 in deficiency notes (short-term bonds) in 1930 to fill relief coffers and another $500,000 in emergency relief bonds in the spring of 1931. Money from the bond sales rested in the hands of the business committee named by the General Assembly that then parceled it out to the city Welfare Department. The previous winter the city tax attorney had informed the city Board of Apportionment that "this past year we have been reluctant to foreclose any liens, because of conditions." The board's response was to press the tax office for more forceful collection. The situation had grown worse: the unpaid property taxes still on the books came to $316,600 for 1930 and an ominous $754,170 for the 1931 tax year. The clear dilemma the city faced was how to continue to provide needed relief without increasing the tax rate. The major businesses, taxpayers, and the general public asked whether the city was doing all it could to pare expenses and still provide for the unemployed. The Buckingham administration girded for the fall election. The battle would be about party patronage and machine-politics-as-usual.[35]

"Mr. Big Businessman, Mr. First Taxpayer . . . admires neither political party. . . . [His] ultimate object [is] making the political game coffee without cream," noted Olmstead, the *Times-Star* columnist. Buckingham had been the manufacturers' candidate in 1929 when he led local Democrats to victory over Behrens, the incumbent Republican, by denouncing GOP inefficiency and corruption. Buckingham was now facing the same charges. In campaigning for reelection, he defended the city's expenditures for unemployment relief. "Is it extravagance to spend $1,500,000 for unemployment relief?" he asked rhetorically in an early campaign speech. "Then the mayor pleads guilty." Moreover, he accused the Republican leaders of the General Assembly of cutting his 1931 bond bill in half in the hope of forcing the city into an unpopular tax increase that would doom the incumbent Democrats. Pointing to the Republican businessmen on the city's Board of Apportionment who had supported his administration's actions, he challenged the Republicans to repudiate their own.[36]

However, he had his own scandal to contend with—the bungling of the Stratford Avenue Bridge contract—just as he had used the Yellow Mill Bridge scandal to beat Behrens in 1929. Buckingham did much more to alienate himself from the electorate; true to his elite background, he dined at the University Club, traveled in a chauffeured car at city expense, and dressed impeccably. The *Sunday Herald* pleaded editorially with the Democratic Party not to renominate Buckingham: "[He] is a capable hand-shaker and a versatile diner-out," the paper noted scornfully. The *Herald* was concerned that Buckingham lacked control of the local Democratic organization. "He seldom gives the politicians a moment's concern. He is safe for Bridgeport's entrenched democracy."[37]

After Buckingham was elected in 1929, the Democrats had solidified their hold on the city by riding Wilbur Cross's coattails to win ten of the twelve common council seats, as well as the three state senate and two state house seats, in 1930. The 1931 campaign season began inauspiciously, with factional battles about new ethnic voters in the Democratic Party who were splitting a number of districts. But the Democrats had won few friends when they had been forced to slash relief payments and cut city payrolls by shortening the school year.

Republicans nominated a relative newcomer for mayor, William Mason, a real estate manager. Mason, a forty-year resident of the city though born in England, counted on his fraternal and business ties. Mason claimed to represent the concerns of local businessmen: "I don't pose as a business man. I am one." The Republicans charged the Democrats with extravagance in city expenditures, attacked the tax burden, and campaigned to reduce the city budget. Mason floated a plan to appoint a committee of "representative businessmen"—Democrat, Republican, and even an Independent or Socialist—to advise him on fiscal matters, a plan applauded by many, including the *Bridgeport Post*. The issue of runaway shops arose in Bridgeport during the 1931 municipal campaign when the Republican Party, campaigning on a lower taxes platform, declared that "high taxation" had driven some industries from the city in the last two years. Finally, Mason pointed out that high tax rates cost everyone, even renters, because 30 cents of every renter's dollar went to city taxes.[38]

Neither Democrats nor Republicans attracted large crowds to their traditional campaign meetings—only sixty people attended a Buckingham speech at the Slovak-American club and only another fifty at the United War Veterans Association, although Buckingham had built quite a reputation for looking after veterans' needs. Republicans too made the rounds of their party's district club rooms and the usual ethnic clubs but to disappointing audiences. Olmstead noted the indifference of the electorate. "Those observers who talk with the man on the street (not the politicians), the man in the barber shop and the men in (mostly out of) the factories report that politicians as a class are undergoing an eclipse which is perhaps a natural tendency of the times. . . . So far Mr. Ordinary Voter . . . is not interested in going to the polls this fall."[39]

Into the electoral arena stepped Jasper McLevy and his slate of stalwart Socialists. The *Herald* soon noted that the Socialist Party was getting crowds of three hundred to six hundred people at its evening street corner rallies. The distinctive style of the Socialist campaign set it apart. The SP had a network of neighborhood clubs and ethnic organizations—notably, the Twelfth District Club on the East Side, which was run by the Polish Socialist Alliance, and the Sixth District Club, with the Workmen's Circle as its base—that held card parties and socials in their club rooms every week, much like the other parties' club activities. But the Socialists also campaigned at a different street corner every night, usually choosing for its rallies the most trafficked intersections in all the city neighborhoods. McLevy also took his campaign message to noontime rallies at major factory gates in the West End, South End, and East Side, places neither of the major parties dared to appear.

The Bridgeport SP revived the basic themes that it had expounded for the last decade and added specific themes related to the depression. The party combined antimachine rhetoric with a working-class vision of what a well-run city should look like. Undergirding the campaign was the idea of the complicity of the Democrats and Republicans in running what McLevy referred to as the "double machine," both parties sharing favorable arrangements and patronage and thus quietly discouraging any true electoral opposition to entrenched privilege. "The best proof of that is the history of the campaign two years ago when many persons contributed equal amounts to both parties' campaign funds," asserted McLevy.[40]

McLevy compared a series of contracting scandals in which "citizens were fleeced of their money" to the incumbent Democrats' expedient of juggling teachers' and municipal employees' salaries to balance the budget. When Democrats pleaded that the city's debt problem was solely the result of their care for the unemployed, the Socialists demanded to know why the Democratic delegation to the state legislature had not voted for either an old-age pension plan or a state unemployment relief plan, both Socialist-sponsored bills with significant support from labor, fraternal, and social service groups. The mayor's favorite work-relief program, the building of a new municipal golf course on land in Fairfield bequeathed by the late D. Fairchild Wheeler, came in for particular ridicule in McLevy's speeches. As the Socialist candidate noted, "While hundreds of thousands of dollars are being sunk in a golf course in the town of Fairfield, the administration can find no funds to provide sewers that are sorely needed in Bridgeport, nor can it find money to improve streets within the city."[41] This theme of neighborhood improvement struck a deep chord in those sections of town and among those residents least able to motor out to the links.

Norman Thomas attracted the largest campaign audience assembled by any party during the 1931 election, about two thousand people gathered at Central High School. Thomas, who had led a municipal reform campaign in New York City in 1929, was credited with prompting the investigation of corruption in the administration of Democrat Jimmy Walker that led to Walker's ouster in 1932. Thomas told the crowd: "There is no more criminal act than graft and corruption in city government, while men, women and children are haunted by the ghastly spectre of starvation and fear of the future." The mainstream politicians in the crowd looked on with worry at the end of the rally, as people broke up into little groups to discuss what Thomas had said instead of leaving the hall.[42]

Thomas articulated the standard by which all politicians should be judged. Efficiency and economy were certainly the goals of the Republican Party and the Citizens' Emergency Committee on Employment, but to the business elite this meant cutting payrolls and limiting relief expenditures. To McLevy and his slate, efficiency and economy meant "better[ing] the living conditions of the working man." The goal at the local level was the "sound and economical administration of the affairs of government in order to realize the ultimate goals of socialization and democratic administration of public utilities." Beyond this, the Bridgeport Socialists added their standard litany of state legislative proposals—old-age pensions, unemployment insurance, minimum wages, and maximum hours—that McLevy and other SP leaders had lobbied for in Hartford for years. Noting that labor had been united against the Republican sheriff Simeon Pease the previous year, McLevy declared that labor would be united for him this year. Unlike two years before, few factory workers wore Buckingham buttons on their coats. As McLevy felt the tide turning in his favor, he declared to the press, "The solid fellow who earns a good wage and goes home to his family at night is with me."[43]

This vision of the respectable worker informed the Bridgeport SP's program. Productivist, honest, mutualistic, family centered, male defined—as sober-minded citizens these self-conscious workingmen saw their task as bringing fairness, honesty, and social justice to the community. At the same time McLevy and his supporters were cognizant of the limitations of socialism in one city, as expressed by the long-time Socialist trade union leader James Maurer of Reading, Pennsylvania: "They [Socialists in city government] cannot do much more than give a clean, honest, efficient, humane administration, free from graft, thereby proving that workers are not all hand and no brain as exploiters of labor would believe. To do that is worthwhile."[44]

The Socialist slate for city offices shows how the SP relied on the members who had stayed with the party through most of the 1920s. Of the twenty-four people listed on the full slate of candidates in 1931 (twenty-two men and two women), some information is available on all but one. The average age of the candidates was fifty-two. For the sixteen whose origins are known, eight were born in the United States (of Yankee, or old immigrant, stock), while the other half were foreign born—two each came from Austria and Denmark and one each from Germany, Latvia, Poland, and Slovakia. Most were skilled craftsmen— seven from the building trades (mostly carpenters), four machinists, one printer, one cigar maker, along with five small retailers, one unspecified factory worker, and one salesman. The two women, Sadie Griffin and Minnie Cederholm, were wives of two of the skilled craftsmen; they listed no occupation, though Sadie Griffin worked in a downtown health food store and Minnie Cederholm was often on union staffs as an organizer. Most candidates had been in the party for some time; they included founders such as seventy-one-year-old Max Schwab, as well as early recruits like Fred Cederholm and McLevy himself. The older Jewish immigrants, like Solomon Snow and George Ribak, were members of the Workmen's Circle. Peter Wojcicki, the Polish-born machinist, and Stephen Havanich, a Slovak cabinetmaker, had links to other ethnic fraternal groups. A new element was added, however, as a number of English machinists and building tradesmen joined the party. As Leicester-born John Shenton explained, he and his family had been supporters of the Labour Party in Britain, and he joined the Bridgeport SP in 1931 because he was convinced that it was the American equivalent.[45]

Local residents responded strongly to Socialist criticisms of the local parties. A full-page "Liberty Bell" ad placed in both the *Morning Telegram* and the *Evening Post* pleaded with voters to repudiate the mainstream politicians: "Bosses Win—You Lose / Tomorrow You are bigger than the Political Bosses or the Spoils system that they Represent—Vote for Jasper McLevy." The ad listed a variety of patronage sins by both Democrats and Republicans against the body politic and was signed with "This advertisement is paid for with the contributions of Nickels, Dimes and Quarters of workers of a local factory. Sick of the old gangs we are going to give you [Jasper] a chance."[46]

The campaign revealed a brooding discontent with politics and politicians in general. The city had lived through a decade of financial improprieties by both the Republican and Democratic Parties. Both mainstream parties faced the disintegration of their neighborhood networks of vote catching. The 1928 presidential election had broken the traditional ties between the local Republicans and new ethnic groups, and the local Democrats had been unwilling to embrace these new ethnic groups. The result was an independent-minded electorate motivated by concern for its economic future. Consider this "Live Letter" from a reader to the *Bridgeport Post,* sandwiched between the more traditional appeals for one of the major candidates: "When the pot calls the kettle black it is time to scrub them both clean. . . . Most voters must keep busy getting their livings and don't have time to mix in politics except election day. You can call us dumb and call us square-head all you want but we don't get mixed in crooked politics and we like to have a clean city all the way from backyards to the City hall. . . . This is not a good time to depend on the hot air that is shot off at the rallies of the old parties. It is a chance for the quiet every day voters to show they got strength to make a good scrubbing." The writer wanted McLevy as his mayor.[47]

The Socialists' critique of machine politics was based on its revulsion at the general commodification of politics—the selling of jobs in return for votes that was at the heart of the patronage system. But the patronage demon was to be found in city contracts let without proper bidding and in unproductive commissioners' slots filled with party cronies, not in honest city workers. This was a position the Socialists had evolved in the Progressive years, but whereas Progressive reformers often opted for administrative, regulatory, and sometimes antidemocratic devices, the Socialists insisted that more democracy, not less, was the remedy. The Socialist Party demanded a higher level of popular participation in government, the opening up of the political process, and an end to secret city board meetings. Socialists opposed business intrusion into the democratic process.

On election day in 1931 the SP captured 35.3 percent of the city vote, only three thousand votes behind the victorious Democrats and well ahead of the Republicans. "People who had not voted in years [were] coming out to the polls," one reporter noted.[48] Indeed, 82.8 percent of the electorate had turned out, far more than ever before in a municipal election. The SP elected three sheriffs, two selectmen, and one common council member, Fred Schwarzkopf from the East

Side's Twelfth District. The youngest of the foreign-born group, Schwarzkopf was an Austrian Jew who had come to Bridgeport as a toddler. "Short, stocky . . . [with] a slight gutteral [*sic*] impediment in his speech," Schwarzkopf had joined the SP as a teenager in 1914, worked as a carpenter, and served as secretary of Carpenters Local #115 in 1917–18.[49] He would be the voice of the party in the common council for the next two years. Finally, the campaign expense reports filed the following week revealed the ways in which each party operated: the Republicans spent $14,399, while the Democrats spent $35,944 gathered from 1,150 contributors (including nearly every Democratic city employee). By contrast the SP spent $798, eschewing elaborate campaign accoutrements and relying on volunteer foot soldiers, not patronage-oriented workers.[50]

* * *

At this point Bridgeport's business community stepped in, proclaiming its own plan for reform. The election results that so inspired Socialist hopes also stimulated business leaders to develop plans to take control of the city's budget. Business elites, clearly worried about the volatility of the Bridgeport citizenry, also distrusted the local Democrats and doubted the GOP's ability to win. In early 1932 the Manufacturers' Association and the Chamber of Commerce created a new entity, the Committee of One Hundred on Municipal Affairs, to investigate city finances. Other groups soon joined them—the East End Business Men's Association, the West End Business Men's Association, and the Federated Council of Business Men, representing small merchants and real estate interests, and finally the Bridgeport Citizens and Taxpayers League (small businesses and home owners)—all interested in cutting taxes. As the Federated Council of Business Men, claiming to represent nine hundred small businesses, stated in a resolution to the common council: "There will be no business recovery until the government applies the pruning knife to government costs, and cuts deeply." The group demanded a 25 percent cut in the tax rate.[51]

The state government had not responded to the pleas of Connecticut mayors for state legislation to raise relief money. Even the emergency appeal of "one of the foremost utility heads in the State" (in all probability, Bridgeport's DeVer H. Warner) while the mayors were meeting with Governor Cross in April 1932 had no immediate effect: "We shall have a serious unemployment situation next winter. . . . In order to meet the requirements in several communities we must have certain state legislation which will both enable the necessary funding and provide possibilities for raising funds by some means other than an increase in property taxes. . . . I doubt whether the private fundraising of last fall can be repeated."[52] Nor did the state apply to the Reconstruction Finance Corporation for loans for relief purposes. Instead, the state tax commissioner pressured the city to undertake a harsher approach to collection of the $673,690 outstanding in personal taxes ($2 yearly for each citizen aged twenty-one and older).[53] It was clear that the city would not survive until the end of the fiscal year (March 31, 1933) without either a special tax levy or drastic cuts in budget or both.

With city coffers nearly empty in late 1932 and a cold winter looming, the local public and private entities moved in separate directions. The Democratic city administration moved to rein in expenditures by cutting salaries and slashing budgets, with the school system taking the brunt of the cuts. The business community's Committee of One Hundred presented its own solution, an immediate 25 percent across-the-board cut in municipal wages and salaries, as well as seeking authorization from the General Assembly to float $1.6 million in city bonds (needed because Bridgeport had already exceeded its statutory bonding limit). But this businessmen's bill was tied to a bold rider that transferred *all* power over taxes, finances, and municipal hiring, as well as disbursement of the bonding revenue, to the existing governor-appointed Board of Apportionment and Taxation (thus extending the 1925 "Ripper Board" and the legacy of the last business challenge to municipal budgeting). This, then, would finally accomplish the business elites' goal of taking the city budget out of public hands.

The proposals of the Committee of One Hundred opened a heated public debate that pitted city officials against business, single teachers against married teachers, public employees against taxpayers, labor against business. The plan even divided the elites. For example, the board of directors of the YWCA, made up of wives of the businessmen leading the Committee of One Hundred, protested the committee's plan to cut city court costs by eliminating Juvenile Court.[54]

"This thing of a cut is not local," observed John J. Egan, the Bridgeport resident who was secretary-treasurer of the Connecticut Federation of Labor (CFL). "It is engineered by the big bankers who have their eye wholly upon cutting the cost of government without considering other costs."[55] Neighborhoods opposed closing fire stations, and many citizens opposed shutting the Bridgeport Normal School, the locally funded teacher-training school that operated as an adjunct to the city high school. Police officers, fire fighters, and teachers resisted the Democratic mayor's proposed flat 20 percent pay cuts and proposed instead a sliding scale. Popular outrage at the Committee of One Hundred's budget and legislative proposals resulted in a deluge of letters to key members of that group, particularly utility company chiefs, who were threatened with boycotts. Married teachers supported a proposed tenure-in-office bill in the General Assembly, while the plan was opposed by young teachers who would be laid off if married teachers stayed. Finally, Rev. Paul F. Keating, pastor of St. Mary's Roman Catholic Church, a predominantly Irish parish, preached from the pulpit against the pay cuts for city workers, reminding his congregation that Catholics—presumably, a large percentage of city employees affected and no doubt Irish as well—were both good citizens and taxpayers and saved the city more than $300,000 by supporting their own schools for more than fifty-six hundred students.[56]

While some common council members pressed for more efficient tax collection, Schwarzkopf, the Socialist council member, spoke up. The SP, he stated, opposed wage cuts and relief cuts and proposed that other operating expenses be cut instead. Once again, Schwarzkopf suggested further reductions in the water rates paid to the Bridgeport Hydraulic Company (the water company had not been cooperative in negotiations with the city for an entire year—the *Herald* claimed that the water company "snickers a bit" whenever the issue was raised). The question, according to Schwarzkopf, was not spending per se but *how* to spend.[57]

Schwarzkopf, who had appealed to the class interests of his neighborhood in his two years on the common council, enjoyed considerable support. He had joined a group of 450 angry East Side residents in opposition to a neighborhood manufacturer who wanted to run freight along abandoned trolley tracks on neighborhood streets. He reminded residents of deaths that had occurred along this street before the New Haven Railroad had been forced to elevate its tracks above street level. At yet another zoning hearing Schwarzkopf led the neighborhood opposition to a businessman's request to build fuel oil storage tanks on his East End property. The *Herald* noted disapprovingly that Schwarzkopf "spent too much time appealing to class prejudice and social standing," using "trick phrases of 'working men's rights' and 'protection of homes.'" The paper conceded, however, that "his discourse" was what the neighborhood people wanted.[58]

Class prejudice was also apparent in the Committee of One Hundred's plans for the city. Interested in saving taxes, yes, but also concerned that the city have the right environment for doing business and be placed in the right hands, local elites felt they were doing the best thing. As DeVer H. Warner, writing on Warner Corset Company stationery, expressed it to J. Henry Roraback, state GOP leader, in asking for his help in the legislation:

> The very best interests of the town and the best element of the town decidedly approve of the [Committee of One Hundred] Bill . . .
> The thing has been handled badly. The town's finances are in a very serious condition. . . . Bridgeport has not grown for a number of years and it is becoming serious; getting a bad name from political and tax standpoint, and those of us that have been less active for a few years past will either have to get into the game pretty soon or move out of town. . . .
> I think what I have said above is stripped of all politics and would be the sentiment of a large majority of the men upon whom the interest and prosperity of the town largely falls.[59]

The General Assembly, dominated by rural and small-town representatives, warmed to the Committee of One Hundred's story of city corruption and extravagance and gave the committee virtually everything it wanted, including increased power for the Board of Apportionment.[60] With bonding privileges extended and the operating budget and control of relief spending now safely in the hands of trusted businessmen, the Board of Apportionment breathed a sigh of relief and set the tax rate at 29.5 mills (only 0.1 mill higher than 1932). The Committee of One Hundred gloated that "the administration of our financial affairs [is] vested in the group of public-spirited men in the Board of Apportionment and Taxation . . . free from political control which might limit the exercise of the power given to them." According to the Socialists, however, this legislative move by businessmen "surrender[ed] the rights of the people to govern themselves by the Democratic methods our forefathers fought for."[61]

* * *

A threatening cloud hung over local politics as Bridgeport readied itself for the 1933 municipal election. The GOP, still reeling from its poor third-place showing in 1931 and further demoralized by the low Hoover vote in Bridgeport in 1932 (though Hoover carried the state), was further handicapped by its complicity with the Committee of One Hundred. The fortunes of the party were similarly in question around the state; while a slate run by the Taxpayers League had won October town elections in Danbury, the Democrats had defeated incumbent Republicans in Norwalk, Milford, West Haven, and even in the GOP bastion of Litchfield County. The Bridgeport Republican Party's campaign slogan was "Pledged to Sound Government"; it mirrored its commitment to work with the Board of Apportionment and Taxation to reduce the city's expenses and tax rate. The GOP nominated John G. Schwarz, Jr., a building supplies dealer, building contractor, and member of the Committee of One Hundred. The forty-six-year-old businessman had held only a few appointive political offices, but he was well known in Masonic circles. "I am not, never have been and never will be a politician," he claimed. "It is evident the people of the city wanted an independent candidate and I am sure I am just that."[62] Schwarz outlined a program of economy that would bring a $500,000 reduction in the city budget, the amount projected to forestall a tax increase. Plagued by defections from its Italian wing, the Republican Party benefited from a renewed organizing effort from middle-class professionals in the new Slavonic Club who attempted to rally their countrymen back to the GOP cause. One spokesman, Gaza Mika, a lawyer, discounted the seeming enthusiasm of the Slavic neighborhoods to vote for McLevy in 1931. "The vast majority of the Slavonic people are individualists," he assured the Bridgeport public, and they would safely vote for the Republicans. The GOP's common council candidates were all white-collar employees or businessmen. In a desperate appeal to ethnic neighborhoods the Republicans cast a wider net for candidates: six Yankees, four Irish Catholics, four Slavs, one Italian, and one German.[63]

The Democratic Party paid relatively little attention to the GOP, except to note the $18,000 that Schwarz had been paid to build the city's new transient relief camp, Camp Warner, in 1933. Mayor Buckingham, tired of the burden of governing, had resigned the mayoralty during the summer to devote full attention to his appointed position on the state Commission for Workmen's Compensation. Choosing acting mayor (and former council member) James Dunn as their mayoral candidate, the Democrats tried to boost their profile by linking it as strongly as they could to the Roosevelt administration and the legislation of the One Hundred Days, until retired general Hugh Johnson, chief of the National

Recovery Administraton, ordered the Democrats to take the NRA's Blue Eagle off their campaign posters.[64] There was no talk of state legislative initiatives, however, for the Democrats had little to show. They had no way of fending off popular discontent with their budget reduction measures, except to blame the GOP for the city's bonding debts. Moreover, the expediency of municipal employee layoffs was wreaking havoc within the party clubs, where many owed their jobs to patronage influence. The narrowness of the interests of the Democratic Party apparatus in the neighborhoods was reflected in the backgrounds of the Democrats' candidates for common council: nine of sixteen were Irish, along with three Yankees, three Germans, and one Italian.[65] During this election campaign the Democrats followed the crowds, copying the SP tactic of speaking to noontime rallies at factory gates.

In their panicked response to the Socialists' growing strength, the local Democrats made antiradicalism their sole campaign issue. "There is no doubt that the issue today is Socialism and nothing else. Socialism in Bridgeport or anywhere is unAmerican, unpatriotic. Even the McLevy buttons are red, the red of socialism," noted one major Democratic Party statement. The newspapers the next day were filled with letters to the editor decrying the Democratic tactic of injecting issues like "unAmerican" into the campaign dialogue. Claiming that a Socialist victory would frighten away prospective factory owners, Democratic ads proclaimed, "Don't Let this Happen!" over a sketch of a closed factory. This tactic did not have the desired effect, however, as the sketch too much resembled a factory closed for the past year of Democratic administration.[66]

Once again, it was the Socialist Party that provided the issues and the fire for a municipal campaign. Its style and substance set it apart from politics as usual. Even the businessman's paper, the *Bridgeport Post*, took note of the differences in the campaigns of the three parties:

> The McLevy headquarters, the Eleventh District Socialist Club rooms on East Main Street, furnishes an unusual contrast with the headquarters of the two old parties. Unlike the other two, it is away from the downtown section of the city and is located in the heart of the East Side, where McLevy and his lieutenants expect to find their greatest support. . . . While Democratic Nominee James L. Dunn has his Stratfield Hotel suite for a headquarters and Republican Nominee John G. Schwarz Jr. holds sway in a new downtown store building, McLevy meets with his campaign pilots in modest quarters, simply furnished and heated by a small stove in the center of the room.[67]

The party had taken particular advantage of the previous year's presidential election to mount a highly visible Socialist campaign in Connecticut, stressing SP state and federal legislative initiatives like old-age pensions, minimum wages and maximum hours legislation, and unemployment insurance. Norman Thomas, the party's presidential candidate, had toured the state in a "Red Special" motorcade along with McLevy as gubernatorial candidate and Devere Allen as candidate for U.S. Senate. They drew large crowds wherever they stopped; the speeches by Thomas and Milwaukee's Daniel Hoan in Bridgeport were broadcast over local radio. McLevy, who was given a column in the *Herald,* hammered away at the political bankruptcy of the mainstream parties: "Democrats and Republicans [are] all brothers under the skin-game—long on platitudes but short on accomplishments," while workers feared for their jobs or for their futures without jobs. Hoan addressed an overflow crowd of four thousand in Bridgeport, while Cross, campaigning for the national ticket, attracted only three hundred to his rally that night in neighboring Fairfield.[68]

New members were attracted to the party after the 1931 showing, and they included a number of enthusiastic, educated young people. Abraham Knepler, recently graduated from Rutgers College, and Jack Bergen, recently graduated from the Yale School of Architecture, were sons of Jewish working-class families who joined the Bridgeport SP in the wake of the 1931 election. As Knepler recalled, "I came into this with enthusiasm. . . . To see the degree of altruism [in the members] struck me, to see the extent to which people could get involved on issues, in the principle of the arguments, the debates," though he noted that some were still so fearful of antiradical backlash that they joined the SP under pseudonyms. Bridgeport Socialists had been disappointed with their results in 1932, as FDR swept the city and carried all Democratic candidates with him. The SP polled only 8.7 percent of the vote in Bridgeport, though this was considerably better than the 2.5 percent Thomas polled nationally. Most important, as Knepler recalled, "1932 served a very important function for the Socialist Party, if not for the community as a whole, in that it provided the first half-way decent opportunity . . . for the propagation of socialist principles, and to get a hearing for it in many places."[69]

In the 1933 municipal campaign the Bridgeport SP literature emphasized a "workerist" image. Its most common leaflet depicted a workingman in overalls exhorting voters: "Let's Go, Bridgeport, Vote Socialist!" McLevy pledged to work for "a program that will . . . ultimately lay the foundation for constructive and sound municipal government, a program that will insure social justice and a program that proposes the social ownership of our municipal utilities." To those who focused on the "Red menace," McLevy pointed out that "the Marxian analysis of the industrial system has come true. The machine has become the master of the man, the man walks the streets by hundreds of thousands because of its development, as Marx predicted it would. . . . What are you going to do? Smash the machine to discredit Marxian philosophy, or are you going to socialize it for the benefit of the human race as Marx proposed?" The Socialists, for their part, distributed "more copies of the National Platform of the Socialist Party . . . than any other single piece of literature," McLevy claimed.[70]

While they confirmed their proletarian image, the Socialists also appealed across class lines. The heated SP campaign stressed taxes, corruption, and potential bankruptcy. When asked what he would do in office, McLevy said he would promptly do what the incumbent Democrats were *not* doing, that is, he would take advantage of new federal funds: "Employment is the most serious problem that is facing us. . . . To secure Federal funds would not only aid in employment but would help many types of merchants as well." In the industrial city, McLevy observed, many suffered when wage earners were out of work, "those taxpayers accommodating the unemployed with living quarters were forced to accept script [*sic*] and the same condition applied to the grocer who furnished the unemployed with food."[71] As in 1931, McLevy linked the public's dissatisfaction with politics as usual to the workings of the "double machine"; thus the "independent voter" had no choice. This explained the appeal of the pro-McLevy "Liberty Bell" ad in 1933: "YOU HAVE ALWAYS WANTED HIM—NOW ELECT HIM."[72]

The SP held club parties, pinochle parties, and picnics and continued its street corner rallies. "There was a lot of give-and-take . . . between speakers and the audience," recalled Knepler of his own soapbox experience. "The crowd, the people were listening and then at some point would interrupt or ask questions . . . like 'What makes you different from the Republicans or the Democrats?' 'What makes you think you wouldn't be as crooked as the others?' . . . and this also sharpened up the thinking of those who spoke."[73] Women Socialists taunted the activists in the Federation of Democratic Women, reminding Bridgeport women that the SP had supported women's suffrage long before the Democratic Party and that women had "equal rights" in the SP. The SP had also been the first party to nominate women candidates for common council, though it should be noted that none was included on the 1933 slate.

But this year the Socialists went beyond rallies on street corners and at factory gates. McLevy was now welcome in Slavic, Italian, Armenian, and Hungarian ethnic halls that had never been identifiably radical. Tensions within Democratic and Republican ethnic ranks for several months had led to feuding between party officials and some ethnic leaders, leading Schwarzkopf to observe that "the foreign element in Bridgeport had been fooled too long by the false leaders among the old party politicians, especially by those leaders who play upon the nationality of those to whom they wish to appeal." The Socialists could always count on their traditional ethnic allies, such as the Workmen's Circle and Polish Socialist Alliance, but now they broadened their ethnic networks.[74] In a last-minute switch Louis Richards, the Italian fraternal leader and long-time Republican who was now disaffected from the local party, endorsed McLevy and his slate.

The party brought in nationally prominent Socialist speakers, such as Frank Crosswaith, the African-American organizer for the International Ladies' Garment Workers' Union (see figure 4), August Claessens of the Rand School, and Hoan, who had been such a hit in Bridgeport in 1932. And when the Democrats brought in the old antiradical general Smedley Butler for a final "Red Menace"

Socialist Campaign Headquarters - 426 East Main St. - Phone 3-3363

Figure 4. Bridgeport Socialist Party rally poster, 1933. (Rare Book, Manuscript, and Special Collections Library, Duke University.)

speech, a "Veterans' McLevy Committee" sent a letter to the editor of the *Bridgeport Post* saying that not every veteran was a Democratic supporter. "NRA strikes" by more than three thousand Bridgeport garment, metal trades, and trucking workers in the months leading up to the election added to the ferment in the city.[75]

Bridgeport Socialists had traveled to Washington in May 1933 to participate in the SP-sponsored Continental Congress of Workers and Farmers, a gathering of unemployed, labor, and community activists. McLevy also endorsed a Connecticut congress scheduled for September, though he and his organization were too busy with their election efforts to attend. Though he refrained from asking for the formal endorsement of the Bridgeport Central Labor Union, McLevy was sure of working people's votes. Even Egan proclaimed before the September 1933 state labor convention, "I vote for a Socialist when he runs for office," while a Hartford building trades leader agreed, stating "I am not a Socialist, I am a Democrat. . . . I vote the Socialist ticket and I am proud of that fact."[76]

The Socialists were victorious, winning more than twenty-two thousand votes (mostly in a straight ballot vote for the whole SP slate), or 48 percent of the vote, in a three-way race. In addition, Bridgeport voters repudiated a number of

Democratic spending priorities, voting, for example, a strong yes on whether to continue the Normal School.[77] As McLevy stated to the press the following day, where reporters found him working at his trade repairing a roof, "My greatest satisfaction in being elected in my tenth mayoralty campaign was to be elected by independent voice of the people." Leo Krzyki, national chair of the Socialist Party, called the McLevy victory "a triumph of real socialism of the 'horny-handed' variety rather than any sort of a passing protest vote." At his inauguration before an audience of twenty-five hundred, McLevy pledged to care for "the victims of the breakdown of the industrial system."[78]

As the *Times-Star* noted in its postelection analysis, the members of the Committee of One Hundred had "devoted their money and their prestige to an attempt to turn back the Socialist tide," but their criticisms of city government were effectively used by McLevy instead.[79] Now bowing to popular decision, both the Committee of One Hundred and the Board of Apportionment pledged their support "in all efforts to give Bridgeport an efficient and economical administration," though they continued to obstruct the Socialist administration for another two years.[80]

The election in Bridgeport was more than a protest vote against incumbents. It was a ringing endorsement of an alternative agenda, an answer to "the quiet discontent of the mass of people," as the columnist Olmstead had put it. In their

Jasper McLevy, 1933. (Photograph by Post Publishing Co., Historical Collections, Bridgeport Public Library.)

success in raising the issue of who pays for social services and who controls the public purse, the Socialists gave shape and direction to public objection to patronage politics and the business-inspired expedient of cutting services and wages. At the same time the Socialists legitimized the grievances of working-class Bridgeport. As Mike Russo, a local Communist Party critic of McLevy's, remembered that election night: "It wasn't a protest vote, it was more than that. . . . This . . . proved that there was this process of becoming radicalized, and they turned to McLevy. . . . They *thought* he was a socialist." The Connecticut Socialist paper, the *Commonwealth,* described the majority of Socialist votes as coming from the "conservative, small home-owning, factory working people who have tried the Democratic and Republican parties for years without protest, and found them wanting."[81]

An engaged electorate, larger than ever before, had spoken in Bridgeport. In 1933, the turnout of the registered voters was 83.5 percent, an impressive response for any local election and the largest turnout to date in any municipal election. A statistical examination of the votes reveals who voted Socialist. (See tables 11 and 12.) While the Socialists in 1931 had not attracted large numbers of low-rent households (the Democrats seem to have retained most of these), the SP had the higher correlation to low-value home owners. This correlation was even stronger in the 1933 election, while low-income renters now also turned to the Socialists. What is clear is that contemporary speculation about a "silk-stocking" protest vote for McLevy was wrong; the correlations between high-income

Table 11. Correlations for 1931 and 1933 Mayoral Vote

	1931			1933		
	Socialist	Democrat	Republican	Socialist	Democrat	Republican
Foreign-born	.28	.24	−.75*	.61	−.42	−.67*
Low-rent household	.10	.37	−.65	.39	−.15	−.73*
Low-value home	.43	.13	−.77*	.53	−.31	−.72*
High-rent household	−.42	−.16	.79*	−.55	.35	.67*
High-value home	−.46	−.16	.84**	−.53	.33	.66*

Relationship of ethnicity to economic variables for foreign-born residents (1930)

High-value home	−.62
Medium-value home	−.24
High-rent household	−.84**
Medium-rent household	−.68*
Low-value home	.61
Low-rent household	.87**

* = Pearson's *r* correlations significant at −.01
** = Pearson's *r* correlations significant at −.001

Sources: City of Bridgeport, *Municipal Register* (Bridgeport, Conn.: City of Bridgeport, 1932); City of Bridgeport, *Municipal Register* (Bridgeport, Conn.: City of Bridgeport, 1934); U.S. Census Bureau, Population, 1930, vol. 3, pt. 1: Reports by States (Washington, D.C.: U.S. Government Printing Office, 1930), table 23.
Note: Calculations were performed with SPSS/PC+.

Table 12. Correlations of Democratic Party Vote in Bridgeport, 1928–40

Year (Campaign)	Foreign-born (1930)	Low-value Home (1930)	Low-rent Household (1930)
1928 (president)	.49	.39	.59
1929 (mayor)	−.23	.11	−.34
1930 (governor)	.14	.43	.24
1931 (mayor)	.24	.13	.37
1932 (president)	.39	.31	.54
1933 (mayor)	−.42	−.31	−.15
1934 (governor)	−.35	−.20	−.12
1935 (mayor)	−.26	−.08	−.11
1936 (president)	.80**	.87**	.87**
1937 (mayor)	−.15	−.11	−.002
1938 (governor)	−.17	−.25	−.05
1939 (mayor)	−.21	−.17	−.08
1940 (president)	.76*	.71*	.95**

* = Pearson's r correlations significant at −.01
** = Pearson's r correlations significant at −.001

Sources: Votes from City of Bridgeport, *Municipal Register,* 1928–40 (Bridgeport, Conn.: City of Bridgeport, 1928–40); U.S. Census Bureau, *Population,* 1930, vol. 3, pt. 1: *Reports by States,* table 23, and vol. 6: *Families,* table 24 (Washington, D.C.: U.S. Government Printing Office, 1930).
Note: Calculations were performed with SPSS/PC+.

indicators and the parties shows that those areas strongly voted Republican in 1931 and 1933. Indeed, in 1933 those areas drifted a bit into the Democratic camp rather than cause the election of a Socialist. On the other hand, the immigrant vote, which divided equally between the Democrats and the SP in 1931, deserted the Democrats for the Socialists in 1933.[82] All indications are that, just as the *Commonwealth* had claimed, the immigrant, low-value home owners—those voters vitally concerned with the well-being of the city budget and worried about taxes on their modest homes—voted Socialist to ensure a fiscally wise administration responsive to the concerns of low-income residents. These were the citizens who viewed big business tax agendas and corrupt political machines in the same light.[83]

* * *

Electoral politics in early 1930s Bridgeport was a cauldron of competing ideological agendas. Early depression era politics at the grassroots had a class character beyond the occasional Roosevelt utterance on behalf of the "forgotten man." The Bridgeport SP successfully raised the related issues of who pays for social services, who controls the public purse, and which services should be funded. That Bridgeport voters had a number of electoral options for lower taxes and still chose the SP meant that low-income taxpayers wanted responsible government, not less government, and were willing to pay for it if other sectors contributed their fair share. The Socialists gave shape and direction to a grassroots challenge to patronage politics and the business-inspired expedient of cutting services and wages. Moreover, their call for greater democracy and public accountability in city government touched a responsive chord with a citizenry disenchanted with the self-interested stance of local corporate leaders.

After November 1933 the Socialists found that they lacked the political tools that they would need to implement their social reform program in the city. In his sober reflection on the political events of 1933 Olmstead noted that the Socialists were elected to offices that had little power. This limited role was the result of the "official reform" movement of the "big business men," who had succeeded legislatively in wresting control of the city budget from elected officials. But the Committee of One Hundred leaders "did not know what to do with the power they had."[84] Although they had succeeded in ending popular control of city finances, "the quiet discontent of the mass of people" as Olmstead put it, gave electoral victory to the Socialist Party. The SP found itself locked in battle with business leaders over fiscal priorities for the next three years.

CHAPTER 6

Captured by City Hall:
The Dynamics of
Accommodation, 1933–36

It was one thing to win an election; it was quite another to win power. The Bridgeport SP learned that painful lesson during the next few years as it attempted to fulfill the expectations of its members, its public, and the business interests that held the strings of the public purse. The Socialists were well aware that creating new priorities for the taxing and financial powers of the city could not be accomplished at the local level alone. Thus they turned their attention to the state and national levels, where redistributive and social spending measures were being debated. In the end, Jasper McLevy and his Socialist administration regained control of essential decision making in the city, but the price they paid was a circumscribed vision of how the city could be remade.

The Bridgeport SP depended on the backing of working people of foreign stock to press forward with its program. But to a large extent this constituency was not organized economically by 1936. Indeed, the shape of labor organization limited what it could do politically. The 1933 strike wave in Bridgeport was the first sustained, and only partially successful, labor action of the depression. Because the development and the fortunes of the Bridgeport Socialist Party were not linked institutionally to union structures in the city—that is, the SP was not a labor party formed by constituent unions to press a political agenda—Bridgeport Socialists succeeded at the polls, even though the majority of working people in the city were not formally organized at their workplaces. The lack of linkage between party and workplace meant that the SP had no organized base upon which to call for support in the difficult task of remaking city hall. Here the limitations of Second International Socialist thinking—that is, seeing separate spheres of organization and action, one political, the other economic; one the sphere of party, the other the sphere of trade union—left McLevy and his followers poorly equipped for serious battle with the city's economic elite. Although the SP came to power amid a nascent wave of union action, that unionism came to a standstill until the CIO era of 1937, after McLevyism had been brought to a halt.

Organizing Labor

More than three thousand Bridgeport workers had engaged in concerted workplace action in the few months before the 1933 municipal election. By August 1933 the National Recovery Administration (NRA) codes had sparked the continued strike wave—workers now walked out in disputes about their employer's interpretations of the codes. In September about 750 women workers at the city's corset factories also struck, winning union recognition for the International Ladies' Garment Workers' (ILGWU) at the Warner and LaResista corset shops. The needle-trades union of the CP-affiliated Trade Union Unity League (TUUL) led a strike at the Mitchell Brothers underwear factory. These were followed by spontaneous strikes at myriad other workshops in Bridgeport—a successful TUUL strike of 250 Hungarian molders, strikes of metalworkers, aircraft workers, cleaners, and dyers—and, finally, a statewide stoppage by 5,000 Teamsters, including several hundred in Bridgeport.[1]

Union activity continued after the city election as well and throughout 1934, often in defense of gains just won. Initially buoyed by the expansion of the economy, recalls from layoff, and NRA-induced wage increases in the summer of 1933, workers found their disputes mediated by state NRA officials who were active New Deal Democrats. These included Milton McDonald, president of the Bridgeport Building Trades Council, and respected "public" representatives like James K. McConaughy, the president of Wesleyan University. The support by Democrats in Washington and in Connecticut drew working people toward the Democratic Party at the state and federal levels, but the attraction faded as the NRA foundered in its futile attempt to negotiate equity between workers and their employers. With no strong enforcement mechanism, neither the state NRA Board nor the federal Labor Relations Board could do more than bring the disputing parties together. Even that assistance disappeared when the National Industrial Recovery Act was invalidated by the Supreme Court in May 1935.[2]

Employers in the metal trades, having learned much from their experiences in World War I and the 1920s, dusted off the company union and other benefit plans. By early 1934 company works councils, which the NRA guidelines considered legitimate collective-bargaining agents, operated at Bridgeport's GE, Singer, Remington Arms, Bullard Machine, and Bridgeport Brass Company plants.[3]

AFL organizers like John J. Egan, the secretary-treasurer of the Connecticut Federation of Labor (CFL), flitted from one hot spot to another, signing workers up in the new and fragile federal locals that the AFL created to deal with the many workers who did not fit craft categories. At the same time organizers from the various AFL unions like the International Association of Machinists (IAM) tried to organize shops with a combination of a craft local for the skilled workers and a federal local for the rest. Egan promoted this arrangement, which he called the "Shop Council Program," as the answer to the AFL's structural limitations; it was, in fact, a faint copy of the radical unions of the World War I years. More successful in spirit, if more marginal in practice, was the effort of the TUUL Steel and Metal Workers Union, which spread its message of industrial unionism from pockets of sympathetic ethnic communities, specifically, the Russians and Hungarians. Many more workers went unorganized.[4]

The IAM made little progress in penetrating the large metalworking shops that dominated the Bridgeport industrial terrain. A good part of the problem internally was the long shadow cast by the events of 1919 and what was viewed as the IAM's betrayal of radical unionism in Bridgeport. "The only thing that has kept the organization apart was the old dissension that happened years ago," reported one union official.[5] "We have more ex-members . . . of the I.A. of M. than any other city in the country," complained the frustrated IAM organizer George Doyle to IAM headquarters in 1934. Some Lodge 30 members wanted to forget the lodge and "just see if they can start with a new charter." In the meantime thirteen machinists, half of Lodge 30's membership, got municipal jobs in early 1934. When the Mechanics Educational Society of America (MESA) came to town, some of the Swedish toolmakers who had once belonged to the IAM joined MESA, saying it "was a new organization, and it didn't cost anything to join, so [they were] going to see what it would do," Doyle reported.[6]

MESA, a militant union of tool-and-die craftsmen from the Detroit area that had dedicated itself to industrial unionism, had begun organizing in the Northeast in early 1934. Mr. R, a GE production worker for fifteen years, recalled that after Doyle failed to bring IAM leaflets around to the GE plant gates as he promised, "I heard about [an] organizer from the Mechanics Educational Society of America. . . . He distributed leaflets at the gate."[7] Mr. R got workers in his department to join; by late spring of 1934 MESA was holding meetings for GE, Remington, and Singer workers and had enrolled nearly one thousand of them. This brief glimmer of organization in the mass-production factories of the city paralleled developments nationwide in 1934, when the stirrings of industrial unionism animated textile and steel workers, West Coast longshoremen, and Minneapolis truckers. Unfortunately for Bridgeport workers, Remington Arms met this challenge by firing the shop-floor leaders. The MESA organizer then left town that fall with the union treasury and never returned. Egan later recalled, "I'm sure he [the MESA organizer] was on the company payroll. I used to see him over at the Elks Club where he was living, and he . . . was talking to the big shot at the Remington. I know he broke the union and then left town." It is impossible to confirm or refute this allegation, but the fact remains that union-minded metalworkers made little progress in these shops until the CIO came to town in late 1936.[8]

Building trades workers, on the other hand, expanded their union power. But the unique nature of their industry and the history of their organizations, along with the continued weakness of the economy, meant that growing union power among construction workers had little effect on the industrial workers around them. The building trades were extremely dependent on government intervention in Bridgeport to maintain their standards and organization. McDonald, who also was president of the Connecticut Building Trades Council in the early 1930s, was adept at alerting federal officials to local contractors on federal projects who ignored standards of union wages and working conditions in violation of the 1930 Davis-Bacon Act. His activity on behalf of the Democratic Party in the state led to his appointment to the state NRA board, where he could also influence decisions regarding prevailing wages.[9]

More important locally was the Socialists' victory in the municipal elections and McLevy's subsequent appointment of Peter Brewster, the business agent for the painters' union, as director of public works. This guaranteed that maintenance and construction work for the city would be unionized. Though the McLevy administration did not have control of relief jobs, the Democrats and Republicans who did control relief heeded federal guidelines, which gave preference for jobs with the Civil Works Administration to building trades union members. The relief agents also appointed union leaders as consultants and supervisors on Federal Emergency Relief Administration jobs. In other words, building trades leaders could gain benefits for their members and power for themselves by lobbying rather than through grassroots organizing, at least in the public sector of their industry.

Thus the idiosyncratic position of the building trades unions within the larger labor movement had a direct effect on the new city administration because many of the SP's elected officials were members of building trades unions, had no experience in organizing workers in mass-production industries, and therefore could not understand the problems that such organizers faced. Construction union members, moreover, were accustomed to negotiating with coalitions of employers' associations, a bargaining pattern that made it easy to envision running the city in cooperation with business associations.

Two other factors immediately limited the Socialists as they took control of city hall. The Bridgeport SP lost its most vocal labor organizers when Fred and Minnie Cederholm broke with McLevy over electoral strategy, as I will discuss shortly. And, before the sit-down strikes of 1937, McLevy had few opportunities to directly intervene on behalf of unionism. Most of his prounion activities were modest. For instance, when long-time SP comrades in the New York garment unions asked him to help them organize garment workers in Bridgeport, the answer was always yes. Both the Amalgamated Clothing Workers of America (ACWA) and the ILGWU invited McLevy to speak on their radio programs on WEVD, the New York City station started in the mid-1920s with the help of the ACWA. Most of the programs on which he appeared also were carried on Bridgeport's radio station WICC, giving McLevy another union audience.[10] In the rare instance when police arrested union picketers, as in the 1935 pocketbook workers' strike in Bridgeport, McLevy and his police chief quickly appeared in city court to see that charges were dismissed. The mayor mediated a few strikes as well and was received with standing ovations at CFL conventions. This is not to say that he could not have done more—Daniel Hoan, the Socialist mayor of Milwaukee, created a precedent when he issued a proclamation giving the city power to shut down factories that tried to operate during a strike, citing a menace to public safety. Many such creative measures could have been forthcoming from Bridgeport City Hall to encourage unionization.[11]

Bridgeport, then, presented a paradox. A volatile electorate willing and able to elect trade unionists to city hall was, at the same time, unable to organize itself at work. This situation owed much to the nature of industrial power in the city at the time, as employers had proved themselves able to quash incipient union organization. Old union structures, unable to adapt to new conditions, also contributed to the impasse. A final significant factor was the situation at city hall itself, where the new Socialist administration quickly became hostage to state legislative measures that limited its action and circumscribed its effectiveness.

Socialist Politics: The First Year

After accepting the standing ovations of the thousands crowded into the Central High School auditorium to witness his inauguration in November 1933, Mayor Jasper McLevy pledged to "carry out our campaign pledge for rehabilitation of the city's financial and social affairs," to seek municipal ownership of utilities, and to care for "the victims of the breakdown of the industrial system."[12] In the flush of victory the SP momentarily forgot that it had not won in a landslide. Antimachine feeling and frustration regarding finances had accompanied the upsurge of class sentiment that had put the Socialists in city hall. Low-income and immigrant residents made up the base of McLevy's support, but other blocs such as native-born and middle-class citizens wanted their agendas fulfilled as well. Middle-class activists in the Taxpayers' League wanted low-cost city government, period. Big business, which viewed the Socialists with a wary eye, still wanted "responsible" government and private control of relief activities. The contradictory nature of these agendas became obvious within the first few months of the McLevy administration.

Power of the purse resided with the Board of Apportionment and Taxation, thanks to the General Assembly's action in the spring of 1933. Together with the Special Welfare Committee, which disbursed the funds from the city's bond sales, the governor-appointed board managed the budget, taxes, and the spending of relief funds raised through bonding. In addition, power still accrued to the traditional parties. Democrats and Republicans whose terms extended to 1934 constituted half of the common council, and they threatened to collaborate in an effort to oust the Socialists at the 1934 election. Moreover, a Republican-dominated state legislature and a Democratic governor still controlled a great part of local affairs.

With his trusted aide Fred Schwarzkopf, the former council member who had just won election as city clerk, McLevy began building his government. He used a series of shrewd appointments and policy initiatives designed to break up the cozy business-as-usual style of city departments while binding cooperative outsiders to the Socialist administration. In addition to appointing Brewster to head public works, McLevy named various Socialist council members to chair the most important municipal boards. But he also named some trusted Democratic and Republican council members to other chairmanships. John J. O'Neil, Jr., the long-time AFL activist in both the typographers' union and the Central Labor Union, was a key Democratic council member who lent support to the McLevy administration in these crucial first months. Much to the chagrin of some SP members, McLevy reappointed businessmen who had shown their nonpartisan interest in the city's welfare, like George Eames, the Singer Manufacturing executive and active Republican who had devoted himself to the Parks and Recreation Board. But other businessmen whose interests and records were contrary to SP campaign goals lost their appointments, including William E. Burnham, an active Republican and industrial executive who had served on the first Ripper Board in the mid-1920s and was still on the Financial Advisory Board. Finally, McLevy's choice for city attorney was Harry Schwartz, a lawyer active in the American Civil Liberties Union (ACLU) and the former director of the Bridgeport Young Men's Hebrew Association; he was not a member of the Socialist Party. Then McLevy set about to reorganize the city.[13]

Within the first eight months the Socialists launched a variety of initiatives to fulfill their promise of efficient government and reorientation of the city government toward the common good. Each initiative antagonized particular business sectors. First was an ordinance forbidding city officials and appointees from engaging in business with the city, a move aimed at the commissioners and Board of Apportionment members who had a monopoly on municipal trade for their particular goods and services. Next McLevy instituted central purchasing of most city supplies and competitive bidding for goods and services and moved to establish a civil service system for municipal employees. The administration also set up a new municipal coal yard, buying the city's fuel wholesale and allowing citizens to make purchases from the yard as well. This rankled the local coal dealers. The Socialists also began lobbying the local banks for a reduction in interest rates for mortgages and personal loans and, with several suburban governments, sued the state Public Utility Commission for a general reduction in water and electrical utility rates for home owners. Finally, the mayor and his common council appointees to the various committees refused to acquiesce on the custom of holding secret meetings of important boards, like the education and appropriations boards, at private clubs like the Black Rock Yacht

Club. They insisted that all deliberations be available for public scrutiny, a demand that ensured their own participation in the doings of the city.[14]

Two major arenas of debate remained unresolved: relief and taxes. The difficulties challenged not only the SP but the business elites who still controlled the Board of Apportionment and the Special Welfare Committee. These business leaders were charged with keeping a rein on city spending, but within a month of the election the Board of Apportionment announced that the city had already accumulated a $500,000 deficit that could not be covered by selling more bonds. The outcry from the public and business community alike was massive, though the board members' defense was that they had cut expenditures as far as possible. Indeed, relief figures show that by December 1933 only 4 percent of the city's population was receiving relief, well below Bridgeport's previous level of care and at that time the lowest of all the state's cities. The board had, in fact, cut relief to the bone.[15] The weary board had little response to McLevy's accusation that it had misled the public by keeping the growing deficit secret during the election season. The city had two choices, according to the board—to levy an interim special tax or move to state receivership. The Socialists declared that the situation was not their fault and that it was "only fair" that the special tax be levied immediately to give their administration a fresh start.

The board members connected to the city's industrial and financial elite resigned themselves to the inevitable, levying a 4.6 mill special tax payable on February 1, two months before the end of the fiscal year. State receivership would have destroyed the city's bond rating while doing little to delay the inevitable municipal responsibility to pay off bonds and interest as well as outstanding bills. Fundamentally, if the city went into state receivership, the General Assembly would hand the city's financial powers to an appointed committee of responsible local citizens. Bridgeport elites had already accomplished this with the special legislation of the previous spring. Underlying that move had been the goal of preventing any radical new administration from repudiating the city's bonds. It would hardly do for the business community, especially the business leaders who now oversaw the city's finances (or who, like Bridgeport's Sumner Simpson of the Raybestos Company, oversaw all city relief programs through the state Emergency Relief Commission), to call attention to the futility of that tactic.[16]

The Manufacturers' Association of Bridgeport split over the issue. A hurriedly organized Special Tax Committee investigated the special tax and recommended to the executive board of the MAB that it seek a court injunction against the tax. But the MAB backed away when members of its executive board, like DeVer C. Warner of the Board of Apportionment and Sumner Simpson and Herman Beach of the Special Welfare Committee, argued that the tax was inevitable and opposed an injunction. MAB resolved to allow individual firms to make the decision to join with the Bridgeport Brass Company, which insisted on pressing a suit. A state court subsequently refused to grant an injunction. What was clear in January 1934 was that manufacturers, both large and small, were opposed to bailing the city out with their tax dollars yet were discouraged by the performance of their colleagues on the city oversight boards. The 4.6 mill special tax went forward.[17] (See table 3, p. 44, for the city's annual tax assessments and tax rates, 1915–40.)

As if to make amends for its lackluster performance, the Board of Apportionment returned to its task with a vengeance, overseeing every major purchase, wrangling with Socialist commissioners about further cost-cutting measures, and continuing the Committee of One Hundred's campaign to cut the cost of government. Its concerns were at odds with the spirit and the substance of the SP's goals for the city. For example, the board quibbled with Brewster about buying essential equipment. When the board suggested buying secondhand equipment to save money, McLevy angrily replied, "I am thoroughly opposed to any more second-hand junk being unloaded onto the city. . . . When this administration took office, we found nothing in the City Yard to do any work with." When two board members wanted to delay voting on this particular item, saying they needed to talk it over in private first, McLevy responded, "In public is the place to talk, not in private."[18]

The board continued to press for further wage cuts for city employees, eyeing teachers' salaries in particular. Because McLevy threatened to veto any salary reductions beyond the 20 percent that had been in effect for the previous eighteen months, the tax board simply reduced the general appropriation to the board of education, causing that body to cut three weeks off the school year. McLevy vetoed this decision. "Bridgeport's children are entitled to a full forty weeks of school," he exclaimed, while the *Bridgeport Herald* deplored this underhanded way of cutting teachers' salaries. The paper noted that now teachers "are getting barely half as much as some of the most useless cops on the police force."[19]

Finally, the Board of Apportionment balked at authorizing money for preparing the utility rate appeal to the state PUC. This last was a delicate situation, because DeVer C. Warner, treasurer of the Bridgeport Hydraulic Company, sat on the board. At this point some board members softened their opposition to the McLevy administration. Francis J. Brennan, a Democratic building contractor, argued in favor of funding the appeal: "This resolution [for money for the rate case] was adopted by a unanimous vote of the Board of Aldermen [*sic*— he meant the common council], and they are the elected representatives of the people. I am not ready to tell them they are wrong all the time." Eventually, the board compromised and authorized some funds.[20]

On the question of relief, the situation grew worse. All relief monies were funneled through the city's Special Welfare Committee, on which the members of the Board of Apportionment and Angus Thorne, head of the city's Department of Public Welfare, also sat. This committee had no Socialist members. The Special Welfare Committee trusted Thorne and allowed his agency to exceed its budget line by tens of thousands of dollars—and without requiring competitive bidding for supplies, the SP noted, which raised the issue of political favoritism.

Federal relief money under the New Deal did little to change the structure of local political power. Federal money helped save Bridgeport's budget but not without political complications. When Roosevelt appointed Harry Hopkins to run the Federal Emergency Relief Administration (FERA) in early 1933, the president's goal was to get relief monies to states and localities quickly. States were required to set up suitable agencies to receive, disburse, and monitor funds to localities. Connecticut was forced to create the Connecticut Emergency Relief Commission (CERC), which replaced the advisory Connecticut Unemployment Commission and was authorized to handle the federal funds. The CERC's role was to review relief procedures in each city, following federal guidelines that stipulated that trained social workers were to certify the amount that each family should receive and certify each city's monthly allotment of funds. In addition, because FERA would provide only a third of state and local relief costs, CERC had to report to the federal government the level of state and local financial support in order to receive its federal grant. While for many states this arrangement meant that the *state* government now provided a substantial amount of money to the localities, Connecticut continued its old arrangement of making the cities and towns bear the burden. Nonetheless, the state commission had total control of federal disbursements; it could and did withhold money if local arrangements or record keeping were deemed deficient.[21]

Thus FERA helped demolish antiquated systems of poor relief and reliance on private charity and replace them with a centralized public organization. Connecticut cities such as Waterbury, which had relied on private funds and private agencies, now had to alter their method of relief and put it in public hands. "Public" hands, however, did not mean elected hands but local relief committees of "public-spirited citizens." Though the CERC was proud of its reputation as a nonpartisan group—Gov. Wilbur Cross appointed four Republicans and one Democrat—its commissioners had little interest in dealing with an interloper political party like the Bridgeport SP.[22] The CERC included some holdover members of the old Unemployment Commission as well as new members like Sumner Simpson, the Bridgeport industrialist. Simpson, chairman of the city's Special Welfare Committee and long-time president of the Community Chest, was then appointed by the CERC as the city's FERA administrator. Thus federal money went from state hands to local Republican industrialist hands, where it often was used for partisan purposes.[23]

Bridgeport's welfare superintendent made all decisions regarding relief recipients, work-relief projects, and levels of pay in consultation with the Special Welfare Committee. Socialist administrators could neither monitor expenditures nor integrate these work projects into their own plans for rebuilding the city and providing services. The Board of Apportionment refused to give the McLevy administration any discretionary funds with which to carry out projects, forcing the administration to apply to the board for each project it wanted. As McLevy complained to the board, "There will be confusion as long as the members of this Board are acting in a dual capacity as members of the Tax Board and as members of the FERA committee. You can approve a project as members of the FERA Board and refuse to approve it as members of the Tax Board."[24]

The situation caused considerable political embarrassment for the mayor. For example, when a severe blizzard buried Bridgeport in February 1934, relief recipients of Civil Works Administration (CWA) jobs put in extra days shoveling the city out. Then McLevy learned that the workers were ineligible to be paid for that work under the CWA and thus would not get checks that week. Anxious unemployed men then demonstrated at city hall, not in front of the homes of the Special Welfare Committee members, calling on the mayor to pay them immediately. The same situation occurred in April when FERA cuts were announced.[25]

McLevy declared war on the Board of Apportionment and ordered audits of all city departments, starting with the Department of Public Welfare and the board of education. After he hired a private auditor who claimed to have uncovered improprieties in the welfare department, McLevy pulled the CERC into the debate, causing the commissioners to seek another auditor's report. The attention given to the situation and the allegation of "political motives" in Bridgeport

Relief workers shoveling snow after the blizzard of February 1934. (Historical Collections, Bridgeport Public Library.)

was enough to cause Eleanor Little, the CERC relief administrator, to press Bridgeport welfare officials for strict adherence to federal guidelines, though she was powerless to change the makeup of the Special Welfare Committee.[26]

The SP scored direct hits in other departments. The audit of the Department of Education uncovered major improprieties there. After the auditors found a shortfall in the trustee account of the superintendent, John Wynkoop, they found fuel oil that had been charged to school accounts but shipped to the homes of board members and employees, excessive travel to "educational conferences," and other misappropriation of funds. Wynkoop was eventually convicted of embezzlement, and charges were instituted against others.[27]

Finally, the Board of Apportionment itself provided McLevy with ammunition when it suddenly notified him in September 1934 of a pending $800,000 deficit in relief and education costs and threatened a tax rate of at least 40 mills in the coming year. Urging retrenchment and economy, the board's letter to McLevy ended with a polite challenge: "If you have any plans to this end, we would appreciate your early advice." McLevy's reply was long and eloquent in its denunciation of the board. "Your board [because of the 1933 Ripper Act] . . . is invested with extraordinary powers, and by the same token, charged with corresponding responsibilities. . . . If your Board feels, as its letter indicates, that it is incapable of adequately performing its duties under the law, then it becomes its plain duty to resign and make way for other citizens determined to carry on intelligently."[28]

All this—the allegations of financial impropriety, the political favoritism in the welfare department, and the budget deficit—made good copy and provided a dramatic backdrop for the 1934 election campaign. Half of the common council seats were up for election, as were state offices. The illusion of the quick fix had faded, the Socialists' accomplishments had been mixed, and the popularity of the mayor was in question. The *Herald* began the campaign season by starting a letter-writing contest, complete with a $10 prize for the best letter. The theme was "Jasper—A Flop or a Phenom?" By printing scores of letters as well as "man-in-the-street" interviews in successive three Sunday issues, the *Herald* captured the sweep of public opinion and revealed rifts within the SP itself. Some letters were severely negative: a former GOP chairman called McLevy a flop for not opposing the special tax of the previous winter. One woman asserted that "people are losing the faith they placed in him and his pedestal is slowly crumbling."

Most, however, supported the initiatives made by the Socialists in the previous nine months and said they would give McLevy more time. They cited "what he is up against": the "board of seven businessmen," "the men who control the financial end," and the lack of home rule. Some thought McLevy too "soft-hearted" in dealing with the welfare and education departments. One placed him next to Franklin Roosevelt, "two men in this country who are under test. . . . Both men . . . are doing their best." Still others were extreme in their praise and hopes: one sent in a photo of McLevy, his craggy Scotsman's face adorned by a penciled-in Lincolnesque beard to show his remarkable resemblance to "Honest Abe." One woman went so far as to state that "when the people cast their votes in the last election, God was there." The winning letter summarized a moderate point of view: McLevy was "honest, . . . an ever-ready fighter, . . . as a conservative socialist, he hates red-hot hasty actions . . . he will always be O Kay!" People expected honest, aggressive but temperate leadership that would lead to a change in the way the city was run.[29]

The most trenchant criticisms came from the Left. Here the internal splits of the previous year were revealed in full. One former Socialist asserted that "McLevy has betrayed his own party," while "A Socialist" noted that "any reformer, a LaGuardia in New York or a Roosevelt in Washington, can do as much or better." One leftist tried to project a more tolerant view of McLevy, noting that there was no hope of changing things, given that "the socialist platform proposes 'legal' methods for changing conditions. Jasper is now learning that 'legal' methods mean capitalist methods"—and claiming that the only hope for the McLevy administration was to put aside those laws. A number of Socialists, former Socialists, and Communists were dismayed at the way in which McLevy had handled the relief strikes in February and April. After the snow shovelers demonstrated in February, McLevy had blamed Communists for stirring up trouble and then retreated from the scene, leaving the police to disperse the crowds after relief workers refused to accept the mayor's explanation of the funding delays.[30] Young SP members were responsible for leading the relief workers during the April protest. In this case the welfare department acted more wisely, handing out temporary vouchers to the men "to keep them over the weekend." In both cases McLevy saw only the work of Communist "agitators," not the serious plight of his constituents—a myopia common, both locally and nationally, to the SP's old guard—predominantly AFL union members who had joined the party before World War I.[31]

The harshest letter came from Sam Krieger, a Communist Party organizer in Bridgeport, who argued that McLevy was "a huge success, a more willing lieutenant than the captains of industry had hoped for! . . . But for the workers of Bridgeport, McLevy has been a monstrous failure and a costly lesson; McLevy carries on political trading with the enemies of the working class; hobnobs with industrialists, fascists and jingoists; sends his police to break strikes and protect strikebreakers." The hyperbole of Krieger's criticism was part and parcel of the Communist Party's radical "Third Period" analysis of the SP as "social fascists," misleaders who would take the working class down the path of reactionary collaboration. Mobilized around unemployment relief, antifascist activity, and shop-floor organizing, the Communists had little patience with reformist electioneering.[32]

Communists and Socialists had been waging a war of soapboxes in cities large and small through the early years of the depression, and rivalry between the two had marred planning for the Free Tom Mooney campaign in 1932 and the Continental Congress of Workers and Farmers of 1933 and now was threatening to undo common efforts in the League Against War and Fascism. Things were so bad in New York and several other cities during the 1932 election that the ACLU was called in to mediate between the two groups. McLevy, who had sat on the national executive committee of the SP since 1928, consistently voted against cooperating with the Communists in any mass organization, though he was willing to cooperate with them in strike support. When an organizer for the United Textile Workers Union warned McLevy after the election that he need-ed to watch out for the CP, McLevy replied, "We of course foresee the possibil-ity of our communist friends attempting their destructive tactics here in Bridge-port. However, we do not in the least fear this condition and will handle it in the proper manner when the time comes."[33]

In March 1933 the Comintern, fearful of fascist developments in Europe, had extended an offer to the Socialist International to put aside their differences and engage in a United Front of the Left. The Communist Party in the United States offered the same to the SP. After some preliminary discussion in the United States, the SP's national committee rejected the offer on a 6-5 vote (McLevy voted no, along with Morris Hillquit, Daniel Hoan, and others, while Norman Thomas led the pro–United Front faction). The SP and CP were roughly the same size at this time, though the SP held a more respectable position in political circles with its belief in a nonviolent transition to socialism, its commitment to parliamentary democracy, and its wariness of the Soviet Union. But the SP itself was rent by ideological disputes and generational tensions that mirrored its conflicts with the CP and caused the SP's old guard to grow even more adamant in rejecting an alliance with Communists. The United Front negotiations were finally scuttled in February 1934 when Communists disrupted a Madison Square Garden rally organized by the SP to protest the plight of Austrian Social Democrats.[34]

A more positive attitude toward the United Front idea existed in some parts of Connecticut. Devere Allen, a Socialist journalist and editor of the Christian-oriented *World Tomorrow,* was active in the Connecticut SP and consistently advocated the United Front. On a grassroots level the issues of fascism and la-bor rights were bringing activists together in a number of cities.[35] In Bridgeport, however, where the SP was strong and where the CP's strength was more nar-rowly based in some neighborhood and ethnic organizations, tolerance for the CP was low in labor and Socialist circles. When the Bridgeport SP rejected a United Front proposal—in fact, the Socialists expelled young members who did cooperate—the CP ran its own slate in the 1933 and 1935 elections. Communists poked fun at McLevy by surreptitiously hoisting a red flag, complete with ham-mer and sickle, over city hall on May 1, 1934, his first May Day in office.[36]

The CP critique by itself did not affect much public opinion in Bridgeport, but it did echo some charges being raised within the Socialist Party itself, both in Bridgeport and at the national level. This was the most recent round in the fundamental, and long-lived, debate about the relationship between reform and revolution. As Devere Allen editorialized soon after the Socialists' 1933 election victory, "The whole problem of municipal socialism is a vexing one, . . . until the State and Federal government is socialist, little can be done on the municipal level." The Bridgeport SP, he warned, should be on the lookout "to guard against [the] temptation" of sticking to "minor matters of clean government." At the same time he emphasized that McLevy was "a conservative Socialist but not a disloyal one." Another column in the same paper, however, criticized McLevy for "the satisfaction he took in the good-will of some of the big industrialists of Bridgeport who congratulated him."[37] At first, Norman Thomas answered critics of McLevy's in measured tones. "I have a lot of confidence in Jasper McLevy personally and in the fundamental soundness of his Socialism," Thomas explained. "He is in a very difficult position, however, and I do not think that his campaign [in 1933] involved many genuine Socialist issues except in so far as attacks on Socialists brought them in. In this position it will be awfully easy, almost unconsciously, to slip."[38]

The long history of municipal socialism had already made apparent the tensions between the electoral strategies of "running to educate" and "running to win," as well as the impossibility of creating "socialism in one city." Yet municipal victories during the Progressive Era had forced the SP to confront the realities of governing. Successful local Socialist groups in other cities had usually taken one of three paths: retreating into ideological rigidity so as not to betray the Socialist ideal—this sometimes took the form of sectarian strife within locals and the expulsion of successful candidates who took a pragmatic approach to their elected responsibilities; abandoning Socialist principles and goals altogether in order to stay in office; or attempting to balance the goals of an eventual cooperative commonwealth with the needs of working-class constituents through ameliorative reforms. During the Progressive Era this included support for labor reform legislation, a positive climate for unionization, and tackling the urban ills that fell most heavily on working-class citizens. Many took the view that the process of replacing "cities for profit" with "cities for living" was a potent educational tool for socialism. Yet this "constructive" socialism, long identified as the politics of the right-wing of the SP such as was practiced by the Milwaukee city government, could become intertwined with and limited to social reformist rhetoric of a more general appeal. Key to the continued viability of these municipal Socialist experiments had been the tentative support given by reform-minded middle-class elements, a more fickle support than the usually solid votes of working-class wards. Many of these political third-party administrations of the Progressive and World War I eras died quickly, some because of internal dissent but more often because the middle and upper classes had combined their electoral efforts to defeat the SP.[39]

The ponderous legacy of this history weighed on the Bridgeport effort. In the eyes of some members of the SP in Bridgeport, McLevy had already slipped into the sell-out mode of running to win. After the near win in 1931 Bridgeport socialists had perceived that the stakes for the next campaign were higher. Dissent over their immediate goals created furor among party members through 1932 and 1933. At the same time the SP moved to enforce discipline and unity within its ranks to prepare for the next election. Operating from their Fifth District club rooms, the long-time Socialists and union activists Fred and Minnie Cederholm led the debate about the proper role for Socialists in campaigns. Among other charges, they accused McLevy of "degrad[ing] the Socialist Party into a vote catching political organization" and questioned the conduct of Socialist sheriffs who had participated in eviction actions in 1932. The Cederholms wanted to forgo winning in order to educate. Emphasizing the organization of workers over the winning of electoral campaigns, they wanted the Socialist International and its concerns to prevail over local election issues. As a Socialist elected to the common council in 1911 and an organizer with the IAM since 1915, Fred Cederholm was, next to McLevy, the best-known and best-regarded member of the SP. Supported by new activists in the Young People's Socialist League (YPSL), the Cederholms at first threatened to disrupt the orderly renomination of McLevy for mayor at the 1933 convention.[40] Instead, they withdrew to carry on what they considered the more important activity, that of organizing workers. Fred Cederholm continued his work with the IAM in Bridgeport, and in 1934 the IAM sent him elsewhere in the state, while Minnie Cederholm became an organizer for the Pocketbook Workers Union and later the ILGWU. They were not involved in the 1933 campaign, though they did not publicly criticize it. In response to the more militant demands of critics within the Socialist Party, the party's local central committee both called for unity and curbed the activity of the Bridgeport YPSL chapter "to prevent them from interfering with the affairs of the parent body."[41] Once installed in city hall, however, the SP could not easily contain its internal tensions. Threatening the party's internal stability was the old guard's fears of Communist "contamination," concern about the influx of new members seeking city jobs, and the objective difficulties of running the city in the tough year of 1934.[42]

External concerns increasingly intruded as well. McLevy was acutely aware of reactionary developments in Europe at the time and drew lessons of caution from the defeat of the Austrian Social Democrats in 1934. The mayor, attending a rally sponsored by the Workmen's Circle, "painted a vivid picture of the menace of fascism" but quietly resolved to keep out of international issues. His thinking was no doubt influenced by the experience of some of his members who helped organize for this event. Jack Bergen, who had addressed the mostly Italian Bridgeport masons' union to ask for its endorsement and attendance at the antifascist rally, was escorted out as the masons sang "La Giovanezza," a Mussolini marching song. McLevy, it seemed, had resolved not to inflame reactionaries if he could avoid it. But a year later his administration refused a gift of Italian-language textbooks from the Mussolini government that had been arranged by the city's Italian fraternal organizations; the textbooks were too ideologically tainted for use in the schools, insisted Bergen, a member of the board of education.[43]

The local SP tensions mirrored the growing ideological and tactical debates that threatened the unity of the Socialist Party nationally. Fissures within the national SP had opened in 1930, through policy disputes between the SP's old guard and the "Militants," new and younger members of the party who admired the Soviet Union and who favored a more activist atmosphere in the party along with greater intervention in trade union affairs. The old guard had for a long time agreed that the party should not intervene in union affairs. As McLevy argued before the national executive committee in the debate about strategy for the AFL convention in 1933, the party "should get into lower organizations if we want to build [the] union movement and will then be able to elect delegates to state and national conventions. If we try to meddle we will be driving a wedge between the AF of L and the SP." For the members of the SP deeply involved in the labor movement, this hands-off principle allowed them to respond to union exigencies rather than submit to party discipline.[44]

McLevy's ability to steer a center course as a voice of trade unionism in the national SP came to an end in May 1934, when the factionalism in the party reached a crescendo. At the party's national convention delegates fought about the adoption of a new declaration of principles. The declaration, written by Connecticut's Devere Allen, contained a strong antiwar statement, attacked "bogus" forms of democracy under capitalism, and, mindful of the rise of fascism in Europe, held out the possibility of having to combat reaction in the United States through armed resistance and the general strike. These points sent old guard members, including McLevy, into paroxysms; these and other debates exacerbated the fight that pitted the old guard against the Militants and members of the Revolutionary Policy Committee. (The Revolutionary Policy Committee, formed in 1934, was even further to the left than the Militants.)[45] When the convention approved the Declaration of Principles, which was later ratified by national voting (with nearly half the membership abstaining from the vote), the old guard, which had been weakened by the death of Hillquit the previous year, lost control of the organization. McLevy narrowly lost his position on the national committee, which now had only one member of the old guard (James Oneal, editor of the *New Leader,* the Socialist newspaper), along with five Militants and four centrists (including Thomas and Hoan).[46]

The Connecticut SP backed the old guard, voting 189-164 against the declaration; Bridgeport provided 103 of the no votes, with 7 voting for the declaration.[47] Devere Allen and Francis Henson—a newcomer affiliated with the National Religion and Labor Foundation in New Haven and a partisan of the SP's Revolutionary Policy Committee—promoted the Declaration of Principles. The uneasy mix of trade unionists, mostly from Bridgeport, and middle-class professionals and intellectuals, many from New Haven and allied with Allen, created social tensions that mirrored ideological disagreements and reflected the class lines of the organization. One example was a semiserious resolution was drawn up at the Connecticut SP convention in September 1934 by some New Haven delegates to correct the mispronunciation of "woids" by Andrew Auth, a member of the Bridgeport Common Council. The resolution called attention to other mispronunciations involving the letter combinations *er, or,* and *ur,* as well as the word *legislature,* by members of the Bridgeport "woiking class."[48] But both Militants and the old guard were mindful of the electoral opportunities in 1934, given the prestige of the Bridgeport SP's victory in 1933. The Connecticut SP went into the 1934 state elections determined to present a unified face.

McLevy had the task of both advancing the SP's state platform and ensuring the election of his Bridgeport candidates to the General Assembly. The Connecticut SP pressed McLevy into service as gubernatorial candidate (the state elections were in alternate years from the municipal races), ran Devere Allen for U.S. Senate, and planned a state campaign geared around the labor and social legislation that had languished in the 1933 General Assembly. McLevy himself put the campaign in perspective in his opening remarks to the SP's state convention, assembled in Bridgeport. He called the 1934 campaign "a life and death struggle between a decaying order and a new and better one." In a new twist the Connecticut SP wrote its platform as an "Open Letter to the Voter," calling for a "cooperative commonwealth" through public ownership of basic industry to combat unemployment and the crisis of capitalism, and listing specific interim legislation that had been on the SP's agenda for years: unemployment insurance, old-age pensions, government support for unionization, a progressive state income tax to relieve the tax burden on low-income citizens, "socialized banking" to reduce mortgage and loan rates, and reapportionment of the state government to bring about greater democratic representation. Allen in particular focused on military and peace issues, citing the dangers of using national guardsmen to break the 1934 textile strike while pointing out to disarmament advocates the need to find jobs for displaced armaments workers. McLevy aimed much of his fire at the "sham liberalism" of Wilbur Cross, the Democratic governor. As McLevy put it, Governor Cross "had failed to make the most of his opportunities. Had he gone before the people with old age pensions and power rates, as he did with his fight for liquor control, he could have accomplished much. . . . [The issue is not] milk and liquor. . . . The real issue is bread and butter!"[49]

The two issues of liquor control and a plan for the regulation of the dairy industry had taken center stage in state politics in both Democratic and Republican camps. With Hugh Alcorn, the state's attorney for Hartford County, as their gubernatorial candidate, the Connecticut Republicans endorsed some moderate reform, for example, old-age pensions, but attacked the New Deal for making the state's citizens "mendicants and beggars"; they called for paying attention to business confidence and industrial recovery. The Democrats, on the other hand, were deeply divided. Cross, the former Yale dean, had become governor in 1931 because his conservative demeanor and rural Yankee background appealed widely across the political spectrum and dispelled the Democrats' image as an Irish machine. However, the New Deal Democrats, led by Arch McNeil of Bridgeport and the old Wilsonian Homer Cummings of Stamford, had been unable to consolidate their organization in Connecticut. Indeed, they had not been able to win the state for Roosevelt in 1932.[50]

Though Cross had campaigned on a pledge to bring "enlightened government" to Connecticut, he had made little in the way of specific proposals. Moreover, he was hamstrung by a Republican General Assembly. Indeed, despite the electoral gains made at the state level in 1930, the entrenched Democrats, led by Hartford's Tom Spellacy, had squandered their potential power and weakened the new governor by making deals with the GOP in return for a series of judicial appointments. Cross had, however, been able to change some of the most backward features of Connecticut government by cementing ties with long-time Democratic labor leaders. He became the first governor ever to address the Connecticut Federation of Labor's annual convention and appointed Joseph Tone, the former labor organizer and New Haven state senator, to serve as commissioner of labor. He also allowed Tone to run the antisweatshop campaign.[51]

In 1934 the deeply divided party finally constructed a compromise slate of Spellacy organization Democrats and New Deal Democrats, with Governor Cross heading the ticket. Cross took to the stump, answering charges of do-nothing policies by blaming the Republican-dominated legislature for blocking his initiatives—true enough, though Cross had not seriously campaigned on behalf of unemployment insurance or old-age pensions. The truth was that Connecticut Democrats had only loosely wrapped themselves in the mantle of the New Deal. Cross himself neglected the task and remained ambivalent about New Deal programs, stating at one point, "I associate largely with Republicans and when I come to the fundamentals of government I find but little disagreement. We all stand for the rights of the state against federal government control."[52] It had been his hostility to federal funding that had placed Connecticut near the bottom of the list for federal relief funds until late 1933. Cross seemed so unappealing a candidate, one who "talked like a parlor liberal and acted like a New Haven banker," according to the *Herald,* that the newspaper predicted that Alcorn, the GOP candidate, would win the election.[53]

The labor vote was fragmented both locally and at the state level and presented some difficulties to both the Democratic and Socialist Parties. In the final days of the campaign J. Nicholas Danz, the maverick president of the Connecticut Federation of Labor and a member of the New London musicians' union, issued a statement denouncing Governor Cross as "an enemy of the laboring class in this state" for using the national guard to quell the 1934 textile strike. Danz urged the twenty-five thousand textile workers of eastern Connecticut to vote for Alcorn instead. During the entire weekend before the election, other CFL officers and Tone, the labor commissioner, tried to repair the damage done by Danz in labor circles. In the fluid situation attending this realignment of electoral coalitions, labor had no unified strategy.[54]

Bridgeport Socialists had a particular need to win in 1934. They knew that they could accomplish their goals only if they could gain some relief from the 1935 General Assembly. As Arnold Freese, the SP state secretary, had reminded Bridgeport members at their thirty-fourth annual picnic in the spring, "The laws that make us slaves or freemen are made in Hartford and Washington. That's where we are headed for."[55] On general state issues McLevy had already made it clear that he wanted a state income tax and opposed a general sales tax. The mayor also had rallied relief workers in Bridgeport to demand that Governor Cross call a special session of the General Assembly in the spring of 1934 to deal with relief issues, to no avail. McLevy accused Bridgeport Democrats of "feather[ing] their nests" with federal emergency relief jobs after being ousted from local office in 1933. They were, he said, using FERA lists to promote Democratic candidates.[56]

In Bridgeport the *Herald* was keen to see the SP win in the local races. A front-page editorial in late October exhorted, "Citizens! Save Your City by Electing Socialist Legislators." The *Herald* held out the tantalizing hope that, with the state senate evenly divided between Democrats and Republicans, three Socialist state senators elected from Bridgeport could hold the balance of power in the upcoming General Assembly. The *Bridgeport Telegram* published straw polls that showed the SP well ahead of other parties, while the *Post* was reduced to lamenting the loss of a favorite Democratic probate judge if Bridgeport citizens pulled the third lever.[57]

Given the growing public debate about the effectiveness of the McLevy administration, the critiques of the Left, and the tension within the national Socialist Party, the 1934 campaign became a referendum on the Bridgeport SP. The atmosphere in Bridgeport had been stirred by the continuing revelations by the SP investigative team, which uncovered improprieties and embezzlement in Democrat-controlled city departments. The city's high school students staged demonstrations against the Democratic board of education, protesting the late afternoon school hours made necessary by the layoff of teachers.[58]

Finally, the public was swayed by McLevy's argument that it would be "good sense to send people to Hartford who will back the mayor that the voters have elected."[59] Despite their internal difficulties, the Democrats won at the state level, though McLevy siphoned 38,000 votes from Governor Cross's winning total. The Socialists won in Bridgeport, with 39.4 percent of the vote in the three-way race; they sent three senators and two representatives to the state capital.[60] However, the Socialist turnout was smaller than in 1933, which revealed both the damage done by the year of municipal stalemate and the continued viability of the mainstream parties on the state and national level.

Socialist Politics: The Second Year

Socialist legislators went to Hartford in January 1935 armed with a legislative agenda to enact their urban reforms and to build a social welfare structure for the state. Above all, they were determined to take back control of the city from the businessmen-dominated boards. The Bridgeport SP's caucus decided its course of action at its December 31 meeting: no deals, no support for the Spellacy organization's Democratic candidate for president pro tem of the senate, and a commitment to make social welfare legislation the top priority, followed by home rule issues for Bridgeport.[61]

At the same time Bridgeport businessmen debated their next move. Given the recent election, DeVer C. Warner told the MAB, "several of our leading citizens have told me . . . it was [best] for the present members of our Tax Board to hand their resignations to the Mayor and let him . . . have full responsibility for tax rates." The question he posed to the MAB was "whether it was best for our Board to continue to carry the responsibility," because McLevy would blame the tax board for any unfavorable financial developments. But Sumner Simpson argued that the tax board had done a marvelous job of cutting city expenses. "This Board was created by the Legislature at the request of the manufacturing interests. . . . Stick to the job, at least for the present." The executive board of the MAB deliberated at length and then voted unanimously to oppose the resignation of the members of the Board of Apportionment and Taxation and to oppose any attempt to repeal the special powers given the board by the 1933 legislature. Business leaders determined to fight for control to the end.[62]

For the moment power rested in the General Assembly, where Bridgeport manufacturers had always gotten what they wanted. But 1935 was different. As had been predicted, the state senate—with seventeen Democrats (all pledged to vote with the Spellacy organization), fifteen Republicans, and three Socialists—stalemated on the election of a senate president pro tem. Through 110 ballots to organize the Senate in January, the results were 17 for the Democratic candidate, 15 for the Republican, and 3 for the Socialist John Taft. On the 111th ballot the Socialists voted for the Republican slate. Governor Cross later reported, with some delight, that the SP senators—Cross called them "three good men"—had come to him the day before the vote to say they could never vote for the organization Democrats, who had shut Cross out as well, and were going to work out an accommodation with the GOP.[63]

Suddenly, many things were possible, though all sides denied the notion of a deal. The Bridgeport delegation then set about to push its social agenda: an old-age pension bill, unemployment insurance, and an income tax instead of the myriad sales taxes proposed by Democrats and Republicans. SP assemblymen cooperated with liberal Democrats in this year of sudden success for social legislation. As Governor Cross later pointed out with pride, the 1935 General Assembly finally passed legislation on issues that had been pending since 1931—a

revived state Board of Mediation and Arbitration, new protective labor legislation for women and minors, new antisweatshop legislation to supplement the
actions of the 1932–33 Labor Department, and a grant of greater regulatory
power to the Public Utilities Commission.

All was not quite perfect on a number of these issues, and the five Socialist
senators and representatives were forced to compromise often with Democrats
and Republicans. For example, the SP considered the child labor provisions of
the state labor bill too weak to warrant support, but the Democrats pushed it
through. Democratic and Republican state legislators then pointed to the bill
as proof that the Federal Child Labor Amendment, up for a ratification vote in
the Connecticut legislature this session, was not needed after all, hamstringing
Socialists and CFL representatives who wanted ratification. Both the SP and the
CFL introduced bills for unemployment insurance, neither of which received
favorable action.[64]

But as enlightened as this General Assembly seemed, the issue of old-age
pensions revealed its limitations. Old-age pensions had been at the core of the
SP legislative agenda throughout the 1920s and had picked up considerable support in the early 1930s.[65] Now in the 1935 General Assembly the Democrats, the
Republicans, and the Socialists, as well as the CFL, had versions of old-age pension bills for consideration. Funding was the issue. The SP wanted an income
tax to cover this and other social welfare expenditures, while Cross pushed hard
for a sales tax, and the Republicans wanted neither. The compromise bill put
forward by the GOP-controlled Judiciary Committee provided a $7 per week
pension limited to indigent citizens older than sixty-five with no family. But the
Republican bill used the most regressive funding system, a $3 annual tax on every
state resident that would replace the $2 yearly personal tax. Socialists and some
Democrats successfully amended the bill in the senate to eliminate its worst
features, but when the Republican-dominated lower house called for reconsideration of the amended bill and hinted at total defeat, the SP state senators initiated a rejection of all amendments. The bill then sailed through the lower
house. In a single legislative maneuver the state got a paltry old-age plan funded not through business or income taxes but through regressive personal taxes,
now increased by $1 per adult, and the SP got a reputation for caving in on the
tax question. This formed the substance of further left-wing criticism of McLevy.
The Socialists' only defense, which many Democrats corroborated, was that the
Republicans were serious about killing anything but their own bill.[66]

Still left as the legislative session drew to a close were the Bridgeport municipal measures, some of which had been reported unfavorably from the Committee on Cities and Boroughs. McLevy forces worried that their January concessions would not be remembered, especially because the old-age pension
debate had not turned out as expected. Business and mainstream party elements
were particularly exercised over Bridgeport's proposed civil service bill and the
repeal of the special powers of the Board of Apportionment. But in the last days

"We Favor the Old Age Pension!" Sixth District Socialist Club, 1935. (Historical Collections, Bridgeport Public Library. Photograph digitally restored by Virginia Blaisdell.)

of the session Bridgeport Socialists got what they wanted—repeal of the Ripper Act of 1933, enactment of a civil service and merit system, authorization to issue refunding bonds, other structural adjustments, and, finally, agreement by the state to take over maintenance of state Route 1 within the city's boundaries. (This one move eliminated the decades-long bridge repair scandals, which involved bridges on that route, and relieved the city's budget of expensive pending repairs.) Socialists returned to the city triumphant.[67]

After eighteen months of stalemate things went well in Bridgeport. Other foes yielded. Sumner Simpson suddenly found it inadvisable to continue as chairman of the local FERA committee and tendered his resignation. Angus Thorne, faced with improprieties in his handling of the Welfare Department, resigned his position. Finally, with the repeal of the Ripper Act provisions, the "Ripper" Board of Apportionment quietly met for the last time on June 20 and disbanded. The new board appointed by McLevy included men of diverse political and business backgrounds, though none had been prominent in the obstructionist politics of the past eighteen months.[68]

As DeVer C. Warner had told the MAB after the 1934 election, he was confident that the McLevy administration "will make a determined effort to reduce the expenditures and to adopt a program of gradual debt reduction."[69] Others were not so sure. While deliberations were going on in Hartford, industrial interests were busy at home, attempting to keep expenses and taxes low, because the business community anticipated a large local tax hike. All pleaded for "the best government at the least cost." The MAB's ultimate fear was that McLevy was "having no stone unturned to get control of the [relief] funds . . . with the view of building up the greatest political machine in the city's history."[70] However, the $2.2 million bonding authorization only allowed the mayor to skirt economic disaster while refusing to give in to the MAB's demand for a reduction in relief allotments. This allowed the Tax Board to set a tax of 31.8 mills for 1935–36, a rate acceptable to large and small taxpayers alike. It was clear that the SP was moving carefully and that local business had adapted itself, however grudgingly, to responsible worker-politicians' control of the city budget.[71]

After its legislative victories in May, the SP eagerly awaited the fall 1935 municipal campaign. The SP renominated most of its officeholders, as well as a few new candidates, like Michael Gratt, a young pharmacist only recently admitted to the party, and a woman common council candidate, the long-time party member Sadie Griffin. The SP platform reiterated the recent legislative accomplishments—return of home rule, civil service, open common council meetings at which the public was invited to participate—and added a call for municipal ownership of public utilities and "planned government in order to build for the future as well as to meet the needs of the present." The SP called for swift implementation of the civil service, especially for the police department, "to fill the places of killed, deceased and elderly officers."[72]

McLevy got appreciative laughs at the soapbox rallies: "They tell you we are not good business men. Of course we are not good business men. We don't get our free fuel, we don't get our cuts on bond issues, we don't stock the city garage with junk machines, we don't put old men on the police and fire departments. Oh, no, we are not good business men." In addition, the McLevyists reaffirmed their allegiance to the national program of the SP, "maintain[ing] that only through socialization of the collectively necessary means of production, transportation and distribution of wealth and through the democratic administration of them by the people for the benefit of all, can the ills of the present social system be eradicated."[73] It was not by choice, they implied, that those goals had to be put off for the present.

Both Democrats and Republicans were demoralized. After a brief flirtation with the possibilities of cooperation, each party decided to go its own way. The new local GOP chairman, J. A. H. Robinson, tried to reassure the state central committee: "Recognizing that our people had gone over to the Socialist column, . . . in repudiation of both of the old parties and past methods of party management, we have used every effort to regain the confidence of our citizens and have made a creditable showing."[74] But Republicans' politics were the politics of the past. The party's candidate for mayor, Clifford Wilson, was a veteran of Bridgeport campaigns, the GOP mayor from 1911 to 1921 who had not held an elected post since he was beaten by the "reform" Democrat Fred Atwater in 1921.

The Democrats were equally bankrupt in the public eye. As mayoral contender the Democrats chose Joseph Wieler, a genial metal polisher whose claim to local fame was his rich baritone, which made him a popular figure in the Germania and Schwaebischer Maennerchor choruses. His popularity with German voters had brought him to the attention of the Democratic Party, where he had won the office of town clerk in the early 1920s and had retained it through the two Buckingham terms. He was so popular that McLevy had appointed him assistant town clerk in 1933 when the Socialist Party candidate won the town clerkship. Wieler was not the most loyal of Democratic candidates in 1935; in fact, the Democrats quietly removed him from the stump when he praised McLevy during a talk before the Taxpayers' League. The only firework set off during the 1935 campaign was a letter to the editor by Minnie Cederholm, the self-described "former socialist leader," taunting McLevy for lost ideals and promises not kept. The Socialists swept the election, gathering more votes— more than 24,000—than they had in 1933 and capturing 55 percent of the vote. Joining forces would not have helped the two major parties; Wilson received 10,363 votes, and the Democrats finished a distant third with only 8,909 votes.[75]

Thus by the mid-1930s the local elites' traditional vehicles—the Democratic and Republican Parties—were bereft of suitable leadership, and the voters had for years decisively repudiated the businessmen who ran for office. The mainstream parties remained viable, however, because they had ties to important political offices and programs at the state and federal levels. The McLevy administration was never free of interference from these state and federal centers of power. For example, Sumner Simpson recommended that John G. Schwarz, Jr., the building supplies dealer, member of the Committee of One Hundred, and GOP mayoral nominee in 1933, replace him as FERA administrator in Bridgeport, and Schwarz got the job. Schwarz's hostility to the Socialist administration and to unions knew no bounds.[76] Local elites gave up their determination to beat the McLevy forces, secure in the knowledge that state structures and fiscal restraints inhibited the actions of the third-party city administration.

Accommodation: 1936 and Beyond

The unwillingness of local citizens to follow the leadership of economic and political elites was one key part of the reconfiguration of officeholding in Bridgeport. But local elites had changed as well. Social and generational transformations, as well as economic development, had altered Bridgeport's economic elite by the late 1930s. Death had claimed key leaders of an older generation that had been influential since the Progressive Era; Fred Atwater and DeVer H. Warner died in the early 1930s. A crude measure of the upper class in the city is the list of names in the local *Blue Book,* the last of which was printed in 1929, itself an indication of the eclipse of the traditional upper class. In 1920, 92 percent of the 587 named in the Bridgeport *Blue Book* lived in the city itself, but by 1929 only 72 percent of the 782 named still lived in the city. Another fifth now lived in the suburb of Fairfield, whereas the rest lived in other adjacent towns.[77]

Bridgeport high society had now turned its attention to New York City because of the "gradual loosening of business ties between the older families and Bridgeport industry." Many local industries had merged with national firms, while others had been disrupted by the depression. Many of the old colonial families, who "derive[d] their wealth from extensive realty holdings, not only in Bridgeport but . . . Ohio holdings, these Ohio lands going back to the time of the Western Reserve" had been maintaining themselves by selling off real estate and were thus further distancing themselves from Bridgeport. "The people of early American stock have been moving out into the outlying communities," noted a staff member of the national YWCA in a survey for the Bridgeport branch. "It is increasingly difficult to get young leadership from this group to serve on boards and committees." Another reported that the social families had "even relinquished control of the Red Cross and Community Chest." The YWCA staffer noted that "the Bridgeport YWCA has no objection to getting leadership from the foreign groups but such leadership develops slowly and is practically not easy to recruit."[78]

Irish Catholic elites, never quite as rich as the old Protestant families, had their Catholic Charitable Bureau, Knights of Columbus, and network of parishes. Though they had evolved cooperative working relationships with the YWCA and YMCA, they would never join these Protestant organizations. Irish Catholics were still not accepted into "society," though the depression had finally opened the doors of some social institutions to them. In fact, in 1932 the Brooklawn Country Club, which was losing members to financial ruin, had let down the barriers to Irish membership, as had the less important Pine Brook Country Club, the Elks, and several yacht clubs. Of course, no other ethnics need apply. The Contemporary Club, Fairfield County Hunt Club, the Art League, and the Garden League still remained exclusive. Irish society had its own social clubs, the Calvert Club, McLean Club, and Junior Guild, the latter patronized by the young families that put on dances and charitable events. However, decisive changes had occurred at the Algonquin Club, the downtown businessmen's club, which had by the late 1930s evolved from a "Yankee stronghold to a conglomerate mixture of Yankees, Irish, Polish, and Italian men."[79]

A socioeconomic elite is not the same thing as a political elite, however. Though the two groups had overlapped at one time, their roles and functions had drifted apart. The political parties had been slowly changing since World War I to include new middle-class ethnics, though social and economic elites still played political roles in the 1920s. When the privatist mode of social welfare funding collapsed under the weight of the depression, many of the charitable activities of the elite ended, cutting off another arena of influence in the

city. The final arena of influence, the control of the city's economy, was loos-
ened by the out-of-town ownership of the city's industries and weakened by the
movement of executives out of the city. The resentment evidenced by Bridgeport workers and some small businessmen toward elites whose factories were
still in Bridgeport, though those elite owners themselves were not, was one
important component of the antibusiness and pro-Socialist sentiment of the
early 1930s. The city was finally in the hands of working-class representatives,
so long as they kept the cost of the city in check and usurped no powers beyond
those acceptable to the city's financial powers.

But the Bridgeport Socialist Party had changed too in the two years that it
had been in power. Although the political moves that Bridgeport Socialists had
made to achieve their legislative victories had been necessary, they represented
a big step onto the slippery slope of compromise. The increasing splits in the
SP nationally removed an important ideological rudder for the local Socialists.
McLevy and the Bridgeport Socialists had always used the broader social welfare initiatives of the national SP platform to guide and strengthen their own
local campaigns. But by 1936, even as some of those reforms were slowly being
implemented by the Second New Deal, the Socialist Party of America was increasingly divided about the nature of those goals. In late 1936 the McLevyists walked away from their commitment to the SP and in doing so lost their
link to far-ranging social change. Though that link had been loosely interpreted in the past, this was a decisive break.

McLevy's move was reluctant at first. As Devere Allen, leader of Connecticut's Militant wing, reported to Norman Thomas, McLevy would only "jump
in on the side of the Old Guard" if pushed by the Militants' actions in Connecticut or at the national level. "Otherwise . . . he has a burning desire to keep
Connecticut building up and out of the national situation as far as possible."[80]
Staying out of the fight was an impossibility. While Allen resigned his position
as editor of the Connecticut SP paper, the *Commonwealth,* in order to organize
for the Militants, McLevy continued to speak at New York events held by the
old guard. He sent Fred Schwarzkopf to the regional gatherings of the new Interstate Conference of the SP, composed of delegates from the state organizations of New York, Massachusetts, Maryland, and Pennsylvania and the Jewish
and Finnish federations. Factionalism continued to build within the SP as Militants and Trotskyists pushed the SP further to the left after the party adopted
the 1934 Declaration of Principles. The problem came to a head in January 1936
when the national executive committee decided to suspend the New York party's charter until it could be determined which faction had the majority. At this
point the Bridgeport SP formally joined the Interstate Conference, and they
issued a joint proposal to the upcoming 1936 SP convention that called for an
end to talk of a United Front, for the purging of all "Communist" elements, and
for a repudiation of the 1934 declaration.

The breaking point came at the SP national convention in May 1936, when the executive committee voted to seat the Militant slate instead of the old guard as the official delegation from New York State.[81] McLevy took to the floor of the convention to criticize the executive committee's action. In a Socialist version of states' rights he argued for "the right of self-determination to states to carry on their own propaganda and their own policies. . . . The only jurisdiction that the National Executive Committee has, or had, was to determine whether or not any state violated the principles and the platform of the party." He went on to castigate the Militants for the decline in party membership after 1934: "They were so busy trying to run the affairs of the state of New York they did not have any time to carry on a program for the building up of the Socialist Party."[82] After the convention New York's old guard regrouped to form the Social Democratic Federation (SDF), and in September the Connecticut SP voted to disaffiliate from the national SP.

New York's old guard was deeply conscious of new currents within the labor movement and was preparing to support Sidney Hillman and David Dubinsky when they placed their unions behind Roosevelt's 1936 campaign. The SDF thus affiliated with the new American Labor Party (ALP) in New York State, which followed the CIO-sponsored Labor's Nonpartisan League in endorsing Roosevelt. Ironically, joining the New York ALP put the SP's anticommunist old guard in a coalition with the Communist Party's Popular Front.

Connecticut Socialists had already seen attempts to form a state labor party fade.[83] The maverick president of the Connecticut Federation of Labor, J. Nicholas Danz, had condemned Governor Cross for sending the national guard to control picketers during the 1934 textile strike, and Danz continued his attacks on both the Democratic and Republican Parties for their cautious attitudes on labor action and labor legislation. In 1935 he aimed his fire at CFL officials who held office in "the two major political parties," noting that "both major parties have not hesitated calling on the military and state police in strike issues. They have turned a deaf ear to the revocation of the injunction law. . . . The people are ready for a change." His solution was a labor party. Though it was a minority movement of eastern Connecticut textile locals and the Hartford Central Labor Union—all representing workers whose strikes had been crushed with the help of state police or national guard intervention—the group nonetheless forged ahead to hold labor party meetings in 1935 and 1936. Their efforts were spurred on by state police intervention in the fierce Remington-Rand strike in Middletown and undeterred by the defeat of a labor party referendum in the Connecticut Federation of Labor. Three hundred people gathered in New Haven in July 1936 to launch the Connecticut Farmer-Labor Party. Like so many other attempts in other states, Connecticut's budding labor party was immediately overwhelmed by the vast outpouring of sentiment for Roosevelt and did not field a ticket in the 1936 elections. After some attempts to lobby as a group for labor legislation, most supporters melded with the new Connecticut CIO's Labor's Nonpartisan League (LNPL). Though some Connecticut Socialists had participated in the July 1936 Farmer-Labor convention, the Bridgeport SP argued that the SP already *was* the labor party of Connecticut.[84]

The Bridgeport Socialists, who did not entertain the notion of affiliation with Democrats or Communists in Connecticut, decided to run a state campaign as usual in 1936, with McLevy as gubernatorial candidate, along with Bridgeport state senate and representative candidates, on the Connecticut SP line. Overwhelmed by the landslide for Roosevelt, who captured 64 percent of the vote in Bridgeport, the Bridgeport Socialists lost their seats in the Connecticut General Assembly to Democrats.[85] The Bridgeport SP became a different organization after the 1936 split with the Socialist Party of America. Though McLevy was elected chairman of the Social Democratic Federation in May 1937, the Bridgeport party delayed its formal affiliation with it. McLevy quietly pulled away from the SDF after 1938. His philosophy may be summed up in his comments to the SDF when the Social Democrats briefly considered reuniting with the SP. According to McLevy, "One of the reasons for the break-up of the S.P. was that instead of trying to build a political party, it wanted to run every trade union, every college and every church. . . . The reasons our Party has gone forward in Connecticut is because it minded its own business and not that of everyone else." Because it had no formal link to a Socialist Party national platform and was unwilling to merge with New Deal or labor Democrats, the Bridgeport organization became more narrowly focused, locally oriented, and unabashedly reformist.[86]

McLevy now had the formula for long-lasting success. He had refrained from criticizing Roosevelt during the 1936 campaign, but now he berated the Connecticut Democrats for their lukewarm attitudes toward labor and denounced the GOP from Alf Landon on down. Two Socialist members of the common council, Mickey Gratt and William Neil, were active in support of CIO locals when the United Electrical and Radio Workers came to town in late 1936. Gratt, in fact, helped organize rallies at GE and received an honorary membership from the United Electrical Workers for his activities. Undoubtedly, it was this visible support from *some* members of the McLevy administration that kept its prolabor record alive.[87] The Bridgeport party, hewing to its municipal platform, was even more successful at the polls, garnering 69 percent of the vote in the municipal election of 1937 and 57 percent in 1939, though the voter turnout declined. (See table 6, p. 95.)

Despite, or perhaps because of, convincing evidence of McLevy's moderation, working-class residents clung to their view of McLevy as representative of their condition and sensitive to their needs. This went beyond mere appearance—one "school kid" told reporters that his family and neighbors were for McLevy ("I'd vote for Jasper because he dresses like we poor kids do")—to feelings of economic vulnerability (another reported, "My mama said we'd have to quit school if our mayor was licked"). In the 1937 city election many factory workers were seen wearing red "Elect McLevy" buttons as they massed to the polls at the end of the working day.[88] While numerous people interviewed by the WPA

Writers' Project in 1938 and 1939 criticized McLevy for some of his actions (McLevy's delay in action on the federal public housing project and McLevy's rejection of wage demands by striking municipal garbage workers), many still supported McLevy. Noted an officer of the metal polishers' union, "I think McLevy's alright. . . . You could always count on . . . Jasper McLevy to address a meeting. . . . No matter what he ran for, I always voted for Jasper. And I'm not considered a Socialist either."[89] The new Bridgeport CIO Labor's Nonpartisan League voted unanimously to endorse McLevy and his slate, calling it the "most progressive" appeal offered by any group at present, clearly a slap at the Democrats. Swedes, in particular, made up the consistent backbone of support: "The Swedes have always been a progressive group. Most of them were Socialists in their native country," while French Canadians and Slovaks were also noted for past electoral support even if they voted Democratic at the national level.[90]

McLevy's "laborist" image followed him to the state level in 1938. In the 1938 gubernatorial contest McLevy used the issues of recent state scandals in connection with construction of the Merritt Parkway and financial improprieties in Waterbury—both involving key state Democratic and Republican Party officials—to pull in more than 25 percent of the vote statewide (48 percent in Bridgeport), enough to allow the Republican candidate, Raymond Baldwin, to defeat Governor Cross by a handful of votes. McLevy's slogan, "The time to reform is now," attracted mostly Democratic voters in the industrial centers of the state and a considerable number of labor voters. The vote was widely perceived as labor's revenge on the state Democratic Party, because it had been cool toward the New Deal.[91] "Two-thirds of the Socialist vote came from the Democrats," a chastened and defeated U.S. Sen. Augustine Lonergan reported to Jim Farley, chair of the national Democratic Party. "I observed a current of radicalism in the State during the campaign."[92]

This state Republican victory over an incumbent Democrat added another win to the GOP column nationally. On the surface it seemed to be part of the conservative backlash nationally against the New Deal in 1938. In Connecticut it signaled the opposite, because a strong SP vote took victory away from the Democrats. In addition, Baldwin was part of a "New Era" Republican Party that ran Polish and Italian ethnics for state office and supported moderate labor legislation, not exactly conservative backlash. But Baldwin's New Era GOP repudiated New Deal economic and social welfare policies, which was most strikingly revealed in his slogan, "There is no substitute for a good job in private industry."[93]

The voter actions at the state level, but even more so locally, raise interesting questions about voter mobilization in general. For one, traditional Democratic and Republican Party stalwarts in Bridgeport were thoroughly demoralized and had given up on mobilization for local elections. One old-timer put it bluntly: "We have carted them [the voters] in for several elections to have them pull the third lever [Socialist]. . . . This time [1937] let them come in themselves."[94]

While turnout dipped in 1937 to 71.7 percent of registered voters, McLevy's majority increased. Turnout was never as spectacular for municipal elections from 1937 on as in the early McLevy years, reflecting a decline in competitiveness, while presidential election turnouts remained high. Bridgeport voters were loyal to FDR, but they never became loyal to the Democrats.

The pattern of voting sheds light on the process of constructing the New Deal voter coalition. It was never consolidated in Bridgeport during the 1930s. While FDR votes in 1936 and 1940 are strongly correlated with such factors as low income and immigrant parentage, no such pattern is evident for state and local races. (See table 12, p. 162.) The Al Smith revolution had produced a massive change in voter mobilization, but the state and local Democratic Party had not captured that vote.

Moreover, voters in Bridgeport were independent voters. In 1937, the only year for which local party registration data exist, the 57,994 registered voters included about 18,000 registered Republicans (31 percent) and 15,500 registered Democrats (26.7 percent). Nearly 40 percent of voters (38.8 percent) had registered without party affiliation, while another 3.4 percent had registered Socialist, which left 42.2 percent of the electorate outside the traditional parties. This is an impressive statement of electoral independence, given the opportunities that still existed for traditional patronage at the state level for both Republican and Democratic activists. In other words, voters who had a viable progressive alternative could turn their backs on traditional parties even as they embraced Roosevelt. This pressure, as well as the stronger organization of the CIO during the World War II years, eventually brought the Democratic Party, both in Bridgeport and statewide, to embrace New Deal social policy and a liberal-labor coalition.

Ethnic Politics during the 1930s

But if class-based voting emerged during the 1930s, it was still in competition with traditional patronage politics, now expanded to include the new ethnics. Ethnic appeals to partisanship remained strong in this era of mobilization of immigrants and the second generation. Federal regulations forced the foreign born who applied for relief to become citizens, thereby adding to the eligible electorate. The political muscle of the new ethnics, which they first flexed during the 1928 presidential campaign, affected local and state politics in the mid-1930s, when ethnic pride swept immigrant cities. Patronage democracy was bolstered by the growing government welfare programs, which many local and state politicians deliberately used to cement voter allegiance and to undercut independent parties.[95]

In addition, the ethnic support for McLevy reveals the fragility of mainstream party politics in Bridgeport. Contrary to the conventional view, ethnic electoral politics did not grow stronger as the 1930s wore on. Instead, ethnic politics in Bridgeport grew more diffuse. Although ethnic clubs still rallied for their candidates—one second-generation new ethnic, Ameriko Scanzillo, a Democrat, captured a state senate seat in the Roosevelt landslide of 1936—most ambitious second-generation ethnic activists were rewarded with county, state, or federal patronage positions, not votes. McLevyism had completely derailed the kind of ethnic pride machine politics that Raymond Wolfinger has interpreted as the norm for this era.[96]

As the city approached the 1937 municipal election, a headline in the *Bridgeport Times-Star* asked readers, "Do People Vote by Racial Blocs at Present?" While noting that both Democrats and Republicans paid careful attention to ticket balancing, the paper reported that appeals on labor issues were more significant to many voters. Moreover, it asserted that the "new generation" resented the question's implication that they were "pro-nationality, rather than American," a reminder that ethnics were aware of the strong anti-immigrant sentiment sweeping the United States at this time.[97]

A growing Americanism pervaded many ethnic communities during the early depression. At a 1932 Pulaski Day celebration held by the Bridgeport branch of the Polish National Alliance, one leader proclaimed his pride that his countrymen Casimir Pulaski and Thaddeus Kosciusko had participated in the American Revolution "and thereby carved on the foundation stones of our national structure the birthright of our countrymen to the enjoyment of the liberties and the opportunities which this nation and its vast territory offers to the various people of Europe, who have come here to develop and finally possess it." He then went on to list the attributes that make Poles "good citizens": being part of the "great army of labor" that built America, building churches and schools, and contributing a growing number of business and professional men.[98] Similarly, that same fall Hungarians, noting that two of their ancestors had taken part in the American Revolution, participated in the city's George Washington Bicentennial Birthday parade. Two years later, as events in Europe were beginning to affect American ethnics, Bridgeport Czecho-Slovakians celebrated the anniversary of the Czecho-Slovak constitution, praising "its success as the only democracy among neighboring dictatorships." This observance is all the more meaningful and indicative of this community's political values because in the 1920s the Bridgeport Slovaks had been split along religious lines—many Catholics had wanted an autonomous Slovakia, and many Protestants supported the 1918 constitution.[99]

The rhetoric of Americanism and democracy, combined with a concern to preserve Polish culture, moved some Poles to desert the Roman Catholic Polish parish in Bridgeport for the Polish National Catholic Church. Citing the practice of demanding money for religious services as well as the past alliance of the Polish Roman Catholic pastor and local Republicans, "the smarter people"—those "against all the hockus pockus [*sic*] of the Catholic religion"—and those "believ[ing] in greater democracy in the Church" moved to the National Catholic Church where the mass was in Polish, not Latin.[100]

The patterns of ethnic community organization had changed in Bridgeport during the 1930s, but they were not channeled into narrow electoral efforts. Most ethnics increasingly looked to American values and searched their European past for antecedents of American democratic values. Traditional ethnic leaders— businessmen and clergy—still had roles to play in their communities, even though they were no longer influential in local politics. They preserved their position by organizing large coalition groups that brought together all organizations in their group on a nonpartisan basis to celebrate their communities; the Polish Alliance and the Slovak Alliance were two examples. A variety of new ethnic veterans' organizations sprang up—the Jewish War Veterans, Czecho-Slovak Legionnaires, American Veterans of Slovak Extraction, Italian War Veterans, Lithuanian Legion of America—that celebrated their participation in either the U.S. military or the liberation army of their homeland to make the world "safe for democracy."[101]

More problematic, however, was the Italian War Veterans' 1935 celebration of the entrance of Italy into the war twenty years earlier. "We are not here today only to celebrate an anniversary, . . . but to celebrate also the birth of a new Italian civilization on the earth," proclaimed a Bridgeport notable of Italian heritage. The Italian community's support for Mussolini, who arguably was the first to tap southern Italians' sense of nationalism, was acceptable to many American businessmen and politicians who were also supportive of Mussolini. But it represented a worrisome trend for Italian-American leftists and unionists who set up national antifascist committees. The massive rallies held in Italian-American communities when Italy invaded Ethiopia, and the ardor with which women gave up their gold wedding rings to Il Duce's military adventures, hinted that Italians were a politically volatile community in the United States. Italians were never a secure part of the New Deal coalition. Similarly, monarchists in the Hungarian community, as well as some disgruntled Slovak autonomists, provided a base for a growing anti-Semitism and conservative politics in Bridgeport in the late 1930s. Ethnic identification could cut two ways, both liberal and reactionary.[102]

Nonetheless, the McLevy administration emphasized the new ethnic rhetoric of Americanism and democracy in the 1936 Bridgeport Centennial, a four-month celebration by every component of Bridgeport's community. The Bridgeport Centennial took on ambitious proportions when the mayor accepted the partnership of the General Electric Company in planning and carrying out the event. GE "loaned" the city one of its top advertising executives to act as general manager for the centennial. This event displayed the organizational strength that McLevyists successfully used in the neighborhoods while also showing the lengths to which McLevy would go to cement his relationship with cooperative industry. It also revealed the political sagacity with which liberal industrialists like the GE management handled the changing political landscape in the 1930s.

One important group of festivities was "Old Home Week," modeled after the

Yankee rituals of 1935 that were part of the state tercentenary celebration. But in 1936 Bridgeport celebrated immigrants. During Old Home Week ethnic groups gathered at Beardsley Park and erected models of their home villages where ethnic foods, dancing, and historical pageants were offered to the public. In addition, each ethnic group had a "day" during the summer months in which to put on a celebration in whatever form the ethnic alliance chose. In subsequent years various ethnicities continued their annual day as a way to celebrate their existence in America and to bridge the distances among the various organizations within their group. Politicians from all parties dutifully attended.[103]

One other main event during the Bridgeport Centennial was Labor Day, which boasted a parade—the first staged in years—put together by the McLevy administration and the city's labor unions. But this Labor Day parade was different: in addition to the usual "Labor Division," participants included a "Civic Division" of ethnic organizations and an "Industrial Division" of ten local companies that entered floats. From the reviewing stand McLevy praised "the part labor has played in the progress of Bridgeport." He was flanked by a representative from the Central Labor Union, a top executive from Remington Arms, the president of the Chamber of Commerce, the GE manager who was

Winning float, Union Division, Labor Day Centennial Parade, 1936. (Photograph by Corbit's Studio, Historical Collections, Bridgeport Public Library.)

general director of the centennial, and a Socialist member of the common council who represented "civic life." The group on the reviewing stand perfectly captured the political accommodation that characterized Bridgeport by 1936.[104]

* * *

By the late 1930s McLevy had subsumed the contest for power between labor and capital—and between Democrats, Republicans, and Socialists—into a vision that held a place for all. It was a sign of the growing power and importance of labor and of ethnics that these groups were central to the process. It is also an indication of the limits of the pursuit of political power in this era. In the latter half of the decade the growing strength of fascism in the world, as well as conservatism in the U.S. Congress, increasingly occupied the attention of many, and the New Deal came to a halt.

In a speech to Bridgeport Swedish groups celebrating the three-hundredth anniversary of their arrival on American shores, McLevy captured that mood in a way that perhaps best revealed his own conception of what was to be done to preserve civilization: "Sweden is the beacon light to the world. It has solved the modern problem of unemployment; it has brought together capital and labor and in the midst of the chaos and misery of Europe, Sweden alone is intelligent in action, magnificent in spirit. . . . It represents civilization in its finest spirit."[105]

Conclusion

The Bridgeport SP's remarkable move from outsider critic to oc-
cupant of city hall was illustrative of the volatility of politics in the early depression years. The party stayed in power in the mid-1930s by using the political
arena for class negotiations with industrial leaders. Even as the McLevyists compromised with local financial and business leaders, for the rest of the 1930s they
served as representatives of the working class in the political process. A feeling
of "us versus them" pervaded working-class sentiment in favor of McLevy, no
matter how much McLevy cooperated with local industrialists.[1]

The politics of the 1930s, especially the nature of the New Deal, has been subjected to extensive analysis, usually in the dichotomous terms of radical or reformist, liberal celebration or corporatist co-optation. The dichotomy of liberation and co-optation has also pervaded much labor historiography of the
depression era, which takes as its point of departure the relationship formed
during the 1930s between unions and the state. While earlier studies credited
the Roosevelt administration with the creation of a labor relations system that
was a unique boon to the labor movement, more recent critical studies have
focused on the limitations of the New Deal's collective-bargaining system and
its effect on the shape and potential of the labor movement. The question of
labor's entanglement in government oversight was thus one side of the New
Deal coin, the other side of which was working people's entanglement in the
Democratic Party.[2]

Critics also argue that Roosevelt and his New Deal, by sweeping the mass of
working people into the Democratic Party, prevented the emergence of a class-
based party that would secure a permanent place for labor in the political system. The question of a labor party in the United States has a long historiogra-

phy itself.[3] But this question remains mired in an essentialist trap, which assumes as a given the emergence of a class-based political system, and the absence of a labor party either defines the American working class positively as pragmatic and job conscious or indicts it as reformist. For the 1930s in particular, any attempt to understand how working people conceived of the political order and their place in it must go beyond either disappointment with or celebration of the reformist character of American working-class ideology, a point made many years ago by David Brody regarding union consciousness.[4]

Some scholars have argued about the nature of the labor consciousness of the 1930s, particularly that of new ethnic workers who are seen as motivated more by the search for security than the search for power in the workplace. Integrating the social history of labor in the 1930s with a social history of political mobilization in the 1930s allows us to gain a new perspective on the putative choice between security or power.[5] The political demands raised by working people in Bridgeport regarding democracy, social policy, taxes, budgets, and unemployment relief reflected a consciousness that *combined* the goals of power and security. In particular, debates about social policy, private versus public action and responsibility, the raising and spending of public funds, and ultimately about the definition of the public good reveal an alternative political ethos expressed by Bridgeport working people that displaced traditional two-party politics during the 1930s.

This is an unusual case of politics in the 1930s. But Bridgeport's uniqueness is precisely what gives this case its value. It demonstrates that, given a solid vehicle for expression, working-class sentiment could be translated into votes outside the two traditional parties. Yet it also illustrates the difficulties in finding that vehicle, which could not be created by a sudden surge of political protest sparked by strikes but had to be built over a long period of time and with deep roots in the community to which it appealed.

This case of highly charged local politics reveals the potential that working-class votes could have. What was missing from Bridgeport in the 1930s was a strongly organized union presence that could provide the powerful base that working-class representatives needed to challenge economic interests and implement the political will of the working-class electorate. Thus our attention turns back to union activity on the shop floor. Many studies—Schatz, Cohen, Gerstle, Lichtenstein, Freeman, Faue, Bruce Nelson, and others—have pointed to the vitality of workplace-based organizing during the early 1930s.[6]

In Bridgeport early attempts to organize key industries like metalworking and electrical products were unsuccessful, due to the lack of a national labor policy and national labor organizations able to shoulder the industrial organizing tasks. That the bulk of the labor support for the SP in Bridgeport came from the AFL building trades, as well as the once-again unionized garment industry, meant that the economic base—not to mention the theoretical base—for labor politics in this metalworking city was limited. That the CIO, through the victory of the United Electrical Workers at GE-Bridgeport, provided a new economic base of power only in 1937, after the SP experiment had run out of steam, adds to the sense of lost opportunity. Moreover, the precarious positions of the UE and other CIO union locals in Bridgeport in the economic downturn of 1937–38 suggests a sobering reconsideration of the picture of workers "on the march" in the 1930s. Staughton Lynd's anthology, "We Are All Leaders," compiles a number of case studies of pre-CIO union formations that reveal the dynamism of 1930s working-class organization. The Lynd collection's usefulness is in its wealth of evidence of the organizational variety created by working people in different industries and in diverse cities. Although most of the essays do not address the question of local politics, they contain hints about confrontations with local authorities about welfare issues and the like.[7] These issues, like the tax issue in Bridgeport, are not often considered in studies of labor politics of the 1930s, but they should be.

Analyses of labor politics in the late 1930s in CIO towns like Akron and Detroit reveal an alarming lack of labor unity at the ballot box. But these studies did not explore existing grassroots political structures in either city, where the complications of traditional ties to, and ethnic solidarities with, the mainstream party candidates may have affected the course of labor politics.[8] Similarly, Cohen's Chicago is a political mystery, with ethnic workers seemingly drawn to the New Deal through FDR's radio voice.

The Bridgeport case reveals one final point, the continuing relevance and potential conservative consequences of powerful ethnic affiliations. Just as ethnic affiliations could be used to create and cement the emerging industrial unions in towns and cities across the land, ethnic links to traditional Democratic and Republican Party machines and patriotic links to conservative European national movements could thwart independent and radical politics of the working class. Where ethnic electoral affiliations were not disrupted as they were in Bridgeport, traditional political modes meant that working-class votes resulted in victory by mainstream Democratic candidates, not labor representatives.

The experience of Bridgeport focuses our attention on the potential for alternative politics in the early years of the depression and at the state and local levels, rather than the more usual focus on 1936 and at the national level. At the same time it reveals the limitations of the local level. Independent electoral parties have never had an easy time moving from the local and state levels to the national level. Bridgeport's experience makes understandable those third parties, like the Milwaukee Socialists and the Minnesota Farmer-Labor Party, which decided to merge with New Deal Democrats in the latter half of the decade, eliding the differences between them in order to hang on to their political and social gains in the face of growing conservative challenges.

McLevyism is best viewed, then, as a working-class variant of New Dealism, one that the architects of the New Deal incorporated in a viable political program. The accommodation reached in Bridgeport, like the bargain attempted between labor and liberal business nationwide, owed as much to the strength of working-class social democratic consciousness as to its weakness. Admitting workers to government, as well as paying for social welfare programs, was not what even liberal industrialists like GE executives had wanted. But it is what they got.

The New Deal was ultimately shaped not by liberals but by conservative business interests and by conservative, mostly southern, Democrats. A New Deal that aimed to incorporate more radical social legislation, restructure political power, and redistribute wealth was halted nationwide by 1938. The ways in which industrialists and state Democratic and Republican leaders limited the political experiment in Bridgeport is a powerful illustration of that complex process.

On the broadest level the Bridgeport story reveals what it meant to be an American, a citizen, and a worker in the 1920s and 1930s. The way that Bridgeport people dealt with many of the issues raised in the political sphere during this time, from simple political recognition to the knotty problems of urban finance, reflected the ways in which working people conceived of themselves and their place in the public sphere. To demand public control of solutions to such matters as unemployment and relief instead of control by private charity and elite decision makers, to demand that employers bear most of the cost of the economic debacle, to make public street corners instead of private club rooms the spaces for political debate, to make the "hyphenate-American" the typical American—these were the real accomplishments of the 1930s.

Notes

Abbreviations

ACWA	Amalgamated Clothing Workers of America
BCC	Bridgeport Chamber of Commerce
CCD	Connecticut Council of Defense
CERC	Connecticut Emergency Relief Commission
FMCS	Federal Mediation and Conciliation Service
HC-BPL	Historical Collections, Bridgeport Public Library
IAM	International Association of Machinists
I.I.	International Institute of Bridgeport
LA-UConn	Labor Archives, University of Connecticut Library
MAB	Manufacturers' Association of Bridgeport
NLRB	National Labor Relations Board
NWLB	National War Labor Board
SPA	Socialist Party of America
WPA-CtSL	Works Progress Administration, Federal Writers' Project–Connecticut, Connecticut State Library
WPA-DC	Works Progress Administration, National Archives
WPA-UConn	Works Progress Administration, Ethnic Studies File, University of Connecticut Library
YWCA-Bridgeport	Young Women's Christian Association (Bridgeport files)
YWCA-National	Young Women's Christian Association (national files)

Introduction

1. Vorse, "Bridgeport and Democracy," 151.

2. Stave, "Great Depression and Urban Political Continuity."

3. Some important works on the social history of politics are Hays, "Politics and Society," and the collected essays in Hays, *American Political History as Social Analysis;* Eley and Nield, "Why Does Social History Ignore Politics?" Also see the overview essay by Kessler-Harris, "Social History." Some early attention to the interaction of state and national politics in the 1930s may be found in Patterson, *New Deal and the States,* and Braeman, Bremner, and Brody, *New Deal,* vol. 2.

Recent scholarly trends in political science and policy studies, such as the state-oriented and "new institutionalism" perspectives, have returned our attention to the structures and organizations that channel or impede actions. They also have paid attention to the ways in which local initiatives influenced national policies. Yet these studies have tended to diminish the roles of ordinary citizens. See Skocpol, "Bringing the State Back in," and March and Olsen, "New Institutionalism." A review of this literature appears in Robertson, "Return to History and the New Institutionalism." In *Protecting Soldiers and Mothers* Skocpol revises her state-centered approach by investigating the influence of middle-class women in bringing about the early welfare legislation in the United States.

4. Careful and sophisticated historically oriented political scientists like Amy Bridges and Martin Shefter, who use New York City in different eras of the nineteenth century as their test cases, argue that the political machine was the solution to class crisis in the nineteenth century, defusing class tensions by building an accommodation among the various social and economic groups in the city (Bridges, *City in the Republic;* Bridges, "Becoming American"; Shefter, "Emergence of the Political Machine"; Shefter, "Trade Unions and Political Machines").

5. Terrence McDonald uses the term *patronage democracy* as a substitute for *machine politics.* See McDonald, "Burdens of Urban History," and Katznelson, "Comment on McDonald"; Teaford, "Finis for Tweed and Steffens"; McDonald and Ward, *Politics of Urban Fiscal Policy;* Brown and Halaby, "Machine Politics in America."

6. Labor politics in the nineteenth century usually revolved around attempts to gain a measure of political power for specific purposes or sometimes larger ideological goals, either by promoting worker candidates within the two major parties or by forming independent parties. A fine overview of labor politics in the nineteenth and twentieth centuries is Brody, "Course of American Labor Politics." Nineteenth-century city studies have proliferated, but see these essential early works: Laurie, *Working People of Philadelphia;* Wilentz, *Chants Democratic;* L. Fink, *Workingmen's Democracy;* Montgomery, "Labor and the Republic in Industrial America." For challenges by radicals see Scobey, "Boycotting the Politics Factory"; Stave, *Socialism and the Cities;* Judd, *Socialist Cities;* Salvatore, *Eugene V. Debs;* Pratt, "Reading Socialist Experience"; Nash, *Conflict and Accommodation;* Bedford, *Socialism and the Workers in Massachusetts.*

7. Oestreicher, "Urban Working-Class Political Behavior"; Katznelson, *City Trenches.* See also Iver Bernstein, "Expanding the Boundaries of the Political"; McCormick, "Ethnocultural Interpretations."

The classic statement of American exceptionalism is Louis Hartz, *Liberal Tradition in America,* and the argument is conveniently summarized in Lipset, "Why No Socialism in the United States?"; Lipset, "Radicalism or Reformism"; and Lipset's essay on the politics of the 1930s, "Roosevelt and the Protest of the 1930s." The analytic contrast of the United States and Western Europe has assumed European class development as the norm and posed American development as the exception. Foner has critiqued this exceptionalism argument in "Why Is There No Socialism in the United States?" as have Wilentz, "Against Exceptionalism," and essays in response by Salvatore and Hanagan. The question has recently been revisited by Kammen in "Problem of American Exceptionalism" and by the essays in Halpern and Morris, *American Exceptionalism?*

8. First to identify the ethnic element in New Deal voting patterns was Lubell, *Future of American Politics.* Other more recent studies include Allswang, *House for All Peoples;* Andersen, *Creation of a Democratic Majority;* Gamm, *Making of New Deal Democrats;* Jensen, "Last Party System."

9. Barrett, "Americanization from the Bottom Up"; Montgomery, *Workers' Control in America,* 32–47, 91–112; Lane, "American Unions, Mass Immigration, and the Literacy Test"; Asher, "Union Nativism and the Immigrant Response." The classic study of nativism and immigration restriction is Higham, *Strangers in the Land.*

10. See Bucki, "Workers and Politics in the Immigrant City." Similar points about Americanization and writing the history of ethnic identity are raised in Conzen, Gerber, Morawska, Pozzetta, and Vecoli, "Invention of Ethnicity"; Barrett and Roediger, "Inbetween Peoples"; Gerstle, "Liberty, Coercion, and the Making of Americans"; Kazal, "Revisiting Assimilation." Jacobson, *Whiteness of a Different Color,* places ethnicity in the context of race in the midtwentieth century.

11. Key works on Progressive Era politics include Wiebe, *Search for Order;* Hays, *Response to Industrialism;* Schiesl, *Politics of Efficiency;* Huthmacher, "Urban Liberalism and the Age of Reform"; Buenker, *Urban Liberalism and Progressive Reform;* Shover, "Progressives and the Working Class Vote in California"; Rodgers, "In Search of Progressivism." Recent labor histories include Kazin, *Barons of Labor;* J. Greene, *Pure and Simple Politics;* Stromquist, "Crucible of Class." Stromquist, in particular, goes beyond the boundaries of labor institutions to explore working-class political action.

12. Two waves of revisionists have analyzed the New Deal. The points of view of the first revisionist debate are presented in Graham, *New Deal: The Critical Issues,* and reviewed in Sitkoff, *Fifty Years Later.* Jensen, "Last Party System," reviews the electoral side of the New Deal system through to its recent disarray. The second revisionist approach is represented by the essays in Fraser and Gerstle, *Rise and Fall of the New Deal Order.*

13. Gieske, *Minnesota Farmer-Laborism;* Haynes, *Dubious Alliance;* Valelly, *Radicalism in the States.*

14. Montgomery, "'New Unionism' and the Transformation of Workers' Consciousness"; Montgomery, "Whose Standards?" My own interpretation of the Bridgeport strikes appears in "Dilution and Craft Tradition."

15. Banks, *First-Person America,* and Anker, "Immigrant Voices from the Federal Writers' Project," discuss the usefulness of WPA interviews, as well as their origin and limitations. Terkel, *Hard Times,* is an important oral history of the 1930s, done in the late 1960s. Painter, *Narrative of Hosea Hudson,* and Nelson, Barrett, and Ruck, *Steve Nelson, American Radical,* use oral history to analyze their subjects; along the way they provide important illustrations of labor and radical activities in the 1930s.

16. As Christopher Tomlins has reminded us, the AFL still surpassed the CIO in numbers at decade's end (Tomlins, "AFL Unions in the 1930s"). Kazin's study, *Barons of Labor,* looks at the political power of building trades workers in Progressive Era San Francisco. A revealing look at labor and city government interactions in the 1930s is Freeman, *In Transit,* on New York City transit workers, though the union in question was a CIO union; see esp. chap. 8.

17. Readers who wish to pursue these details are invited to consult my dissertation, "Pursuit of Political Power."

Chapter 1: *Connecticut's Industrial Fortress*

1. Twain, *Connecticut Yankee in King Arthur's Court,* 37–38.

2. See the historical narrative and photographs in Palmquist, *Bridgeport: A Pictorial History,* and the photographs in Procter and Matuszeski, *Gritty Cities,* 70–89. For the history of Bridgeport and Connecticut mechanics and inventors, see Roe, *English and American Tool Builders,* 183–84, 211–13. A recent spatial analysis of Bridgeport growth in the late nineteenth and early twentieth centuries is Macieski, "Place in Time."

3. U.S. Census Bureau, *Population* (1920), vol. 1, tables 46–47; U.S. Census Bureau, *Census of Manufacturers,* 1919, table 190.

4. See company histories in Waldo, *History of Bridgeport and Vicinity,* 1:153–92; Danenberg, *Story of Bridgeport,* 125–40.

5. Diary entry, Nov. 4, 1919, Daniel Nash Morgan Papers. Morgan was a retired Bridgeport banker and businessman who had served as treasurer of the United States during the second Cleveland administration.

6. Waldo, *History of Bridgeport and Vicinity,* 2:78–80; *Who's Who in Connecticut,* 297; King obituary, *New York Times,* May 14, 1926.

7. *Herald,* April 25, 1920.

8. Federal income tax returns for 1924 revealed that Warner paid the highest tax in the city (*Herald,* September 6, 1925; Warner obituary, *Post,* September 24, 1934).

9. Waldo, *History of Bridgeport and Vicinity*, 2:24–25, quote on p. 25.

10. *Herald*, August 22, 1915.

11. D. H. Warner to Mrs. William T. Hincks, May 8, 1911, DeVer H. Warner Personal Correspondence, Warner Corset Company Papers.

12. *Herald*, October 2, 1927.

13. Warner to A. E. Lavery, May 11, 1910; Warner to C. Westley Abbott, November 18, 1910; Willis F. Hobbs (president, MAB) to Warner, December 22, 1911, all in Warner Personal Correspondence, Warner Corset Company Papers.

14. Some prominent businessmen who rallied around King were associates of Warner's. For example, Albert E. Lavery, an officer of the Bridgeport Hydraulic Company, described by Warner as "my confidential man in matters of general policy," was active in the Republican Party. Guy P. Miller, at this time a manager in the Bridgeport Brass Company, was the Republican common council member from the Fifth District, the silk-stocking ward; in the 1920s he would become an officer in the Bridgeport Hydraulic Company (Warner to Charles G. Sanford, January 18, 1910, Warner Personal Correspondence, Warner Company Papers). Unfortunately, this collection contains Warner's correspondence for the years 1910 and 1911 only. We thus have merely a small record of Warner's activity in city politics.

15. *Post*, November 4, 1923; Simpson obituary, *Herald*, June 14, 1953; Moody's Investment Service, *Moody's Manual—Industrials*. See also table 1, p. 13.

16. Waldo, *History of Bridgeport and Vicinity*, 2:51–52; Burpee, *Burpee's The Story of Connecticut*, 3:471. Eames's penchant for city beautification had earned him the sobriquet "Father of Bridgeport Parks," a not-inconsiderable honor in the Park City. See DeVer H. Warner to Eames, April 29, 1910, Warner Personal Correspondence, Warner Corset Company Papers, for an example of their cooperation to expand park services for the working people of the city over the opposition of wealthy property owners. Warner declared it a case of "the classes against the masses."

17. Lancaster, "Democratic Party in Connecticut." Also see Seitz, "Connecticut: A Nation in Miniature," on both Connecticut and Bridgeport.

18. *Evening Farmer*, November 8, 1911.

19. On the 1915 plan see the *Herald*, June 20, 1915. The proposal had been drawn up in 1917 by a Wilson-appointed board on the order of the common council. The board included the King supporters Lucien T. Warner and Guy P. Miller, thus dooming its chances. On the 1917 plan see City of Bridgeport, *Bridgeport City Manager Charter, 1917*; *Herald*, June 24, July 15, and August 12, 1917.

20. The antidemocratic, centralizing thrust of Progressive Era municipal reform is argued in Hays, "Politics of Reform in Municipal Government." Also see Schiesl, *Politics of Efficiency*; Weinstein, *Corporate Ideal in the Liberal State*, chap. 4.

21. The patterns in Bridgeport reveal the inaccuracy of the traditional bifurcation of immigration waves into "old" (e.g., immigration from 1840 to 1880, mostly northern and western European) and "new" (1890–1920, predominantly eastern and southern European). See Daniels, *Coming to America*, esp. 183–84, for a discussion of the misleading nature of the nomenclature of "old" and "new" immigrants, including its exclusion of immigrants from Africa and Asia.

22. Bucki, "Pursuit of Political Power," 180–85. Also see Embardo, "'Summer Lightning,' 1907," though my interpretation differs significantly. Far from being a repudiation of radicals as Embardo contends, the strike actually established a strong radical presence in the Hungarian community. The subsequent history of the Socialist Party, the Socialist Labor Party, the IWW, and even the postwar Communist Party in this community can be traced to the effects of this strike.

23. *Herald*, August 2, 1914, pp. 1, 10; O'Grady, *Immigrants' Influence on Wilson's Peace Policies*, passim.

24. *New York Times*, July 15, 1915; Hatch, *Remington Arms in American History*, 203–13; Hewes, *Women as Munition Makers*, 29–32; Connecticut Bureau of Labor Statistics, *Annual Report, 1916, 1917, 1918, 1919, 1920*.

25. *Herald*, August 22, 1915.

26. Hewes, "Bridgeport on the Rebound," 50. The first president of the BCC was George E. Crawford, a self-made entrepreneur who owned the largest commercial laundry in the state; the board of directors included businessmen from all political persuasions (Minute Books, May 17, 1915, April 24, 1916, and February 12, 1917, BCC Papers; Waldo, *History of Bridgeport and Vicinity,* 2:210–13). For brief accounts of activities of the earlier business groups, see *Post,* January 18, 1911, and Janick, "Government for the People," 168–71. DeVer H. Warner and his business associates alternately supported the new chamber organization and quarreled with it. Thus Warner was not in the leadership of the chamber, but its leaders solicited his support.

27. Waldo, *History of Bridgeport and Vicinity,* 2:79; Hewes, "Bridgeport on the Rebound," 49–51; City of Bridgeport, *Official Proceedings of Common Council,* 1916–17, 277–78.

28. Interview with R. Schmidt (financial secretary of the Polishers and Buffers Union from 1914 to 1923), by P. K. Russo, n.d. [1939–40], Box 112, WPA-CtSL Papers.

29. Montgomery, "The 'New Unionism'"; Bing, *Wartime Strikes and Their Adjustment,* 291–97 (national statistics) and 73–81 (Bridgeport strikes).

30. Portions of this section, along with more extensive citations, were previously published as Bucki, "Dilution and Craft Tradition." Also see Montgomery, "Whose Standards?" which analyzes the Bridgeport strikes but overestimates the degree of unity between skilled and unskilled workers during the war.

31. *Herald,* August 22, 1915.

32. *Herald,* September 12, 1915.

33. Potter, "War Boom Towns—Bridgeport"; *Machinists' Monthly Journal,* April 1915, p. 343, and *Machinists' Monthly Journal,* March 1916, pp. 261–62; *Post* and *Evening Farmer,* July–September 1915, daily issues.

34. *Herald,* August 22, 1915; *Post,* September 3, 1915.

35. The ILGWU organizers who set up the Corset Workers' Union at the Warner Company and other corset companies opened a Hungarian branch of this local; soon the Italian women demanded their own branch. But the garment union soon acknowledged the potential for interethnic discord, as well as the encouragement of nativism among American workers, that such arrangements sometimes provoked (*Post,* August 17, 1915; *Ladies' Garment Worker,* February 1916, p. 13).

36. *Post,* August 25, 1915.

37. *Herald,* September 5, 1915; Waldo, *History of Bridgeport and Vicinity,* 1:300; *International Molders Journal* 52 (November 1916): 974.

38. *Evening Farmer,* July 21, 1915; *Herald,* September 5, 1915.

39. These remarks were made by an unnamed Bridgeport representative to the Second Yama Conference on industrial relations, cited in Gitelman, "Being of Two Minds."

40. Bowen, "Conquest of Bridgeport." Note that the IAM, buoyed by the success of the Bridgeport Eight-Hour Day campaign, made the eight-hour day a basic goal while organizing elsewhere in the nation in the spring of 1916. The Socialist Fred Cederholm, a long-time Bridgeport IAM member and former member of the common council, led the 1915 IAM strikes and then was blacklisted by the city's employers. In 1917 he was appointed to the IAM national staff and assigned to other cities during the war period. He returned to Bridgeport in the 1920s (*Evening Farmer,* October 20, 1917).

41. The quote appears in "Interview with Industrial Worker Mr. P.," interview by M. G. Sayers, [n.d., 1939?], Box 135, WPA-CtSL Papers; *Bridgeport Post,* December 18, 1958 (obituary); L. Herman Lavit, son of Sam Lavit, interview by author, Bridgeport, October 22, 1987. Lavit, born Samuel Lavitsky in Russia, had emigrated with his family to Argentina when he was a small child. He had come to New York City as a teenager to live with relatives, tramped for jobs around the region, and finally settled in Bridgeport in 1909.

42. "A.W. Reports" (typewritten reports of an IAM informer to the MAB) April–September 1916, MAB Papers. See also *Machinists' Monthly Journal,* November 1916, p. 1134. The Scandinavian Lodge was formed because of the success of a recently established Swedish local of the carpenters' union

and because a few machine shops employed a large number of Swedish machinists. Sketchy mention of the ethnic lodges in IAM statements indicated that their memberships remained small (fewer than one hundred each) and consisted of skilled machinists, not less-skilled production workers (Entry 142, Box 1, February 9, 1918, Military Intelligence Records).

43. L. Herman Lavit interview.

44. Interview with Mr. Pederson by Vincent Frazzetta, January 1941, File 109:22, Box 26, WPA-UConn Papers. He is identified only as "Mr." Pederson.

45. Interview with Sidney Johnson by George Fisher, October 1939, File 109:22, Box 26, WPA-UConn Papers.

46. Pederson interview. Pederson also liked the fact that the small shops were friendly toward unions. He noted too that relations between Swedes and Norwegians in Bridgeport were strained because Swedes did not consider Norwegians to be ambitious or educated workers.

47. Bullard, "Organization Plan That Typifies Modern Management"; "Bullard Maxi-Pay Plan"; *Herald*, July 28, 1918, October 19, 1930. Copies of Bullard Company employee pamphlets are in CCD Records. Also see Bullard Company Board of Directors Minute Books, vol. 2, p. 48, and vol. 3, p. 73, Bullard Company Papers.

48. George Bowen to Federal Conciliator McWade, April 30, 1917, File 33-347, FMCS Records.

49. For example, the IAM Polish Lodge 782, led by skilled Polish machinists, printed a Polish-language announcement in the IAM Lodge 55 newspaper, *Bridgeport Labor Leader,* explaining that membership was now open to all who worked in the machinist trades, regardless of skill, and offered a machinists' school through the union to learn all aspects of the craft (*Herald*, June 24, 1917).

50. "Strong Plea for Permanent Adjustment"; *Herald,* July 7, 1918. Particular points in employer testimony and union arguments are in Transcript, Case 132, pp. 20–28, 261, 833, 900, NWLB Records. Also see Entry 141, Box 1, July 23, 1918, Military Intelligence Records.

51. This issue had been raised during the strikes in the summer of 1915 by none other than Samuel Gompers himself, the "responsible" union voice, who darkly hinted at foreign involvement in fomenting munitions strikes. Gompers was roundly criticized in labor circles for his statements. He later claimed that he was misquoted and denied having mentioned either Germans or Bridgeport in his remarks to the press. In fact, a Gompers memo in his files, dated July 19, 1915, noted that he had received evidence that it was "rich Clan na Gael men" who were interested in fomenting munitions strikes (*New York Herald,* June 18, 1915; Gompers memo, July 19, 1915, and Gompers to Ernest Bohm [secretary of the New York City Central Labor Union], July 28, 1915, Reel 79, AFL-Gompers Papers [microfilm edition]). Also see Confidential Memo, September 27, 1915, for attempts by conservative Connecticut AFL leaders to protect Gompers in his fight with antiwar activists in the AFL (File "Subversive Activities during World War I," Box 123, National Civic Federation Papers).

52. *Herald,* October 22, 1916.

53. *Evening Farmer,* August 14 and October 20, 1917; Waldo, *History of Bridgeport and Vicinity,* 1:290; *Post,* May 5, 1918 (note that the numbers of enemy aliens included Slovak and Polish immigrants who happened to have been born in the German or Austro-Hungarian empires); Fraser, "Yankees at War"; Connecticut State Council of Defense, *Report, December 1918; Post,* February 10, 1917.

54. The Bridgeport SP included Russian, Hungarian, Lithuanian, Jewish, Finnish, Greek, and Polish branches (Local 3 Minute Books, May–July 1915, June 1916, March–June 1917, McLevy-Schwarzkopf Papers).

55. *Telegram,* November 20 and 26, 1917; *Survey* 39 (December 8, 1917): 296; SP Minutes, October 27, 1917, McLevy-Schwarzkopf Papers; *Evening Farmer,* October 20, 1917; Grubbs, *Struggle for Labor Loyalty.*

56. *Herald,* October 15 and 22, July 21, and November 5, 1916; *Post,* October 10, 1917; *Post,* March 9 and October 26, 1919. For similar Polish activities see Borkowski, "Role of Pittsburgh's Polish Falcons"; also see Buczek, *Immigrant Pastor,* 48–53, for similar recruitment efforts in the Polish community of New Britain, Connecticut. For Slovak women's efforts see Report, Mrs. M. V. Gombar to Ella Fleck, n.d. [Spring 1918], Ella Fleck Papers.

57. Governor's secretary to Murray, April 11, 1917, File 117, Box 257, Governor Holcomb Papers.

58. Renkiewicz, "Polish American Workers, 1880–1980," 123–24; Gerson, *Woodrow Wilson and the Rebirth of Poland,* 46–54; Vassady, "The 'Homeland Cause'"; Barany, "The Magyars"; *Herald,* August 2, 1914, and May 23, 1915; *Post,* May 13, 1915; Park, *Immigrant Press and Its Control,* 311, 431–32. No copies of the Magyar-language *Bridgeport* survive.

59. *Telegram,* July 5, 1918.

60. Editorial from *Bridgeport Times,* quoted in *New York Call,* August 31, 1918.

61. A copy of the common council ordinance is in Box 46, File K18, CCD Records. For similar activities throughout the state, see Fraser, "Yankees at War," passim.

62. Wriston, *Report of the Connecticut State Council of Defense;* Banit, "War Machine," 52–68 and passim; "Springfield and Bridgeport," 185–86, 216–17.

63. National War Labor Board, "Findings in re employers v. employees in munitions and related trades, Bridgeport, Connecticut," Transcript Case 132, Box 20, NWLB Records. For an overview of NWLB philosophy see Bing, *Wartime Strikes and Their Adjustment,* esp. 73–81; Connor, *National War Labor Board,* esp. chaps. 7 and 8; and McCartin, *Labor's Great War.* For the national IAM view of the Bridgeport situation, see *Machinists' Monthly Journal,* August 1918, pp. 764–66.

64. See "Investigation of Night Workers," Women's Council, April 1918, Box 376, File T62, CCD Records, for patterns among Bridgeport women munitions workers. Greenwald, *Women, War, and Work,* surveys and analyzes women's wartime work experiences; see esp. pp. 116–28 for women's experiences in railroad machine shops.

65. *Labor Leader,* September 16 and October 24, 1918. The Bridgeport American Labor Party won 2 percent of the vote, with the Bridgeport SP winning its usual 4 percent.

66. *Bridgeport Progress,* February 15, 1919, BCC Papers; *Herald,* March 30, 1919; *Connecticut Labor Press,* March 29, 1919. IAM Women's Lodge 1196 became active in the cause of women's suffrage, and four members, led by the lodge president Elsie Ver Vane, were arrested during the Washington, D.C., watch-fire demonstrations in January 1919 ("In the Name of Right and Justice").

67. *Herald,* July 20 and 27, 1919; *Bridgeport Labor Leader,* July 24 and 31, 1919.

68. For example, the strike waves in Waterbury, Connecticut, and Lawrence, Massachusetts, revealed similar interethnic unity (Bucki, *Metal, Minds, and Machines,* 77–79; Vecoli, "Anthony Capraro and the Lawrence Strike of 1919"). An overview of the interconnectedness and contradictions in ethnic and class awareness during the 1919 strikes appears in Montgomery, "Nationalism, American Patriotism, and Class Consciousness."

69. *Herald,* August 10, 1919. Strike reports taken from *Herald* accounts, July–September 1919. Also see Connecticut Bureau of Labor Statistics, "Strikes and Lockouts," *Annual Report,* 1919–20, 57–66; Connecticut Federation of Labor, "Organizing Report of Secretary I. M. Ornburn," *Proceedings of the Annual Convention,* 1920, 9; *Labor Leader,* September 25, 1919; *Machinists' Monthly Journal,* September 1919, p. 853; *Machinists' Monthly Journal,* October 1919, p. 953.

70. In contrast, both Dubofsky, *State and Labor in Modern America,* and McCartin, *Labor's Great War,* discount the more radical sensibilities of American workers in this era, and downplay the effects of worker activism on the establishment and decision making of the NWLB.

71. *Herald,* May 16, 1920 (both quotes); *(Bridgeport) Progressive Labor News,* May 6 and July 22, 1920. On the Amalgamated Metal Workers of America (AMWA), see Savage, *Industrial Unionism in America,* 284–301; *Progressive Labor News,* January 22 and March 18, 1920; New York State Legislature, *Revolutionary Radicalism,* 1:934–41. Note that AMWA delegates were among the many members of left-wing union formations who participated in conventions that formed the new Workers' Party in 1920–22 (Oneal and Werner, *American Communism,* 116–18, 124–25). The *Bridgeport City Directory,* 1921 and 1922, listed an AMWA Local Españo No. 34. Note that Lavit spoke fluent Spanish, the result of his childhood in Argentina (L. Herman Lavit interview, 1987).

72. *Herald,* May 16, 1920.

73. Connecticut Bureau of Labor Statistics, *Annual Report,* 1922, p. 49; *Herald,* October 24 and 31, 1920; File 170-1284, FMCS. The information on Vernon is from the *Herald,* June 3, 1928. Vernon had allegedly changed his name during the war to evade the draft. Blacklisted, he never worked

again in Bridgeport. When he returned to the Bridgeport area late in the decade, he started an ill-fated chicken farm. He died under suspicious circumstances in 1928. He had evidently never lost his interest in radical politics; the police investigating his death found a copious library of "Bolsheviki" books and pamphlets in his house.

74. "Interview with Industrial Worker Mr. P."

75. Ibid.; *Herald,* November 9, 1919; *Post,* November 8, 9, 10, and 12, 1919, and January 3 and 4, 1920; Shubert, "Palmer Raids in Connecticut"; Preston, *Aliens and Dissenters,* 5–8, 208–37; Murray, *Red Scare,* 190–222.

76. Report by police superintendent to Capt. Peter Hall, 3d Precinct, February 21, 1921, Bridgeport Police Records; Files 10110-2283/9,/29–31,/32,/96, Box 3078, and File 10261-179, Box 3209, Military Intelligence Records; *Herald,* October 31, 1920, and May 1, 1921; *Post,* May 2, 1921. The *Post* noted that "capitalism was denounced" at the May Day meeting (report on Sacco and Vanzetti meeting, superintendent of police PJF to John G. Stanley, Board of Police Commissioners, September 21, 1921, in Bridgeport Police Records). The meeting took place at the Casino Theater on September 18; there was no local newspaper coverage.

77. Police report, April 12, 1921, Bridgeport Police Records. The city police department's detective division operated a "Red squad" of sorts through at least 1923, reporting on radical meetings of all stripes and keeping tabs on known radicals, mostly at the behest of the Hartford office of the Federal Bureau of Investigation. The records are silent on whether the police intervened directly in any radical or union activity.

78. Jacoby, *Employing Bureaucracy,* 177, 328 n. 29; Douglas, *Real Wages in the United States,* 445; Soule, *Prosperity Decade,* chap. 5; Beney, *Cost of Living in the United States,* 44–45, 62–63; U.S. Department of Labor, Women's Bureau, *Home Work in Bridgeport, Connecticut;* Diamond, "Connecticut Study of Street Trades"; "Shop Committees in Bridgeport"; *Herald,* September 4, 1921. Also see various clippings, Box 135, WPA-CtSL Papers. General overviews of the unemployment situation and coping strategies of industry and government are Klein, *Burden of Unemployment,* and Feder, *Unemployment Relief in Periods of Depression,* 293–324.

79. *Herald,* November 23, 1919. The council's proposals also included a cooperative store along the British model.

80. *Herald,* April 18 and May 2, 1920, and January 9 and July 31, 1921; *Post,* May 1, 1921; *Times,* November 1 and 3, 1921; Morris, *Conflict within the AFL,* 72–74. Lists of strikes appear in Connecticut Bureau of Labor Statistics, *Annual Report,* 1920–22, pp. 49–52.

81. *Herald,* June 19, July 10, and September 11 and 18, 1921. The "slave auction" technique gained prominence when a similar auction on the Boston Common by Urbain Ledoux, "Mr. Zero," was reported in the national press (Chenery, "Mr. Zero, the Man who Feeds the Hungry"; Laidler, "The Month: Labor in America").

82. Similarly, after a personal appeal by the head of the city's Board of Charities, the Bridgeport chamber rescinded its previous negative vote on the bonds, citing "the matter of giving immediate relief to the unemployed, not only in providing for their physical wants, but in giving them assurance that the city has sufficient funds available for any emergency" (Minutes, May 4, 1921, BCC Papers).

83. *Herald,* March 6, May 15, June 26, and July 3, 1921; Minute Books, January 8 and May 5, 1921, MAB Papers. Also see Executive Board Minutes, March 4, 1921, for MAB concerns about "combatting the Communist movement" in the midst of the unemployment crisis, and MAB, *Bulletin No. 1991* (July 22, 1921, also in the MAB Papers), for instructions to members on how to conduct layoffs and keep the goodwill of employees. Sam Lavit and Edward Belfonte, an Italian foreman, led the unemployed workers' protest, while city officials pleaded with the men to understand that they had to agree with the Special Relief Commission's new rules in order to get the funds at all (*Herald,* July 17 and 24 and August 7, 1921). Also see Angus P. Thorne, "Report of Special Relief Commission," in City of Bridgeport, *Municipal Register,* 1922, 168–90.

The report noted that only ex-servicemen and men with families were given relief, and only those who could prove a legal settlement (i.e., no aliens) in the city were provided with relief. However, aliens whose children could claim a legal settlement in Bridgeport were given work. Relief recipients, who could own neither property nor an automobile, were paid in a combination of cash and orders to local merchants. The fund provided work for an average of 961 men a week from July to December 1921, reaching a peak of 1,305 families on relief in December when the money ran out. See Minute Books, December 6, 1920, May 9, 1921, and January 5, February 6, and March 27, 1922, Bridgeport Board of Public Charities. Note that many cities had similar splits between city administrations and local business in regard to relief issues. See Klein, *Burden of Unemployment*.

84. *Herald*, July 10 and September 11, 1921.

Chapter 2: *Manufacturers, Politics, and Postwar Problems*

1. Speech to 1929 NAM convention, quoted in Prothro, *Dollar Decade*, 97. For business activities in the 1920s also see Allen, *Only Yesterday*, chaps. 6 and 7; Leuchtenberg, *Perils of Prosperity*, chaps. 5 and 10; Hicks, *Republican Ascendancy*, chap. 5.

2. The term *class legislation* was part of populist rhetoric and referred to laws on behalf of business special interests. Ironically, when business interests referred to class legislation, they meant regulatory laws and prolabor legislation. On business lobbying in the 1920s see Prothro, *Dollar Decade*, 151–64; Bonnett, *Employers' Associations*, 298, 326–34; Hicks, *Republican Ascendancy*, 50–87. The success of the congressional progressive-labor bloc in thwarting business's legislative goals in the early 1920s is detailed in Walling, *American Labor and American Democracy*, pt. 1, 66–169.

3. *Connecticut Industry* 1 (February 1923): 5.

4. *Connecticut Industry* 2 (July 1924): 4.

5. Mitchell, "Social Legislation in Connecticut," 71–128, 158–73; Hicks, *Republican Ascendancy*, 220 n. 9; *Connecticut Industry* 6 (January 1928): 5–7. For Roraback's business and political career see Dahill, "Connecticut's J. Henry Roraback." The governor from 1925 to 1931, John H. Trumbull, was president of Trumbull Electric Manufacturing Company in Plainville and was a director of a number of other corporations. During his terms as governor he became a director of Connecticut Light & Power Company. The lieutenant governor from 1928 to 1931 was Ernest E. Rogers, president of the Connecticut Chamber of Commerce in 1926. While a state senator earlier in the decade, Rogers was both vice president of the state Chamber of Commerce and chairman of the state Senate Appropriations Committee.

6. For example, the moderate liberal program advanced in 1922 by New Haven's GOP leader, Isaac Ullman, and supported by Windsor Locks's Frank Healey and Bridgeport's John T. King, was easily overwhelmed by the conservative majority on the first day of the GOP convention. The Ullman program called for equal rights for women, the extension of child welfare work, protection of depositors of private banks, extended home rule for municipalities, increased taxes on certain "power [utility] interests," and curbs on private utilities' use of the state's natural resources—a liberal, though hardly radical, program. King's interest seems mainly to have been political rivalry rather than strong ideological support for these issues (*Hartford Courant*, August 4 and September 14, 1922; Dahill, "Connecticut's J. Henry Roraback," 141–54).

7. Janick, *A Diverse People*, 24–28; Lancaster, "Rotten Boroughs and the Connecticut Legislature"; Lancaster, "Background of a State 'Boss' System"; Mitchell, "Social Legislation in Connecticut," 158–73. The state Labor Department, run by Roraback's righthand man, Harry MacKenzie, for most of the 1920s was particularly negligent. The economist Ewan Clague, investigating industrial conditions in the state, flatly told the Consumers League of Connecticut that the Labor Department's annual reports were "absolutely worthless" and that its field workers displayed "general incompetence" (Ewan Clague to Consumers League, August 5, 1931, Box 4, File 60, Consumers League of Connecticut Papers).

8. City of Bridgeport, "Report of the Board of Apportionment," and "Statement of Indebtedness," *Municipal Register*, 1914–15, and *Municipal Register*, 1918–19.

9. F. H. Duncomby to Governor Lake, June 24, 1921, Box 282, Governor Lake Papers. The reports of the legislative hearings are in *Hartford Courant*, April 8 and 15, 1921; *Telegram*, April 15, 1921; *Post*, June 28, 1921.

10. Miscellaneous letters, "Bridgeport File," Box 282, Governor Lake Papers. The heated rivalry between King and Roraback, the state GOP leader, stemmed from Roraback's battle with King about the 1920 state committeeman position and was credited with fueling anti-King sentiment in Hartford.

11. Minutes, August 30, 1921, BCC Papers. The *Herald* of September 4, 1921, reported rumors that about three hundred members had quit the chamber over this issue. The BCC Papers contain no information on this. While yearly membership figures are unavailable, the chamber's membership totaled 1,244 after a membership drive in 1919 (Minutes, May 13, 1919, BCC Papers). By contrast, the other major business group, the Manufacturers' Association, had about 110 members (*Bridgeport Star*, April 16, 1925).

12. *Herald*, July 10, September 10 and 18 and October 9 and 16, 1921; Atwater obituary, *Post*, February 23, 1933 (HC-BPL clipping file).

13. *Herald*, July 31 and October 23, 1921; *Post*, November 6, 1921; *Times*, November 3, 1921.

14. *Times*, October 31 and November 3, 7, and 9, 1921; *Post*, November 7, 8, and 9, 1921. In addition to specific citations, information about this and subsequent electoral campaigns in Bridgeport was derived from reading three newspapers, the *Herald*, the *Post*, and the *Times*, for the six weeks before each election.

15. Minutes, January 6, 1922, Bridgeport Board of Apportionment Records.

16. Minutes, February 10, 1922, and February 9, March 21, and May 11, 1923, Board of Apportionment Records. The board of education protested that Bridgeport was appropriating only 22.4 percent of the city budget to schooling, compared to a national average of 39 percent.

17. Minutes, November 21 and 23, 1921, and January 18 and February 8, 1922, Board of Apportionment Records. Spending for poor relief, charity, and unemployment relief during Wilson's last year came to 6.9 percent of the city budget, while in Atwater's first year it totaled 8.1 percent; by contrast, normal expenditures for these categories averaged 2.9 percent (calculated from City of Bridgeport, "City Treasurer's Report," *Municipal Register*, 1921, 1922, 1923, 1924, 1925).

18. Minutes, January 23 (quote) and March 29, 1922, MAB Papers.

19. Minutes, July 13, 1923, MAB Papers.

20. *Post*, December 18, 1921.

21. Minutes, September 20, 1920. The chamber never took a formal stand on this issue, voting in May 1922 not to take part in the charter revision effort (Minutes, May 31, 1922, BCC Papers).

22. *Herald*, October 7, 1923. Also see *Herald*, September 3 and October 15, 1922, and September 30, 1923; *Post*, November 6, 1922, and September 24, 1923; City of Bridgeport, *Proposed Charter for the City of Bridgeport, November 6, 1923*. On the national movement toward commission government, see Rice, *Progressive Cities*, esp. 84–99.

23. Atwater obituary, *Post*, February 23, 1933 (HC-BPL clipping file); the Cornell quote is from the *Herald*, September 30, 1923.

24. *Herald*, October 21 and November 4, 1923; Behrens's obituary, *Times-Star*, April 5, 1940 (HC-BPL clipping file).

25. The arrest of Wilson's former tax collector, Howard F. Smith, on charges of embezzlement during the Wilson administration, helped Atwater's case but not enough (*Times*, November 3, 1923; *Herald*, November 11, 1923).

26. *Times*, November 7, 1923 (King quote); *Herald*, November 25, 1923 (Eames quote).

27. He was inaugurated December 3, 1923. See City of Bridgeport, *Municipal Register*, 1924, 30–33; *Post*, November 17, 1923.

28. The delegation to the mayor included George Eames, Willis F. Hobbs, and Guy P. Miller (Minutes, November 19 and December 3, 1923, MAB Papers).

29. Connecticut Tax Commissioner, *Supplementary Report of the Tax Commissioner, 1923 and 1924*, p. 12; *Times*, February 12, 1925.

30. Connecticut Chamber of Commerce, *Report of the Joint Committee on Taxation and State Finance;* Connecticut Chamber of Commerce, *Finances of Connecticut;* Manufacturers' Association of Connecticut, *Report Submitted to the Directors;* Clarence Heer, "Trends in Taxation and Public Finance"; National Industrial Conference Board, *State and Local Taxation of Business Corporations.*

31. *Connecticut Industry* 2 (July 1924): 4.

32. Prothro, *Dollar Decade,* 20–36 (Emery is quoted on p. 20); Fay, *Business in Politics,* 143–53.

33. The Yale economist F. R. Fairchild reported that Connecticut compared favorably with other states in terms of taxes. He particularly noted that the state had kept its indebtedness to less than $1 per capita (compared to other states' average of $8) (*Connecticut Industry* 2 [December 1924]: 13–20).

34. G. Miller, "Local Taxation of Manufacturing Property," 7–8.

35. Ibid.

36. Blodgett, "Property Tax Troubles Ad Lib"; Connecticut Tax Commissioner, *Report of the Tax Commissioner for the Biennial Period 1923 and 1924.* See also report of the MAC Taxation Committee, *Connecticut Industry* 2 (July 1924): 5–8.

37. Connecticut Tax Commissioner, *Supplementary Report of the Tax Commissioner 1923 and 1924.* Also see *Connecticut Industry* 3 (January 1925): 5–6, and *Connecticut Industry* 3 (March 1925): 5–9, for Blodgett's additional recommendations to alter categories of property that were particularly open to misinterpretation and abuse, especially the personal property tax on equipment and stocks on hand (inventory).

38. *Herald,* February 8 and 15, 1925.

39. The Warners never made a definitive statement repudiating their alliance with King. Though the Warner company posted hefty profits during the war, the net income of 1922–25 did not absorb the shortfalls of 1921 and 1926 (federal and state tax returns, Financial Records, Warner Corset Company Papers). On the tax litigation see *Times,* February 11, 1925; *Herald,* July 12 and 19, 1925; Minutes, June 6, 1923, Board of Apportionment Records; Hearing Docket #3697 (October 17, 1921) and #3892 (March 5, 1923), Connecticut Public Utility Commission Records. In addition, the Hydraulic Company's contract with the city was due to expire in 1926, and it faced prolonged negotiations over this as well.

40. *Herald,* March 29, 1925; Minutes, March 31, 1925, Board of Apportionment Records.

41. *Hartford Courant,* April 16, 1925.

42. Minute Books, January 31, 1925, BCC Papers.

43. Minute Books, January–April 1925, BCC Papers; *Herald,* February 22, 1925. Also see coverage of the hearings in *Telegram,* April 16 and 17, 1925, and *Times,* April 16, 1925.

44. *Herald,* February 15, 1925; Executive Board Minutes, March 12, 1925, *Bulletin No. 4601* (April 17, 1925), MAB Papers. Winter's testimony was immediately challenged by the small manufacturer Carl Siemons, a member of the Manufacturers' Association and also a Behrens appointee to the Board of Apportionment, who said that his opinion and those of other small manufacturers had not been sought (*Star,* April 16, 1925).

45. *Times,* April 15 (Blodgett quote), May 12 and 21, 1925; *Hartford Courant,* May 14 and 22 and June 3, 1925; *Telegram,* May 14, 1925; *Herald,* May 17, 1925. Note that some GOP leaders were concerned with the negative public reaction to the state GOP should the bill pass. See Harvey P. Bissell (Bridgeport customs inspector) to Roraback, May 8, 1925, and F. L. Wilder (state senator from New Haven) to Sen. Hiram Bingham, April 25, 1925, both in Roraback Papers. No replies from Roraback are attached.

46. John Leverty, a Democrat and president of a wholesale drug firm, and Anker S. Lyhne, an RVL member and president of Bridgeport Metal Goods Company, were two other Atwater appointees who remained. New board members were D. Fairchild Wheeler, a Democrat, former president of the chamber, and president of the city's largest mortgage and realty firm; William Winter, active in the RVL before moving to neighboring Fairfield and also in real estate; and Willis Hobbs, a member of RVL and president of the Bridgeport Hardware Manufacturing Company. The final

member, John J. Phelan, a Democrat who served as county coroner, was considered a neutral appointment. The two members not from the elite were Leverty and Phelan (*Herald*, June 28, 1925; *Dau's Blue Book for New Haven, Bridgeport, Waterbury; New Haven, Bridgeport and Waterbury Blue Book*).

47. Behrens to Trumbull, November 18, 1925, and Trumbull to Behrens, November 20, 1925, Box 323, Governor Trumbull Papers.

48. City of Bridgeport, "Annual Message of the Mayor," June 2, 1924, in *Municipal Register*, 1924, 43. Note that while the 1920 census reported that 24.6 percent of Bridgeport families owned their home, that figure had risen to 29.7 percent by 1930, surely not a majority. But this figure is misleading, because many homes were owner-occupied, multiple-family houses whose owners rented apartments to other working-class families (U.S. Census Bureau, *Population*, 1920, vol. 2, p. 1288; *Population*, 1930, vol. 4: *Families*, p. 219).

49. *Herald*, June 28 (King quote) and October 18 (Behrens quote), 1925.

50. *Star*, November 2, 1925.

51. *Herald*, May 3 and 17 and September 6, 1925.

52. The *Herald*'s Sunday circulation in 1925 was 36,000, compared to the *Post*'s circulation of 46,000 daily and 20,000 on Sunday (N. W. Ayer and Sons, *Directory of Newspapers and Periodicals*, 1926).

53. *Herald*, June 28, 1925, November 6, 1921, and September 30, 1923.

54. *Herald*, October 18, 1925 (Cullinan quote); *Herald*, October 25, 1925; the King quote is from a leaflet, Republican Town Committee, "To the Voters of the City of Bridgeport" [1925], in McLevy Scrapbook, McLevy-Schwarzkopf Papers.

55. *Times*, October 30, 1925.

56. *Bulletin No. 4730* (October 31, 1925), MAB Papers.

57. *Star*, November 2, 1925. King had become less involved in Bridgeport politics and had spent months in Europe before returning for the city election of 1925. King was implicated in a series of Harding administration scandals and was indicted in early 1926, along with the former attorney general, Harry Daugherty, and the alien property custodian, Thomas W. Miller, on charges of conspiracy to defraud the federal government, income tax evasion, and perjury. King took ill soon after receiving the indictments and died in May 1926. He was fifty-one. His estate was valued at $876,000 (Banit, "War Machine," 38; *New York Times* obituary, May 14, 1926; *Post*, April 2 and 21, 1926; Allen, *Only Yesterday*, 151–52).

58. *Star*, November 4, 1925.

59. On the issue of public permits see W. Parker Seeley (assistant city attorney under Mayor Wilson) to Police Superintendent Flanagan, May 20, 1921, advising that the administration was not interested in continuing to require permits, in the Bridgeport Police Records. Also see American Civil Liberties Union, *Police and the Radicals*. Of the eighty-eight who replied to the ACLU, only twenty-seven officials said that *any* radical meetings, whether public or private, were being held in their cities. On the New Haven story see Waldman, *Labor Lawyer*, 164–74.

60. "Political universe" refers to the shape of the electorate; see Burnham, "Changing Shape of the American Political Universe." For overviews of the System of 1896 see Burnham, *Critical Elections*; Burnham, "The System of 1896"; Kleppner, *Who Voted?* 1–12, 55–82; Sundquist, *Dynamics of the Party System*, 134–169; Kousser, *Shaping of Southern Politics*; Skowronek, *Building a New American State*. McGerr, *Decline of Popular Politics*, discusses the decline of the System of 1896.

61. The roles of the Bridgeport industrialists Walter B. Lashar and Sumner Simpson, financial backers of the *Post/Telegram* and the *Times-Star*, respectively, are detailed in the acerbic history of Bridgeport newspapers by Wilson, "Journalism," and Wilson, *History of Fairfield County*, 1:350–53. See *Herald*, October 21, 1928, and *Post*, November 26, 1930, for biographies of Richard Howell, editor of the *Herald* during the 1920s. Circulation numbers in N. W. Ayer and Sons, *Directory of Newspapers and Periodicals* (1920–40), show circulation figures for the *Post* of 41,000 to 47,000 daily, and the *Times-Star* 17,000 to 30,000 daily. The *Herald* attained a Sunday circulation of 69,000 statewide.

62. The positions of the national Democratic and Republican Parties are summarized in Burner, *Politics of Provincialism,* and Huthmacher, *Massachusetts People and Politics.* Buenker, *Urban Liberalism and Progressive Reform,* details the successes of both Democrats and Republicans in creating these urban, cross-class coalitions in the pre–World War I period; see esp. pp. 9–31.

63. *Herald,* September 3, 1922. Note, though, that some Republican members of Congress were open to labor issues. See Zieger, *Republicans and Labor.*

64. King did not bolt the party for Teddy Roosevelt's Progressive campaign in 1912, though he later became a Roosevelt booster. For an overview of progressive Republicans in Connecticut, see Janick, "Government for the People." There is no evidence that the Healey-Ullman group made common cause with the national labor progressives in the 1920s GOP. For an overview of the Connecticut GOP in the 1920s, see Dahill, "Connecticut's J. Henry Roraback," esp. 190–226; Mitchell, "Social Legislation in Connecticut," 71–128; "Reminiscences of J. Henry Roraback" (August 1942–January 1943); Schiff, "Colonel Isaac Ullman"; *Hartford Courant,* August 4 and 30 and September 13 and 14, 1922. On the 1924 campaign see *Telegram,* November 4, 1924; *Herald,* October 19, 1924.

65. Lancaster, "Background of a State 'Boss' System"; Lancaster, "Democratic Party in Connecticut"; *Herald,* November 5 and 12, 1922.

66. Benedict M. Holden (Hartford) to Roraback, December 24, 1919, in Roraback Papers. The Knights of Columbus was overwhelmingly Irish at this time.

67. Janick, "Senator Frank B. Brandegee" (Roraback is quoted on p. 450); *Herald,* November 6, 1921. The Yale professors Irving Fisher and Henry Farnam led a coalition of academics in opposition to Brandegee because of his stand on the League of Nations. The Connecticut Women's Suffrage Association (CWSA) split over Brandegee, who opposed women's suffrage; key GOP women leaders of the CWSA stayed with the party, while the rest worked to defeat Brandegee. The senator ran 25,000 votes behind his party in Connecticut, though he still won reelection. Also see Nichols, *Votes and More for Women.*

68. Driscoll ms., 1939, Box 113, WPA-CtSL Papers.

69. Cornelius J. P. Murphy, letter to the editor, *Herald,* November 6, 1921.

70. *Herald,* November 9, 1924.

71. "Your friend and admirer" [anonymous] to Roraback, July 17, 1922, Roraback Papers; *Connecticut Labor News,* September 13, 1924.

72. *Herald,* January 23, 1927. More evidence of KKK activity in Connecticut is found in clippings, Box 134, WPA-CtSL Papers; *Herald,* October 7, 1923, and October 12, 19, and 26, 1924; *Telegram,* October 28, 1924; *Times,* October 5, 1925; *Danbury Herald,* May 27, 1928.

73. *Telegram,* March 14, 1921.

74. Palmquist, "Stoker Mayor of Bridgeport," sheds interesting light on the difficulty of breaking the elite lock on the mayor's office; an Irish Democrat who was a stoker at a local mill had been elected Bridgeport mayor in 1903 for one term. At various points in the 1920s the Ku Klux Klan publicly warned the Bridgeport Democrats not to nominate an Irish Catholic for mayor (*Herald,* October 2 and 9, 1927).

75. Dahl, *Who Governs?* For a useful overview of the role of city council members and changes in their authority and functions in the metropolises by the late nineteenth century, see Teaford, *Unheralded Triumph,* 15–41.

76. I could not trace 25 percent of the Democratic list. I gathered candidates' names from the *Municipal Register* and newspaper accounts of elections, and where necessary I used the city directory for occupations. I determined ethnicity by analyzing names and using information from newspapers and church or club memberships (where available), which serve as indicators of ethnic background. The obvious difficulties of distinguishing names from the various British Isles necessitated lumping them together, though many were, according to the scattered evidence, Irish in background. Curiously, with the occasional exception of the Democratic *Times* and *Times-Star,* newspapers rarely featured information on the council candidates. Presumably, they were already known to their districts, less important, or assumed to be the recipients of a straight-ticket vote.

77. As an example, four candidates listed their occupation as carpenter in the 1920s. Of these, the two Republican candidates appear on the membership rolls of Carpenters Local #115, though there was no newspaper identification of this. Of the two Democratic candidates, neither was enrolled in #115 during the 1920s. One Republican member of the common council from 1925 to 1931 was a charter member of the typographers union (see Central Labor Union of Bridgeport and Vicinity, *Centennial Illustrated History; Times,* November 7, 1921, and November 3, 1923; and *Post,* November 4, 1923, for biographical statements on candidates running for city office).

78. Occupations found in *Bridgeport City Directory,* 1921–29.

79. However, the GOP women did sponsor a "Colored Women's Political Club" in 1920 (*Herald,* December 5 and 12, 1920, September 4 and 11, 1921, and November 9, 1924). Nichols, *Votes and More for Women,* 121, describes splits between GOP women in Bridgeport and Henry Roraback; also see the *Herald* for April 4, 1920, and September 9, 1928, for feminist dissent from the mainstream Connecticut GOP.

80. *Evening Star,* September 7, 1925; *Herald,* May 2, 1920, and September 11, 1921; *Times,* October 18, 1923.

81. Interview with Mrs. O by John P. Driscoll, 1939, Box 113, WPA-CtSL Papers.

82. *Herald,* April 24, 1927. See City of Bridgeport, *Articles of Association,* lists for 1920s, for the registration of the various Democratic and Republican clubs. The literature written during the 1920s and 1930s about the structure of party politics in the city is extensive. See Zink, *Government of Cities,* 211–14; Peel, *Political Clubs of New York City,* 71–86, 120–137, 148–222; Salter, *Boss Rule,* on the GOP machine in Philadelphia. For party clubs in earlier eras see McGerr, *Decline of Popular Politics,* 23–27, 79–83.

83. *Times,* December 13, 1924.

84. Interview with Mrs. X by M. G. Sayers and P. K. Russo, n.d. [1939],File 1, Box 119, WPA-CtSL papers.

85. *Telegram,* October 29, 1924; *Times-Star,* October 31, 1927; *Herald,* February 8, 15, 1925.

86. *Herald,* February 8, March 22, and October 11, 1925, and August 21, 1927.

87. On the Hebrew Republican Club see *Herald,* November 16, 1924, and February 8 and June 7, 1925. Listings of officers of this club, as well as those of the Democratic and Republican Twelfth District clubs, are in City of Bridgeport, *Articles of Association,* vols. 12–14 (1920–24). I traced occupations through the *Bridgeport City Directory* for these years. Aside from the Jewish club, ethnic issues seemed to have intruded very little on this district up to 1928; the only ethnic club listed is the Twelfth District Italo-American Political Club in 1921, but evidence suggests that it was still-born.

Chapter 3: Ethnics in the 1920s

1. Interview with Igor Bella by Kubisek, 1938, Box 93, WPA-CtSL Papers.

2. The literature on immigrant patterns and community formation is vast. See the general survey by Bodnar, *The Transplanted.* Also see Bodnar, Simon, and Weber, *Lives of Their Own;* Higham, *Ethnic Leadership in America;* J. Smith, *Family Connections;* Barton, *Peasants and Strangers;* Cummings, *Self-Help in Urban America,* esp. the essays by Renkiewicz, Stolarik, and Stipanovich.

3. Miaso, *History of the Education of Polish Immigrants;* Pienkos, *PNA;* Wlodarski, *Origin and Growth.*

4. On national Slovak organizations see Stolarik, "Immigration and Urbanization," passim. For Bridgeport see Frazzetta, "Hallett Street Block Survey," Box 93, WPA-CSL.

5. On Poles see Pienkos, *PNA,* 80 ff.; Borkowski, "Role of Pittsburgh's Polish Falcons." On Slovaks see Stolarik, "The Slovaks," 929; *Bridgeport Times-Star,* August 22, 1927; Stolarik, "A Place for Everyone"; Elizabeth Yatzevitch, field visit report, March 5–7, 1923, and "1919 Survey," both in I.I. Records.

6. As one example, see the report on the Polish Socialist Alliance in Park and Miller, *Old World Traits Transplanted,* 137–38.

7. M. Epstein, *Jewish Labor in U.S.A.;* Liebman, *Jews and the Left,* 283–305; Ethel M. Freedman, interview by author, Fairfield, March 12, 1985.

8. *Post,* October 14, 1934, May 22, 1935, and July 26, 1942 (HC-BPL clipping file); Havadtoy, *Down in Villa Park;* Geller, "Bridgeport, the Ethnic City"; Puskás, *From Hungary to the United States,* 155; Lengyel, *Americans from Hungary;* Rákóczi Aid Association, *Golden Jubilee Book.*

9. Unidentified clip, August 25, 1932 (HC-BPL clipping file); *Herald,* September 29, 1929; Emil Napolitano ms., Box 114, WPA-CtSL Papers; Briggs, *Italian Passage.* The famed anticlericalism of Italians was partly rooted in hostility toward the church's anti-Mazzini role in the unification struggle (Vecoli, "Prelates and Peasants"). Mussolini in the 1920s was arguably the first to appeal successfully to a southern Italian nationalism.

10. Grucci interview by Emil Napolitano, 1939, Box 114, WPA-CtSL Papers.

11. Connecticut Bureau of Labor Statistics, "Italian Difficulty at Bridgeport"; interviews with Grucci and Louis Richards, Napolitano, 1939, Box 114, WPA-CtSL Papers. The early condemnation of the padrone system, as detailed in Koren, "Padrone System and Padrone Banks," was mirrored in early historiography on immigrants. This gave way in the 1960s and 1970s to a positive assessment of the padrone system among some historians. Compare Nelli, "Italian Padrone System in the United States," and V. Greene, *American Immigrant Leaders,* 170. A more nuanced view is Peck, "Reinventing Free Labor."

12. See Wytrwal, *America's Polish Heritage,* 227–35; Pienkos, *PNA.* Bukowczyk, "Transformation of Working-Class Ethnicity," suggests that the search for customers and accommodation to corporate antiunionism merged to create this conservative milieu in Polonia during and immediately after World War I. He contends that the competition for customers by Polish and Jewish grocers during World War I contributed to anti-Semitic activity in the Polish community. This has an obvious parallel in later Hungarian and Slovak anti-Semitism. Also see Wolkovich, *Bay State "Blue" Laws and Bimba,* for an example of how a Lithuanian Communist leader became caught between two rival Lithuanian fraternal organizations in Brockton in a dispute with anti-Soviet and secular versus clerical overtones.

13. *Herald,* May 5, 1929. The information on leftist activities in the Hungarian community is from leaflets and reports filed in Detective Division, Bridgeport Police Records, 1921–32. See esp. the report by Patrolman Robert F. Hoffman to Capt. Hall, January 16, 1921. Also see more generally Beynon, "Crime and Custom of Hungarians," 758; Benkart, "Religion, Family, and Community Among Hungarians," 166–67; Roucek, "Hungarians in America."

14. 1936 Survey, I.I. Records; Becker ms., 1937, and Gaffney ms., both in File 109:20, Box 26, WPA-UConn Papers. Pospelova is quoted in Report, June 1923, Minute Books, YWCA-Bridgeport.

15. Breckinridge, *New Homes for Old,* 201–18; *Post,* June 5, 1926, May 15, 1933, and March 1, 1938 (BPL Clipping file); *Herald,* May 27, 1928.

16. "Among the Foreign-born," *Bulletin of the Foreign-Language Information Service* 1 (December 1922): 10, cited in Nelli, *Italians in Chicago,* 169; interview with Sackett 1939, Box 115, WPA-CtSL Papers; *Times-Star,* October 24, 1927; ad for Hungarian *Bridgeport* in *Bridgeport City Directory,* 1931, p. 146; *Herald,* January 21, 1925.

17. Benkart, "Religion, Family, and Community," 139, 177–79, 181–85, 191–92; unidentified clippings, April 25, July 20, 22, 1934 (HC-BPL clipping file). The unnamed Hungarian is quoted in Frazzetta ms., 1940, File 109:11, Box 21, WPA-UConn Papers.

18. Roucek, "Passing of American Czechoslovaks," p. 623; "American Sport and the Immigrant Worker," *(New York) Advance,* September 9, 1927, p. 5; Frazzetta ms., 1938, Box 114, WPA-CtSL Papers; Pienkos, *One Hundred Years Young,* 117–23.

19. East Side block survey, pp. 76–77, Frazzetta ms., 1939, Box 18, and interview with Mrs. S. by P. K. Russo, March 1940, File 109:11, Box 21, both in WPA-UConn Papers; Frazzetta ms., 1938, Box

114, WPA-CtSL Papers. Gabaccia, *From Sicily to Elizabeth Street,* notes that areas of second settlement preserved family networks and did not disrupt community life.

20. Miss Wiley survey, 1919, I.I. Records. This quote probably referred to the flight of both Yankee and Irish-American families.

21. Interview with Mrs. Hallie J., [n.d., 1939?] Box 115, WPA-CtSL Papers.

22. Gerald H. Beard to John R. Brown, January 20, 1921, Folder 17, Box 1, Beard Papers.

23. Havadtoy, *Down in Villa Park.*

24. Interview with Meresko by Frazzetta, 1939, Box 18, WPA-UConn Papers.

25. The transportation survey was done by the Manufacturers' Association of Bridgeport in the expectation that buses would replace the trolleys (Minute Books, February 28, 1923, MAB Papers). W. B. Lashar, a prominent manufacturer who also invested in a bus company, bid for five miles of new motorized bus routes that would cross the East Side. He noted that these would be used mostly by "the people who go to and from their work in the factories" (*Evening Star,* April 17, 1925; Robert McLevy [nephew of Jasper McLevy], interview by author, Bridgeport, May 16, 1983.

26. The examples are myriad, but see Orsi, *Madonna of 115th Street,* and Vecoli, "Prelates and Peasants."

27. On St. Anthony see *Telegram,* June 15, 1929, and June 20, 1930 (HC-BPL clipping file); on Mount Carmel see *Herald,* July 17, 1927; on Faetana see *Herald,* September 12, 1920; unidentified clipping, September 1931 (HC-BPL clipping file). Rudolph Vecoli has noted that although these *festas* centered around saints and the mass, they do not belie the noted anticlericalism of Italian communities in the United States. The contributions collected on saints' days went to the mutual aid society, not the church. The priest and the church remained institutionally weak during this period in the Italian community (Vecoli, "Prelates and Peasants").

28. However, some city residents like "Old Irritability" thought things had gotten out of hand; the fireworks were too loud and violated "our day of religion" (letter to the editor, *Times-Star,* September 3, 1928).

29. Interview with anonymous Italian by Frazzetta, September 1939, Box 114, WPA-CtSL Papers. For a similar example elsewhere see Harney, "Montreal's King of Italian Labour."

30. Interview with Louis Richards by Frazzetta, December 1938, Box 114, WPA-CtSL Papers.

31. Unidentified clip, August 25, 1932 (HC-BPL clipping file). The D'Elia family, influential for three decades, started from a grocery business; after World War I it branched into the insurance and foreign exchange business, while Frank and his son became active in the Sons of Italy.

32. *Post,* October 12, 1908. Note that no copies of *Il Sole* survive. Richards by this time had established himself as an undertaker, a profession he pursued for the rest of his life. Undertaking was the career of choice for more than one Italian leader. The Abriola brothers, Louis and Antonio, from the southern province of Basilicata, came to the United States as children, apprenticed as barbers, and set up their shops in Bridgeport in the late 1890s. Both eventually trained as undertakers, set up separate businesses, and later brought modern mortuary practices to Italians in place of traditional European ways. Louis and his son Louis, Jr., were active Republicans, while Antonio became an active Democrat with a small but loyal following. Another of Louis's sons, Salvatore, a barber, became active in union circles and Socialist electoral politics in the 1920s (*Post,* October 6, 1935, March 26, 1939, and March 9, 1942; *Telegram,* January 9, 1952 [HC-BPL clipping file]).

33. *Herald,* September 9, 1928 (Schwaebischer Maennorchor outing). Also see *Telegram,* October 27, 1924; *Herald,* November 11, 1923, October 19, 1924, September 27, 1925, and October 23, 1927; *Times-Star,* April 5, 1940; *Who's Who in Connecticut,* 23; "Your friend and admirer" to J. Henry Roraback, April 10, 1925, Roraback Papers.

34. See, for example, Shea and Stoj, "Pulaski Democratic Club of New Britain, Connecticut."

35. "Reminiscences of J. Henry Roraback—His Political Philosophies," p. 22. While noteworthy, this attention to new ethnics was modest by regional standards. John Buenker contends that, compared to neighboring Rhode Island, the Connecticut GOP did rather little to embrace new ethnics (Buenker, "The Politics of Resistance").

36. Names gathered from lists of city board members, City of Bridgeport, *Municipal Register,* 1920–30.

37. *Post,* January 8, 1928; *Black Rock News,* November 4, 11, and 19, 1927; *Herald,* October 14 and 21, 1923; *Times-Star,* November 9, 1927.

38. In Connecticut city court judges could be nominated by anyone for a two-year term. The General Assembly's Judiciary Committee then reviewed these names and made its recommendation to the Assembly, which then rendered a final vote. Thus the party in control of the legislature, the GOP in this case, controlled these offices (Bailey, *Children Before the Courts of Connecticut,* 43). Peel, *Political Clubs of New York City,* 251–56, notes that in New York City Irish and Jewish political activists worked out a similar deal for sharing power.

39. For the Polish club see Zygmunt J. Czubak to Roraback, April 25, 1924, Roraback Papers. Czubak, a lawyer, was the only professional listed as an officer; the others whose occupations I could find were a real estate–mortgage agent, two craftsmen, and a jitney operator (City of Bridgeport, *Articles of Association,* 14:196, and occupational listings in the 1924 city directory). Also see *Articles of Association,* 1920–30, passim, for the date of incorporation and the names of officers of each ethnic association.

40. Interview with Liberat Dattolo by Frazzetta, 1939, Box 95, WPA-CtSL Papers.

41. Peel, *Political Clubs of New York City,* 251–67.

42. "Agli Elettori Italiani," *La Sentinella,* October 31, 1925, p. 1. I am indebted to Andrea Graziozi for translating this item. D'Elia, running for city sheriff, Petriello, running for town selectman, and Abriola, running for common council from the Tenth District were all elected in this year of the Republican sweep. Antonio Abriola, running for sheriff on the *Democratic* ticket, was not acknowledged by the newspaper and did not win.

43. City of Bridgeport, *Articles of Association,* 12:461 (July 14, 1921); *Herald,* November 4, 1923, and September 27, 1925. Mormino, *Immigrants on the Hill,* 177–88, reviews the record of political success of Italians as analyzed by a number of case studies of Italian immigrant communities. He notes that in the medium-sized cities like Buffalo, St. Louis, Kansas City, Rochester, and Utica before 1920, the Italian communities were relatively unsuccessful in gaining political power, even if their *prominenti* were recognized. His study showed that St. Louis Italians followed the same successful organizational path as the Bridgeport Italian community in the 1920s. Also see Maiale, *Italian Vote in Philadelphia,* 122–25.

44. Interview with Mr. Pareni, by Frazzetta, 1938, Box 114, WPA-CtSL Papers.

45. *Herald,* January 30, 1927.

46. October 3, 1927, in City of Bridgeport, *Official Proceedings of the Common Council,* 1926–27, p. 515. The Democratic Party had not given up on the Italian community, and Antonio Abriola remained a staunch advocate.

47. *Herald,* January 30, 1927. This suspicion of ethnics was reinforced in the 1926 publication by Daniel Brewer, *Conquest of New England,* 328, who warned New England Yankees of the continued dangers of improperly assimilated immigrants.

48. *Herald,* May 1, 1927, state edition.

49. *Herald,* November 5, 1922, and September 25, 1921.

50. Czubak to Roraback, June 16, 1924, Roraback Papers; *Herald,* February 8, 1925. Similarly, the Italian community was briefly split by this GOP rivalry, with Louis Richards remaining loyal to the state GOP leadership (Alex Creedon [Hartford] to Roraback, January 12, 1925, Roraback Papers).

51. Murberg is quoted in *Herald,* October 2, 1921; the Abraham Lodge is quoted in *Herald,* October 11, 1925.

52. Changes in immigration law in 1922 no longer automatically conferred citizenship on an adult woman who married an American citizen or whose husband became a citizen. After 1922 immigrant women had to apply for citizenship themselves. Thus women's naturalization lagged. Only in 1934 were children granted citizenship based on either parent's American citizenship; before this time only the father's status counted. See Kansas, *Citizenship of the United States of America.*

53. Interview with John Wadsworth by Frazzetta, 1938, Box 114, WPA-CtSL Papers; Andersen, *Creation of a Democratic Majority,* 40–41, 88; Gavit, *Americans by Choice,* 236–38. Unfortunately, voter lists for elections in the 1920s and 1930s in Bridgeport do not exist, so it is impossible to carry out a systematic appraisal of ethnic representation among the city's voters. This lack of involvement in the electoral life of the nation and the lack of partisan affiliation, called "nonimmunization" by political scientists, defined the large numbers of eligible voters who had few loyalties to existing political arrangements.

54. Figures from U.S. Census Bureau, *Population,* 1920, vol. 3: *Population by States,* p. 162; Bridgeport Registrar of Voters Office, *Book of Elections,* 1920, 1927.

55. Schoonmaker, *Actual Government of Connecticut,* 23–24, 111–12; Harris, *Registration of Voters in the United States,* 199, 222–23; Republican Party of Connecticut, *Republican Handbook of Connecticut.*

56. Stephen Bucki, interview by author, Fairfield, March 23, 1985. The quote appears in Connecticut Bureau of Labor Statistics, *Condition of Wage Earners, 1927–28,* 115. I have been unable to find statutory evidence of a twentieth-century use of the personal tax requirement to bar voters, though it could have been used in that way. The office of the Connecticut Secretary of State has acknowledged that the history of the law and its meaning are ambiguous. See T. Joseph Loy, Office of Secretary of State, to Mrs. Clifford J. Durr, October 31, 1974 (copy in author's possession).

57. Low voting turnouts became a subject of concern and study for political scientists in the 1920s. In their famous 1924 study, *Non-Voting,* the University of Chicago political scientists Charles Merriam and Harold Gosnell surveyed residents of that city who had not voted in the previous year's mayoral election. Ethnicity was an important variable, and the poor in general were less likely to vote than the better-off (Merriam and Gosnell, *Non-Voting,* 36–37, 40–44).

58. "This is the day of newspaper reading and radio broadcasting," not rallies (*Times-Star,* November 9, 1927). See McGerr, *Decline of Popular Politics,* for the general argument regarding national decline in popular politics by the 1920s, esp. pp. 184–210 on the 1920s debate about the "vanishing voter."

59. *Telegram,* October 31 and November 4, 1924.

60. *Herald,* March 27, August 14, September 4 and 18, October 2, 23, and 30, and November 6, 1927; *Times-Star,* November 1 and 8, 1927; Connelly, "Plan for the Taxation of Property"; Behrens's statements to common council, October 3, 1927, in *Official Proceedings of the Common Council, 1926–27,* 513–14. The Republicans circulated newspaper articles from 1915 reporting on manufacturer Atwater's opposition to the eight-hour day, the goal of the citywide strikes of the day. Atwater claimed an eight-hour day would only give workers more time to "loaf around the corner saloon" (*Herald,* November 6, 1927). Note that the Socialist candidate Jasper McLevy had first raised this issue in the 1921 municipal campaign.

61. Critical election theory has come under attack in recent years as rigid, mechanical, and insensitive to more complex components of people's political motivations and actions. See Lichtman, *Prejudice and the Old Politics,* for the argument that religion alone, rather than a holistic ethnocultural worldview, stands out most strongly as a motivating factor in the 1928 vote. Socioeconomic position also seems to have been a stronger factor than previously supposed. Basic works on this debate include Lubell, *Future of American Politics;* Key, "Theory of Critical Elections," which includes data for Connecticut in this period; Burnham, *Critical Elections;* Burnham, "System of 1896"; Alvarez and True, "Critical Elections and Partisan Realignment," which includes data on Hartford.

62. *Herald,* October 28, 1928; editorial, *Hartford Times* October 20, 1928, as quoted in Rosengren, "Connecticut Government and Politics," 92–93.

63. *Herald,* October 21, 1928.

64. The Hoover ad appears in *Times-Star,* October 29, 1928; the Howell column appeared in *Herald,* September 9, 1928. See also Peel and Donnelly, *The 1928 Campaign,* 78.

65. *Herald,* October 21, 1928.

66. Roraback to Lawrence Richey, Republican National Committee, December 5, 1928, as quoted in Dahill, "Roraback," 204–7.

67. *Herald,* August 19 (reporting on *Catholic Transcript*) and October 21, 1928; *Post,* November 4, 1928.

68. See national convention voting record in *Congressional Quarterly,* 1976, p. 157; Lancaster, "Democratic Party in Connecticut." The Bridgeport delegation was strongly pro-Smith. At the state convention the Bridgeport Democrats, led by John Cornell, had unsuccessfully promoted Edward Buckingham, a former mayor, for lieutenant governor (*Herald,* September 4, 1927, and April 29, August 26, and September 8, 1928).

69. *Herald,* August 19, September 9, and October 21 and 28, 1928; *Times-Star,* October 25 and 26 and November 5, 1928.

70. *Herald,* September 30 and October 28, 1928; *Times-Star,* November 2, 1928. On labor in the national campaign see Bornet, *Labor Politics in a Democratic Republic.* On the favorable labor legislation gained under Republican rule, see Zieger, *Republicans and Labor,* esp. 87–108 and 216–77 on Hoover's labor position.

71. Socialist Party of America, *Intelligent Voter's Guide,* 11, 175.

72. *Herald,* August 26, 1928.

73. *Herald,* September 23, 1928.

74. The editorial appeared in *Herald,* October 28, 1928. The SP national campaign is represented in its *Intelligent Guide.* Also see Bornet, *Labor Politics in a Democratic Republic.,* 80–99, 189–206. Locally, see *Herald,* August 26, September 9, 16, and 23, October 14 and 28, and November 4, 1928. Note that the Workers (Communist) Party and the Socialist Labor Party ran candidates for top state offices but not for local offices.

75. Roraback to Richey, December 5, 1928, quoted in Dahill, "Roraback," 204.

76. *Herald,* August 12, 1928. On media coverage of the contest, including ethnic media, see Casey, "Scripps-Howard Newspapers," 209–31; Bornet, *Labor Politics in a Democratic Republic.,* 170–71.

77. *Herald,* October 21, 1928 (Swedes); the Fourth District club is quoted in *Herald,* August 26, 1928; list of incorporators of Hoover Republican Club, City of Bridgeport, *Articles of Association,* 16:166–67 (September 5, 1928). The Roraback report is quoted in Dahill, "Roraback," 205.

78. *Herald,* October 28, 1928.

79. *Times-Star,* September 1 and 3, 1928; *Herald,* September 23 (quote) and October 28, 1928.

80. *Times-Star,* October 25, 1928. One study of Italian Republican politics in Philadelphia noted the disastrous consequences of the local *professionalisti* attempts to keep their constituents in the GOP camp in 1928: "Stones and tomatoes came at us from every direction." The leaders were too far removed from grassroots sentiment (Maiale, *Italian Vote in Philadelphia,* 84–89, quote on p. 84).

81. *Herald,* August 12, 19, and 26, September 9 and 30, and October 21, 1928. Roraback attributed success with African Americans to the successful drive to win back voters lost in the early stage of the campaign (Roraback to Richey, December 5, 1928, in Dahill, "Roraback," 204). On black politics nationally see Bornet, *Labor Politics in a Democratic Republic,* 169–70; Weiss, *Farewell to the Party of Lincoln.*

82. *Herald,* October 28, 1928; *Times-Star,* November 5, 1928.

83. *Black Rock Beacon,* August 31 and September 7, 14, and 28, 1928; *Bridgeport Times,* February 2, 1926; Waldo, *History of Bridgeport and Vicinity,* 2:34–35.

84. *Herald,* October 28, 1928; Bridgeport Registrar of Voters, *Book of Elections,* 1920–40.

85. *Black Rock News,* October 12, 1928. On the national trends see Andersen, *Creation of a Democratic Majority,* chap. 2.

86. Dattolo interview by Frazzetta, 1939, Box 95, WPA-CtSL Papers. Note that in the original, he had named Louie Abriola as the Democratic activist, either his mistake or that of the recorder.

87. See city council candidate profiles, *Times-Star,* November 2, 3, and 5, 1928. Nagy was also one

of the incorporators of the Twelfth District Slovak Democratic Club, organized in May 1928 (City of Bridgeport, *Articles of Association,* 16:414).

88. *Herald,* October 28 and November 11, 1928; *Times-Star,* November 7, 1928; Peel and Donnelly, *The 1928 Campaign,* 78.

89. *Herald,* November 11, 1928; *Who's Who in Connecticut,* 44; interview with Edward T. Buckingham by Nolan, 1940, Box 112, WPA-CtSL Papers; *Times-Star,* October 12 and 15, 1929.

90. *Times-Star,* November 5 and 6, 1929.

91. *Herald,* October 27, 1929.

92. *La Sentinella,* October 26 and November 2, 1929. My thanks to Maureen Miller for translating these items. *La Sentinella* was edited by Michele Altieri. Also see the similar endorsement in a new newspaper, *La Vittoria,* March 12, 1929.

93. *La Sentinella,* November 9, 1929.

94. *Post,* September 29, 1931; Frazzetta ms., 1938, Box 114, WPA-CtSL Papers. In reporting a shooting incident involving Italians at the new Bellvede Athletic Club in 1929, the *Herald* of August 25, 1929, alleged that it was one of those "gambling and bootleg dive[s]" that had become "useful allies of politicians, as recruiting stations for voters and as sources of income for party campaign funds."

Chapter 4: Working People, 1922–32

1. The quotation is from Lynd and Lynd's study of Muncie, Indiana, *Middletown,* p. 53, which remains the most important contemporary work on life in the 1920s.

2. The traditional narrative of American workers in the 1920s is Irving Bernstein, *Lean Years.* For new perspectives on workers in the 1920s, see Stricker, "Affluence for Whom?"; Montgomery, "Thinking about American Workers in the 1920s"; Montgomery, *Fall of the House of Labor,* chap. 9; Frank, *Purchasing Power.*

3. As recorded by the sociologist Ewa Morawska, who surveyed eastern European workers in the steel town of Johnstown, Pennsylvania. Morawska termed this attitude *"morskoje plavanije,"* a swimming at sea with alternating waves of high and low (Morawska, *For Bread with Butter,* 216).

4. In 1939 Bridgeport wage earners numbered 29,419 and produced $160.3 million worth of goods, down slightly from the 1929 figures (U.S. Census Bureau, *Census of Manufacturers,* 1920, vol. 9: *Manufactures, For States,* table 33, p. 191; U.S. Census Bureau, *Census of Manufacturers,* 1929, vol. 3: *Reports by States,* table 2, p. 90; U.S. Census Bureau, *Census of Manufacturers,* 1939, vol. 3: *Reports by States,* table 2, p. 145).

5. Overviews of the Bridgeport economy can be found in the monthly "Business Pattern" report published in the Manufacturers' Association of Connecticut's magazine, *Connecticut Industry,* and in the Bridgeport Chamber of Commerce's monthly newsletter, *Bridgeport Progress.*

6. *Connecticut Industry,* February 1930, p. 18.

7. U.S. Census Bureau, *Census of Manufacturers,* 1919.

8. Peter J. Wojcicki (son of Peter P. Wojcicki), interview by author, Stratford, Conn., March 14, 1985.

9. Interview with Stephen Havanich by Frazzetta, 1940, Box 93, WPA-CtSL Papers. Also see Morawska, *For Bread with Butter,* 194–95, 239, on this connection between German and eastern European workers in the search for better jobs. Jewish men, however, felt that they were discriminated against in metalworking factories, which hired few of them (Reich ms., 1939, Box 115, WPA-CtSL Papers).

10. Interview with Mr. H.S. by William J. Burke, March 1940, File 109:19, Box 25, WPA-UConn Papers.

11. Italian interview #1 (mason quote), Italian interview #2 (tailor anecdote), both by Frazzetta, 1940, Box 114, WPA-CtSL Papers.

12. Italian interview #1 (mason quote); Havanich interview by Frazzetta, Box 93; Italian inter-

view #3 (tailor and barber) by Frazzetta, 1940, Box 114, all in WPA-CtSL Papers; Polish interview #4 (barber) by Frazzetta, 1940, File 109:19, Box 25, WPA-UConn Papers.

13. Interview with Mr. A.T. by Burke, March 1940, Box 114; Vincent Frazzetta, "The Slovak Community of Bridgeport," n.d. [1940], Box 93, both in WPA-CtSL Papers.

14. See discussion of the brass company's personnel policies later in the chapter. Hareven, *Family Time and Industrial Time,* describes the continuing ties of family and ethnicity that bypassed the personnel procedures of the Amoskeag Mills in the 1920s.

15. "Report of Interview with State Employment Service," Bridgeport YWCA, n.d. [1938?], Reel 109:4, YWCA-National. The state employment agent said "she hated to see an Italian girl come in but could always place an attractive, trained *Protestant*" [emphasis in original].

16. For general overviews of women's manufacturing jobs in the early twentieth century, see Kessler-Harris, *Out to Work,* chaps. 5, 6, and 8. Studies of women's work patterns before the war noted that native-born American and Irish-American women predominated in sales work (Consumers League of Connecticut, *The Department Store Girl,* pamphlet, January 1915, copy in Consumers League of Connecticut Papers; State of Connecticut, *Report of the Commission to Investigate the Condition of Wage-Earning Women and Minors;* Oppenheimer, *Female Labor Force in the United States;* Klaszynska, "Why Women Work").

17. See U.S. Census sources; Connecticut Department of Labor Statistics, *Report on the Condition of Wage Earners, 1922,* 56–58. For a similar employment pattern see Johnson, "Negro Population of Waterbury, Connecticut."

18. Rockefeller's managerial model, embodied in the Special Conference Committee (SCC), is reviewed in Jacoby, *Employing Bureaucracy,* 180–89. Other important overviews of employer philosophy and practice in this era are Brody, "Rise and Decline of Welfare Capitalism"; Irving Bernstein, *Lean Years,* 144–89; Brandes, *American Welfare Capitalism;* Dunn, *Company Unions.*

19. Jacoby, "Industrial Labor Mobility in Historical Perspective," argues that at the national level economic stability and technological change, plus the end of immigration, were responsible for the decline of job turnover and the resulting employment stability in the 1920s, not the efficacy of the personnel policies and welfare capitalism so touted in the era. The Bridgeport data may be found in Minute Books, Report, December 22, 1922, and Minutes, September 19, 1921, December 29, 1922, and March 24, 1926, MAB Papers.

20. A classic management statement of the open shop's innocence and evenhandedness is Merritt, *The Open Shop and Industrial Liberty.* Merritt, the associate counsel for the League for Industrial Rights, got his start as a Connecticut lawyer suing the Danbury Hatters Union (Bonnett, *Employers' Associations in the United States,* 449–74). A critical evaluation is Zimand, *Open Shop Drive.* See p. 43, where Zimand notes that Merritt's League for Industrial Rights had successfully lobbied for legislation for "social control of industrial warfare" in ten states, including Connecticut.

21. For an overview of these industrial relations plans in the 1920s, see Burton, *Employee Representation.* Note the extent to which employers used the rhetoric of democracy, echoing the wartime goals so appealing to workers. See the various essays in Lichtenstein and Harris, *Industrial Democracy in America,* esp. Montgomery, "Industrial Democracy or Democracy in Industry?" and McCartin, "'An American Feeling.'"

22. The "Bridgeport Plan" is described in Manufacturers' Association of Bridgeport, *Bridgeport Employees Committees,* and Aborn and Shafter, "Representative Shop Committees." Specific company plans are detailed in Bullard, "Organization Plan That Typifies Modern Management"; company pamphlets by Singer Manufacturing Company, Remington–UMC Company, and Bridgeport Brass Company, all at Baker Library, Harvard University.

23. "Shop Committees in Bridgeport." Only small shops had found the committees to be unworkable or unnecessary and had allowed them to wither (J. A. Kingman [advertising secretary, Locomobile Company] to C. J. Hicks, November 6, 1918, "Corporate Matters" Box, Locomobile Company Papers; *Herald,* May 2, 1920).

24. *Connecticut Industry,* December 1923, p. 14–19; Bridgeport Brass Company, "Historical Sketch of Bridgeport Brass Company 1865–1925," 13; *Connecticut Industry,* December 1924, p. 37–38; Robert H. Booth, service manager, Bridgeport Brass Company, to J. Henry Roraback, January 18 and 25 and March 23, 1922, Roraback Papers.

25. National studies of management strategies showed a similar trend. See Jacoby, *Employing Bureaucracy,* 189–99. Also see the roundtable on company unionism and welfare work in Laidler and Thomas, *New Tactics in Social Conflict,* 96–140. Responses of Connecticut companies are in Reports, Box 109, National Civic Federation Papers.

26. However, there was no indication that management had introduced a works council at the Bridgeport plant, as it had at other plants such as those in Lynn and Schenectady. On GE industrial relations policy generally, see Bruère, "West Lynn"; Budenz, "Wife in Name Only," "Genesis at West Lynn," "Jonah's Whale at West Lynn," "Jehu's Driving at West Lynn," and "'Democracy' à la General Electric"; Ripley, *Life in a Large Manufacturing Plant;* Broderick, *40 Years With General Electric;* Schatz, *Electrical Workers,* chap. 1; Montgomery, *Fall of the House of Labor,* 438–57. Also instructive are the exchanges between Robert Dunn and Charles M. Ripley in Laidler and Thomas, *New Tactics in Social Conflict,* 127–32, 136–40.

27. On GE's history in Bridgeport see *Bridgeport Works News,* Golden Anniversary Issue, September 1974, and various issues from 1926 to 1929; *Herald,* October 15 and November 19, 1922, and May 8, 1927.

28. Interview with GE worker Mr. R. by P. K. Russo, 1939, Box 133, WPA-CtSL Papers.

29. *Herald,* August 22, 1915; Selekman, Walker, and Couper, *Clothing and Textile Industries,* 68; International Ladies' Garment Workers' Union (hereafter ILGWU), "Report of the G.E.B. to the 16th Convention," *Proceedings,* 1922, 74; ILGWU, "Report of G.E.B. to the 19th Convention," *Proceedings,* 1928, 257–65.

30. Interview with Mr. P., 1939, Box 135, WPA-CtSL Papers; Bucki, "Dilution and Craft Tradition," 143–44; L. Herman Lavit, son of Sam Lavit, interview by author, Bridgeport, October 22, 1987. Note that the Bridgeport ACWA's cooperation with employers who accepted the union was a familiar one in the 1920s. The ACWA deemed cooperation necessary in the cutthroat competition of the clothing market. See Fraser, *Labor Will Rule,* chaps. 6–7.

31. Report by Anthony Capraro, n.d. [early 1924]; Report, April 14, 1924; Local 223 to Sidney Hillman, May 25, 1925, all in Box 2, Capraro Papers; Amalgamated Clothing Workers of America, *Documentary History,* 1924, pp. 46–47; *(New York) Advance,* issues of June–August 1923, May–June 1925, January–March 1926; *Herald,* April 19 and May 3, 1925; *Times,* April 30 and May 1, 1925, and February 9, 1926; *Star,* May 6, 1925; Agent Anna Weinstock Report, June 1923, File 170-2072, FMCS Records.

32. For examples of union strategy in this era that relied on public or government support, see the discussions in Hardman, *American Labor Dynamics,* 121–38. Witte, *Government in Labor Disputes,* 125–45, points out the crucial arena of local and state courts in intervening in labor disputes to the detriment of union activity, a practice on the rise in the 1920s.

33. *Herald,* May 3, 10, and 17, and June 7 and 21, 1925. Nothing seems to have come of this project.

34. The Amalgamated Textile Workers (ATWA) was formed in April 1919 by workers' committees from Lawrence, Massachusetts; Paterson and Passaic, New Jersey; and New York on the heels of textile strikes that spring. The ACWA supported the founding convention of the ATWA. ATWA was regarded as a dual union by the AFL United Textile Workers, a conservative, craft-oriented union. By the fall of 1919 the ATWA claimed a membership of fifty thousand, including locals in Norwalk, Rockville, and Stafford Springs, Connecticut. Textile unionism had a long history of fragmented organizations, and the ATWA was not able to overcome these tendencies. It did, however, provide a base for the amalgamation efforts of the Workers (Communist) Party in the mid-1920s (Savage, *Industrial Unionism,* 250–76; Brooks, "United Textile Workers of America," 58–79, 220–45, 250–73; ACWA, *Documentary History,* 1920, 215–17; Goldberg, *Tale of Three Cities,* passim; Fox, *Amalgamation*).

35. The 1928 strike was Lavit's last activity for the labor movement; an item in the *Herald* of August 19, 1928, describes him as a "former labor leader."

36. It should be noted that this was not all that different from the ACWA's internal methods in the 1920s, but as we have seen, the Bridgeport ACWA carried out more strikes and involved more new immigrant workers (Lorwin, *American Federation of Labor*, 213–18, 226–42, 426; Morris, *Conflict within the AFL*, 55–85; Schneider, *Workers' (Communist) Party and American Trade Unions;* Montgomery, *Fall of the House of Labor*, chap. 9).

37. Ornburn is quoted in Connecticut Federation of Labor (hereafter CFL), *Proceedings*, 1922, 22. General information on Danaher appears in *Who's Who in Connecticut*, 1933, 75. Danaher first became counsel for the CFL in 1900. He once described his initiation into the labor movement through his brother, an organizer for the Knights of Labor (CFL, *Proceedings*, 1934, 269). O'Meara is quoted in CFL, *Proceedings*, 1926, 10.

38. On labor lobbying and social legislation generally in Connecticut, see Mitchell, "Social Legislation in Connecticut," 138–58, 174–221, 248–73. On CFL positions see CFL, *Proceedings*, 1920–30, passim.

39. *Bridgeport Telegram*, November 26, 1917.

40. Egan, "What Is Wrong with the Machinists Today?"

41. *Herald*, July 29, 1923.

42. Campaign pamphlet [ca. 1943], Section G, Reel 94, Socialist Party of America Papers (microfilm edition); *Commonwealth*, September 1928; *Post*, October 30, 1933 (quote); Minutes, October 11, 1900, Minute Books, Branch 10, Local Bridgeport, Socialist Party, McLevy-Schwarzkopf Papers; Geo. Waldo, Jr., to Morris Hillquit, February 8, 1911, Frame 504, Morris Hillquit Papers (microfilm edition). McLevy is given credit for the passage of the workers' compensation bill in Foucher and Eams, "Labor Movement in Connecticut," 27–28. Both Foucher and Eams, and Moret, *Brief History of the Connecticut Labor Movement*, provide only limited information on their subjects. On constructive socialism see S. Miller, *Victor Berger*.

43. Morris Sigman to Gompers, April 12, 1923, and Gompers reply, File 9, Box 1, Sigman Papers; *Justice*, March 30, 1923; Egan, "What Is the Matter with the Machinists Today?"

44. CFL, *Proceedings*, 1925, 30, 43; *Herald*, September 6 and 13, 1925.

45. The nonunion contractors in nearby New Haven began to threaten the Bridgeport unions by the end of the 1920s (*Connecticut Industry*, October 1923, p. 10, and November 1923, p. 10).

46. Local 115 membership rolls, 1920–30; Local 1013 membership rolls, 1920–30, and minute books, passim, Brotherhood of Carpenters Records. Overviews of labor relations in the building trades and the internal dynamics of the carpenters' union are Haber, *Industrial Relations in the Building Trades;* Christie, *Empire in Wood;* Galenson, *United Brotherhood of Carpenters*. For a view of a smaller "empire" in the 1920s see Erlich, *With Our Hands*, 85–113.

47. For general ethnic profiles of the building trades unions, see Haber, *Industrial Relations in the Building Trades*, 298–99; M. Epstein, *Jewish Labor in U.S.A.*, 1:373–75, and 2:324–36. For Bridgeport details see Brotherhood of Painters and Decorators Local 190 Minute Books, 1926–30, passim. Lists of union officers are in *Bridgeport City Directory* and Connecticut Bureau of Labor Statistics, *Annual Report*, for the 1920s.

48. Kipnis, *American Socialist Movement*, 94, 102–6; Minutes, October 11, 1900, SP Branch 10, in "Socialist Party" Box, McLevy-Schwarzkopf Papers; *Commonwealth*, December 1932, p. 1; *Post*, November 2, 1929.

49. While Morris Hillquit of the national party provided the wording of a bill, McLevy gathered more than four hundred local union endorsements for the Hillquit bill, instead of the employers' liability bill that the CFL was considering, and McLevy then lobbied the General Assembly to ensure its passage (Geo. Waldo, Jr., to Morris Hillquit, February 8, 1911, Frame 504, Morris Hillquit Papers [microfilm edition]; *Commonwealth*, September 1928, n.p.).

50. "Editorial: Connecticut Socialism." Beardsley quoted the article in the *International Socialist Review* and also claimed that 70 percent of SP members in the state were Catholics.

51. Olmstead, "The Great Jasper," 88–89, 101; Hunter, "Trade Unions and the Socialist Party." On the ideology of Second International socialism generally, see Lichtheim, *Short History of Socialism*, and Gay, *Dilemma of Democratic Socialism*.

52. On the PSA see *Commonwealth*, May 1931, p. 3. The PSA had been organized in the United States independently of the American Socialist movement. The PSA remained separate from the SPA until 1911, when the two national organizations merged. Many state and local branches continued to remain separate from SPA chapters in many localities (H. Gluski, "Report of Polish Translator-Secretary," n.d. [1913], Reel 94, series 3, section 1, SPA Papers). Bridgeport World War I activities are in Minutes, various dates, 1915, Branch 10 and Local 3, SP, in McLevy-Schwarzkopf Papers. The language branches were Polish, Jewish, Finnish, Greek, German, Slovak, Lithuanian, Russian, and Hungarian.

53. Robert McLevy, interview by author, Bridgeport, May 16, 1983. The son of Charles McLevy (Jasper's brother), Robert McLevy was the business agent for the Bridgeport carpenters' union from the 1960s to the 1980s. For political endorsements see Minutes, passim, of Carpenters Local 115, and Painters Local 190, 1920s.

54. *Herald*, June 5, 1921.

55. *Times-Star*, February 2, 9, and 13, 1926.

56. Schwarzkopf to Wm. Henry, February 7, 1929, Reel 11, SPA Papers.

57. The portrait of the SP candidates comes from the lists of candidates in City of Bridgeport, "Election Results," *Municipal Register*, 1921–30, supplemented where possible by addresses and other information contained in newspaper accounts of the various candidates. I then looked the names up in that year's city directory to find occupations. Names omitted from the list are those appearing only on the 1922 and 1924 campaign lists, when the SP opened its slate to nonmembers from the labor movement.

58. *Commonwealth*, December 1932, p. 1; *Post*, November 2, 1929. Information on Schwab comes from miscellaneous correspondence in Collection 3, Socialist Labor Party, Reel 4, Socialist Collection at the Tamiment Library (microfilm).

59. Profiles of these men come from *Commonwealth*, June 1931, p. 1, and November 1931, p. 3; *Post*, November 2, 1929, and November 3, 1941. Schwarzkopf's collection of socialist literature is in Special Collections, University of Bridgeport Library.

60. Information on Wojcicki comes from Peter J. Wojcicki interview. The Havanich biography is in the Slovak community survey, 1940, Frazzetta ms., Box 93, WPA-CtSL Papers. Havanich is listed as a member of IWW Local #300 in Detective Files, Bridgeport Police Records.

61. *Herald*, February 25, 1925.

62. "Ethnic Files," I.I. Records. Though the number of members that the International Institute reported is probably inflated, the PSA represented a popular position on Polish politics in this period, namely, support for the Pilsudski regime. Bridgeport WPA surveys reported the popularity of Gen. Josef Pilsudski. Interviewers found a picture of General Pilsudski on the walls of numerous Polish homes (Frazzetta ms., Box 93, WPA-CtSL Papers). Occupations are derived from the *Commonwealth*, May 1931, p. 3; and the 1931 city directory.

63. The influx of large numbers of eastern and southern European immigrants into the party only began during the war period, and many of these left between 1919 and 1921. Some remained, however, and by 1929 the Bridgeport party reported that it had dues-paying members in the Polish Socialist Alliance (20), Jewish Socialist Verband (no number), and the Finnish branch (26) (Leinenweber, "Class and Ethnic Bases of New York City Socialism"; Laslett, *Labor and the Left*; Montgomery, *Fall of the House of Labor*, 281–302). On Bridgeport membership see PSA Annual Report, December 31, 1929, Reel 13; List of Secretaries—Jewish Verband, January 4, 1929, and Exec. Sec. to Plunkitt, March 26, 1929, Reel 11, SPA Papers (microfilm).

64. The exception here is Fred Cederholm, the IAM organizer, whose craft had undergone extensive attack by metal trades employers and whose workplaces were bastions of the American Plan.

65. Dawson, "Parameters of Craft Consciousness"; Emmons, "Aristocracy of Labor."

66. *Bridgeport Labor Leader,* October 24, 1918; *Herald,* November 3, 1918. Neither ticket did well in that election, with the SP earning 4 percent of the vote, the ALP 2 percent.

67. *Bridgeport Labor Leader,* October 24, 1918 (list of candidates); *(Hartford) Labor Standard,* March 1, May 15, September 1, and October 1, 1919; *Connecticut Labor Press,* November 8, 1919, and January 31, February 7, March 13, and April 10, 1920; Fine, *Labor and Farmer Parties,* 377–97; *Bridgeport Herald,* October 10, 1920, July 24, 1921, and September 6, 1925; CFL, *Proceedings,* 1919, 17–18, 31–34; "Who Is This A. J. Muste?"; Janick, "Government for the People," 268–74. M. Toscan Bennett, elite Hartford lawyer, and his wife, Josephine Bennett, a leading National Women's Party activist, were two leaders and funders of the new effort to promote the Connecticut Farmer-Labor Party and went on to help finance Brookwood Labor College in 1921.

68. *Herald,* October 15 and 22, 1922. The slate is listed in City of Bridgeport, *Municipal Register,* 1923, 331–37. Total votes calculated from top of ticket (senate race).

69. For general background see Weinstein, *Decline of Socialism,* 272–323; Walling, *American Labor and American Democracy.*

70. Weinstein, *Decline of Socialism,* 324–32, describes the negative outcome for the national SP.

71. The Connecticut electors for La Follette–Wheeler were Helen Hill Weed, suffrage activist and daughter of the late E. J. Hill, the Republican member of Congress; Roger Sherman Baldwin of Woodbury, a gentleman farmer and son of Simon Baldwin, an ex-governor; Richard Howell of Bridgeport, general manager of the *Bridgeport and Waterbury Herald;* J. P. Farrell of Hartford, an official of the Brotherhood of Railway Firemen and Engineers; C. H. Newton of New London, who represented the SP; and Walter Davis of Hamden, an IAM activist who represented the SP (*Herald,* August 24, 1924).

72. The CFL vote was 48 yes, 32 no, 17 "not voting," and 14 marked as "absent" (*Connecticut Labor News,* September 6, 1924; CFL, *Proceedings,* 1924).

73. Note that three were marked as absent for the vote. The Bridgeport Carpenters Local 115, in nonpartisan fashion, endorsed all labor men running in the race: Milton McDonald, John J. O'Neil, Jr., Jasper McLevy, "Bro. John Gallagher" (running as a Democrat only), and "Bro. Healy" (running as a Republican only) (Local 115 Minutes, August 12 and 26 and October 21, 1924).

74. *Herald,* August 24, and October 5 and 12, 1924; *Labor News,* July 19, August 9, all September and October issues, and November 1, 1924; *Hartford Courant,* September 4 and 5, 1924.

75. *Herald,* November 2, 1924.

76. The Walling biographical details are in S. Miller, *Victor Berger,* 54–56, 83, 151–52; Weinstein, *Decline of Socialism,* 119, 130, 172; DeLeon, *American Labor Who's Who,* 239. On the campaign see *Telegram,* October 27–30 and November 3, 1924; *Herald,* October 19 and 26 and November 2, 1924; *Times,* October 20 and 21, 1924. Note that Walling, in *American Labor and American Democracy,* makes no mention of his own campaign.

77. *Telegram,* November 1, 1924; MacKay, *Progressive Movement of 1924,* 170–74.

78. *Herald,* November 9, 1924; *Telegram,* November 3, 1925; *Connecticut Labor News,* November 8, 1924.

79. *Herald,* November 16, 1924, and March 8, 1925; *Times,* November 7, 1924; CFL, *Proceedings* 1925.

80. For example, the *Herald* of August 23, 1929, reported the successes of the British Labour Party, devoting full pages to Ramsay MacDonald's "rise from humble lad to England's Prime Minister" and suggesting similar social remedies for the United States.

81. *Herald,* August 25, 1929; *Bridgeport Progress,* October 2, 1929.

82. Connecticut Unemployment Commission, *Measures to Alleviate Unemployment,* 34–35; Fearon, *War, Prosperity, and Depression,* 205–8. In early 1934, when the U.S. Census Bureau again conducted a special census of Bridgeport, it found 12,193 totally unemployed workers (18 percent of the workforce), with another 3,830 (6.2 percent) on federal relief projects. Thus the overall unemployment rate was 24.2 percent, with the men's rate at 27.3 percent and women's at 17.5 percent (Federal Emergency Relief Administration, "Survey of the Occupational Characteristics of

Persons Receiving Relief, Bridgeport, May 1934," typescript in U.S. Department of Labor Library, Washington, D.C. [1934]).

83. Connecticut Unemployment Commission, "Analysis of Situation Regarding Needs and Funds for Unemployment Relief," typescript report, May 13, 1932, Box 380, Governor Cross Papers-Hartford; "Bridgeport Industrial Activity Report," *Bulletin* 6246 (December 29, 1933) and *Bulletin* 6396 (December 19, 1934), MAB Papers; Manufacturers' Association of Connecticut, *Unemployment and Its Remedies,* 127–28. Figures in Beney, *Cost of Living,* tables on pp. 62–98, show that the cost of living in Bridgeport declined for all household expenditures except heating and cooking gas and car fare.

84. Information on large Bridgeport firms comes from Moody's Investment Service, *Moody's Manual—Industrials; New York Times,* March 9, 1932: 37.

85. *GE Bridgeport Works News,* September 19, 1930, pp. iii–iv.

86. Bridgeport newspaper clipping files, Box 134, WPA-CtSL Papers. Unfortunately, the entire 1933 run of the *Herald* is missing from the Bridgeport Public Library, and I have found no extant copies elsewhere.

87. Connecticut Unemployment Commission, *Measures to Alleviate Unemployment,* 20–22; Executive Board Minutes, September 2, 1932, MAB Papers. Later surveys in Connecticut, such as E. Wight Bakke's New Haven study, also pointed to the diverse responses to unemployment, especially of higher status workers and middle classes (Bakke, *Citizens without Work,* passim).

88. Connecticut Unemployment Commission, Statement by Edward H. Goss of Waterbury's Scoville Company, *Measures to Alleviate Unemployment,* 20.

89. International Institute, "Annual Report 1933," in Minute Books, YWCA-Bridgeport.

90. Rodnick ms., Box 135, WPA-CtSL Papers. On the segmented nature of women's work see Milkman, "Women's Work and Economic Crisis"; Ware, *Holding Their Own,* chap. 2; Helmbold, "Downward Occupational Mobility."

91. Hallett Street Block Survey, pp. 20–21 (first quote), Frazzetta ms., Box 93; Clinton Avenue Survey (second quote), Box 119, both in WPA-CtSL Papers.

92. Quote is in interview with Mrs. Kurmery by P. K. Russo, April 1940, File 109:11, Box 21, WPA-UConn Papers; Pearl Russo, interview by author, Brookline, Mass., September 28, 1983.

93. *Herald,* March 27 (Mrs. S. quote), March 13, August 7, and October 9 and 23, 1932.

94. The Polish National Alliance (PNA), for example, sustained its membership levels through massive membership drives in the early 1930s, even as many were dropping out because they couldn't pay their insurance premiums. In 1930 forty-two thousand members purchased new PNA policies throughout the country, while about thirty thousand either canceled theirs or were terminated for nonpayment. The PNA had invested most of its assets in real estate mortgages in the Chicago area, was thus forced to foreclose on many of them, and was stuck with excess and devalued property (Pienkos, *PNA,* 140).

95. Cohen, *Making a New Deal.* See membership numbers for fraternal organizations in Fraternal Monitor, *Statistics, Fraternal Benefit Societies,* 1930–40. On the IWO see Sabin, *Red Scare in Court,* 10–24; Keeran, "International Workers Order"; Frank Fazekas, interview by author, Stratford, Conn., May 22, 1982.

96. *Herald,* October 9 and 23, 1932; *Black Rock Beacon,* September 18, 1931.

97. *Post,* January 24, 1964; *Herald,* October 31, 1937; unidentified clip, March 21, 1932, HC-BPL clipping file.

98. *Post,* March 5 and 10, 1931, April 29, 1937, May 7, 1939, and December 17, 1940 (HC-BPL clipping file); *Telegram,* May 5, 1931; "1936 survey," I.I. Records. Note that other, larger Swedish communities carried out similar voluntary relief efforts but were harder hit by the depression. For example, in Chicago the collapse of the "Swedish" banks in the city wiped out many Swedes and Swedish organizations' funds (Lindmark, "Swedish-Americans and the Depression Years").

99. *Black Rock Beacon,* September 18 and December 18, 1931, and March 11 and August 19, 1932; unidentified clipping, October 16, 1932, HC-BPL clipping file.

100. *Herald,* March 8, 1931; *Commonwealth,* March 1931, p. 3; File 170-6114, FMCS Records.

101. Labor Research Association, *Labor Fact Book 1,* 137–38; Daniel J. Leab, "'United We Eat'"; *Hartford Daily Times,* February 10, 1931; *Herald,* April 27 and August 31, 1930, August 2, 1931, and July 10, 1932; *Times-Star,* April 7, 1933; Lombardo, "Connecticut in the Great Depression," 49–50; Files 10110-2661:28 and 10110-2661:32, Military Intelligence Papers; miscellaneous letters and telegrams in "Communist Party" file (Box 379), "Bridgeport" file (Box 384), "Trade Union Utility [*sic*] League" file (Box 383), Governor Cross Papers-Hartford.

102. Brotherhood of Carpenters and Joiners District Council Minutes, various dates, 1930–32; J.A.M. to District Council, October 17, 1933 (in Minute Books); Carpenters Local 115 Minutes, September 16, 1930, and January 20, 1931, all in Brotherhood of Carpenters Papers; CFL, delegate reports, *Proceedings,* 1932. Carpenters everywhere faced similar challenges. For example, see Erlich, *With Our Hands,* 114–21. On union relief funds see Irving Bernstein, *The Lean Years,* 44–45.

103. Egan is quoted in *Times-Star,* September 8, 1931; CFL, *Proceedings,* 1931, 30–31; Carpenters Local 115 Minutes, July 1 and September–October 1930; Swedish Carpenters Local 1013 Minutes, October 10, 1930, Brotherhood of Carpenters Papers; *Herald,* October 26 and November 2, 1930; Connecticut Secretary of State, *Register and Manual, 1931,* 512.

104. U.S. Department of Labor, *Employment of Women in the Sewing Trades of Connecticut—Preliminary Report;* Bilevitz, "Connecticut Needle Trades"; Shepherd, "Robbing the Working Girl"; Hearings, Labor Committee, February 16, 1933, Legislative Division, Connecticut State Library; Minutes, Industrial Relations Committee, September 28, 1932, MAB Papers. The antisweatshop campaign was part of a larger attempt by Cross's Democratic administration to bolster its liberal credentials, to reveal how the 1931 GOP-dominated legislature had cut the Labor Department's budget, and to propose labor laws for the consideration of the 1933 General Assembly.

105. Manufacturers' Association of Connecticut, *Elimination of the Sweatshop,* 1.

106. *Connecticut Industry,* January 1933, p. 8.

107. Cross, *Connecticut Yankee,* 284–85; Manning, *Employment of Women in the Sewing Trades.*

108. Seidman, *Needle Trades,* 192–98; *Advance* (November 27, 1931): 7; Jack C. Bergen, interview by author, Bridgeport, September 3, 1982.

109. For an overview of the NRA strike wave see Irving Bernstein, *Turbulent Years,* 37–91. On the ACWA strikes see *Commonwealth,* June 1933, p. 1; *Advance* 15 (March–December 1933 issues); Amalgamated Clothing Workers of America, Local 125, *The Shirt and Clothing Workers of Connecticut, 1933–1943* (New Haven, Conn.: ACWA, 1943); interview with Mamie Santora, n.d. [1939?], Box 134, WPA-CtSL Papers. For the ILGWU activity see *New York Times,* August 16 and 22, 1933; *Post,* September 15, 1933; *Times-Star,* September 20 and October 14, 1933; Report, File 692, NLRB Records; ILGWU, *Proceedings,* 1934, 120–24; interview with M. H. S. Isenstadt, 1939, Box 133, WPA-CtSL Papers.

110. Unidentified clipping, July 31, 1933, McLevy scrapbook, McLevy-Schwarzkopf Papers. The Stylecraft strike is detailed in File 170-8085, FMCS Records; Buckingham ms., Box 92, and Bridgeport Labor File, Box 134, both in WPA-CtSL Papers.

Chapter 5: Capturing City Hall

1. Michael Russo, interview by author, Brookline, Mass., September 28, 1983. Descriptions of the election night celebration are in *Bridgeport Times-Star,* November 7, 1933; *Bridgeport Post,* November 8, 1933.

2. Patterson, *America's Struggle against Poverty,* chap. 2; Bucki, "Evolution of Poor Relief Practice in Nineteenth-Century Pittsburgh"; Katz, *In the Shadow of the Poorhouse,* chaps. 1–8.

3. National events are surveyed in Schwarz, *Interregnum of Despair.*

4. Manufacturers' Association of Connecticut, *Unemployment and Its Remedies,* 134–38. This document echoed recommendations from the New England Council and the National Association of Manufacturers.

5. For overviews of business activity in the employee welfare arena in this era, see Berkowitz and McQuaid, *Creating the Welfare State*, 1–34, 54–68; Brandes, *American Welfare Capitalism, 1880–1940*; Brody, "Rise and Decline of Welfare Capitalism"; Zahavi, *Workers, Managers, and Welfare Capitalism.*

6. Berkowitz and McQuaid, *Creating the Welfare State*, 92–95; Schatz, *Electrical Workers*, 53–61. The full text of Swope's address, as well as the plans and comments of others, including the U.S. Chamber of Commerce, appears in Beard, *America Faces the Future*. Swope's address is also reprinted in *Monthly Labor Review*, November 1931, pp. 45–53.

7. Hook, "Industry's Obligation to the Unemployed"; Hook, "The Unemployed—What Shall We Do with Them?" address to American Society of Mechanical Engineers, December 2, 1931, New York; *Connecticut Industry*, July 1932, p. 7; Connecticut Unemployment Commission, *Measures to Alleviate Unemployment*, 92–94; Jacoby, *Employing Bureaucracy*, 212–15; Irving Bernstein, *Lean Years*, 89–90.

8. *Connecticut Industry*, February 1931, p. 4 (Hubbard quote); MAC, *Unemployment and Its Remedies*, 134–35 (Goss quote).

9. The state unemployment commission, chaired by Hook, was the successor to the state Emergency Committee on Unemployment, which he also chaired. The Manufacturers' Association of Connecticut's Special Committee on Unemployment Relief, which prepared the report *Unemployment and Its Remedies*, included three Bridgeport members: George S. Hawley, president of the Bridgeport Gas Light Company; A. E. North, treasurer of the Bullard Company; and William R. Webster, chairman of the board of Bridgeport Brass Company.

10. Note that no general tax on employers to fund relief efforts was forthcoming from the Connecticut General Assembly until it was compelled to implement an unemployment insurance plan under provisions of the federal Social Security Act in 1936.

11. Report of Helen Gifford, Bridgeport YWCA, to National YWCA Office, September 1931, Reel 167.2, YWCA-National.

12. Frank Fazekas, interview by author, Stratford, Conn., May 22, 1982. Enthusiastic workers at the Bridgeport Works, 92 percent of whom had voted in favor, saw GE's unemployment fund as a hedge against dangerously unstable times. But Bridgeport GE found that it had to start its unemployment benefit plan in December 1930, two months before its planned inauguration, because of layoffs; management had already reduced maximum benefits to $15 a week (*GE Bridgeport Works News*, June 20, 1930, pp. 1–3, August 15, 1930, pp. 1–38, and December 19, 1930, p. 1).

13. Bingham is quoted in Schwarz, *Interregnum of Despair*, 16.

14. Mitchell, "Social Legislation in Connecticut," 329–63; Cross, *Connecticut Yankee*, 250–55; Governors' Conference, *Proceedings of the Governors' Conference, 1932*, copy in Box 15, File 175, Wilbur Cross Papers-Yale.

15. "How the Cities Stand," 74.

16. "Conference of Mayors," April 15, 1932, typescript in Box 380, File "Emergency Committee for Employment," Governor Cross Papers-Hartford.

17. *GE Bridgeport Works News*, October 17, 1930, p. 3 and December 19, 1930, p. 2. The average employee contribution was $6.38 (*Post*, November 14, 1931).

18. *Post*, February 15, 1931; H. Almon Chaffee to R. I. Neithercut, December 3, 1931, and report of Bridgeport Subcommittee on Industrial Employment, August 28, 1931, both in Box 16, Connecticut Unemployment Commission Papers.

19. *Herald*, March 13, 1932. Indeed, the 1932 fund drive yielded only $350,000, compared to the previous year's total of $551,079 ("Summary Report on Relief Status in New England for Welfare and Relief Mobilization Committee," 1932, report in Box 380, Governor Cross Papers-Hartford).

20. Lubove, *Professional Altruist*, chap. 7; United Way of America, *People and Events*, 21–57; Norton, *Cooperative Movement in Social Work*, 112–30, 154–72; Carter, *Gentle Legions*, 279–80; Brilliant, *United Way*, 18–26; Katz, *In the Shadow of the Poorhouse*, 156–57.

21. *Connecticut Industry,* August 1932, p. 15.

22. For January–July 1932 Bridgeport reported $924,966 in relief expenditures, with $855,166 coming from public funds and only $69,800 from private sources (Connecticut Unemployment Commission, *Measures to Alleviate Unemployment,* p. 67; MAC, *Unemployment and Its Remedies,* tables 17–18, pp. 112–13).

23. Colcord, Koplovitz, and Kurtz, *Emergency Work Relief,* 11–30.

24. The new work-relief program instituted in June 1931 had new rules: wages of 35 cents an hour for the male breadwinner of a household, with the number of hours allowed per week dependent on the number of dependents in that household. The wages were paid only in scrip, which would be honored by merchants and grocers throughout the city. In September 1931, 842 men were employed on these work details, down from a high of 1,222 in the early phase of the program. In addition, the city continued to give direct food and fuel supplies to families in need and paid rent if a relief family received an eviction notice (Colcord, Koplovitz, and Kurtz, *Emergency Work Relief,* 48–53; *Post,* February 15, 1931; Minutes, January 29, February 3, 6, 17, and 24, and April 6, 1931, Board of Apportionment Minute Books; *Herald,* July 26, 1931; Angus P. Thorne, "Survey, August 10, 1932," File "Relief Surveys," Box 383, Governor Cross Papers-Hartford).

Connecticut state law prohibited "aliens" (noncitizens) from obtaining "settlement" in any of the towns of the state, settlement being the legal determination that one's well-being was the responsibility of that town. Settlement laws were quite stringent, in that one had to have lived in the town or city for at least four years before applying for relief and not to have taken relief during any of those four years. The state took responsibility for "unsettled" residents (Heisterman, "Statutory Provisions Relating to Legal Settlement").

25. Schlesinger, *Age of Roosevelt,* 252; also see Irving Bernstein, *Lean Years,* 310–11.

26. Leff, *Limits of Symbolic Reform,* 14–15; Chatters, "Municipal Finance"; Kantowicz, *Polish-American Politics in Chicago,* 156–60. Ridley and Nolting's *What the Depression Has Done to Cities* provides examples of specific areas of municipal activity. The fullest account of the tax strike issue is in Beito, *Taxpayers in Revolt,* though his stated thesis that tax delinquency tapped a widespread "anti-big-government" sentiment falls short. From his evidence "anti-big-government" sentiment was clearly apparent among large real-estate interests but not necessarily among small property owners. Small property owners, whether working class or middle class, may have been moved by antimachine sentiment, but this does not mean that they rejected an expanded government role, especially in this time of crisis.

27. Hoan, *Taxes and Tax Dodgers,* 3–4, 16.

28. Orloff and Skocpol, "Why Not Equal Protection?"

29. The MAC statement is quoted in *Connecticut Industry,* February 1931, p. 4. MAC noted that Massachusetts governor Ely and others were now calling for a moratorium on their labor laws in order to keep industry from moving out of state (MAC, *Unemployment and Its Remedies,* 130).

30. Bridgeport Brass Company and Singer Manufacturing Company both received reductions in their 1933 tax bills after appealing their assessments to the city tax attorney. The Bridgeport Gas Light Company had in 1929 received a final settlement on its 1920s taxes, which saved the company nearly $5 million (Minutes, September 10, 1929, March 2, 1933, Board of Apportionment Minute Books).

31. Connecticut Unemployment Commission, *Measures to Alleviate Unemployment,* 88–89.

32. *Connecticut Industry,* January 1932, cover page; Moses, "Death—and Taxes," quoted in Schwarz, *Interregnum of Despair,* 110, and Thomas quote on 127 (see also 106–41); Fearon, *War, Prosperity, and Depression,* 123–25. For a national context for these tax debates see Leff, *Limits of Symbolic Reform,* 16, 48–90; Schlesinger, *Age of Roosevelt,* 252–55. Note that by the late 1920s, states only occasionally used personal income and corporate income taxes (Patterson, *New Deal and the States,* 3–25, 31).

33. *Congressional Record,* May 12, 1930, p. 8742, as quoted in Sundquist, *Dynamics of the Party System,* 201–2.

34. Alan H. Olmstead, *Bridgeport Times-Star,* December 30, 1933, in clipping scrapbook, McLevy-Schwarzkopf Papers.

35. Angus P. Thorne, "Survey," August 10, 1932, in File "Relief Surveys," Box 383, Governor Cross Papers-Hartford; *Herald,* July 26, 1931; Minutes, February 4, 1931, Board of Apportionment Minute Books; City of Bridgeport, *Municipal Register,* 1932, 88, and *Municipal Register,* 1933, 96.

36. Olmstead, *Times-Star,* September 11, 1931; Buckingham is quoted in *Times-Star,* October 21, 1931.

37. Meeting, November 27, 1929, Board of Apportionment Minute Books; *Times-Star,* October 27, 1931 (HC-BPL clipping file). Background on Buckingham is provided in *Who's Who in Connecticut,* 1933, 44; interview with Buckingham by Nolan, February 1940, Box 112, WPA-CtSL Papers; endorsements by the editors of the society paper *Bridgeport Life,* October 10 and 17, 1931 (HC-BPL clipping file); editorial, *Herald,* October 11, 1931, p. 1 (last quote).

38. *Herald,* August 16 and October 11, 1931; *Times-Star,* October 22, 1931; *Post,* October 9, November 1 and 2, 1931; Howard S. Challenger to J. H. Roraback, July 22, 1931, Roraback Papers. Also rather wisely, the GOP ticket dumped John F. Maloney, who had been city sheriff for sixteen years, deeming his "iron-fisted method of tax collection" a liability.

39. *Herald,* October 18 and 25, 1931; Olmstead, *Times-Star,* September 11, 1931.

40. *Herald,* October 18, 1931.

41. *Herald,* November 1, 1931; Socialists' platform appears in *Herald,* July 9, 1931.

42. *Bridgeport Telegram,* October 30, 1931; Johnpoll, *Pacifist's Progress,* 61–67.

43. *Commonwealth,* December 1931, p. 1; McLevy is quoted in *Herald,* November 1, 1931.

44. Maurer, *It Can Be Done,* 305.

45. *Herald,* July 9, 1931; Shenton is quoted in *Sunday Post,* November 19, 1933.

46. The "Liberty Bell" ad ran in *Post* and *Telegram,* November 2, 1931.

47. *Post,* November 2, 1931.

48. *Times-Star,* November 4, 1931.

49. Olmstead, "The Great Jasper," 160.

50. *Post,* November 18, 1931 (McLevy scrapbook). The Communist Party also ran a municipal slate, which received 178 votes. It did not report campaign expenses.

51. *Black Rock Beacon,* February 12 and July 29, 1932; unidentified clip [1932], in "Committee of 100," HC-BPL clipping file; *Post,* September 8, 9, and 20, and October 30, 1932; Board of Directors' Minutes, February 10 and June 27, 1932, BCC Papers. Note that the tax rate had been raised only 1 mill since 1929.

52. This was a letter to Mayor Buckingham, read by Buckingham at the mayors' conference. Buckingham noted that the letter writer wished to remain anonymous ("Mayors Conference," April 15, 1932, Box 380, Governor Cross Papers-Hartford).

53. Minutes, March 18, 1932, Board of Apportionment Minute Books.

54. Board of Directors Minutes, January 30, 1933, Minutes Books, YWCA-Bridgeport. The female-led YWCA had long championed the needs of low-income women and children in the city, though usually with a sense of noblesse oblige. In the 1920s the Y sponsored a day-care center for children of immigrant women who had to work, and the Y's International Institute served women in immigrant communities with English and citizenship classes.

55. *Post,* January 15, 1933. Also see *Post,* January 7, 1933.

56. Unidentified clip, January 23, 1933 (wooden scrapbook, McLevy-Schwarzkopf Papers).

57. Unidentified clip, February 24, 1933 (clipping scrapbook, McLevy-Schwarzkopf Papers); *Post,* January 19, 1933; *Herald,* March 20 and August 7, 1932; *Commonwealth,* February 1933, p. 1; Minutes, February 2, 1932, Board of Apportionment Minute Books.

58. *Herald,* April 12 and August 7, 1932.

59. DeVer H. Warner to Roraback, April 6, 1933, Roraback Papers.

60. Brief reports of actions on Bridgeport bills by the General Assembly's Committee on Cities and Boroughs is contained in Committee Hearings, 1933 General Assembly, Legislative Division,

Connecticut State Library. The committee approved all proposals by the Committee of One Hundred while reporting unfavorably most other approaches (*Post,* April 1, 1933 [McLevy scrapbook]).

61. Committee of One Hundred is quoted in *Post,* June 16, 1933 (HC-BPL clipping file); the Socialists are quoted in *Commonwealth,* April 1933. p. 4. Bridgeport sold $871,000 in 1933 city bonds through a New York City bond syndicate (*New York Times,* June 24, 1933). No list of buyers was published.

62. *Bridgeport Life,* October 28, 1931.

63. Mika is quoted in *Post,* October 25, 1933; *Post* and *Times-Star* daily issues, September–November 1933; candidate biographies appear in *Times-Star,* October 30 and 31 and November 1, 2, and 3, 1933.

64. *Post,* October 28 and 29, 1933.

65. See candidate backgrounds in *Times-Star,* October 30 and 31 and November 1, 2, and 3, 1933.

66. The Democrats are quoted in *Times-Star,* November 1, 1933; Democrat ad in *Post,* November 4, 1933.

67. *Post,* November 2, 1933.

68. McLevy column, *Herald,* September 25, October 23, and November 6, 1932.

69. Abraham Knepler, interview by author, Bridgeport, September 29, 1982. The Connecticut SP reported dues-paying membership of six hundred at the end of the year (1932 Membership report, Reel 26, SPA Papers). No exact figures exist for Bridgeport membership at this time. The national SP campaign is covered in Johnpoll, *Pacifist's Progress,* 93–105.

70. 1933 leaflet, Reel 94 Section G, SPA Papers; *Post,* October 20, 1933; McLevy is quoted in Olmstead, "Great Jasper," 162; McLevy to H. L. Springer (Sayre, Penn.), November 29, 1933, "McLevy Letterbox," McLevy-Schwarzkopf Papers.

71. *Bridgeport Life,* October 28, 1933, pt. 2, p. 1 (first quote); *Post,* October 18, 1933 (second quote). Indeed, Cross, a Democrat, was refusing to call a special session of the state legislature to pass enabling legislation so that Connecticut cities could apply for federal money (*Sunday Post,* September 3, 1933).

72. *Post,* November 6, 1933.

73. Knepler interview, September 29, 1982.

74. For Schwarzkopf speech to one thousand attending the SP annual picnic, see *Commonwealth,* July 1933, p. 4; interview with Ethel M. Freedman, Fairfield, March 12, 1985.

75. Campaign details, in addition to specific citations, were gathered from daily issues of the *Post* and *Times-Star,* September–November 1933; *Commonwealth,* August 1933, p. 4, and October 1933, p. 1; "The Third Lever," campaign pamphlet, 1933, Reel 94 Section G, SPA Papers. The 1933 issues of the *Bridgeport Sunday Herald* have not survived.

76. Jack C. Bergen, interview by author, Bridgeport, September 3, 1982; Shannon, *Socialist Party of America,* 227–35. McLevy signed the call for the national meeting (copy of call in File 10110-2666:49, Entry 65, Box 3100, Military Intelligence Records). Papers relating to the Connecticut congress are in Box 9, Alfred Bingham Papers. The Egan quote was in the context of a debate about a motion by a coalition of Socialist trade unionists to endorse the upcoming Connecticut Congress of Workers and Farmers, a spinoff of the successful Socialist Continental Congress of Workers and Farmers the previous spring. The convention eventually voted no because Communists were also participating in the congress. McLevy was one of the signers of the call for the Connecticut congress (Connecticut Federation of Labor, "Proceedings," 1933, typescript, in Connecticut State AFL-CIO Papers). Also see interview with R. Schmidt, officer of a metal polishers' local in Bridgeport, by P. K. Russo, n.d. [1939], Box 112, WPA-CtSL Papers.

77. *Times-Star,* November 8, 1933. Voting results listed in City of Bridgeport, *Municipal Register,* 1934. The Normal School, a training school for teachers run alongside the city high school, had long been a priority with Bridgeport voters; it was reopened in 1923 after voters repudiated the last business attempt to take over city hall.

78. McLevy and Krzyki are quoted in *New York Times*, November 9, 1933; for McLevy inauguration quote see *Post*, November 13, 1933.

79. *Times-Star*, November 8, 1933. The campaign expenses reported by the three parties for the 1933 election were Democrats, $20,890; Republicans, $13,630; and Socialists, $1,890. No one made note of the CP campaign, which garnered 204 votes (*New York Times*, November 23, 1933).

80. *Post*, November 9, 1933.

81. Olmstead, *Times-Star*, December 30, 1933; Michael Russo interview; *Commonwealth*, November 1933, pp. 1, 4.

82. Note that these data are consistent with the data presented by Stave in "Great Depression and Urban Political Continuity," 173–74, though my emphasis is different. Stave chose to focus on the conservative "continuity" that the Bridgeport SP was supposed to represent. Though he may have been closer to the mark on the later years of McLevy's reign (McLevy was mayor until 1957), the evidence I have examined does not support his contention about the early years. Some small and medium-sized businesses may have supported the SP in the early years, but the record shows that major industrialists fought the SP in its first term.

83. At the same time investments in municipal bonds by many ethnic organizations around the country may have led ethnic voters to be more aware of city finances. For example, in Minneapolis the Croatian Fraternal Union had urged its members to get involved in politics to protect their benefits (Rachleff, "Class, Ethnicity, and the New Deal," 93).

84. Olmstead, *Times-Star*, December 30, 1933 (clipping in wooden scrapbook, McLevy-Schwarzkopf Papers).

Chapter 6: Captured by City Hall

1. These various strikes are detailed in the September–November 1933 issues of the *Post;* the September 1933 issues of the *Times-Star;* "Labor file," Box 133, WPA-CtSL Papers; File 176-466, FMCS Records; "Truck Strike" file, Box 392, Governor Cross Papers-Hartford.

2. Irving Bernstein, *Turbulent Years,* 217–317; Lorwin and Wubnig, *Labor Relations Boards; Herald,* March 18 and September 30, 1934. No records of the Connecticut NRA board survive.

3. *Herald,* April 22, 1934; Remington Arms Company, *Bonus Plan;* Bridgeport Brass Company, "Company Handbook," 1938, in Box 718:5:1a, Bridgeport Brass Company Collection; *Post,* November 28, 1933; Minutes, April 11 and October 1, 1934, MAB Papers; Balderston, *Executive Guidance of Industrial Relations,* 58–65; Jacoby, *Employing Bureaucracy,* 207–33.

4. Connecticut Federation of Labor (hereafter CFL), *Proceedings,* 1934, 76–77. See AFL list of charters, courtesy of the George Meany Labor Archives, Washington, D.C., in Labor Vertical File, LA-UConn; Bridgeport IAM organizing reports in Reel 150, IAM Records (microfilm edition); "Labor 1934" file, Russo ms., Box 133, WPA-CtSL Papers.

5. CFL, Bridgeport IAM report, *Proceedings,* 1933.

6. George A. Doyle to A. O. Wharton, June 3, 1934, Reel 2, IAM Records (microfilm). The IAM expected individual workers to pay $5 to join, plus dues of $1.75 a month even before any effective action had been taken to organize their workplace, something many workers could not afford and would not do. MESA, by contrast, had only token dues at this stage.

7. Interview with Mr. R. by P. K. Russo, 1939, Box 133, WPA-CtSL Papers.

8. Interview with John J. Egan by Russo, 1939, Box 133, WPA-CtSL Papers. The distrust resulting from the MESA incident impeded organization for years afterward. One observer reported that Slovak workers on Bridgeport's East Side distrusted Irish union organizers (this description fit most union spokesmen in the city), whom they suspected of trying to get them fired (Hallett St. Block Survey, Frazzetta ms., 1939, Box 93, WPA-CtSL Papers). I could find no information about this incident in MESA publications. The December 1934 issue of *MESA Voice* reported that the MESA organizer in question was working in New York. MESA had established locals in Bridgeport, New Haven, and Torrington, Connecticut, in 1934 (*Herald,* April 15 and September 16, 1934; Rodnick

ms., Box 135, WPA-CtSL Papers). For a history of the organization see Dahlheimer, *History of the Mechanics Educational Society;* M. Smith, "Militant Labor in Detroit."

9. *Post,* September 3, 1933; Bridgeport Carpenters District Council Minutes, January 8 and December 3 and 17, 1934, and February 4, 1935, Brotherhood of Carpenters Records. For information on the contours of collective bargaining in the 1930s building trades, see Haber, "Building Construction"; Slichter, *Union Policies and Industrial Management,* passim.

10. International Ladies' Garment Workers' Union (hereafter ILGWU), *Proceedings,* 1934, 172, 183; Morris Novik (WEVD) to McLevy, January 25, 1937, McLevy Letterbox #1, McLevy-Schwarzkopf Papers.

11. The text of Hoan's proclamation is in *New Commonwealth,* November 1935, p. 4; Schwarzkopf to George Rhodes (Reading, Pa.), May 18, 1936. Also see *Herald,* November 4, 1934 (United Textile Workers); "Election Congratulation file," 1933 and 1935; August Claessens to McLevy, April 3, 1935, and McLevy to Claessens, April 20, 1935 (in regard to support for Pocketbook Workers drive); McLevy to Bernard Schub (ILGWU, New Haven), November 8, 1935, all in McLevy-Schwarzkopf Papers; CFL, *Proceedings,* 1935.

12. *New York Times,* November 8, 1933; *Bridgeport Post,* November 13, 1933.

13. *Commonwealth,* January 1934, p. 1–2; *Herald,* December 10, 1933 (clipping in Box 4, Norman Thomas Papers); *Post,* December 31, 1933, and January 2, 1934; *Telegram,* January 1, 1934.

14. Lobbying for lower interest rates was a wise move, because it was solicitous of both home owners and small businessmen. Indeed, later in 1934 the Federated Business Men's Council took up the same issue. There is no record that anything was accomplished along these lines (*Herald,* November 4, 1991). On public board meetings see *Commonwealth,* February 1934, p. 1, June 1934, p. 4, July 1934, pp. 1–3, and August 1934, p. 18.

15. Connecticut Emergency Relief Commission (hereafter CERC), *Report of the Emergency Relief Commission,* appendix 11, 110–11. Bridgeport had not yet received federal money to cover expenses or to implement new relief, though funds were pending as they were passed through a new state commission.

16. Sumner Simpson exemplified the interlocking financial and industrial interests represented by the political appointments of this era. In 1930, in addition to being president of the Raybestos-Manhattan Company and its Canadian and European divisions, he was vice president and director of the First National Bank of Bridgeport (the bank that handled city finances) and a director of the Bridgeport People's Savings Bank, the D. M. Read Department Store, the Bridgeport Gas Light Company, the Bridgeport Hardware Manufacturing Company, the Bridgeport Housing Company, and a few local building and loan companies (*Directory of Directors*). While his company might have moved operations elsewhere, his other financial interests were directly tied to the continued economic viability of Bridgeport.

17. Minutes, January–February 1934, Board of Apportionment Minute Books; *Herald,* December 31, 1933, and January 7 and 14, 1934; *Telegram,* January 3, 1934 (McLevy clipping files); Executive Board Minutes, January 10 and 29, 1934, MAB Papers; William Hogan to Kenneth Wynne (executive secretary to Governor Cross), April 14, 1935, Box 395, Governor Cross Papers-Hartford. The tax set for 1934–35 was held at 29.3 mills.

18. Minutes, November 19 and December 20, 1934, Board of Apportionment Minute Books.

19. This was one issue on which the Board of Apportionment did not have the five votes it needed to override the mayor's veto (*Herald,* October 7, 1934; McLevy to Board of Apportionment, September 20, 1934, McLevy Box, Mayors' Files, City Archives; Minutes, February 24, 1934, Board of Apportionment).

20. Board of Apportionment to F. Schwarzkopf, April 25, 1934, in Minutes, April 25, 1934, Board of Apportionment Records; also see Minutes, May 10, 18, 1934, Board of Apportionment Records; *Herald,* March 3, 1935 (McLevy clipping file). The debate had some immediate results, as the United Illuminating Company suddenly announced a reduction in electricity rates.

21. Connecticut, along with other New England states, received the lowest per capita amount

of federal money. The national per-family payment averaged $23.90 and in nearby New York it was $45.12, while Connecticut averaged less than $15. Bridgeport's average family relief payment was $10.06 in summer, $15.16 in winter. Bridgeport's relief expenditures, for the period January 1, 1933, to June 30, 1934, totalled slightly more than $3 million; Bridgeport taxes paid for 44.5 percent of that sum, with the federal government covering another 45.8 percent, and the state only 9.7 percent (Patterson, *New Deal and the States,* 50–55; Bane, "Public Welfare"; CERC, *Experience of the Emergency Relief Commission,* 112–13; Minutes, February 9, 1934, Bridgeport Board of Apportionment).

22. Eleanor Little, relief administrator for the CERC, encouraged local committees to put their city's mayor on the committee, because they would need the city's cooperation and matching funds, but Bridgeport elites did not heed this advice (CERC, *Experience of the Emergency Relief Commission,* 9; Little, "Relief Without Politics").

23. Hopkins complained to Newton Brainard, chairman of CERC, that the FERA office had received numerous reports that the administration of relief in Connecticut was "thoroughly Republican, and that is being used for partisan purposes," while firmly suggesting that Brainard not "tolerate any political interference or discrimination in our work" (Harry Hopkins to Newton Brainard, December 22, 1933, CWA Box 7, WPA-DC Records). Also see Robert T. O'Connell (Meriden, Conn.) to Louis M. Howe, December 11, 1933, Box 15, OF 300, Franklin D. Roosevelt Papers, for O'Connell's complaints that Republicans and anti-FDR Democrats controlled relief money in the state.

24. Minutes, November 19, 1934, Board of Apportionment Minute Books.

25. See letters and telegrams asking CWA to cover snow shovelers, February 23, 1934, CWA Box 7, WPA-DC Records; Minutes, February 21, 1934, Board of Apportionment Minute Books.

26. This did not, however, return control of relief to the mayor. The state audit cleared the welfare superintendent of wrongdoing in the short term. When the welfare superintendent dragged his feet on this issue and then interfered with or overruled the newly hired case supervisor, Eleanor Little, relief administrator for the CERC, listened more sympathetically to the Socialist city administration (Eleanor Little to Jacob Becker [CWA, Washington], February 28, 1934, CWA Box 7; Eleanor Little to Robert Lansdale [FERA, Washington], August 3, 1934, FERA Box 43, both in WPA-DC Records; Minutes, March 20, May 15, June 21, July 17, and December 21, 1934, Box 1A, CERC Records).

27. *Commonwealth,* March 1934, p. 2, April 1934, p. 3, June 1934, pp. 1 and 4; *Herald,* May 6, September 16 and 21, October 7, and November 4, 1934; Olmstead, "The Great Jasper," 197–204.

28. Minutes, September 17, 1934, Board of Apportionment Minute Books; McLevy to Board of Apportionment, September 22, 1934, McLevy Box, Mayors' Files, City Archives; *Herald,* September 23, 1934.

29. All quotes are from *Herald,* August 26 and September 2 and 9, 1934.

30. Mike Russo, organizer of the Unemployed Council, recalled that he and Will Weinstone of the national office of the Communist Party had just climbed onto hydrants in order to address the crowd of five hundred when "police just started clubbing everybody" (Mike Russo, interview by author, Brookline, Mass., September 28, 1983). The *Herald* at first sympathized with the mayor and repeated his negative comments about the CP organizers but then printed letters from readers disputing this official view and blaming the police for the disorder (*Herald,* March 11 and 18, 1934). The SP continued to state its version, accusing the Communists of throwing "pieces of broken sidewalk" at the police ([Schwarzkopf] to Dr. Philip Nemoff [West New York, N.J.], n.d. [summer 1934], McLevy-Schwarzkopf Papers).

31. *Herald,* April 29, 1934. Jack Bergen, the Socialist board of education member and a FERA supervisor, was severely reprimanded for his part in leading the April demonstration (Jack C. Bergen, interview by author, Bridgeport, September 3, 1982). Key to these decisions was that the city literally had no money in February but received new federal funds and local tax payments after April 1. Bridgeport SP members, mostly YPSL activists, were later involved in organizing an un-

employed workers union, but it never reached the scale of SP efforts in other cities. See Rosenzweig, "'Socialism in Our Time,'" for the national Unemployed Workers Union.

32. Krieger, himself an old Wobbly, "loved action and that sort of thing." He had recently helped organize and obtain legal counsel for some Greek sailors who had jumped ship in Bridgeport harbor; later in 1934 he, along with other party members and local activists from the League Against War and Fascism, was arrested by city police for protesting the visit to the city by the German consul general of New York (M. Russo interview; *Daily Worker,* November 3, 12, and 20, and December 20, 1934). McLevy's reason for refusing a rally permit for the league's protest was, he insisted, a defense of free speech. Jack Bergen, the local SP secretary and a board of education member, suggested that McLevy's hesitancy over this issue was connected to his unwillingness to antagonize any city constituency. Two of the large German-American fraternal groups in Bridgeport had arranged the rally for the German consul general and the crew of a large German ship docked in New York harbor, and there was little anti-Nazi activity or sentiment in the city at that time (Jack C. Bergen, interview by author, Bridgeport, Conn., December 16, 1983). Communist Party activists also agitated against McLevy for meeting with Gen. Josef Haller when he visited the city as a guest of Polish organizations.

33. American Civil Liberties Union, *Annual Report, 1932–33,* 19–20; Minutes, SP national executive committee meeting, January 27–28, 1933, copy in McLevy Letterbox #5, McLevy-Schwarzkopf Papers; the McLevy comment on the local CP appears in McLevy to Leonard Greene (Lawrence, Mass.), November 17, 1933, McLevy-Schwarzkopf Papers.

34. Johnpoll, *Pacifist's Progress,* 111–16; Labor Research Association, *Labor Fact Book 3,* 147–51; Warren, *Alternative Vision,* 145–48. On the CP's offer to form a United Front with the SP, and then a Popular Front, see Ottanelli, *Communist Party of the United States,* 49–135.

35. For example, instances of cooperation were numerous in the late 1920s and early 1930s in New Haven, where the CP had majority strength in the Workmen's Circle (which the Communists took into the International Workers Order in the 1930s) and influence in the Central Labor Council through the painters' union (Kreas, *My Life and Struggle for a Better World,* 71–91).

36. Michael Russo considered it a mistake to compete with the Bridgeport SP in elections at that time and tried to continue United Front discussions. Only in 1936, with the mobilization of new ethnic working-class neighborhoods and the organization of the CIO in Bridgeport, did the CP move beyond its strength in the Hungarian and Russian communities to forge an effective broad-based coalition in the city on labor and social issues (M. Russo interview, September 1983).

37. "Bridgeport's Victory—A Portent?"; "Ex Cathedra," 626. The "big industrialists" were not named.

38. Thomas to Sam Romer (New York City), December 19, 1933, Box 4, Norman Thomas Papers. Six months later Thomas admitted that he was "not altogether happy about the Bridgeport situation, [but] Devere Allen and others have called to my attention the facts about the laws binding McLevy" (Thomas to Alden R. Whitman [Bridgeport], June 21, 1934, Box 5, Norman Thomas Papers).

39. Of the many studies of Socialist politics in the Progressive Era, the most useful are Judd, *Socialist Cities;* Stave, *Socialism and the Cities;* S. Miller, *Victor Berger and the Promise of Constructive Socialism;* Weinstein, *Decline of Socialism in America;* Pratt, "Reading Socialist Experience"; Olson, "Milwaukee Socialists, 1897–1941."

40. Fred Cederholm (chair, Fifth District) to P. J. Cooney (Socialist sheriff), August 16, 1932, McLevy Letterbox #6, McLevy-Schwarzkopf Papers; Resolution, Fifth District Club, n.d. [1933], in "Election Congratulation file," McLevy-Schwarzkopf Papers; *Herald,* May 12, 1940; Bergen interview, September 1982. Also see George Ribak interview by Bruce Stave, 1972, typescript, HC-BPL.

41. The evidence is incomplete, but apparently in 1934 the Bridgeport YPSL, meeting at the hall of the Polish Socialist Alliance, carried some of the points raised by the Cederholms until the YPSL members too were discouraged by the parent body from further participation. The Polish Socialist Alliance itself had a falling-out with the Bridgeport local and discontinued its active involve-

ment (*Herald,* September 9, 1934; Bergen interview, September 1982; Abraham E. Knepler, interview by author, Bridgeport, September 29, 1982). One YPSL member, Kieve Liskofsky, was expelled from YPSL (*Commonwealth,* August 1934, p. 6; SP City Central Committee, Communique from Jack C. Bergen [secretary SP—Bridgeport], October 19, 1932, in McLevy Letterbox #6, McLevy-Schwarzkopf Papers; Minutes, July 11, November 21, 1932, Third District Club Minute Book, in Socialist Party Box, McLevy-Schwarzkopf Papers). For hints of the controversy see "General Action Committee" to McLevy, August 3, 1934, McLevy Letterbox #5, and Frank Fraczek (an activist in the Polish Branch) to James Oneal (editor, *New Leader*), September 24, 1935, copy in McLevy Letterbox #5, both in McLevy-Schwarzkopf Papers. Fraczek calls McLevy "Bridgeport's 'Little Stalin.'" The only extant copy (June 1934) of the short-lived Bridgeport YPSL paper, the *Torch,* is in Sterling Library, Yale University. Informants provided no further information about these events.

42. Elected Socialists sometimes had a difficult time adjusting to their new status; for example, the local party felt it necessary to discipline Fred Schwarzkopf "to reduce the swelling of his head," by denying him an elected party post in 1934 (*Herald,* January 28, April 15, and May 6, 1934).

43. *Commonwealth,* March 1934, p. 2; Bergen interview, December 1983); *New Commonwealth,* November 1935, p. 4. The support for Mussolini was strong in Bridgeport's Italian community. Michael Russo, organizer for the Communist Party and a favorite son in that community because of his earlier success as a sculptor, related how, when he mounted a soapbox on the East Side to denounce Mussolini's invasion of Ethiopia in 1935, he was physically attacked by the crowd (M. Russo interview, March 1990).

44. Minutes NEC, January 28–27, 1933, typescript in McLevy Letterbox #5, McLevy-Schwarzkopf Papers; Shannon, *Socialist Party of America,* 236; Johnpoll, *Pacifist's Progress,* 108–11.

45. For example, in one resolution criticizing the NRA as detrimental to American unionism, one paragraph also critiqued the internal weakness of the labor movement and the harm done by the craft form of organization, a stand that again prompted McLevy's unswerving opposition. McLevy argued for increased SP activity within the trade unions to combat their inadequacies: "Start out and do our own job and do it well. And when we do that, then, Comrades, we are going to be in a position where we will have the rank and file you speak about in the Socialist Party and in the trade union movement both fighting on the economic and political fields for the principles and the ideals we stand for." He was supported by nearly every union member at the convention, and the offending paragraph was struck from the resolution (Socialist Party of America (hereafter SPA), *1934 Convention Proceedings,* p. 241, Reel 77, SPA Papers). McLevy left very little in the way of formal correspondence or public statements regarding internal party affairs; when he did speak up, it was always on trade union issues or in opposition to the United Front. See Dilling, *Red Network,* 337–38, for a list of Revolutionary Policy Committee activists.

46. Shannon, *Socialist Party of America,* 214–18, 235–41; SPA, *1932 Convention Proceedings, 1934 Convention Proceedings,* both in Reel 77, SPA Papers; Levinson, "Labor Turns to Politics"; Johnpoll, *Pacifist's Progress,* 87–134. Note that Shannon groups the centrists under one term, "Progressives," whereas Johnpoll separates them into two wings, reformers and pragmatists. Shannon counted two old guard members on the national executive committee in 1934, as he included James Graham there, whereas Johnpoll categorizes him as a centrist. Warren, *Alternative Vision,* takes issue with Johnpoll's interpretation and defends Norman Thomas and the Militants' program.

47. A desperate message from the Committee for the Preservation of Socialist Policies (an old guard vehicle) asked the Bridgeport SP how the rest of its three hundred members would vote; Schwarzkopf informed the committee that the rest were too busy with the local and state campaign to vote on the referendum. This revealed an alarming lack of interest in national affairs and the beginning of Bridgeport's distancing itself from the national party (George H. Goebel to Fred Schwarzkopf, August 23, 1934, and Schwarzkopf to Goebel, August 24, 1934, McLevy Letterbox #1, McLevy-Schwarzkopf Papers; Shannon, *Socialist Party,* 240).

48. *Herald,* September 16, 1934.

49. McLevy is quoted in the *Herald,* October 14, 1934. Also see *Commonwealth,* July 1934, p. 1, and August 1934, p. 3; *Herald,* September 9 and 16, October 14, and November 4, 1934.

50. Griffen, "Roraback of Connecticut"; Cross, *Connecticut Yankee*, 222–26; Rosengren, "Connecticut Government and Politics," 141–42; Spencer, "Homer S. Cummings."

51. Cross, *Connecticut Yankee*, 277–98; *New York Times*, January 5 and March 12, 1933; Mitchell, "Social Legislation in Connecticut," 229–45; *Herald*, March 8, 1931.

52. Lockard, "Role of Party in the Connecticut General Assembly," 172, as quoted in Patterson, *New Deal and the States*, 158; Jeffries, *Testing the Roosevelt Coalition*, 3–50.

53. *Herald*, November 4, 1934.

54. Technically, Cross was out of state on vacation when the textile strike, part of a northeastern strike wave among textile workers, began; his lieutenant governor ordered out the national guard. Cross then returned to the state, recalled only part of the guard, and sent Labor Commissioner Tone to mediate the dispute. Cross did, however, send out more guardsmen after "flying squadrons" of strikers attempted to spread the strike throughout all the eastern Connecticut mills (Cross, *Connecticut Yankee*, 305–11; *Herald*, September 9 and 23, October 28, and November 4, 1934).

55. *Herald*, April 29, 1934.

56. *Herald*, November 4, 1934. Further complicating the election efforts was that some building trades leaders resented McLevy's interference with the workings of the Welfare Department and called upon CERC officials to keep FERA's local relief committee in place. Though the SP had claimed credit for the preferential treatment that unemployed union craftsmen had received on work-relief details, it seemed that some local unions had made their own deals with Democrats and Republicans (M. F. Feier [Local 2, Bricklayers] to Eleanor Little, July 26, 1934, and Albert Walkley [Bridgeport Building Trades Council], July 27, 1934, both in FERA State Files, Box 47, WPA-DC Records; *Herald*, September 9, 30, 1934; Knepler, "Socialism's Forward March—Bridgeport")

57. *Herald*, October 21, 1934; *Telegram*, October 25, 1934; *Post*, October 23, 1934.

58. The students argued that the new school schedule interfered with their after-school jobs, which they needed (*Herald*, October 14, 1934).

59. *Herald*, October 21, 1934.

60. The three Socialist state senators were Audubon Secor, forty-eight, an engineer; Albert Eccles, fifty-two, an engraver; and John M. Taft, thirty-six, an artisan. The representatives were Harry Bender, forty-three, a factory inspector, and Jack C. Bergen, twenty-eight, an architect. Their occupations made them stand out in the sea of lawyers and small businessmen who made up the General Assembly (*Connecticut Register and Manual, 1935*).

61. After 79 percent of voters pulled the lever to repeal the Ripper Act of 1933, the Socialists made home rule a leading goal (*New Commonwealth*, January 1935, p. 3).

62. DeVer C. Warner to Alpheus Winter (MAB manager), November 23, 1934; Sumner Simpson to George S. Hawley (MAB president), November 28, 1934; Minutes, November 28, 1934, in Minute Books, all in MAB Papers.

63. Cross, *Connecticut Yankee*, 316. As Jack Bergen pointed out, the decision was a sound one. If the SP had voted with the Democrats to organize the state senate, the overwhelmingly Republican House would have stymied all progress during that term (Bergen interview, September 1982)

64. Cross, *Connecticut Yankee*, 322–41; *New Commonwealth*, first March issue, 1935, p. 4; *New Commonwealth*, second March issue, 1935, p. 4; *New Commonwealth*, first April issue, 1935, p. 3, *New Commonwealth*, second April issue, 1935, p. 1; *Sunday Herald*, January 13, 1935; Lockard, "Role of Party in the Connecticut General Assembly," 288–89; Connecticut SP Legislative Bulletin, March 25, 1935, McLevy-Schwarzkopf Papers. Congress had passed a constitutional amendment on child labor, and the amendment was making its way through state legislatures. It was never ratified by the required number of states.

65. The issue had been first introduced in Connecticut in 1915 by Julius Stremlau of the CFL and the Fraternal Order of Eagles. Information on the creation of a Connecticut coalition of the SP, the CFL, and fraternal groups to win an old-age pension plan in the state is in *Commonwealth*, March 1931, p. 1; *Commonwealth*, June 1931, p. 1; Bridgeport Painters Local 190 Minutes, March 21, May 2, 1930, Brotherhood of Painters; Bridgeport Carpenters Local 115 Minutes, April 8, 1930, Brotherhood of Carpenters; *Carpenter*, July 1931, p. 33; *Herald*, March 22 and May 17, 1931, and October 21, 1934;

CFL, *Proceedings*, 1931, 23–25. For national developments on this issue see Irving Bernstein, *Lean Years*, 237–39, 484–85; A. Epstein, "Older Worker"; Patterson, *New Deal and the States*, 12.

66. *New Commonwealth*, first February issue, 1935, p. 1; *New Commonwealth*, second February issue, 1935, p. 1; *Post*, March 16, 1935; *Hartford Courant*, April 18, 19, and 24, 1935. For leftist criticism of the Bridgeport SP's actions see Browder, *Communism in the United States*, 280–81; Devere Allen to Norman Thomas, September 20, 1935, Box 9, Thomas Papers. Cross won only a small cigarette sales tax and some minor revisions of business taxes. The SP income tax was not even debated. An overview of Connecticut labor and social legislation in this era is Mitchell, "Social legislation in Connecticut," 391–445, 463–69.

67. *Times-Star*, January 11, 1935; *New Commonwealth*, first May issue, 1935, p. 4; *New Commonwealth*, second May issue, 1935, p. 3; *New Commonwealth*, June 1935, p. 1; Clifford Wilson to Governor Cross, May 2, 1935, Box 395, Governor Cross Papers-Hartford; William J. Flood to J. Henry Roraback, April 12, 1935, Roraback Papers.

68. The new board assembled on September 5, 1935, to begin its new duties. Board members included Bernard Ashmun, president of Armstrong Manufacturing and member of the executive board of the MAB; Joseph Schultz, general manager of Jenkins Brothers Valve Company, an out-of-town firm that had been supportive of McLevy in the past; one moderate-sized wholesaler; two owners of building contracting firms; and William S. Mason, the real estate manager who had been the GOP mayoral candidate in 1931. McLevy's appointments were deliberately nonpartisan (Minutes, June 20 and September 5, 1935, Board of Apportionment Minute Books).

69. Warner to Alpheus Winter, November 23, 1934, Minute Books, MAB Papers.

70. Note that the refunding bonds were to be used to cover the maturing bonds from previous years. McLevy would repay some outstanding bonds within the next year. Manufacturers' statements are in Minutes, executive board meeting, January 3, 1935, MAB Papers; annual meeting, February 5, 1935, Board of Apportionment Minute Books.

71. *New Commonwealth*, second February issue, 1935, p. 1; *New Commonwealth*, first March issue, 1935, p. 1; CERC Minutes, February 19, March 21, 1935, Box 1A, CERC Records; *Herald*, March 17 and 31, 1935.

72. A merit civil service was considered important for the sort of nonpatronage government envisioned by the SP. It also eliminated the problem of job seekers' flooding the party or of party members' squabbling among themselves, as had happened in other municipalities when the Socialists took over (Olson, "Milwaukee Socialists"; Pratt, "Reading Socialist Experience"). On the police department appointments see "Polly-ticks Says," *Herald*, October 20, 1935.

73. The 1935 municipal platform of the Bridgeport SP appears in Reel 94, Section G, SPA Papers. Pertinent coverage is in *New Commonwealth*, first September issue, 1935, p. 6; *New Commonwealth*, October 1935, p. 1; *Herald*, October 13 and 20, 1935. The split in the national SP was not mentioned.

74. J. A. H. Robinson to Roraback, February 25, 1935, Roraback Papers.

75. *Herald*, October 13 and 20, 1935; *Post*, November 6, 1935. The voter turnout was slightly lower than in the 1933 election (78.5 percent compared to 83.5 percent in 1933). An indication of party enthusiasm for the campaign was evident in the expenditures reported by each party: SP, $3,448; Democrats, $5,025; and GOP, $12,144 (a far cry from the large sums spent on the 1933 race) (*New Commonwealth*, December 1935, p. 1). As one state Democratic leader wrote to James Farley, the national party chief, the following year, "In Bridgeport there does not seem to be a man strong enough within the [Democratic] Party to dominate the situation and I firmly believe that if any place requires a good deal of hard work it is here" (John M. Bailey [Hartford] to James Farley, September 15, 1936, Box 38, OF 300, FDR Papers). Democrats were very worried about the president's chances in Bridgeport in 1936.

76. Schwarz quickly alienated the buildings trades union leaders who had been supportive of Simpson and Thorne, firing union carpenters and replacing them with nonunion men. McLevy wanted him dismissed, but the Connecticut Emergency Relief Commission kept him on as FERA

administrator until the program was replaced by the WPA in early 1936 (Minutes, April 16, 1935, Box 1A, CERC Records; *New Commonwealth,* first April issue, 1935, p. 1; *New Commonwealth,* second April issue, 1935, p. 4; Albert Walkley [Bridgeport Building Trades] to FERA [Washington], July 16, 1935, FERA State Box 46, WPA-DC Records).

77. *Dau's Blue Book for New Haven, Bridgeport, Waterbury,* 1920; *New Haven, Bridgeport and Waterbury Blue Book,* 1929.

78. Buckingham ms., n.d., Rourke ms., 1939, J. P. Driscoll ms., 1939 (all in Box 113), WPA-CtSL Papers; reports by Margaret B. Gerard, October 3, 1935, and March 18, 1939, Reel 167.2, YWCA-National.

79. Rourke interviews, 1939 (Box 112), Buckingham ms., n.d. (Box 113), Rourke ms., 1939 (Box 113), J. P. Driscoll ms., 1939 (Box 113); Fisher ms., n.d. (Box 116), and M. V. Rourke ms., 1939 (Box 116), WPA-CtSL Papers.

80. Allen to Thomas, November 26, 1935, Box 9, Thomas Papers.

81. The New York old guard had received the votes of the Connecticut and Maryland delegates and most of those of the Massachusetts and Pennsylvania delegates. Nonetheless, the vote was 9,449 to 4,809 against New York's old guard.

82. SPA, *1936 Convention Proceedings,* 1936, pp. 224–26, Reel 77, SPA Papers.

83. The national literature on the labor party phenomenon is voluminous. See Lovin, "Persistence of Third-Party Dreams"; Lovin, "Ohio 'Farmer-Labor' Movement in the 1930s"; Lovin, "Fall of Farmer-Labor Parties"; Lovin, "CIO Innovators, Labor Party Ideologues"; Waltzer, "Party and the Polling Place"; Davin, "Very Last Hurrah?"; Gieske, *Minnesota Farmer-Laborism;* Valelly, *Radicalism in the States;* D. Miller, *New American Radicalism.*

84. After much debate at the 1935 Connecticut Federation of Labor convention, the CFL voted to hold a referendum on the labor party question. When the mail referendum, in which only one hundred of the CFL's 585 locals participated, revealed that only twenty-nine had voted for a labor party, the CFL put the issue to rest. Danz was defeated for reelection at this convention as well. Information on this episode in Connecticut labor history is from CFL, *Proceedings,* 1935, 3, 14, 63–64; CFL, *Proceedings,* 1936, 10–17; *New Commonwealth,* July 1935, p. 2; *New Commonwealth,* first September issue, 1935, p. 1; *Herald,* June 21, 1936; *Hartford Times,* July 1, July 30, August 12, September 3, and November 27, 1935, and January 21, 1936 (all clippings in Box 199, WPA-CtSL Papers); Sherman, "Connecticut Forms a Labor Party"; "For a Labor Party in Connecticut" (1935), Box 6, File 1, and "Call for a Connecticut Farmer-Labor Party Conference" (1936), in Box 9, Folder 76, both in Alfred Bingham Papers; *New Haven Journal-Courier,* July 13, 1936; Nathaniel Sherman (New Haven) to Albion Hartwell (New York City), October 25, 1936, Box 11, File 7, Mary Van Kleeck Papers; Fred Schwarzkopf to S. M. Levitas, November 21, 1935, McLevy-Schwarzkopf Papers.

85. McLevy and his slate received 16 percent of the vote cast, considerably better than the 4 percent that Norman Thomas received on the presidential line.

86. McLevy is quoted in Minutes, SDF Executive Board, September 17, 1938, McLevy Letterbox #2, McLevy-Schwarzkopf Papers. I gleaned information about Bridgeport's involvement in SDF from the extensive correspondence in McLevy Letterboxes #1, #2, and #5, McLevy-Schwarzkopf Papers; Series 3, State and Local files, Reel 94, Section G, and SDF Files, Reel 120, SPA Papers; 1936 correspondence between Devere Allen and Norman Thomas, Reel 6, Thomas Papers (microfilm edition); *Herald,* August 9, 1936; *New Commonwealth,* all issues, September 1935 through March–April 1936; *Socialist Call,* June 5, 1937. For background see Shannon, *Socialist Party of America,* 242–46; Johnpoll, *Pacifist's Progress,* 135–77.

87. *Herald,* June 28, 1936; *Times-Star,* October 25, 1937.

88. *Herald,* October 31 and November 7, 1937. The paper interviewed schoolchildren on their parents' political views. The paper noted that for the first time, the polls were open until 6 P.M. in a municipal election, crediting this fact for the large factory turnout.

89. Interview with R. Schmidt by P. K. Russo, 1939, Box 112, WPA-CtSL Papers.

90. Interview with Miss Anderson by Vincent Frazzetta, 1939, Box 26, File 109:22, WPA-UConn

Papers; interview with Mrs. Y. by Russo, 1939, Box 92, WPA-CtSL Papers; *Herald,* September 13, 1936, and October 31, 1937. Also see congratulatory telegram from Labor's Nonpartisan League of Connecticut, November 2, 1937, "Election Congratulation file," McLevy-Schwarzkopf Papers. The Connecticut LNPL's endorsement was a critical, not a positive, one, however; LNPL members noted they were too new to run their own candidates.

91. The state Democratic convention had denied nominations to Labor Commissioner Joseph Tone and other New Deal Democrats, though Governor Cross was renominated. See Connecticut Democratic analyses both before and after the election in Box 42 and Box 15, OF 300, FDR Papers. The strong fear of the McLevy labor vote, conveyed by Democratic Party workers, as well as reports that factory workers throughout the state were putting up McLevy posters and wearing McLevy buttons during the last week of the campaign, is convincing evidence of both a "throw the rascals out" mood and pro–New Deal sentiment among rank-and-file workers. Most of these Democratic reports to Jim Farley urged him to do something about mainstream Connecticut Democratic "coolness" toward the New Deal. Roosevelt, however, kept hands off the Connecticut Democrats.

92. Lonergan to Farley, November 29, 1938, Box 42, OF 300, FDR Papers. Workers in numerous factories, including WPA workers on state projects, wore McLevy buttons in the final days of the campaign (Cross, *Connecticut Yankee,* 415; various letters from Connecticut Democratic leaders in Boxes 15 and 42, OF 300, FDR Papers; see esp. David E. FitzGerald to Farley, October 24 and November 4, 1938, Box 42, and William J. Fitzgerald [Norwich] to Ed Dolan, November 14, 1938, Box 15).

93. Raymond Baldwin, transcript of oral autobiography, 1969–70, 485–491, quote on p. 488. Note that Baldwin needed the 3,000 votes he received on the Union Party line to clinch his close win. On the 1938 elections across the nation see Leuchtenburg, *Franklin D. Roosevelt and the New Deal,* 252–74; Jeffries, *Testing the Roosevelt Coalition;* Burns, *Roosevelt: The Lion and the Fox,* 358–80.

94. *Post,* November 7, 1937.

95. Much New Deal literature has noted the persistence of the machine: Dorsett, *Franklin D. Roosevelt and City Bosses;* Allswang, *Bosses, Machines and Urban Politics;* Stave, *New Deal and the Last Hurrah.* For other examples of manipulation of New Deal relief funds for political advantage, see Trout, *Boston, the Great Depression, and the New Deal,* chaps. 7–8, and Argersinger, *Toward a New Deal in Baltimore.*

96. Wolfinger analyzes nearby New Haven in "Development and Persistence of Ethnic Voting."

97. *Times-Star,* October 29, 1937.

98. *Herald,* October 23, 1932.

99. *Post,* August 21, 1932, and October 29, 1934; *Herald,* October 30 and November 6, 1932. For a further look at the contested discourse of "Americanism" in this era, see Gerstle, *Working-Class Americanism.*

100. Frazzetta ms., Bridgeport, December 1939, Box 25, File 109:19; interview with CIO leader, New Britain [n.d.], Box 49, File 153:7, both in WPA-UConn Papers.

101. See ethnic clipping files, HC-BPL.

102. Slovak residents of the East Side also began to express resentment of African Americans, who were increasingly moving into East Side neighborhoods ("Slovaks of Bridgeport," Frazzetta ms., 1939, Box 93, WPA-CSL). Also see Hungarian interviews, Box 21, File 109:11, WPA-UConn Papers; *Sunday Post,* May 8, 1938. For other examples of ethnic influences on right-wing attitudes and intolerance, see Bayor, *Neighbors in Conflict;* Maiale, *Italian Vote in Philadelphia;* Stack, *International Conflict in an American City.*

103. See Bridgeport Centennial Clipping File, HC-BPL, for particulars. A description of the Yankee bias of the Connecticut tercentenary is in Ducoffe-Barone, "Inventing Tradition." John Bodnar, in *Remaking America,* analyzes the various commemorative impulses in American communities, including native-born and ethnic celebrations of pioneers and patriotism, from the late

nineteenth through the twentieth centuries. However, he neglects the *internal* dynamics within ethnic communities that decided which themes to emphasize.

104. *Herald,* September 6, 1936; *Post,* September 8, 1936; *GE Bridgeport Works News,* September 11, 1936. p. 1.

105. *Post,* July 12, 1938.

Conclusion

1. Although McLevy never again did as well at the state level as he did in 1938, he and his Socialist Party organization were reelected again and again to city hall, until 1957 when Democrats finally defeated him by a narrow margin. That election was marked by Socialist accusations of Democratic voter fraud. Stave, "Great Depression and Urban Political Continuity," presents data that show that McLevy's grassroots support in 1957 remained that same low-income, immigrant electorate that had voted for the SP in 1933, a remarkable continuity of voter alignment that failed in 1957 because it was no longer the majority.

2. The positive, though not completely uncritical, view of the New Deal labor system is represented by Irving Bernstein, *Turbulent Years.* Critical studies that stress the corporatist nature of American labor include Radosh, "Corporate Ideology of American Labor Leaders"; Weinstein, *Corporate Ideal in the Liberal State;* Milton, *Politics of U.S. Labor;* Tomlins, *State and the Unions;* Fraser, "'Labor Question'"; Davis, *Prisoners of the American Dream.* More recently, Staughton Lynd's anthology, *"We Are All Leaders,"* argues that national bureaucratic unions quashed local radical unions during their formative years. Montgomery, "American Workers and the New Deal Formula," stresses the simultaneously liberating and co-optive nature of the New Deal labor relations system. Dubofsky, *State and Labor in Modern America,* argues that labor gained more than it lost from state intervention on behalf of peaceful industrial relations.

3. Some key works are Fine, *Labor and Farmer Parties;* Lovin, "Persistence of Third Party Dreams"; Lovin, "Fall of Farmer-Labor Parties"; Brody, "On the Failure of U.S. Radical Politics"; Davin, "Very Last Hurrah?"

4. Brody, "Labor and the Great Depression." The "job-conscious" label was imposed theoretically by Selig Perlman, *Theory of the Labor Movement,* in 1928.

5. Bodnar, "Immigration, Kinship, and the Rise of Working-Class Realism," argues that the search for security, rather than the search for power, was the goal of ethnic workers in the 1930s. Fraser, "'Labor Question,'" posits a similar argument.

6. Schatz, *Electrical Workers;* Cohen, *Making a New Deal;* Gerstle, *Working-Class Americanism;* Lichtenstein, *Most Dangerous Man in Detroit;* Freeman, *In Transit;* Faue, *Community of Suffering and Struggle;* B. Nelson, *Workers on the Waterfront.*

7. See, especially, the articles by Feurer, "Nutpickers' Union," and Borsos, "'We Make You This Appeal.'" Note that one essay, Davin, "Very Last Hurrah?" addresses labor politics.

8. D. Nelson, "CIO at Bay"; Lovin, "CIO Innovators, Labor Party Ideologues."

Bibliography

Archival Collections

Alfred Bingham Papers, MSS 148, Manuscripts and Archives, Sterling Memorial Library, Yale University, New Haven, Conn.

Amalgamated Clothing Workers of America Papers, Labor-Management Documentation Center, M. P. Catherwood Library, Cornell University, Ithaca, N.Y.

American Federation of Labor Records: The Samuel Gompers Era. (Microfilm edition, Microfilming Corporation of America, 1979)

Anthony Capraro Papers, Immigration History Research Center, University of Minnesota, Minneapolis

Benjamin Schlesinger Papers, International Ladies' Garment Workers' Union Archives, New York, N.Y.

Bridgeport Municipal Records, City Archives, City Hall
 Board of Apportionment and Taxation Minute Books, 1921–36
 Board of Public Charities Minute Books, 1919–22, 1930–34
 Mayors' Files, McLevy Box
 Office of Town Clerk, Articles of Association, 1920–30
 Police Department, Detective Files
 Registrar of Voters, *Book of Elections*

Bridgeport Public Library, Historical Collections
 Alan H. Olmstead Papers
 Bridgeport Area Chamber of Commerce Papers
 Bridgeport Brass Company Collection
 Bridgeport Centennial Clipping File
 Bullard Company Papers
 Ella G. Fleck Papers
 Jasper McLevy and Frederick Schwarzkopf Papers
 Locomobile Company Papers
 Manufacturers' Association of Bridgeport Papers (Manufacturers' Association of Southern Connecticut)
 Newspaper Clipping Files
 Warner Corset Company Papers, DeVer H. Warner Personal Correspondence, 1910–11
 Young Women's Christian Association of Bridgeport Papers

Brotherhood of Carpenters and Joiners, Bridgeport Locals 115, 1013, and District Council Records, in possession of Carpenters Local 99, Bridgeport, Conn. (These records have since been transferred to Historical Collections, Bridgeport Public Library.)

Brotherhood of Painters and Decorators Local 190 Minute Books (1926–30, 1935–41), in possession of Painters Local 1719, Bridgeport, Conn.

Connecticut State AFL-CIO Papers, Historical Manuscripts and Archives, University of Connecticut Libraries, Storrs

Connecticut State Archives, Connecticut State Library, Hartford
    Connecticut Council of Defense Records, RG 30
    Connecticut Public Utility Commission Records
    Emergency Relief Commission, RG 32
    Governors' Papers, RG 5: Wilbur L. Cross, 1931–38; Marcus Holcomb, 1915–20; Everett J. Lake, 1921–23; Charles A. Templeton, 1923–25; John H. Trumbull, 1925–30
    Labor Committee Hearings, General Assembly Legislative Division Records
    Unemployment Commission, RG 31
    Works Progress Administration Federal Writers' Project, RG 33

Consumers League of Connecticut, RG B-77, Schlesinger Library, Radcliffe College, Cambridge, Mass.

Daniel Nash Morgan Papers, RG 69:41, Archives, History, and Genealogy Division, Connecticut State Library, Hartford

David Dubinsky Papers, International Ladies' Garment Workers' Union Archives, New York, N.Y.

Gerald H. Beard Papers (1862–1921), RG 65, Divinity School Library, Yale University, New Haven, Conn.

J. Henry Roraback Papers, in possession of Dr. Edwin Dahill, West Hartford, Conn.

International Association of Machinists Records, Microfilm 550, State Historical Society of Wisconsin, Madison

International Institute of Bridgeport Records, in possession of International Institute of Connecticut, Inc., Bridgeport, Conn. (These records have since been transferred to Historical Collections, Bridgeport Public Library.)

Mary Van Kleeck Papers, Accession #573, Archives of Labor History and Urban Affairs, Wayne State University, Detroit, Mich.

Morris Hillquit Papers, Microfilm Edition, State Historical Society of Wisconsin, Madison

Morris Sigman Papers, International Ladies' Garment Workers' Union Archives, New York, N.Y.

National Archives, Washington, D.C., and Suitland, Md.
    Federal Mediation and Conciliation Service, RG 280
    Military Intelligence G-2, Department of War, RG 165
    National Labor Relations Board, RG 25
    National Recovery Administration, RG 9
    National War Labor Board, RG 2
    President's Organization on Unemployment Relief, RG 73
    Works Progress Administration, RG 69

National Civic Federation Papers, Manuscripts Division, New York Public Library, New York City

Norman Thomas Papers, MSS 79-1880, Manuscripts Division, New York Public Library, New York City (also microfilm edition)

President Franklin D. Roosevelt Papers, OF 300: Official File, Franklin D. Roosevelt Library, Hyde Park, N.Y.

Socialist Collection, Tamiment Library, 1872–1956, Microfilm edition, Glen Rock, N.J.: Microfilming Corporation of America

Socialist Party of America Papers, Microfilm edition, Glen Rock, N.J.: Microfilming Corporation of America

Wilbur Lucius Cross Papers, MSS 155, Manuscripts and Archives, Sterling Memorial Library, Yale University, New Haven, Conn.

Works Progress Administration Federal Writers' Project–Connecticut Papers, University of Connecticut Libraries, Historical Manuscripts and Archives, Storrs (rearranged photocopies of ethnic material from Connecticut WPA Federal Writers' Project, Connecticut State Library)

Young Women's Christian Association, Records Files Collection, National Board Archives, New York, N.Y.

Government Publications

Bailey, William B. *Children Before the Courts of Connecticut.* U.S. Department of Labor, Children's Bureau. Washington, D.C.: U.S. Government Printing Office, 1918.

Bridgeport, City of. Office of Town Clerk. *Articles of Association.* Bridgeport, Conn.: City of Bridgeport, 1920–30.

————. *Bridgeport City Manager Charter, Special Election, Aug. 11, 1917.* Bridgeport, Conn.: City of Bridgeport, 1917.

————. *Municipal Register.* Bridgeport, Conn.: City of Bridgeport, 1915–40.

————. *Official Proceedings of the Common Council.* Bridgeport, Conn.: City of Bridgeport, 1915–36.

————. *Proposed Charter for the City of Bridgeport, November 6, 1923.* Bridgeport, Conn.: City of Bridgeport, 1923.

Connecticut Bureau of Labor Statistics. *Annual Report,* 1916, 1917, 1918, 1919, 1920, 1920–22, 1929. Hartford: State of Connecticut, 1916–29.

Connecticut Bureau of Labor Statistics. "Italian Difficulty at Bridgeport." *Sixteenth Annual Report* (1900): 221–24.

Connecticut Bureau of Labor Statistics. *Report on the Condition of Wage Earners, 1922.* Hartford: State of Connecticut, 1922.

Connecticut Bureau of Labor Statistics. *Report on the Condition of Wage Earners, 1927–28.* Hartford: State of Connecticut, 1928.

Connecticut Emergency Relief Commission. *Experience of the Emergency Relief Commission with Relief Administration in Connecticut.* Hartford: State of Connecticut, 1937.

————. *Report of the Emergency Relief Commission to the Governor, January 1933–December 1934.* Hartford: State of Connecticut, 1934.

Connecticut Secretary of State. *Connecticut Register and Manual, 1931.* Hartford: State of Connecticut, 1931.

Connecticut Secretary of State. *Connecticut Register and Manual, 1935.* Hartford: State of Connecticut, 1935.

Connecticut State Council of Defense. *Report of the Connecticut State Council of Defense, December 1918.* Hartford: Connecticut State Council of Defense, 1919.

Connecticut, State of. *Report of the Commission to Investigate the Condition of Wage-Earning Women and Minors.* Hartford: State of Connecticut, 1913.

Connecticut Tax Commissioner. *Report of the Tax Commissioner for the Biennial Period 1923 and 1924.* Taxation Document No. 211. Hartford: State of Connecticut, 1924.

————. *Supplementary Report of the Tax Commissioner, 1923 and 1924.* Supplement to Taxation Document No. 211. Hartford: State of Connecticut, 1925.

Connecticut Unemployment Commission. *Measures to Alleviate Unemployment in Connecticut.* Hartford: State of Connecticut, 1932.

Connelly, William F. "A Plan for the Taxation of Property in the City of Bridgeport." In *Taxation Document No. 216.* Connecticut Tax Department. Hartford: State of Connecticut, 1926.

Governors' Conference. *Proceedings of the Governors' Conference, Twenty-Fourth Annual Session, Richmond, Va., April 25–27, 1932.* Washington, D.C.: Governors' Conference, 1932.

Manning, Carol. *The Employment of Women in the Sewing Trades of Connecticut.* Bulletin No. 109. U.S. Department of Labor. Women's Bureau. Washington, D.C.: U.S. Government Printing Office, 1935.

New York. Office of the Governor. *Conference on Unemployment and Other Interstate Industrial Problems.* Albany: State of New York, 1931.

New York State Legislature. Joint Committee Investigating Seditious Activities (Lusk Committee). *Revolutionary Radicalism: Its History, Purpose, and Tactics.* 4 Vols. Albany: J. B. Lyons, 1920.

Nolen, John. *Better City Planning for Bridgeport.* Bridgeport, Conn.: City Plan Commission, 1916.

U.S. Census Bureau. *Abstract for Connecticut, 1910* (Washington, D.C.: U.S. Government Printing Office, 1911).

U.S. Census Bureau. *Census of Manufacturers,* 1919, 1929, 1939. Washington, D.C.: U.S. Government Printing Office, 1919, 1929, 1939.

U.S. Census Bureau. *Population.* Thirteenth Census (1910), Fourteenth Census (1920), Fifteenth Census (1930), Sixteenth Census (1940). Washington, D.C.: U.S. Government Printing Office, 1910, 1920, 1930, 1940.

U.S. Department of Labor. Women's Bureau. *The Employment of Women in the Sewing Trades of Connecticut—Preliminary Report.* Bulletin No. 97. Washington, D.C.: U.S. Government Printing Office, 1932.

———. *Home Work in Bridgeport, Connecticut.* Bulletin No. 9. Washington, D.C.: U.S. Government Printing Office, 1919.

U.S. Internal Revenue Service. *Statistics of Income 1926.* Washington, D.C.: U.S. Government Printing Office, 1926.

———. *Statistics of Income, 1930.* Washington, D.C.: U.S. Government Printing Office, 1930.

Wriston, Henry W. *Report of the Connecticut State Council of Defense.* Hartford: State of Connecticut, 1919.

Interviews

Baldwin, Raymond. Oral Autobiography [transcript]. Interview by Morton Tenzer. October–December 1969 and January 1970. Historical Manuscripts and Archives, University of Connecticut Libraries, Storrs.

Bergen, Jack C. Interviews by author. Tape recordings. Bridgeport, Conn., September 3, 1982, and December 16, 1983.

Bucki, Stephen J. Interviews by author. Fairfield, Conn., March 23, 1985, and October 25, 1989.

Donnelly, Jack K. Interview by author. Tape recording. Bridgeport, Conn., November 2, 1987.

Fazekas, Frank. Interview by author. Tape recording. Stratford, Conn., May 22, 1982.

Freedman, Ethel M. Interview by author. Tape recording. Fairfield, Conn., March 12, 1985.

Knepler, Abraham E. Interviews by author. Tape recordings. Bridgeport, Conn., September 29, 1982, and October 4, 1982.

Lavit, L. Herman. Interview by author. Tape recording. Bridgeport, Conn., October 22, 1987.

McLevy, Robert. Interview by author. Bridgeport, Conn., May 16, 1983.

Russo, Michael A. Interviews by author. Tape recordings. Brookline, Mass., September 28, 1983 and March 1, 1990.

Russo, Pearl Kosby. Interviews by author. Tape recordings. Brookline, Mass., September 28, 1983, and March 1, 1990.

Veteran Connecticut Trade Unionists. Panel: "Personal Recollections." Tape recording. New Haven, Conn., September 23, 1983. Personal possession of author.

Wojcicki, Peter J. Interview by author. Stratford, Conn. March 14, 1985.

Newspapers and Periodicals

(New York) Advance, 1923–36
Black Rock (Conn.) Beacon, 1931–32
Black Rock (Conn.) News, 1927–28
Bridgeport Evening Farmer

Bridgeport Labor Leader, 1918–20
Bridgeport Life, 1930–33
Bridgeport Post (and *Telegram*), 1920–36
Bridgeport Progress, 1919–31
Bridgeport Progressive Labor News
Bridgeport Star
Bridgeport Sunday Herald, 1920–36
Bridgeport Times
Bridgeport Times-Star (*Bridgeport Times* in 1925), 1925–36
Bridgeport Works News
Carpenter, 1920–36
Commonwealth (Connecticut), 1925–34
Congressional Quarterly
Congressional Record
Connecticut Industry, 1924–36
Connecticut Labor News (*Connecticut Labor Press,* 1919–21), 1919–25
Daily Worker
Danbury (Conn.) Herald
General Electric Bridgeport Works News, 1926–30, 1936
Hartford Courant
International Molders Journal
Justice, 1919–35
La Sentinella, 1925, 1928
La Vittoria
Labor Age, 1921–30
Labor Herald, 1922–25
Labor Leader
(Hartford) Labor Standard, 1918, 1919, 1922
Ladies' Garment Worker, 1915–18
Machinists' Monthly Journal, 1920–30
MESA Voice
Monthly Labor Review
New Commonwealth (Connecticut), 1935
New Haven Journal-Courier
New York Call
New York Herald
New York Times
Socialist Call
Survey

Books, Articles, and Pamphlets

Aborn, Willard G., and William L. Shafter. "Representative Shop Committees." *Industrial Management* 58 (July 1919): 29–32.
Allen, Frederick Lewis. *Only Yesterday: An Informal History of the Nineteen-Twenties.* New York: Blue Ribbon, 1931.
Allswang, John M. *Bosses, Machines and Urban Politics.* New York: Kennikat, 1977.
———. *A House for All Peoples: Ethnic Politics in Chicago, 1890–1936.* Lexington: University Press of Kentucky, 1971.
Alvarez, David J., and Edmond J. True. "Critical Elections and Partisan Realignment: An Urban Test Case." *Polity* 5 (Summer 1973): 563–76.

Amalgamated Clothing Workers of America. *Documentary History of the Amalgamated Clothing Workers of America.* Vols. 1–11. New York: Amalgamated Clothing Workers of America, 1914–36.

Amalgamated Clothing Workers of America. Local 125. *The Shirt and Clothing Workers of Connecticut, 1933–1943.* New Haven, Conn.: ACWA, 1943.

American Civil Liberties Union. *Annual Report, 1932–33.* New York: ACLU, 1933.

———. *The Police and the Radicals: What 88 Police Chiefs Think and Do About Radical Meetings.* New York: ACLU, 1921.

Andersen, Kristi. *The Creation of a Democratic Majority, 1928–1936.* Chicago: University of Chicago Press, 1979.

Anker, Laura. "Immigrant Voices from the Federal Writers' Project: The Connecticut Ethnic Survey, 1937–1940." In *The Mythmaking Frame of Mind: Social Imagination and American Culture.* Ed. James Gilbert, Amy Gilman, Donald M. Scott, and Joan W. Scott. 270–302. Belmont, Calif.: Wadsworth, 1993.

Argersinger, Jo Ann E. *Toward a New Deal in Baltimore: People and Government in the Great Depression.* Chapel Hill: University of North Carolina Press, 1988.

Asher, Robert. "Union Nativism and the Immigrant Response." *Labor History* 23 (Summer 1982): 325–48.

Bakke, E. Wight. *Citizens without Work.* New Haven, Conn.: Yale University Press, 1940.

Balderston, C. Canby. *Executive Guidance of Industrial Relations: An Analysis of the Experience of 25 Companies.* Philadelphia: University of Pennsylvania Press, 1935.

Bane, Frank. "Public Welfare." In *What the Depression Has Done to Cities.* Ed. Clarence E. Ridley and Orin F. Nolting. 14–17. Chicago: International City Managers' Association, 1935.

Banks, Ann, ed. *First-Person America.* New York: Alfred A. Knopf, 1980.

Barany, George. "The Magyars." In *The Immigrants' Influence on Wilson's Peace Policies.* Ed. Joseph P. O'Grady. 140–72. Lexington: University Press of Kentucky, 1967.

Barrett, James R. "Americanization from the Bottom Up: Immigration and the Remaking of the Working Class in the United States, 1880–1930." *Journal of American History* 79 (December 1992): 996–1020.

Barrett, James R., and David Roediger. "Inbetween Peoples: Race, Nationality, and the 'New Immigrant' Working Class." *Journal of American Ethnic History* 16 (Spring 1997): 3–44.

Barton, Josef J. *Peasants and Strangers: Italians, Rumanians, and Slovaks in an American City, 1890–1950.* Cambridge, Mass.: Harvard University Press, 1975.

Bayor, Ronald H. *Neighbors in Conflict: The Irish, Germans, Jews, and Italians of New York City, 1929–1941.* Baltimore, Md.: Johns Hopkins University Press, 1978.

Beard, Charles A., ed. *America Faces the Future.* Boston: Houghton Mifflin, 1932.

Bedford, Henry F. *Socialism and the Workers in Massachusetts, 1886–1912.* Amherst: University of Massachusetts Press, 1966.

Beito, David T. *Taxpayers in Revolt: Tax Resistance During the Great Depression.* Chapel Hill: University of North Carolina Press, 1989.

Beney, M. Ada. *Cost of Living in the United States, 1914–1936.* NICB Studies No. 228. New York: National Industrial Conference Board, 1936.

Berkowitz, Edward, and Kim McQuaid. *Creating the Welfare State: The Political Economy of Twentieth-Century Reform.* 2d ed. New York: Praeger, 1988.

Bernstein, Irving. *The Lean Years: A History of the American Worker, 1920–1933.* Boston: Houghton Mifflin, 1960.

———. *The Turbulent Years: A History of the American Worker, 1933–1941.* Boston: Houghton Mifflin, 1969.

Bernstein, Iver. "Expanding the Boundaries of the Political: Workers and Political Change in the Nineteenth Century." *International Labor and Working-Class History* 32 (Fall 1987): 59–75.

Beynon, Erdmann D. "Crime and Custom of the Hungarians of Detroit." *Journal of Criminal Law and Criminology* 25 (January–February 1935): 755–74.

Bibliography

Bilevitz, William. "The Connecticut Needle Trades." *Nation,* November 16, 1932, pp. 475–77.

Bing, Alexander. *Wartime Strikes and Their Adjustment.* New York: E. P. Dutton, 1921.

Blodgett, William. "Property Tax Troubles Ad Lib." *Connecticut Industry,* January 1924, pp. 5–9.

Bodnar, John. "Immigration, Kinship, and the Rise of Working-Class Realism in Industrial America." *Journal of Social History* 14 (Fall 1980): 45–59.

———. *Remaking America: Public Memory, Commemoration, and Patriotism in the Twentieth Century.* Princeton, N.J.: Princeton University Press, 1992.

———. *The Transplanted: A History of Immigration in Urban America.* Bloomington: Indiana University Press, 1985.

Bodnar, John, Roger Simon, and Michael P. Weber. *Lives of Their Own: Blacks, Italians, and Poles in Pittsburgh, 1900–1960.* Urbana: University of Illinois Press, 1982.

Bonnett, Clarence E. *Employers' Associations in the United States: A Study of Typical Associations.* New York: Macmillan, 1922.

Borkowski, Joseph A. "The Role of Pittsburgh's Polish Falcons in the Organization of the Polish Army in France." *Western Pennsylvania Historical Magazine* 54 (October 1971): 359–74.

Bornet, Vaughn Davis. *Labor Politics in a Democratic Republic: Moderation, Division, and Disruption in the Presidential Election of 1928.* Washington, D.C.: Spartan Books, 1964.

Borsos, John. "'We Make You This Appeal in the Name of Every Union Man and Woman in Barberton': Solidarity Unionism in Barberton, Ohio." In *"We Are All Leaders": The Alternative Unionism of the Early 1930s.* Ed. Staughton Lynd. 238–93. Urbana: University of Illinois Press, 1996.

Bowen, George. "The Conquest of Bridgeport." *Machinists' Monthly Journal,* May 1916, pp. 553–54.

Braeman, John, Robert H. Bremner, and David Brody, eds. *The New Deal.* Vol. 2: *The State and Local Levels.* Columbus: Ohio State University Press, 1975.

Brandes, Stuart D. *American Welfare Capitalism, 1880–1940.* Chicago: University of Chicago Press, 1976.

Breckinridge, S. P. *New Homes for Old.* New York: Harper and Brothers, 1921.

Brewer, Daniel Chauncey. *The Conquest of New England by the Immigrant.* New York: G. P. Putnam's Sons, 1926.

Bridgeport Brass Company. "A Historical Sketch of Bridgeport Brass Company, 1865–1925." Pamphlet reprinted from *Metal Industry* 23 (August 1925).

———. *Industrial Manual.* Bridgeport, Conn.: Bridgeport Brass, 1919.

———. *Sick Benefit Association of the Bridgeport Brass Company—By-Laws.* Bridgeport, Conn.: Bridgeport Brass, 1917.

Bridgeport City Directory. Bridgeport, Conn.: Price and Lee, 1920–40.

"Bridgeport's Victory—A Portent?" *World Tomorrow,* November 23, 1933, pp. 627–28.

Bridges, Amy. "Becoming American: The Working Classes in the United States Before the Civil War." In *Working-Class Formation: Nineteenth-Century Patterns in Western Europe and the United States.* Ed. Ira Katznelson and Aristide R. Zolberg. 157–96. Princeton, N.J.: Princeton University Press, 1986.

———. *A City in the Republic: Antebellum New York and the Origins of Machine Politics.* Ithaca, N.Y.: Cornell University Press, 1984.

Briggs, John W. *An Italian Passage: Immigrants to Three American Cities, 1890–1930.* New Haven, Conn.: Yale University Press, 1978.

Brilliant, Eleanor L. *The United Way: Dilemmas of Organized Charity.* New York: Columbia University Press, 1990.

Broderick, John Thomas. *40 Years with General Electric.* Albany, N.Y.: Fort Orange Press, 1929.

Brody, David. "The Course of American Labor Politics." In *In Labor's Cause: Main Themes on the History of the American Worker.* 43–80. New York: Oxford University Press, 1993.

———. "Labor and the Great Depression—Interpretive Prospects." *Labor History* 13 (Spring 1972): 231–44.

————. "On the Failure of U.S. Radical Politics: A Farmer-Labor Analysis." *Industrial Relations* 22 (Spring 1983): 141–63.

————. "The Rise and Decline of Welfare Capitalism." In *Workers in Industrial America: Essays on the Twentieth Century Struggle.* 48–81. New York: Oxford University Press, 1980.

Browder, Earl. *Communism in the United States.* New York: International Publishers, 1935.

Brown, M. Craig, and Charles N. Halaby. "Machine Politics in America, 1870–1945." *Journal of Interdisciplinary History* 17 (Winter 1987): 587–612.

Bruère, Robert W. "West Lynn." *Survey* 56 (April 1, 1926): 21–27, 49.

Bucki, Cecelia. "Dilution and Craft Tradition: Bridgeport, Connecticut, Munitions Workers in 1915–1919." *Social Science History* 4 (February 1980): 105–24.

————. "Dilution and Craft Tradition: Munitions Workers in Bridgeport, Connecticut, 1915–1919." In *The New England Working Class and the New Labor History.* Ed. Herbert G. Gutman and Donald M. Bell. 137–56. Urbana: University of Illinois Press, 1987.

————. *Metal, Minds, and Machines: Waterbury at Work.* Waterbury, Conn.: Mattatuck Historical Society, 1980.

————. "Workers and Politics in the Immigrant City in the Early Twentieth Century U.S." *International Labor and Working-Class History* 48 (Fall 1995): 28–48.

Buczek, Daniel S. *Immigrant Pastor: The Life of the Right Reverend Monsignor Lucyan Bójnowski of New Britain, Connecticut.* Waterbury, Conn.: Heminway, 1974.

Budenz, Louis Francis. "'Democracy' à la General Electric." *Labor Age* 16 (July 1927): 15–16.

————. "Genesis at West Lynn." *Labor Age* 16 (February 1927): 15–17.

————. "Jehu's Driving at West Lynn." *Labor Age* 16 (April 1927): 15–17.

————. "Jonah's Whale at West Lynn." *Labor Age* 16 (March 1927): 15–17.

————. "Wife in Name Only." *Labor Age* 16 (January 1927): 2–3.

Buenker, John D. "The Politics of Resistance: The Rural-Based Yankee Republican Machines of Connecticut and Rhode Island." *New England Quarterly* 47 (June 1974): 212–37.

————. *Urban Liberalism and Progressive Reform.* New York: Charles Scribner's Sons, 1973.

Bukowczyk, John J. "The Transformation of Working-Class Ethnicity: Corporate Control, Americanization, and the Polish Immigrant Middle-Class in Bayonne, N.J., 1915–1925." *Labor History* 25 (Winter 1984): 53–82.

"Bullard Maxi-Pay Plan." *American Machinist* 44 (May 25, 1916): 922.

Bullard, S. H. "Organization Plan That Typifies Modern Management." *Industrial Management* 60 (December 1920): 441–44.

Burner, David. *The Politics of Provincialism: The Democratic Party in Transition, 1918–1932.* New York: W. W. Norton, 1967.

Burnham, Walter Dean. "The Changing Shape of the American Political Universe." *American Political Science Review* 59 (March 1965): 7–28.

————. *Critical Elections and the Mainsprings of American Politics.* New York: W. W. Norton, 1970.

————. "The System of 1896: An Analysis." In *The Evolution of American Electoral Systems.* Ed. Paul Kleppner. 147–202. Westport, Conn.: Greenwood, 1981.

Burns, James MacGregor. *Roosevelt: The Lion and the Fox, 1882–1940.* New York: Harcourt Brace Jovanovich, 1956.

Burpee, Charles Winslow. *Burpee's The Story of Connecticut.* 4 Vols. New York: American Historical Co., 1939.

Burton, Ernest Richmond. *Employee Representation.* Baltimore, Md.: Williams and Wilkins, 1926.

Carter, Richard. *The Gentle Legions: National Voluntary Health Organizations in America.* 1961. Reprint, New Brunswick, N.J.: Transaction Publishers, 1992.

Casey, Ralph D. "Scripps-Howard Newspapers in the 1928 Presidential Campaign." *Journalism Quarterly* 7 (September 1930): 209–31.

Central Labor Union of Bridgeport and Vicinity. *Centennial Illustrated History of the City of Bridgeport, Connecticut and the Central Labor Union of Bridgeport and Vicinity and Its Affiliated Organizations.* Bridgeport, Conn.: Central Labor Union of Bridgeport, 1900.

Chatters, Carl H. "Municipal Finance." In *What the Depression Has Done to Cities.* Ed. Clarence E. Ridley and Orin F. Nolting. 1–6. Chicago: International City Managers' Association, 1935.

Chenery, William L. "Mr. Zero, the Man Who Feeds the Hungry." *Survey* 47 (October 1, 1921): 15.

Christie, Robert A. *Empire in Wood: A History of the Carpenters' Union.* Ithaca, N.Y.: Cornell University Press, 1956.

Clark, Florence M. "Employment Conditions and Unemployment Relief." *Monthly Labor Review* 40 (March 1935): 626–34.

Cohen, Lizabeth. *Making a New Deal: Industrial Workers in Chicago, 1919–1939.* New York: Cambridge University Press, 1990.

Colcord, Joanna C., William Koplovitz, and Russell H. Kurtz. *Emergency Work Relief: As Carried Out in Twenty-Six American Communities, 1930–1931.* New York: Russell Sage Foundation, 1932.

Connecticut Chamber of Commerce. *The Finances of Connecticut.* N.p., n.d. [1921].

———. *Report of the Joint Committee on Taxation and State Finance to the Connecticut Chamber of Commerce.* New Haven: Connecticut Chamber of Commerce, 1917.

Connecticut Federation of Labor. *Proceedings of the Annual Convention.* Bridgeport: Connecticut Federation of Labor, Annual, 1920–32, 1934–36.

Connor, Valerie Jean. *The National War Labor Board: Stability, Social Justice, and the Voluntary State in World War I.* Chapel Hill: University of North Carolina Press, 1983.

Consumers' League of Connecticut. *The Department Store Girl and Her Friend in "the Five and Ten."* Pamphlet. N.p.: Consumers League of Connecticut, 1915.

Conzen, Kathleen Neils, David A. Gerber, Ewa Morawska, George E. Pozzetta, and Rudolph J. Vecoli. "The Invention of Ethnicity: A Perspective from the U.S.A." *Journal of American Ethnic History* 12 (Fall 1992): 3–41.

Cross, Wilbur L. *Connecticut Yankee: An Autobiography.* New Haven, Conn.: Yale University Press, 1943.

Cummings, Scott, ed. *Self-Help in Urban America: Patterns of Minority Business Enterprise.* Port Washington, N.Y.: Kennikat, 1980.

Dahl, Robert A. *Who Governs? Democracy and Power in an American City.* New Haven, Conn.: Yale University Press, 1961.

Dahlheimer, Harry. *A History of the Mechanics Educational Society of America in Detroit from Its Inception in 1933 through 1937.* Detroit, Mich.: Wayne State University Press, 1951.

Danenberg, Elsie Nicholas. *The Story of Bridgeport.* Bridgeport, Conn.: Bridgeport Centennial, 1936.

Daniels, Roger. *Coming to America: A History of Immigration and Ethnicity in American Life.* New York: HarperCollins, 1990.

Dau's Blue Book for New Haven, Bridgeport, Waterbury. 12th ed. New York: Dau's Blue Books, 1920.

Davin, Eric Leif. "The Very Last Hurrah? The Defeat of the Labor Party Idea, 1934–36." In *"We Are All Leaders": The Alternative Unionism of the Early 1930s.* Ed. Staughton Lynd. 117–71. Urbana: University of Illinois Press, 1996.

Davis, Mike. *Prisoners of the American Dream: Politics and Economy in the History of the U.S. Working Class.* London: Verso, 1986.

Dawson, Andrew. "The Parameters of Craft Consciousness: The Social Outlook of the Skilled Worker, 1890–1920." In *American Labor and Immigration History, 1877–1920s: Recent European Research.* Ed. Dirk Hoerder. 135–55. Urbana: University of Illinois Press, 1983.

DeLeon, Solon. *The American Labor Who's Who.* New York: Hanford Press, 1925.

Diamond, H. M. "Connecticut Study of Street Trades." *American Child* 4 (August 1922): 97–103.

Dilling, Elizabeth. *The Red Network: A "Who's Who" and Handbook of Radicalism for Patriots.* Chicago: Elizabeth Dilling, 1934.

Directory of Directors in the State of Connecticut. 12th ed. Boston: Bankers Service, 1931.

Dorsett, Lyle W. *Franklin D. Roosevelt and the City Bosses.* Port Washington, N.Y.: Kennikat, 1977.

Douglas, Paul H. *Real Wages in the United States, 1890–1923.* Boston: Houghton Mifflin, 1930.

Dubofsky, Melvyn. *The State and Labor in Modern America.* Chapel Hill: University of North Carolina Press, 1994.

Ducoffe-Barone, Deborah. "Inventing Tradition: The Connecticut Tercentenary Medal and Card of 1935." *Connecticut History* 32 (1991): 1–24.

Dun, R.G. *Reference Book, March 1920.* New York: R. G. Dun, 1920.

Dunn, Robert W. *Company Unions: Employers' "Industrial Democracy."* New York: Vanguard, 1927.

"Editorial: Connecticut Socialism." *International Socialist Review* 14 (March 1914): 562–63.

Egan, John J. "What Is Wrong with the Machinists Today?" *Machinists' Monthly Journal,* April 1924, pp. 178–79.

Eley, Geoff, and Keith Nield. "Why Does Social History Ignore Politics?" *Social History* 5 (May 1980): 249–71.

Embardo, Robert J. "'Summer Lightning,' 1907: The Wobblies in Bridgeport." *Labor History* 30 (Fall 1989): 518–35.

Emmons, David. "An Aristocracy of Labor: The Irish Miners of Butte, 1880–1914." *Labor History* 28 (1987): 275–306.

Epstein, Abraham. "The Older Worker." *Annals of the American Academy of Political and Social Science* 154 (March 1931): 28–31.

Epstein, Melech. *Jewish Labor in U.S.A.* 1950/1953. Reprint, New York: KTAV Publishing, 1969.

Erlich, Mark. *With Our Hands: The Story of Carpenters in Massachusetts.* Philadelphia: Temple University Press, 1986.

"Ex Cathedra." *World Tomorrow* 16 (November 23, 1933): 628.

Faue, Elizabeth. *Community of Suffering and Struggle: Women, Men, and the Labor Movement in Minneapolis, 1915–1945.* Chapel Hill: University of North Carolina Press, 1991.

Fay, Charles Norman. *Business in Politics: Considerations for Business Leaders.* Cambridge, Mass.: Cosmos Press, 1926.

Fearon, Peter. *War, Prosperity, and Depression: The U.S. Economy, 1917–1945.* Lawrence: University Press of Kansas, 1987.

Feder, Leah Hannah. *Unemployment Relief in Periods of Depression.* 1936. Reprint, New York: Arno, 1971.

Feurer, Rosemary. "The Nutpickers' Union, 1933–34: Crossing the Boundaries of Community and Workplace." In *"We Are All Leaders": The Alternative Unionism of the Early 1930s.* Ed. Staughton Lynd. 27–50. Urbana: University of Illinois Press, 1996.

Fine, Nathan. *Labor and Farmer Parties in the United States, 1828–1928.* New York: Rand School of Social Science, 1928.

Fink, Leon. *Workingmen's Democracy: The Knights of Labor and American Politics.* Urbana: University of Illinois Press, 1983.

Foner, Eric. "Why Is There No Socialism in the United States?" *History Workshop Journal* 17 (1984): 57–80.

Fox, Jay. *Amalgamation.* Labor Herald Library No. 5. Chicago: Trade Union Educational League, 1923.

Frank, Dana. *Purchasing Power: Consumer Organizing, Gender, and the Seattle Labor Movement, 1919–1929.* New York: Cambridge University Press, 1994.

Fraser, Steve. "The 'Labor Question.'" In *The Rise and Fall of the New Deal Order, 1930–1980.* Ed. Steve Fraser and Gary Gerstle. 55–84. Princeton, N.J.: Princeton University Press, 1989.

———. *Labor Will Rule: Sidney Hillman and the Rise of American Labor.* New York: Free Press, 1991.

Fraser, Steve, and Gary Gerstle, eds. *The Rise and Fall of the New Deal Order, 1930–1980.* Princeton, N.J.: Princeton University Press, 1989.

Fraternal Monitor. *Statistics, Fraternal Benefit Societies.* Rochester, N.Y.: Fraternal Monitor, 1930–40.

Freeman, Joshua B. *In Transit: The Transport Workers Union in New York City, 1933–1966.* New York: Oxford University Press, 1989.

Gabaccia, Donna. *From Sicily to Elizabeth Street: Housing and Social Change Among Italian Immigrants, 1880–1930.* Albany: State University of New York Press, 1984.

Galenson, Walter. *The United Brotherhood of Carpenters: The First Hundred Years.* Cambridge, Mass.: Harvard University Press, 1983.

Gamm, Gerald H. *The Making of New Deal Democrats: Voting Behavior and Realignment in Boston, 1920–1940.* Chicago: University of Chicago Press, 1989.

Gavit, John P. *Americans by Choice.* New York: Harper Brothers, 1922.

Gay, Peter. *The Dilemma of Democratic Socialism: Eduard Bernstein's Challenge to Marx.* New York: Columbia University Press, 1952.

Geller, Herbert F. "Bridgeport, the Ethnic City." Reprints of Ethnic History Series from *Bridgeport Sunday Post,* 1977–80. Bridgeport Board of Education, Bridgeport, Conn., 1981.

Gerson, Louis L. "The Poles." In *The Immigrants' Influence on Wilson's Peace Policies.* Ed. Joseph P. O'Grady. 272–86. Lexington: University of Kentucky Press, 1967.

———. *Woodrow Wilson and the Rebirth of Poland, 1914–1920.* New Haven, Conn.: Yale University Press, 1953.

Gerstle, Gary. "Liberty, Coercion, and the Making of Americans." *Journal of American History* 84 (September 1997): 524–58.

———. *Working-Class Americanism: The Politics of Labor in a Textile City, 1914–1960.* New York: Cambridge University Press, 1989.

Gieske, Millard. *Minnesota Farmer-Laborism: The Third Party Alternative.* Minneapolis: University of Minnesota Press, 1979.

Gitelman, H. M. "Being of Two Minds: American Employers Confront the Labor Problem, 1915–1919." *Labor History* 25 (Spring 1984): 189–216.

Goldberg, David J. *A Tale of Three Cities: Labor Organization and Protest in Paterson, Passaic, and Lawrence, 1916–1921.* New Brunswick, N.J.: Rutgers University Press, 1989.

Graham, Otis L., Jr., ed. *The New Deal: The Critical Issues.* Boston: Little, Brown, 1971.

Greene, Julie. *Pure and Simple Politics: The American Federation of Labor, 1881 to 1917.* New York: Cambridge University Press, 1998.

Greene, Victor R. *American Immigrant Leaders, 1800–1910: Marginality and Identity.* Baltimore, Md.: Johns Hopkins University Press, 1987.

Greenwald, Maurine Weiner. *Women, War, and Work: The Impact of World War I on Women Workers in the United States.* Westport, Conn.: Greenwood, 1980.

Griffen, Bulkley S. "Roraback of Connecticut." *New Republic,* November 26, 1930, pp. 41–43.

Grubbs, Frank L., Jr. *The Struggle for Labor Loyalty: Gompers, the A.F. of L., and the Pacifists, 1917–1920.* Durham, N.C.: Duke University Press, 1968.

Haber, William. "Building Construction." In *How Collective Bargaining Works.* Ed. Harry A. Millis. 183–228. New York: Twentieth Century Fund, 1942.

———. *Industrial Relations in the Building Trades.* Cambridge, Mass.: Harvard University Press, 1930.

Halpern, Rick, and Jonathan Morris, eds. *American Exceptionalism? U.S. Working-Class Formation in an International Context.* New York: St. Martin's, 1997.

Hanagan, Michael. "Response to Wilentz's 'Against Exceptionalism.'" *International Labor and Working Class History* 26 (Fall 1984): 31–36.

Hardman, J. B. S. *American Labor Dynamics in the Light of Post-War Developments.* New York: Harcourt, Brace, 1928.

Hareven, Tamara K. *Family Time and Industrial Time: The Relationship between the Family and Work in a New England Industrial Community.* New York: Cambridge University Press, 1982.

Harney, Robert F. "Montreal's King of Italian Labour: A Case Study of Padronism." *Labour/Le Travailleur* 4 (1979): 57–84.

Harris, Joseph P. *Registration of Voters in the United States.* Washington, D.C.: Brookings Institution, 1929.

Hartz, Louis. *The Liberal Tradition in America.* New York: Harcourt, Brace and World, 1955.

Hatch, Alden. *Remington Arms in American History.* New York: Rinehart, 1956.

Havadtoy, Magdalene. *Down in Villa Park: Hungarians in Fairfield.* West Hartford, Conn.: News Press, 1976.

Haynes, John Earl. *Dubious Alliance: The Making of Minnesota's DFL Party.* Minneapolis: University of Minnesota Press, 1984.

Hays, Samuel P. *American Political History as Social Analysis: Essays.* Knoxville: University of Tennessee Press, 1980.

———. "Politics and Society: Beyond the Political Party." In *The Evolution of American Electoral Systems.* Ed. Paul Kleppner. 243–67. Westport, Conn.: Greenwood, 1981.

———. "The Politics of Reform in Municipal Government in the Progressive Era." *Pacific Northwest Quarterly* 55 (October 1964): 157–69.

———. *The Response to Industrialism, 1885–1914.* Chicago: University of Chicago Press, 1957.

Heer, Clarence. "Trends in Taxation and Public Finance." President's Research Committee on Social Trends. In *Recent Social Trends in the United States.* 2:1331–90. New York: McGraw-Hill, 1933.

Heisterman, Carl A. "Statutory Provisions Relating to Legal Settlement for Purposes of Poor-Relief." *Social Service Review* 7 (March 1933): 95–106.

Helmbold, Lois Rita. "Downward Occupational Mobility During the Great Depression: Urban Black and White Working-Class Women." *Labor History* 29 (Spring 1988): 135–72.

Hewes, Amy. "Bridgeport on the Rebound." *Survey* 37 (October 14, 1916): 49–51.

———. *Women as Munition Makers: A Study of Conditions in Bridgeport, Connecticut.* New York: Russell Sage Foundation, 1917.

Hicks, John D. *Republican Ascendancy, 1921–1933.* New York: Harper and Brothers, 1960.

Higham, John. *Strangers in the Land: Patterns of American Nativism, 1860–1925.* New York: Atheneum, 1965.

Higham, John, ed. *Ethnic Leadership in America.* Baltimore, Md.: Johns Hopkins University Press, 1978.

Hiller, Ernest T. *The Strike: A Study in Collective Action.* Chicago: University of Chicago Press, 1928.

Hoan, Daniel W. *Taxes and Tax Dodgers.* Chicago: Socialist Party of America, 1933.

Hook, James W. "Industry's Obligation to the Unemployed." *Mechanical Engineering* 53 (October 1931): 707–13.

———. "The Unemployed—What Shall We Do with Them? A Complete Plan of Unemployment Relief for the Future." Address to American Society of Mechanical Engineers, December 2, 1931, New York City. Pamphlet. Miscellaneous Publications on Unemployment, Mudd Library, Yale University, New Haven, Conn.

"How the Cities Stand." *Survey* 68 (April 15, 1932): 71–75, 92.

Hunter, Robert. "The Trade Unions and the Socialist Party: Part X—The Bridgeport Plan." *Miners Magazine* 12 (April 29, 1912): 10–11.

Huthmacher, J. Joseph. *Massachusetts People and Politics, 1919–1933.* Cambridge, Mass.: Harvard University Press, 1959.

———. "Urban Liberalism and the Age of Reform." *Mississippi Valley Historical Review* 49 (September 1962): 231–41.

International Ladies' Garment Workers' Union. *Proceedings of the Convention, 15th (1920)–23rd (1937).* New York: ILGWU, 1920–37.

"In the Name of Right and Justice." *Suffragist* 7 (January 25, 1919): 8–9.

Jacobson, Matthew Frye. *Whiteness of a Different Color: European Immigrants and the Alchemy of Race.* Cambridge, Mass.: Harvard University Press, 1998.

Jacoby, Sanford M. *Employing Bureaucracy: Managers, Unions, and the Transformation of Work in American Industry, 1900–1945.* New York: Columbia University Press, 1985.

———. "Industrial Labor Mobility in Historical Perspective." *Industrial Relations* 22 (Spring 1983): 261–82.

Janick, Herbert. *A Diverse People: Connecticut, 1914 to the Present.* Chester, Conn.: Pequot Press, 1975.

———. "Senator Frank B. Brandegee and the Election of 1920." *Historian* 35 (May 1973): 434–51.

Jeffries, John W. *Testing the Roosevelt Coalition: Connecticut Society and Politics in the Era of World War II.* Knoxville: University of Tennessee Press, 1979.

Jensen, Richard. "The Last Party System: Decay of Consensus, 1932–1980." In *The Evolution of American Electoral Systems.* Ed. Paul Kleppner. 203–41. Westport, Conn.: Greenwood, 1981.

Johnpoll, Bernard K. *Pacifist's Progress: Norman Thomas and the Decline of American Socialism.* Chicago: Quadrangle, 1970.

Johnson, Charles S. "The Negro Population of Waterbury, Connecticut: A Survey." *Opportunity: Journal of Negro Life* 1 (November 1923): 298–302, 338–42.

Judd, Richard W. *Socialist Cities: Municipal Politics and the Grass Roots of American Socialism.* Albany: State University of New York Press, 1989.

Kammen, Michael. "The Problem of American Exceptionalism: A Reconsideration." *American Quarterly* 45 (March 1993): 1–43.

Kansas, Sidney. *Citizenship of the United States of America.* New York: Washington Publishing, 1936.

Kantowicz, Edward R. *Polish-American Politics in Chicago, 1888–1940.* Chicago: University of Chicago Press, 1975.

Katz, Michael B. *In the Shadow of the Poorhouse: A Social History of Welfare in America.* New York: Basic, 1986.

Katznelson, Ira. *City Trenches: Urban Politics and the Patterning of Class in the United States.* New York: Pantheon, 1981.

———. "Comment on McDonald's 'The Burdens of Urban History.'" *Studies in American Political Development* 3 (1989): 30–51.

Kazal, Russell A. "Revisiting Assimilation: The Rise, Fall and Reappraisal of a Concept in American Ethnic History." *American Historical Review* 100 (April 1995): 437–71.

Kazin, Michael. *Barons of Labor: The San Francisco Building Trades and Union Power in the Progressive Era.* Urbana: University of Illinois Press, 1987.

Keeran, Roger. "The International Workers Order and the Origins of the CIO." *Labor History* 30 (Summer 1989): 385–408.

Kessler-Harris, Alice. *Out to Work: A History of Wage-Earning Women in the United States.* New York: Oxford University Press, 1982.

———. "Social History." In *The New American History.* Ed. Eric Foner. 163–84. Philadelphia: Temple University Press, 1990.

Key, V. O. "A Theory of Critical Elections." *Journal of Politics* 17 (February 1955): 3–18.

Kipnis, Ira. *The American Socialist Movement, 1897–1912.* New York: Columbia University Press, 1952.

Klaszynska, Barbara. "Why Women Work: A Comparison of Various Groups in Philadelphia, 1910–1930." *Labor History* 17 (Winter 1976): 73–87.

Klein, Philip. *The Burden of Unemployment: A Study of Unemployment Relief Measures in Fifteen American Cities, 1921–22.* New York: Russell Sage Foundation, 1923.

Kleppner, Paul. *Who Voted? The Dynamics of Electoral Turnout, 1870–1980.* New York: Praeger, 1982.

Knepler, Abraham. "Socialism's Forward March—Bridgeport." *Commonwealth,* August 1934, p. 11.

Koren, John. "The Padrone System and Padrone Banks." *Bulletin of the U.S. Department of Labor* 9 (March 1897): 113–27.

Kousser, J. Morgan. *The Shaping of Southern Politics: Suffrage Restriction and the Establishment of the One-Party South, 1880–1910.* New Haven, Conn.: Yale University Press, 1974.

Kreas, Saul. *My Life and Struggle for a Better World.* New Haven, Conn.: Saul Kreas and Joelle Fishman, 1977.

Labor Research Association. *Labor Fact Book 1.* New York: International Publishers, 1931.

Labor Research Association. *Labor Fact Book 3.* New York: International Publishers, 1936.

Laidler, Harry W. "The Month: Labor in America." *Labor Age* 10 (November 1921): 18–19.

Laidler, Harry W., and Norman Thomas, eds. *New Tactics in Social Conflict.* New York: Vanguard, 1926.

Lancaster, Lane W. "The Background of a State 'Boss' System." *American Journal of Sociology* 35 (March 1930): 783–98.

———. "The Democratic Party in Connecticut." *National Municipal Review* 17 (August 1928): 451–55.

———. "Rotten Boroughs and the Connecticut Legislature." *National Municipal Review* 13 (December 1924): 678–83.

Lane, A. T. "American Unions, Mass Immigration, and the Literacy Test, 1900–1917." *Labor History* 25 (Winter 1984): 5–25.

Laslett, John H. M. *Labor and the Left: A Study of Socialist and Radical Influences in the American Labor Movement, 1881–1924.* New York: Basic, 1970.

Laurie, Bruce. *Working People of Philadelphia, 1800–1850.* Philadelphia: Temple University Press, 1980.

Leab, Daniel J. "'United We Eat': The Creation and Organization of the Unemployed Councils in 1930." *Labor History* 8 (Fall 1967): 300–315.

Leff, Mark H. *The Limits of Symbolic Reform: The New Deal and Taxation, 1933–1939.* New York: Cambridge University Press, 1984.

Leinenweber, Charles. "The Class and Ethnic Bases of New York City Socialism, 1904–1915." *Labor History* 22 (Winter 1981): 31–56.

Lengyel, Emil. *Americans from Hungary.* Philadelphia: J. B. Lippincott, 1948.

Leuchtenburg, William E. *Franklin D. Roosevelt and the New Deal, 1932–1940.* New York: Harper and Row, 1963.

———. *The Perils of Prosperity, 1915–32.* Chicago: University of Chicago Press, 1958.

Levinson, Edward. "Labor Turns to Politics." *Nation,* June 8, 1932, pp. 648–50.

Lichtenstein, Nelson. *The Most Dangerous Man in Detroit: Walter Reuther and the Fate of American Labor.* New York: Basic, 1995.

Lichtenstein, Nelson, and Howell John Harris, eds. *Industrial Democracy in America: The Ambiguous Promise.* New York: Cambridge University Press, 1993.

Lichtheim, George. *A Short History of Socialism.* New York: Praeger, 1970.

Lichtman, Alan J. *Prejudice and the Old Politics: The Presidential Election of 1928.* Chapel Hill: University of North Carolina Press, 1979.

Liebman, Arthur. *Jews and the Left.* New York: John Wiley, 1979.

Lindmark, Sture. "The Swedish-Americans and the Depression Years, 1929–1932." *Swedish Pioneer Historical Quarterly* 19 (January 1968): 3–31.

Lipset, Seymour Martin. "Radicalism or Reformism: The Sources of Working Class Politics." In *Consensus and Conflict: Essays in Political Sociology.* 187–252. New Brunswick, N.J.: Transaction Books, 1985.

———. "Roosevelt and the Protest of the 1930s." *Minnesota Law Review* 68 (December 1983): 273–98.

———. "Why No Socialism in the United States?" In *Radicalism in the Contemporary Age,* Vol. 1: *Sources of Contemporary Radicalism.* Ed. Seweryn Bialer and Sophia Sluzar. 31–149. Boulder, Colo.: Westview, 1977.

Lorwin, Lewis L. *The American Federation of Labor: History, Policies, and Prospects.* Washington, D.C.: Brookings Institution, 1933.

Lorwin, Lewis L., and Arthur Wubnig. *Labor Relations Boards.* Washington, D.C.: Brookings Institution, 1935.

Lovin, Hugh T. "CIO Innovators, Labor Party Ideologues, and Organized Labor's Muddles in the 1937 Detroit Elections." *Old Northwest* 8 (Fall 1982): 223–43.

———. "The Fall of Farmer-Labor Parties, 1936–1938." *Pacific Northwest Quarterly* 62 (January 1971): 16–26.

———. "The Ohio 'Farmer-Labor' Movement in the 1930s." *Ohio History* 87 (Autumn 1978): 419–37.

————. "The Persistence of Third-Party Dreams in the American Labor Movement, 1930–1938." *Mid-America* 58 (1976): 141–58.

Lubell, Samuel. *The Future of American Politics.* 3d ed. New York: Harper and Row, 1965.

Lubove, Roy. *The Professional Altruist: The Emergence of Social Work as a Career, 1880–1930.* Cambridge, Mass.: Harvard University Press, 1965.

Lynd, Robert S., and Helen Merrill Lynd. *Middletown: A Study in Modern American Culture.* New York: Harcourt, Brace, and World, 1929.

Lynd, Staughton, ed. *"We Are All Leaders": The Alternative Unionism of the Early 1930s.* Urbana: University of Illinois Press, 1996.

MacKay, Kenneth Campbell. *The Progressive Movement of 1924.* Columbia University Studies in History, Economics, and Public Law No. 527. New York: 1947.

Maiale, Hugo V. *The Italian Vote in Philadelphia between 1928 and 1946.* Philadelphia: University of Pennsylvania Offset Press, 1950.

Manufacturers' Association of Bridgeport. *Bridgeport Employees Committees.* Bridgeport, Conn.: MAB, 1920.

Manufacturers' Association of Connecticut. *The Elimination of the Sweatshop.* Hartford, Conn.: MAC, 1933.

————. *Report Submitted to the Directors of the Manufacturers' Association by a Committee to Study the Subject of Taxation and Make Recommendation as to the Action of This Association Upon Taxation Question.* Hartford, Conn.: MAC, 1921.

————. *Unemployment and Its Remedies.* Hartford, Conn.: MAC, 1933.

March, James G., and Johan P. Olsen. "The New Institutionalism: Organizational Factors in Political Life." *American Political Science Review* 78 (September 1984): 734–49.

Maurer, James H. *It Can Be Done: The Autobiography of James Hudson Maurer.* New York: Rand School Press, 1938.

McCartin, Joseph A. "'An American Feeling': Workers, Managers, and the Struggle Over Industrial Democracy in the World War I Era." In *Industrial Democracy in America: The Ambiguous Promise.* Ed. Nelson Lichtenstein and Howell John Harris. 67–86. New York: Cambridge University Press, 1993.

————. *Labor's Great War: The Struggle for Industrial Democracy and the Origins of Modern American Labor Relations, 1912–1921.* Chapel Hill: University of North Carolina Press, 1997.

McCormick, Richard L. "Ethnocultural Interpretations of Nineteenth-Century American Voting Behavior." In *The Party Period and Public Policy: American Politics from the Age of Jackson to the Progressive Era.* 29–63. New York: Oxford University Press, 1986.

McDonald, Terrence J. "The Burdens of Urban History: The Theory of the State in Recent American Social History." *Studies in American Political Development* 3 (1989): 3–55.

McDonald, Terrence J., and Sally K. Ward, eds. *The Politics of Urban Fiscal Policy.* Beverly Hills, Calif.: Sage, 1984.

McGerr, Michael E. *The Decline of Popular Politics: The American North, 1865–1928.* New York: Oxford University Press, 1986.

Merriam, Charles Edward, and Harold Foote Gosnell. *Non-Voting: Causes and Methods of Control.* Chicago: University of Chicago Press, 1924.

Merritt, Walter Gordon. *The Open Shop and Industrial Liberty.* N.p., 1922.

Miaso, Józef. *The History of the Education of Polish Immigrants in the United States.* Trans. Ludwik Krzyzanowski. New York: Kosciuszko Foundation, 1977.

Milkman, Ruth. "Women's Work and Economic Crisis: Some Lessons of the Great Depression." *Review of Radical Political Economics* 8 (Spring 1976): 73–97.

Miller, Donald L. *The New American Radicalism: Alfred M. Bingham and Non-Marxian Insurgency in the New Deal Era.* Port Washington, N.Y.: Kennikat, 1979.

Miller, Guy P. "Local Taxation of Manufacturing Property." *Connecticut Industry,* August 1923, pp. 7–8.

Miller, Sally M. *Victor Berger and the Promise of Constructive Socialism, 1910–1920.* Westport, Conn.: Greenwood, 1973.

Milton, David. *The Politics of U.S. Labor: From the Great Depression to the New Deal.* New York: Monthly Review Press, 1982.

Montgomery, David. "American Workers and the New Deal Formula." In *Workers' Control in America: Studies in the History of Work, Technology, and Labor Struggles.* 153–80. New York: Cambridge University Press, 1979.

———. *The Fall of the House of Labor: The Workplace, the State, and American Labor Activism, 1865–1925.* New York: Cambridge University Press, 1987.

———. "Industrial Democracy or Democracy in Industry? The Theory and Practice of the Labor Movement, 1870–1925." In *Industrial Democracy in America: The Ambiguous Promise.* Ed. Nelson Lichtenstein and Howell John Harris. 20–42. New York: Cambridge University Press, 1993.

———. "Labor and the Republic in Industrial America: 1860–1920." *Le Mouvement Social* 111 (April–June 1980): 201–15.

———. "Nationalism, American Patriotism, and Class Consciousness among Immigrant Workers in the United States in the Epoch of World War I." In *"Struggle a Hard Battle": Essays on Working-Class Immigrants.* Ed. Dirk Hoerder. 327–51. DeKalb: Northern Illinois University Press, 1986.

———. "The 'New Unionism' and the Transformation of Workers' Consciousness in America, 1909–22." *Journal of Social History* 7 (Summer 1974): 509–29.

———. "Thinking about American Workers in the 1920s." *International Labor and Working-Class History* 32 (Fall 1987): 4–38.

———. "Whose Standards? Workers and the Reorganization of Production in the United States, 1900–1920." In *Workers' Control in America: Studies in the History of Work, Technology, and Labor Struggles.* 113–38. New York: Cambridge University Press, 1979.

Moody's Investment Service. *Moody's Manual—Industrials.* New York: Moody's, 1921.

Morawska, Ewa. *For Bread with Butter: The Life-Worlds of East Central Europeans in Johnstown, Pennsylvania, 1890–1940.* New York: Cambridge University Press, 1985.

Moret, Marta. *A Brief History of the Connecticut Labor Movement.* Storrs: University of Connecticut Labor Education Center, n.d. [1982].

Mormino, Gary Ross. *Immigrants on the Hill: Italian-Americans in St. Louis, 1882–1982.* Urbana: University of Illinois Press, 1986.

Morris, James O. *Conflict within the AFL: A Study of Craft versus Industrial Unionism, 1901–1938.* Ithaca, N.Y.: Cornell University Press, 1958.

Murray, Robert K. *Red Scare: A Study of National Hysteria, 1919–1920.* Minneapolis: University of Minnesota Press, 1955.

Nash, Michael. *Conflict and Accommodation: Coal Miners, Steel Workers, and Socialism, 1890–1920.* Westport, Conn.: Greenwood, 1982.

National Civic Federation. *Profit Sharing by American Employers.* New York: E. P. Dutton, 1921.

National Industrial Conference Board. *State and Local Taxation of Business Corporations.* New York: NICB, 1931.

Nelli, Humbert. "The Italian Padrone System in the United States." *Labor History* 5 (Spring 1968): 153–67.

———. *Italians in Chicago, 1880–1930: A Study in Ethnic Mobility.* New York: Oxford University Press, 1970.

Nelson, Bruce. *Workers on the Waterfront: Seamen, Longshoremen, and Unionism in the 1930s.* Urbana: University of Illinois Press, 1988.

Nelson, Daniel. "The CIO at Bay: Labor Militancy and Politics in Akron, 1936–1938." *Journal of American History* 71 (December 1984): 565–86.

Nelson, Steve, James R. Barrett, and Rob Ruck. *Steve Nelson, American Radical.* Pittsburgh: University of Pittsburgh Press, 1981.

Bibliography

New Haven, Bridgeport, and Waterbury Blue Book. 15th ed. New York: Blue Books, 1929.

Nichols, Carole. *Votes and More for Women: Suffrage and After in Connecticut.* New York: Haworth, 1983.

Norton, William J. *The Cooperative Movement in Social Work.* New York: Macmillan, 1927.

N. W. Ayer and Sons. *Directory of Newspapers and Periodicals.* Philadelphia: N. W. Ayer and Sons, 1920–40.

O'Grady, Joseph P., ed. *The Immigrants' Influence on Wilson's Peace Policies.* Lexington: University of Kentucky Press, 1967.

Oestreicher, Richard. "Urban Working-Class Political Behavior and Theories of American Electoral Politics, 1870–1940." *Journal of American History* 74 (March 1988): 1257–86.

Oneal, James, and G. A. Werner. *American Communism: A Critical Analysis of Its Origins, Development, and Programs.* New York: E. P. Dutton, 1947.

Oppenheimer, Valerie Kincade. *The Female Labor Force in the United States: Demographic and Economic Factors Governing Its Growth and Changing Composition.* 1970. Reprint, Westport, Conn.: Greenwood, 1976.

Orloff, Ann Shola, and Theda Skocpol. "Why Not Equal Protection? Explaining the Politics of Public Social Spending in Britain, 1900–1911, and the United States, 1880s–1920." *American Sociological Review* 49 (December 1984): 726–50.

Orsi, Robert A. *The Madonna of 115th Street: Faith and Community in Italian Harlem, 1880–1950.* New Haven, Conn.: Yale University Press, 1985.

Ottanelli, Fraser M. *The Communist Party of the United States: From the Depression to World War II.* New Brunswick, N.J.: Rutgers University Press, 1991.

Painter, Nell Irvin. *The Narrative of Hosea Hudson: His Life as a Negro Communist in the South.* Cambridge, Mass.: Harvard University Press, 1979.

Palmquist, David W. *Bridgeport: A Pictorial History.* Virginia Beach, Va.: Donning, 1981.

Park, Robert E. *The Immigrant Press and Its Control.* New York: Harper and Brothers, 1922.

Park, Robert E., and Herbert A. Miller. *Old World Traits Transplanted.* New York: Harper and Brothers, 1921.

Patterson, James T. *America's Struggle against Poverty, 1900–1985.* Cambridge, Mass.: Harvard University Press, 1986.

———. *The New Deal and the States: Federalism in Transition.* Princeton, N.J.: Princeton University Press, 1969.

Peck, Gunther. "Reinventing Free Labor: Immigrant Padrones and Contract Laborers in North America, 1885–1915." *Journal of American History* 83 (December 1996): 848–71.

Peel, Roy V. *The Political Clubs of New York City.* New York: G. P. Putnam's Sons, 1935.

Peel, Roy V., and Thomas C. Donnelly. *The 1928 Campaign: An Analysis.* New York: Richard R. Smith, 1931.

Perlman, Mark. *The Machinists: A New Study in American Trade Unionism.* Cambridge, Mass.: Harvard University Press, 1961.

Perlman, Selig. *A Theory of the Labor Movement.* New York: Macmillan, 1928.

Pienkos, Donald E. *One Hundred Years Young: A History of the Polish Falcons of America, 1887–1987.* Boulder, Colo.: East European Monographs, 1987.

———. *PNA: A Centennial History of the Polish National Alliance of the United States of North America.* Vol. 168. Boulder, Colo.: East European Monographs, 1984.

Potter, Zenas F. "War Boom Towns—Bridgeport." *Survey* 35 (December 4, 1915): 237–41.

Preston, William, Jr. *Aliens and Dissenters: Federal Suppression of Radicals, 1903–1933.* Cambridge, Mass.: Harvard University Press, 1963.

Procter, Mary, and Bill Matuszeski. *Gritty Cities.* Philadelphia: Temple University Press, 1978.

Prothro, James Warren. *The Dollar Decade: Business Ideas in the 1920's.* Baton Rouge: Louisiana State University Press, 1954.

Puskás, Julianna. *From Hungary to the United States, 1880–1914.* Budapest: Akademiai Kiado, 1982.

Rachleff, Peter. "Class, Ethnicity, and the New Deal: The Croatian Fraternal Union in the 1930s." In *The Ethnic Enigma: The Salience of Ethnicity for European-Origin Groups*. Ed. Peter Kivisto. 89–113. Philadelphia: Balch Institute, 1989.

Radosh, Ronald. "The Corporate Ideology of American Labor Leaders from Gompers to Hillman." *Studies on the Left* 6 (November–December 1966): 66–88.

Rákóczi Aid Association. *Golden Jubilee Book*. Bridgeport, Conn.: Rákóczi Aid Association, 1938.

Remington Arms Company. *Bonus Plan*. Bridgeport, Conn.: DuPont, 1935.

Remington Arms–UMC Company. *Organization and By-Laws for Employees' Departmental and General Committees*. Bridgeport, Conn.: Remington Arms, 1919.

"Reminiscences of J. Henry Roraback: He Was a Leader in Defeat as in Victory." *Connecticut State Journal* 9 (November 1942): 15, 30–36.

"Reminiscences of J. Henry Roraback: His Part in the Republican National Picture." *Connecticut State Journal* 9 (October 1942): 13, 30–33.

"Reminiscences of J. Henry Roraback: His Political Philosophies and Theories of Government." *Connecticut State Journal* 9 (August 1942): 12, 22–24.

"Reminiscences of J. Henry Roraback: Legislative Management in the '20's and the Modern Trend." *Connecticut State Journal* 10 (January 1943): 12, 21–23.

"Reminiscences of J. Henry Roraback: Making Decisions and Sticking to Them Were His Forte." *Connecticut State Journal* 9 (September 1942): 21, 40–45.

"Reminiscences of J. Henry Roraback: A Striking Comparison to the Late David E. Fitzgerald." *Connecticut State Journal* 9 (December 1942): 13, 24.

Renkiewicz, Frank. "Polish American Workers, 1880–1980." In *Pastor of the Poles: Polish American Essays Presented to Right Reverend Monsignor John P. Wodarski*. Ed. Stanislaus A. Blejwas and Mieczyclaw B. Biskupski. 116–36. New Britain, Conn.: Polish Studies Program Monographs, 1982.

Republican Party of Connecticut. State Central Committee. *Republican Handbook of Connecticut*. Hartford: Republican Party of Connecticut, 1930.

Rice, Bradley Robert. *Progressive Cities: The Commission Government Movement in America, 1901–1920*. Austin: University of Texas Press, 1977.

Ridley, Clarence E., and Orin F. Nolting, eds. *What the Depression Has Done to Cities*. Chicago: International City Managers' Association, 1935.

Ripley, Charles M. *Life in a Large Manufacturing Plant*. Schenectady, N.Y.: General Electric, 1919.

Robertson, David Brian. "The Return to History and the New Institutionalism in American Political Science." *Social Science History* 17, no. 1 (Spring 1993): 1–36.

Rodgers, Daniel T. "In Search of Progressivism." *Reviews in American History* 10 (December 1982): 113–32.

Roe, Joseph Wickham. *English and American Tool Builders*. New Haven, Conn.: Yale University Press, 1916.

Rosenzweig, Roy. "'Socialism in Our Time': The Socialist Party and the Unemployed, 1929–1936." *Labor History* 20 (Fall 1979): 485–509.

Roucek, Joseph Slabey. "Hungarians in America." *Hungarian Quarterly* 3 (Summer 1937): 358–66.

———. "The Passing of American Czechoslovaks." *American Journal of Sociology* 39 (March 1934): 611–25.

Sabin, Arthur J. *Red Scare in Court: New York versus the International Workers Order*. Philadelphia: University of Pennsylvania Press, 1993.

Salter, J. T. *Boss Rule: Portraits in City Politics*. New York: McGraw-Hill Book, 1935.

Salvatore, Nick. *Eugene V. Debs: Citizen and Socialist*. Urbana: University of Illinois Press, 1982.

———. "Response to Wilentz's 'Against Exceptionalism.'" *International Labor and Working Class History* 26 (Fall 1984): 25–30.

Savage, Marion. *Industrial Unionism in America*. New York: Ronald Press, 1922.

Schatz, Ronald W. *The Electrical Workers: A History of Labor at General Electric and Westinghouse, 1923–60*. Urbana: University of Illinois Press, 1983.

Schiesl, Martin. *The Politics of Efficiency: Municipal Administration and Reform in America, 1800–1920.* Berkeley: University of California Press, 1977.

Schiff, Judith A. "Colonel Isaac Ullman: Philanthropist, Politician, and Patriot." *Jews in New Haven: A Publication of the Jewish Historical Society of New Haven* 2 (1979): 32–40.

Schlesinger, Arthur M., Jr. *The Age of Roosevelt: The Crisis of the Old Order, 1919–1933.* Boston: Houghton Mifflin, 1957.

Schneider, David M. *The Workers' (Communist) Party and American Trade Unionism.* Baltimore, Md.: Johns Hopkins University Press, 1928.

Schoonmaker, Nancy M. *The Actual Government of Connecticut.* New York: National Woman Suffrage Publishing, 1919.

Schwarz, Jordan A. *The Interregnum of Despair: Hoover, Congress, and the Depression.* Urbana: University of Illinois Press, 1970.

Scobey, David. "Boycotting the Politics Factory: Labor Radicalism and the New York City Mayoral Election of 1884." *Radical History Review* 28–30 (1984): 280–326.

Scott, Joan. "Social History and the History of Socialism: French Socialist Municipalities in the 1890s." *Le Mouvement Social* 111 (1980): 145–53.

Seidman, Joel. *The Needle Trades.* New York: Farrar and Rinehart, 1942.

Seitz, Don C. "Connecticut: A Nation in Miniature." *Nation,* April 18, 1923, pp. 461–65.

Selekman, B. M., Henrietta Walker, and W. J. Couper. *The Clothing and Textile Industries in New York and Its Environs.* New York: Committee on Regional Plan of New York and Its Environs, 1925.

Shannon, David A. *The Socialist Party of America: A History.* New York: Macmillan, 1955.

Shea, Jonathan, and Christine Stoj. "The Pulaski Democratic Club of New Britain, Connecticut." In *Pastor of the Poles: Polish American Essays Presented to Right Reverend Monsignor John P. Wodarski.* Ed. Stanislaus A. Blejwas and Mieczyclaw B. Biskupski. 137–52. New Britain, Conn.: Polish Studies Program Monographs, 1982.

Shefter, Martin. "The Emergence of the Political Machine: An Alternative View." In *Theoretical Perspectives on Urban Politics.* Ed. Willis D. Hawley. 14–44. Englewood Cliffs, N.J.: Prentice-Hall, 1976.

———. "Trade Unions and Political Machines: The Organization and Disorganization of the American Working Class in the Late Nineteenth Century." In *Working-Class Formation: Nineteenth-Century Patterns in Western Europe and the United States.* Ed. Ira Katznelson and Aristide R. Zolberg. 197–296. Princeton, N.J.: Princeton University Press, 1986.

Shepherd, William G. "Robbing the Working Girl." *Collier's,* November 12, 1932, pp. 10–11.

Sherman, Nathaniel. "Connecticut Forms a Labor Party." *Nation,* July 31, 1935, p. 131.

"Shop Committees in Bridgeport." *Industrial Relations-Bloomfield's Labor Digest* 8 (September 3, 1921): 804–7.

Shover, John L. "The Progressives and the Working Class Vote in California." *Labor History* 10 (Fall 1969): 584–601.

Shubert, Bruce B. "The Palmer Raids in Connecticut: 1919–1920." *Connecticut Review* 5 (October 1971): 53–69.

Singer Manufacturing Company. *Organization and By-Laws for Employees' Committees.* Bridgeport, Conn.: Singer Manufacturing, 1920.

Sitkoff, Harvard, ed. *Fifty Years Later: The New Deal Evaluated.* New York: Alfred A. Knopf, 1985.

Skocpol, Theda. "Bringing the State Back in: Strategies of Analysis in Current Research." In *Bringing the State Back In.* Ed. Peter B. Evans, Dietrich Rueschemeyer, and Theda Skocpol. 3–37. New York: Cambridge University Press, 1985.

———. *Protecting Soldiers and Mothers: The Political Origins of Social Policy in the United States.* Cambridge, Mass.: Harvard University Press, 1992.

Skowronek, Stephen. *Building a New American State: The Expansion of National Administrative Capacities, 1877–1920.* New York: Cambridge University Press, 1982.

Slichter, Sumner H. *Union Policies and Industrial Management.* Washington, D.C.: Brookings Institution, 1941.

Smith, Judith E. *Family Connections: A History of Italian and Jewish Immigrant Lives in Providence, Rhode Island, 1900–1940.* Albany: State University of New York Press, 1985.

Smith, Matthew. "Militant Labor in Detroit." *Nation,* May 16, 1934, pp. 560–62.

Socialist Party of America. *The Intelligent Voter's Guide: Official 1928 Campaign Handbook of the Socialist Party.* Chicago: Socialist National Campaign Committee, 1928.

Soule, George. *Prosperity Decade: From War to Depression, 1917–1929.* New York: Rinehart, 1947.

Spencer, Thomas T. "Homer S. Cummings and the 1932 Presidential Campaign." *Connecticut Historical Society Bulletin* 48 (Winter 1983): 1–9.

"Springfield and Bridgeport." *New Republic,* September 14, 1918, pp. 185–86.

"Springfield and Bridgeport—Second Phase." *New Republic,* September 21, 1918, pp. 216–17.

Stack, John F., Jr. *International Conflict in an American City: Boston's Irish, Italians, and Jews, 1935–1944.* Westport, Conn.: Greenwood, 1979.

Stave, Bruce M. "The Great Depression and Urban Political Continuity: Bridgeport Chooses Socialism." In *Socialism and the Cities.* Ed. Bruce M. Stave. 157–83. Port Washington, N.Y.: Kennikat, 1975.

———. *The New Deal and the Last Hurrah: Pittsburgh Machine Politics.* Pittsburgh: University of Pittsburgh Press, 1970.

———, ed. *Socialism and the Cities.* Port Washington, N.Y.: Kennikat, 1975.

Stolarik, M. Mark. "A Place for Everyone: Slovak Fraternal-Benefit Societies." In *Self-Help in Urban America: Patterns of Minority Business Enterprise.* Ed. Scott Cummings. 130–41. Port Washington, N.Y.: Kennikat, 1980.

———. "The Slovaks." In *Harvard Encyclopedia of American Ethnic Groups.* Ed. Stephen Thernstrom. 926–34. Cambridge, Mass.: Harvard University Press, 1980.

Stricker, Frank. "Affluence for Whom? Another Look at Prosperity and the Working Classes in the 1920s." *Labor History* 24 (Winter 1983): 5–33.

Stromquist, Shelton. "The Crucible of Class: Cleveland Politics and the Origins of Municipal Reform in the Progressive Era." *Journal of Urban History* 23 (January 1997): 192–220.

"Strong Plea for Permanent Adjustment." *Iron Age* 102 (August 8, 1918): 332–34.

Sundquist, James L. *Dynamics of the Party System: Alignment and Realignment of Political Parties in the United States.* Rev. ed. Washington, D.C.: Brookings Institution, 1983.

Teaford, Jon C. "Finis for Tweed and Steffens: Rewriting the History of Urban Rule." *Reviews in American History* 10 (December 1982): 133–49.

———. *The Unheralded Triumph: City Government in America, 1870–1900.* Baltimore, Md.: Johns Hopkins University Press, 1984.

Terkel, Studs. *Hard Times: An Oral History of the Great Depression.* New York: Pantheon, 1970.

Tomlins, Christopher L. "AFL Unions in the 1930s: Their Performance in Historical Perspective." *Journal of American History* 65 (March 1979): 1021–42.

———. *The State and the Unions: Labor Relations, Law, and the Organized Labor Movement in America, 1880–1960.* New York: Cambridge University Press, 1985.

Trout, Charles H. *Boston, the Great Depression, and the New Deal.* New York: Oxford University Press, 1977.

Twain, Mark. *A Connecticut Yankee in King Arthur's Court.* 1889. Reprint, New York: Penguin, 1986.

United Way of America. *People and Events: A History of the United Way.* Alexandria, Va.: United Way, 1977.

Valelly, Richard M. *Radicalism in the States: The Minnesota Farmer-Labor Party and the American Political Economy.* Chicago: University of Chicago Press, 1989.

Vassady, Bela, Jr. "The 'Homeland Cause' as Stimulant to Ethnic Unity: The Hungarian American Response to Károlyi's 1914 American Tour." *Journal of American Ethnic History* 2 (Fall 1982): 39–64.

Vecoli, Rudolph J. "Anthony Capraro and the Lawrence Strike of 1919." In *Pane e Lavoro: The Italian American Working Class.* Ed. George E. Pozzetta. 3–28. Toronto: Multicultural History Society of Ontario, 1980.

———. "Prelates and Peasants: Italian Immigrants and the Catholic Church." *Journal of Social History* 2 (Spring 1969): 217–68.

Vorse, Mary Heaton. "Bridgeport and Democracy." *Harper's,* January 1919, pp. 145–54.

Waldman, Louis. *Labor Lawyer.* Mount Vernon, N.Y.: S. A. Jacobs, Golden Eagle Press, 1944.

Waldo, George C., Jr. *History of Bridgeport and Vicinity.* 2 Vols. New York: S. J. Clarke, 1917.

Walling, William English. *American Labor and American Democracy.* New York: Harper and Brothers, 1926.

Waltzer, Kenneth. "The Party and the Polling Place: American Communism and an American Labor Party in the 1930s." *Radical History Review* 23 (Spring 1980): 104–29.

Ware, Susan. *Holding Their Own: American Women in the 1930s.* Boston: Twayne, 1982.

Warren, Frank A. *An Alternative Vision: The Socialist Party in the 1930s.* Bloomington: Indiana University Press, 1974.

Weinstein, James. *The Corporate Ideal in the Liberal State, 1900–1918.* Boston: Beacon, 1968.

———. *The Decline of Socialism in America, 1912–1925.* New York: Monthly Review Press, 1967.

Weiss, Nancy J. *Farewell to the Party of Lincoln: Black Politics in the Age of FDR.* Princeton, N.J.: Princeton University Press, 1983.

"Who Is This A. J. Muste?" *World Tomorrow* 12 (June 1929): 253.

Who's Who in Connecticut. New York: Lewis Historical Publishing, 1933.

Wiebe, Robert H. *The Search for Order, 1877–1920.* New York: Hill and Wang, 1967.

Wilentz, Sean. "Against Exceptionalism: Class Consciousness and the American Labor Movement." *International Labor and Working Class History* 26 (Fall 1984): 1–24.

———. *Chants Democratic: New York City and the Rise of the American Working Class, 1788–1850.* New York: Oxford University Press, 1984.

Wilson, Lynn W. "Journalism." In *History of Bridgeport and Vicinity.* Ed. George C. Waldo Jr. 2:356–61. New York: S. J. Clarke, 1917.

Wilson, Lynn Winfield. *History of Fairfield County, Connecticut, 1639–1928.* 3 Vols. Chicago: S. J. Clarke, 1929.

Witte, Edwin E. *The Government in Labor Disputes.* New York: McGraw-Hill, 1932.

Wlodarski, Reverend Stephen. *The Origin and Growth of the Polish National Catholic Church.* Scranton, Pa.: Polish National Catholic Church, 1974.

Wolfinger, Raymond E. "The Development and Persistence of Ethnic Voting." *American Political Science Review* 59 (December 1965): 896–908.

Wolkovich, William. *Bay State "Blue" Laws and Bimba.* Brockton, Mass.: Forum Press, n.d.

Wytrwal, Joseph A. *America's Polish Heritage: A Social History of the Poles in America.* Detroit, Mich.: Endurance Press, 1961.

Zahavi, Gerald. *Workers, Managers, and Welfare Capitalism: The Shoeworkers and Tanners of Endicott Johnson, 1890–1950.* Urbana: University of Illinois Press, 1988.

Zieger, Robert H. *Republicans and Labor, 1919–1929.* Lexington: University of Kentucky Press, 1969.

Zimand, Savel. *The Open Shop Drive: Who Is Behind It and Where Is It Going.* New York: Bureau of Industrial Research, 1921.

Zink, Harold. *Government of Cities in the United States.* New York: Macmillan, 1939.

Dissertations, Theses, and Unpublished Papers

Banit, Thomas. "The War Machine: Bridgeport, 1914–1918." Master's thesis, University of Bridgeport, 1973.

Benkart, Paula Kaye. "Religion, Family, and Community among Hungarians Migrating to American Cities, 1880–1930." Ph.D. diss., Johns Hopkins University, 1975.

Brooks, Robert R. R. "The United Textile Workers of America." Ph.D. diss., Yale University, 1935.

Bucki, Cecelia F. "Evolution of Poor Relief Practice in Nineteenth-Century Pittsburgh." Master's paper, History Department, University of Pittsburgh, 1977.

———. "The Pursuit of Political Power: Class, Ethnicity, and Municipal Politics in Interwar Bridgeport, 1915–1936." Ph.D. diss., University of Pittsburgh, 1991.

Dahill, Edwin McNeil, Jr. "Connecticut's J. Henry Roraback." Ed.D. diss., Columbia University, 1971.

Federal Emergency Relief Administration. "Survey of the Occupational Characteristics of Persons Receiving Relief, Bridgeport, May 1934." Typescript, U.S. Department of Labor Library. Washington, D.C., 1934.

Foucher, M. S., and Patricia Eams. "The Labor Movement in Connecticut: An Introductory History." Unpublished manuscript, Connecticut State AFL-CIO Papers, 1955–56.

Fraser, Bruce. "Yankees at War: Social Mobilization on the Connecticut Homefront, 1917–1918." Ph.D. diss., Columbia University, 1976.

Janick, Herbert F., Jr. "Government for the People: The Leadership of the Progressive Party in Connecticut." Ph.D. diss., Fordham University, 1968.

Little, Eleanor Howell. "Relief Without Politics." Unpublished paper. [Hartford, Conn.], [1937?].

Lockard, W. Duane. "The Role of Party in the Connecticut General Assembly, 1931–1951." Ph.D. diss., Yale University, 1952.

Lombardo, Peter J., Jr. "Connecticut in the Great Depression, 1929–1933." Ph.D. diss., Notre Dame University, 1979.

Macieski, Robert Leon. "A Place in Time: The Shaping of City Space in Bridgeport, Connecticut, 1890–1919." Ph.D. diss., Boston College, 1994.

Mitchell, Rowland L., Jr. "Social Legislation in Connecticut, 1919–1939." Ph.D. diss., Yale University, 1954.

Olmstead, Alan H. "The Great Jasper." Manuscript. Olmstead Papers. Bridgeport, Conn., 1943–44.

Olson, Frederick I. "The Milwaukee Socialists, 1897–1941." Ph.D. diss., Harvard University, 1952.

Palmquist, David. "The Stoker Mayor of Bridgeport." Unpublished paper, Bridgeport, Conn., n.d.

Pratt, William C. "The Reading Socialist Experience: A Study of Working Class Politics." Ph.D. diss., Emory University, 1969.

Rosengren, Arne. "Connecticut Government and Politics." Master's thesis, Wesleyan University, 1949.

Stolarik, Marian Mark. "Immigration and Urbanization: The Slovak Experience, 1870–1918." Ph.D. diss., University of Minnesota, 1974.

INDEX

Abraham Lodge No. 89 of B'nai B'rith, 84
Abriola, Antonio, 92, 94, 218n.32, 219nn.42, 46
Abriola, Louis, 82, 218n.32, 219n.42, 221n.86
Abriola, Salvatore, 218n.32
ACLU. *See* American Civil Liberties Union
ACWA. *See* Amalgamated Clothing Workers of America
Adiletta, Joseph, 98
administrative state, 56
ads, political, 88–90
AFL. *See* American Federation of Labor
African Americans: and election of 1928, 93; and election of 1929, 97; General Electric and, 108; job distribution, 106; in labor force (1920–30), 102; La Follette and, 124; migration to industrial regions, 3; political participation, 80, 83; in prewar Bridgeport, 18, 20 (table); Roraback and, 221n.81; Slovak resentment of, 242n.102; in Socialist Party, 158; as strikebreakers, 39; women's political club, 216n.79
Aheppa Society, 60
aircraft workers strike, 165
Alcorn, Hugh, 180
Algonquin Club, 53, 93, 188
Allen, Devere: and election of 1933, 157; on McLevy, 189; Socialist Party declaration of, 179–80; on United Front, 176–77
Allyn House (state GOP headquarters), 80
ALP. *See* American Labor Party
Al Smith revolution, 92–94, 96, 98, 125, 193
Altieri, Michele, 82, 98
Amalgamated Clothing Workers of America (ACWA): cooperation with employers, 224n.30; immigrants and, 225n.36; La Fol-

lette and, 124; McLevy administration and, 167–68; in 1930s, 134; Sacco and Vanzetti rally, 38; strikes, 23, 110–11, 112
Amalgamated Metal Workers of America (AMWA), 37–38, 39, 209n.71
Amalgamated Textile Workers Union, 110–11, 112, 224n.34
American Civil Liberties Union (ACLU), 169, 176
American Committee for Relief in Ireland, 60
American exceptionalism, 2, 3, 204n.7
American Federation of Labor (AFL): defines labor movement, 6; Egan as voice of, 114; and election of 1928, 90; labor party and, 123; local politics and, 113; McLevy in, 115; membership drives, 24; proclamation of, in 1923, 100; response to ethnic separateness, 25; rubber workers and, 37; Socialist Party and, 178; stance on immigration restrictions, 3; strike by, in 1933, 165–66
—craftsmen: political positions of, 6–7; in Socialist Party, 8, 119–22; wartime activities of, 23
Americanism, 29–36, 194, 195
Americanization: ethnic survival by, 100; interplay of immigrant groups and, 3; Italian goal of, 82; new ethnics and, 78; in 1920s, 68–69; political effects of, 84; second generation and, 74–75; working-class politics and, 2; during World War I, 29–36
American Labor Party (ALP), 34, 122, 190, 209n.65, 227n.66
American Legion, 38
American Plan, 106, 226n.64

CECELIA BUCKI is an associate professor of history at Fairfield University. She received her doctoral degree from the University of Pittsburgh, where she studied with David Montgomery. She has published in *International Labor and Working-Class History, Social Science History, Labor History,* and the anthology *Labor Histories.* A native of Bridgeport, she has been actively involved in researching and preserving Connecticut local history and labor history.

The Working Class in American History

The University of Illinois Press
is a founding member of the
Association of American University Presses.

Composed in 10.5/12.5 Adobe Minion
by Jim Proefrock
at the University of Illinois Press
Manufactured by Thomson-Shore, Inc.

University of Illinois Press
1325 South Oak Street
Champaign, IL 61820-6903
www.press.uillinois.edu